THE HOUND AND THE HAWK

17 mar 05

John Cummins was born in 1937. He has been a teacher of Spanish at the Universities of St Andrews and Birmingham, and he was head of the Department of Spanish at the University of Aberdeen until his retirement in 1995. He is also an expert on Renaissance manuscripts. He lives in Angus, Scotland.

Also by John Cummins

The Spanish Traditional Lyric

The Journal of Christopher Columbus (ed)

Francis Drake: The Lives of a Hero

THE HOUND
AND THE HAWK

The Art of Medieval Hunting

John Cummins

PHOENIX
PRESS

PHOENIX PRESS
5 UPPER SAINT MARTIN'S LANE
LONDON WC2H 9EA

To the Blairs Syndicate, Stonehaven:

Ian Cameron,
Fred Dey,
John Donald,
Brian Jones,
Mick Mickelburgh,
Ian Robertson,
Bill Russell;

not forgetting Corrie, Dougal, Jet, Max,
Pirate, Rebel, Sable, Sam, Struan, Sweep, Toby . . .

A PHOENIX PRESS PAPERBACK

First published in Great Britain
by Weidenfeld & Nicolson in 1988
This paperback edition published in 2001
by Phoenix Press,
a division of The Orion Publishing Group Ltd,
Orion House, 5 Upper St Martin's Lane,
London WC2H 9EA

A CIP catalogue record for this book
is available from the British Library.

Printed and bound in Great Britain by
Butler & Tanner Ltd, Frome and London

ISBN 1 84212 097 2

Contents

Illustrations

Acknowledgements

In the preparation of this book I have enjoyed the cooperation of the staffs of numerous institutions: the British Library; the Bodleian Library, Oxford; the National Library of Scotland; the Bibliothèque Nationale, Paris; the Bibliothèque de l'Arsénal; the Musée Condé, Chantilly; the Jagd- und Fischereimuseum, Munich; the Kunsthistorisches Museum, Vienna, and in particular the Waffensammlung; the Österreichische Nationalbibliothek, Vienna, especially the Handschriftensammlung; the Museum of Hunting in Schloss Markegg, Austria; the Biblioteca Nacional, Madrid; the Biblioteca del Palacio, Madrid; the Library of the Academia de la Historia, Madrid; the Library of the Monastery of San Lorenzo del Escorial; and the Library of the University of Aberdeen.

My thanks are due to Messrs Hutchinson and Co. for permission to print Peter Dronke's translations of three German and Serbian lyrics at the end of Chapter 20, and to the Chicago University Press for allowing me to include lines from Richmond Lattimore's translation of the *Iliad* early in the same chapter. With the exception of these passages, and others out of copyright, translations from foreign and medieval sources are my own.

I have drawn extensively on the assistance of friends and colleagues in my own University, who have translated passages, interpreted problems, loaned books from their own libraries, written letters, obtained microfilms on my behalf and helped with paleographical obscurities. They include Dr Patrick Edwards and Mr Thomas Pearce of the Department of Classics; Dr Donal Byrne of the Department of History of Art; Dr Barry Cooper of the Department of Music; Dr Seumas Grannd of the Department of Celtic; Dr Stephen Parkinson of the Department of Linguistics; Dr Jürgen Thomaneck, Dr James Mellis, Dr Gordon Burgess and Mrs Margaret Stone of the Department of German; and Professor James Laidlaw, Dr Alison Saunders and Dr John Dunkley of the Department of French.

I have also received important suggestions or practical help from Ing. Theo Maiwald of the Österreichische Falknerbund; Dr Kurt Lindner, Bamberg; Dr Rosemary Combridge of the School of European Languages and Literatures, Queen Mary College, London; Mr Daniel C. de W. Rogers of the Department of Spanish, University of Durham; and Gerard and Liselotte Beran, who made my stay in Vienna memorable by their hospitality and by introductions and enquiries which greatly furthered the progress of my research.

ACKNOWLEDGEMENTS

If I had medals to award, however, or if treasure and titles were in my gift, they would go to Mrs Doreen Davidson and Miss Elizabeth Weir, of the Languages Secretariat of the University of Aberdeen.

John Cummins
King's College, Old Aberdeen, Scotland

Introduction

De chiens, d'oyseaulx, d'armes, d'amours,
Pour une joye, cent douloivs.

Gace de la Vigne, whose long poem *Le Roman des Déduis* (*The Pleasures of Hunting*) includes this pessimistic and thoroughly misleading couplet,[1] was writing for aristocratic readers: for a medieval warrior class, the *defensores*, defenders of that tripartite society whose spiritual welfare was in the hands of the clerics, the *oratores*, and which was fed by the efforts of the *laboratores*, the tillers of the soil. He links in a single line, probably without thinking too much about it, the three consuming preoccupations of that class: warfare, their accepted function; courtly love, their principal cerebral interest; and hunting with hounds or hawks, their constant peacetime exercise. Gaston III, Count of Foix, called Gaston Phoebus because of his golden hair, makes just the same linkage in decrying and praising his own accomplishments in his *Livre de chasse*, saying, 'All my life I have taken special delight in three things: arms, love and hunting.' He modestly renounces all claims to expertise in the first two, but has no doubts of his mastery of the third.[2]

In this love of hunting, the medieval aristocrat usually had before him the example of his monarch. The rulers of Europe – the Emperor Frederick II, Alfonso XI and Pedro the Cruel of Castile, Henry IV of England, Philip Duke of Burgundy, the Emperor Maximilian I, and James IV of Scotland are among the most notable examples – maintained immense establishments of hounds, falcons or both, partly for the entertainment of visiting dignitaries, but essentially for their own amusement and exercise. Nearly every page of the accounts of James IV of Scotland's Lord High Treasurer includes items of expense on hunting: falconers' wages, horses and clothing; the purchase of dogs, nets, hawk-bells, arrowheads, leashes; the building of a mews; the transport of venison to Edinburgh; payments to beaters; the carriage of the King's bed from the capital to his hunting lodge. In the thirty years from 1488 to 1508 the names of forty-eight different royal falconers appear in the accounts.[3]

King Fernando of Portugal had forty-five mounted falconers, as well as huntsmen and other falconers on foot, and 'used to say that he would not rest until he housed a hundred falconers in a single street in Santarem'.[4] From Alfonso XI's *Libro de la montería* one can assemble a list of twenty-six named huntsmen, merely as casual mentions in the hunting anecdotes. A register of the correspondence of the Emperor Frederick II for 1239–40 mentions more than fifty of his falconers by name (they include an Englishman and his son);[5] Francesco Sforza, Duke of Milan, wept for grief when his favourite falcon died, and the poets of the court produced memorial verses. Maximilian I had hundreds of huntsmen and kennel-men, with separate staffs in the various Austrian provinces, and at least 1500 hounds.[6]

Whether in the detailed practical manuals or in the imaginative work in which hunting figures as narrative or symbol, medieval literature on the theme is permeated by a sense of dedicated enjoyment, the fulfilment of an enduring compulsion to retain a link with nature in a period barely emerging from the primitive, when immersing oneself in the forests of Europe could still create the illusion of being amid a limitless wilderness with infinitely renewable sources of game. Planning the chase was a mental challenge, taking part in it was physically and emotionally satisfying, and the spoils provided delight for the stomach. Something so enjoyable, so self-indulgent, and so expensive had to be explained and justified.

One defence was the avoidance of the idleness which nurtures bodily and spiritual evils. Pero López de Ayala, Chancellor of Castile, the greatest medieval Spanish authority on falconry, tells us that all men

> should avoid idleness, for it causes sin; when man is not occupied in good and honest things, thoughts are born in his heart from which arise misery and mortification, and from this misery comes desperation, which is the root of damnation. It also brings evil to the body, for when a man is idle, without exercising his limbs and experiencing changes of air, his bodily humours grow stale and he is subject to sickness and diseases. . . . To avoid these evils, those engaged in the education of the sons of kings and princes thought it good that they should go through the countryside for a few hours every day, taking fresh air and exercise.[7]

Not only the royal amateur – the professional huntsman, too, is saved from damnation: Gaston Phoebus argues that 'a good huntsman can never be prey to any of the Seven Deadly Sins':

> Firstly, all sin springs from idleness, for when a man is idle and remains in his bed or his chamber, he is drawn to imagining the

pleasures of the flesh, for he does nothing but remain in one place with thoughts of pride or avarice or anger or idleness or gluttony or lust or envy, for man's imaginings lean more easily to evil than to good, because of his three enemies, the world, the flesh and the Devil. And I shall prove to you that the good huntsman cannot be idle or engage in these evil visions or the wicked deeds to which they give rise, for at night he will lie down thinking only of his sleep and of rising in the morning to do his job diligently, without thought of sin.[8]

The essence of the poem *Sir Gawain and the Green Knight* is in the contrast between the alternating scenes of energetic hunting by Sir Bertilak, full of vigour, sunlight and purpose, and the languid ease of Sir Gawain, lounging in his bed and open to the corrupting overtures of Lady Bertilak. As Chaucer's parson reminds us, 'Slepynge long in greet quiet is eek a greet norice to Leccherie.'[9]

Allied with the avoidance of sin is a more positive view: that the wild beasts retain something which man has lost, and which, by implication, he may somehow regain, or at least perceive, in studying, hunting and defeating them. This is most apparent in that comprehensive and delightful work of French practicality cum high-mindedness, the *Livres du Roy Modus et de la Reine Ratio*, in which Queen Reason intervenes in the teaching of King Method to compare the sensual faculties of man with those of the beasts:

The five natural senses are these: hearing, sight, smell, taste and touch. Now compare man with the beasts! Is there a man who hears as keenly as the boar or the mole? Is there a man who sees as clearly as the lynx, which can see through a wall four feet thick? A man whose sense of smell equals that of the vulture, which scents its prey seven leagues away? A man whose sense of taste equals that of the stag, which perceives the virtue and evil in every plant, and eats nothing which will harm it? Is there a man whose touch is as subtle as the spider's, which feels the finger before the finger touches it?

All these senses God gave to Adam, in greater perfection than to any other animal, and God sent Queen Reason to guide him, but in the Fall of Man she was rejected, and so these senses were lost, 'and for that reason the animals were left with greater sensual abilities than man. This is why you marvel at the senses of the beasts, as you would not had Adam but believed in me.'[10]

A second justification is that the hunt prepares a man for war, maintaining in peacetime a range of skills, both mental and physical, which he may need quite soon in battle. Mr Jorrocks, Surtees' heroic Master of

Hounds, didn't know it, but in his cheerful description of the hunt as 'the sport of kings; the image of war without its guilt, and only five-and-twenty per cent of its danger' he was echoing the words of many noble and royal predecessors.[11] Ramón Llull, the Catalan whose book on chivalry served as a guide to so many successors, asserted that a knight should constantly exercise his body by hunting wild beasts, the hart, boar and wolf.[12]

At the mere semantic level, the military associations are conveyed unconsciously: the boar or bear is the 'enemy'; the head-on encounter is a 'joust'; the waiting archers form a 'battle-line'. At other levels comparisons are more rational and explicit, as in the explanation by Alfonso XI of Castile, which takes as its starting-point the knight's accepted functions:

> For a knight should always engage in anything to do with arms and chivalry, and if he cannot do so in war, he should do so in activities which resemble war. And the chase is most similar to war, for these reasons; war demands expense, met without complaint; one must be well horsed and well armed; one must be vigorous, and do without sleep, suffer lack of good food and drink, rise early, sometimes have a poor bed, undergo cold and heat, and conceal one's fear.[13]

The hunt, especially that of the boar, often reproduced the physical demands of man-to-man combat, training a man in the management of sword and spear,[14] and at the tactical level of deploying one's forces it was a useful war-game for those in charge. 'If kings need to know how best to choose a field of battle to their own advantage, and to consider the positioning of their battle-line, so does the hunter when he has to hunt an area new to him,' says John I of Portugal. He devotes a long chapter to a meticulous exploration of the common factors to be considered: contour, amount of cover, availability of men, even the direction of the wind, which is crucial in hunting since it can carry the scent of the quarry to the hounds and also betray the hunter to the quarry; in battle it is usually beneficial to fight into the wind, as it refreshes the soldiers and improves their breathing, but if there is dust it is better to have one's back to the wind, and let the dust blind the enemy.[15]

From one brief and ancient treatise, the *De Arte Bersandi* of Guicennas, one can deduce that the hunt was not only a peacetime pleasure, but also a necessity in time of war; a group of men might set out not knowing whether their weapons would be needed for killing a deer or an enemy. One had to be prepared for both: 'The archers (possibly crossbowmen in this case) should have a quiver with five arrows and three darts; the arrows for shooting at beasts and the darts to defend themselves in the event of need. If they are not in a zone of war, let them carry two flat-headed arrows for shooting at birds.'[16]

Exercise, the avoidance of sin, a training for war: all necessary aspects of the princely education, of which hunting was therefore an integral part. Indeed, Theodore of Antioch, who translated the Arab falconer Moamin's treatise for the Emperor Frederick II, concluded in his preface that 'the only amusement appropriate to kings is hunting'.[17] Part of its appropriateness is the possibility it offers of the visual magnificence by which kingly and aristocratic dignity may be demonstrated. In the eyes of the late Middle Ages kings and noblemen are not as other men are; the structure of society which sets them apart is divinely ordained, and their superiority must be made clear by pomp, pageant, ceremony, procession and other physical glories. Pero López de Ayala, no stranger to splendour as Castilian ambassador to the courts of France and Aragon, defends falconry partly on these grounds, and cites Aristotle in support: 'There are other benefits: a virtue which the philosopher, in the Fourth Book of his *Ethics*, calls *magnificentia*, which is the grandeur of great men; for it is a noble and grand thing for a great lord to have falcons and goshawks, for, kept as they should be, they add splendour both to his house and in the field when they precede him in his riding and hunting.' In the Italian ducal palaces whole rooms were decorated with hunting scenes celebrating the exploits of their owners.[18]

The most splendid hawks and hounds available were often given from one monarch to another, richly accoutred as proof of the status of the giver and a tribute to that of the recipient. King Fernando of Portugal gave the Moorish King of Granada six alaunts and six running-hounds, all with richly decorated collars, silver gilt muzzles, and leashes woven of golden thread; the gift was conveyed by seven of the royal huntsmen, and completed by thirty hunting-spears with silver blades and decorations.[19] To honour distinguished guests, one took them hunting. In the mid-fourteenth century the Order of Teutonic Knights, in order to attract pilgrim knights to assist in their crusading, feasted them liberally and took them on bear- and elk-hunts in the great German forests.[20] Pero López quotes many opinions of foreign, especially French and Aragonese, falconers, and describes their methods — obviously a reflection of the hunting entertainments provided for him as Castilian ambassador.

Practical men grow lyrical in describing the music of horn and hound (see Chapter 12, pp. 160–71) and the stirring visual glories of the hunt. John I of Portugal comes close to blasphemy in his description of bear-hunting:

> such a beautiful thing to witness that no man seeing it could have so little spirit of the huntsman in his heart that he would not, in his delight, forget all other duties, for in truth this sight is so splendid as to be comparable to experiencing the glory of God; for if wise men say

that those who are in glory have neither hunger nor thirst, and feel neither weariness nor pain, then truly this sight is as we say, for those who see it cannot, we are sure, feel any of these things.[21]

Here it is difficult to distinguish between royal magnificence and subjective pleasure, but none of the various justifications can obscure the fact that men hunted because it was a *déduit*, a delight. The specific joys of the hunt, the skills of tracking and harbouring game, the empathy with the hounds and hawks, the security in the recurring rhythm of the seasons in a turbulent world, the esoteric ritual and secret catechisms of vocabulary, the fulfilment brought by the successful attuning of mind, eye and muscle will emerge elsewhere in this book.

Also apparent in practical manuals and imaginative fiction is the delight in good fellowship. The hunt is a social occasion; it is preceded and followed by good food and jollity, with plentiful wine for aristocrats and employed huntsmen alike. A vitual constituent is the 'assembly' or 'gathering' (Fig. 3), which

shuld be makyd in a faire mede, wel grene, with faire trees . . . alle about, . . . and a clere wel or some rennyng breke besides. And it is cleped gaderyng because that alle men and houndes for the huntyng gadren hem thider; . . . and alle the officers that parten from home shuld bryng thider al that hem neden overychon in his office wel and plenteously, and shuld lay the towailes and boordclothes all about upon the grene gras, and sette divers metis upon a grete plater after the lordis pouere, and some shuld ete sittyng and some standynge, some lenyng upon her elbowes; some shuld drynk and some laugh, some jangle, some borde, some play, and shortly do alle manere of disportis of gladnesse.[22]

Even merrier is the roistering supper which follows the hunt. Gace de la Vigne provides a lively picture of the hunt suppers of the French court and the wine-fuelled arguments which followed them:

Later you may hear hunters talk of their sport,
And for me there can be no finer pastime in the world.
I believe no ears ever heard such dazzling marvels;
Even the King has to smile a little at what he hears.
Still, I shall forbear to suggest that untruths are said
– However much the ill-natured may hint at falsehood –
For in hunting there are feats so frequent and so testing
That the layman would refuse them credence.[23]

Gaston Phoebus, too, loves the boastful arguments about exploits of men and hounds, and concludes that 'in the end, wine will be their peace-maker.'[24] So, too, in fiction: when the Châtelain de Coucy came to dine at the Castle of Favel, 'they drank their good wines freely, and all the talk was of arms and war, of hounds and hawks and tournaments.'[25]

Man hunted originally as a necessity, and clearly the joyful consumption of what one had killed remained important in the Middle Ages and later. Look, for instance, at the ending of Folgore da San Gemignano's sonnet, one of a series written in celebration of a fellowship of Sienese nobles:

> Then, going home, you'll closely charge the cook:
> 'All this is for tomorrow's roast and stew:
> Skin, lop and truss: hang pots on every hook:
> And we must have fine wine and white bread too,
> Because this time we mean to feast: so look
> We do not think your kitchens lost on you.'[26]

The dead boar or deer was often brought home with fanfares and triumph.[27] A recurring feature is the giving of the spoils to women: one often finds James IV sending venison home to his Queen,[28] and the King of France, in Gace de la Vigne's *Déduis*, gives venison to the various aristocratic ladies of the area in which the stag is taken.[29] It was common for ladies to watch the hunting from a vantage point; in the case of park hunts, from the roof of the castle itself. The illustrations in Maximilian I's *Teuerdank* show the Emperor intrepidly spearing chamois on the Alpine cliffs, watched from a safer position by the ladies of his court.[30]

Women themselves sometimes engaged actively in hunting (Fig. 13). The stag chase in *La Chasse*, a poem by Jacques de Brézé, High Seneschal of Normandy, is organized efficiently and forcefully from the saddle by 'Madame', not named in the poem itself, but identifiable as Princess Anne de Beaujeu, daughter of Louis XI.[31] John Coke's *Debate betwene the Heraldes* refers to ladies shooting driven game, admittedly in rather artificial circumstances: '. . . we have also small parkes made onely for the pleasure of ladyes and gentylwomen, to shote with the longe bowe, and kyll the sayd beastes'. His French predecessor, author of the *Débat des héraulx*, is rather haughty about this decadent practice: 'Killing a beast in a park is not hunting; if it is in a park it is caught already. It is not to be wondered at that the English ladies kill them with the bow, for the poor beasts go where they want them to go, of necessity.'[32]

Something of the same garden party atmosphere pervades the Devon-shire hunting tapestries (Fig. 9). These include scenes of strenuous bloodi-ness in a landscape crowded with elegantly dressed aristocrats. It is difficult to assess which of these are hunters and which spectators, but clearly the ladies, and many of the gentlemen, have not been charging through river and thicket in pursuit of boar, bear or deer. These glorious works, like Madame's participation in de Brézé's hunt, are to some degree an idealization; they amalgamate sports which took place at different seasons and in different terrains, mingling active participant with passive spectator, the chase with certain aspects of social intercourse, in a way suggestive of the symbolic associations of the two. Clearly there was female participation in certain forms of hunting, especially falconry, and female interest in other forms, but for women to take part in the rigours of classic *par force* hunting, as opposed to its social preliminaries and aftermath, must have been a rarity. The medieval practical manuscripts, lavishly illustrated, depict only men, hounds and their quarry. John I of Portugal's *Livro da montaria*, devoted largely to the boar-hunt, alludes nowhere to women; nor does Alfonso XI of Castile, in the stirring descriptions of week-long pursuits of the bear through the snows of the Sierra de Gredos.

However, when the practical element in a picture or a work of hunting literature is less than total, women and eroticism are usually the first things to creep in. The social side of hunting provides a setting for amorous dalliance, as a closer look at the Devonshire tapestries shows (Fig. 9). Courtly socializing and aristocratic, but nevertheless bloody, sport are superimposed in a way which makes us compare the activity of the hunter, or of his hounds and hawks, with the sexual predatoriness of the courtiers, whose minds are in some cases occupied with things other than the unmaking of a deer. For a large hunt the whole court – men, women, servants, huntsmen, cooks, musicians – might move to a hunting lodge or a tented village. James IV's treasurer makes payment to 'Johne Hertsede, pailyoun [pavilion] man, to take forth the palyonis and pas to Strivelin with them to the Kingis passing to hunting'.[33] The poem *Guillaume de Dole* shows us the hunters returning to such a camp to wash for a meal; in the absence of towels,

> They borrow the ladies' white chemises,
> And take their chance to put their hand
> On many a white thigh.[34]

Hunting, as we shall see, is a rich source of erotic imagery; the combination of love-making and the chase can vary from a tapestry of hunting scenes in which erotic activity is a by-product to a mural about love in which the hunt is a supporting motif; from a romance or lyric poem in which a falcon or stag plays a minor functional or symbolic role to a long allegory in which the theme of courtly love is worked out in the setting and terminology of the hunting field.

The hunt, with its searches and disappointments, its quests for animals either elusive or frightening, also furnishes material for moral and religious symbolism. The pragmatic Gaston Phoebus would probably have derided this connection, but it is clear that every person of high birth in the Middle Ages was strongly aware of hunting, that the hunters included many of those who wrote, read or listened to imaginative literature, and that a proper appreciation of much of that literature was impossible without a detailed knowledge of the organization and conventions of the hunt. Moreover, this relationship was probably a reciprocal one. If the influence of the practical on the literary was so evident, it is not outlandish to suppose that in the minds of the more imaginative an awareness of the literary may have strongly conditioned the delight in the practical. The extent of literary uses of hunting motifs and symbols, especially those involving the chase of the deer in the later Middle Ages, suggests that for an impressionable aristocrat, brought up from his youth to appreciate such literature, embarking on a hunt must have been a kind of participatory theatre, wrapped in evocative associations: of white or white-footed harts which are really transformed princes; of devilish boars; of mysterious hermitages deep in the woods; of animals or hawks which lead the hunter away from his familiar environment and into the nebulous geography and landscape of Arthurian legend, where logic is obscured by mists and peril springs unheralded; of golden tresses, even, high on moated battlements. These literary associations must have been accentuated by the setting chosen for the gathering, described by Phoebus and the *Master of Game* in terms so similar to those of the conventional *locus amoenus* in which many allegorical narratives begin.

There were fundamental differences between hunting with hounds and falconry. In hunting with hounds, the hunter's animate auxiliaries were, broadly speaking, constant; the ritually distinguished variations of the sport emanate from the varied nature of the quarry. The variations in the falconer's sport, in contrast, are based on the differing size, speed, and characteristics of flight of the hunting-birds themselves. Hunting the deer, boar and bear involved pitting numerous hounds against a single opponent, often out of sight; falconry was a single combat, in full view. The falconer became deeply involved with his bird in its taming and training period, but once launched from his fist the bird depended for its success on its own skills; the huntsman worked with his hounds throughout, guiding, encouraging, weighing up the meaning and validity of their cries, adding or withdrawing hounds as the state of the chase warranted. The loss of a hound might lessen the effectiveness of a pack, but could not destroy it; a man seeing his falcon disappear into its native element, where he could not follow, saw vanish with it the work of his nights and days over a long preceding period and his hope of sport for the rest of that season. These factors cause differences in the way in which medieval writers approach their subjects, and in the symbolism based on these activities.

The medieval writers who preface their treatises with a justification of hunting do so in the secure knowledge of the massive support for their views in the society, and above all in the class, for which they write. There was a view in learned ecclesiastical circles that hunters were wicked,[35] but the higher clergy, generally of noble birth themselves, commonly disregarded it. Popes and cardinals were great hunters, viewing the chase as an adjunct of power. Domenico Boccamazza, who wrote a *Trattato della caccia*, was chief huntsman to Pope Leo x.[36] In England archbishops and bishops were often given permission to take limited numbers of deer in the royal forests when passing through on the king's business, and abbeys and priories were liberally treated by the Crown in the granting of permits to take lesser game.

The Church was not above a little poaching: the Abbot of Peterborough, convicted of trespass and poaching in the Forest of Peterborough, is only one of several cases.[37] The monks of Paisley were allowed by the Steward family to hunt with sword and bow and arrow, accompanied by greyhounds and other dogs, but there was an area of preserved forest in which they had to keep their dogs leashed and unstring their bows. They were also forbidden to take hawks or falcons, which were reserved for the laird, but were given the hides of all the deer taken in the forest of Fereneze.[38]

There is plentiful evidence of such receipt by the Church of the spoils of royal and aristocratic hunting. In 1140 the family of de Moreville granted to the monks of Kelso the right to feed swine and cut timber in the forest of Kilvinnen, and to claim a tenth of the hides of red and fallow deer taken there.[39] David I of Scotland gave to the monasteries of Selkirk, Kelso and Dunfermline one tenth of all the venison and hides from his forest of Lammermuir, to the monks of Scone one tenth of the deer taken in the forests north of the River Tay, to those of Jedburgh one tenth of all venison from Teviotdale; Edward I gave thirty carcasses to the Bishop of St Andrews in 1291 and six to John, Abbot of Geddesworth, in 1292;[40] Robert I and David I of Scotland made annual gifts of five deer to the Priory of Coldingham;[41] James IV sent venison to the Bishop of Glasgow.[42] One English description specifies that the Master of Game should actually count out a tithe of the bag 'and delyvere it to the procatours of the chirch that owen to have it'.[43] The Abbey of Châalis was the main source from which the King of France borrowed large numbers of mastiffs for his boar-hunting (see Appendix I, p. 257).

In 1275 Sir William le Baud made a grant to the Dean and Canons of St Paul's, London, of a fallow doe once yearly on the day of the Conversion of St Paul, and of a buck on the saint's commemoration day. Sir William and his family offered the carcass before the high altar to the canons, who wore garlands of flowers on their heads, and the antlers were borne around the church on a spear to the accompaniment of hunting-horns; the custom was preserved into the reign of Queen Elizabeth.[44]

It is difficult to know wheer one should interpret such gifts and grants of venison as a way of quelling ecclesiastical opposition, or simply as a disinterested and jovial disposal of one's plenty. Many writers not only do not question the rightness of their sport, but do not even raise the point. Moreover, they reveal in their straightforward imparting of their knowledge and skills a generally unassertive conviction that the world, while not ideal, is there for man's fulfilment; an uncomplicated awareness that, whatever ambitious dealings are being conducted elsewhere by men more venal, devious and corruptible, as long as the hunter concentrates on his innocent and ancient craft he will do no harm to others, nor they to him. The way to salvation is through the fields and forests, and the hunter has a lucky foreknowledge of Paradise in his waking and his going to rest:

> Now shall I preve how hunters lyven in this world most joyfully of eny other men. For whan the huntere ryseth in the mornyng he sawe a swete and fayre morow, and the clere wedir and bryght and hereth the songe of the smalle fowles, the whyche syngen swetely with grete melodye and ful of love, everich in his langage in the best wyse that he may, . . . and whan the sonne is arise he shall see the fressh dewe uppon the smale twygges and grasse, and the sunne which by his vertu shal make hem sheyne, and that is grete lyking and joye to the hunters hert.
>
> . . . And whan he hath wel ete and wel dronke he shal be al glad and wel, and wel at his eese, than he shal goo to take the eyre in the evenyngis of the nyght for the grete hete that he hath had, . . . and goo lye in his bed in faire fressh clothez, and shal slepe wel and stedfastly al the nyght without any evel thought of eny synne, wherfore I say that hunters goon in to Paradis whan thei dey, and lyven in this world most joyful of eny other men.
>
> . . . And men desyren to leve long in this world in helthe and in joye, and after deth helthe of mannys sowle, and hunters han alle thise thingges. And therfore be ye alle hunters, and ye shal do as wise men.[45]

1

'The Moost Resonable Beest and beste knowynge of eny beest that evere God made'

Nowe wil I telle you of the nature of hundes the which hunt-eth ... and furst of hure noble condicions that be so grete and merveillous in some hundes that ther is no man that may leve [i.e. believe] it. ... An hound is trewe to his lord or to his maystere, ... an hounde is of greet undirstondyng and of greet knowynge, a hounde has greet strength and grete bounte, An hounde is a wise beast and a kynde, an hounde hath greet mynde and greet smell-yng, ... an hounde is of greet wurthynes and of greet sotilte, ... an hounde is of good obeysaunce, for he wil lerne as a man al that a man wil teche hym, a hounde is ful of good sport, ... Houndes ben hardy for oon hounde dare wel kepe his maisters hous and his beest and also he wil kepe al his maistres goodes, and rathere he wil be dede than eny thing be lost in his kepyng.[1]

That is the sweepingly approving view of a master hunter, Edward, Duke of York, as expressed in his *Master of Game*. The *Boke of St Albans*, which loves making lists above all else, and approaches serious matters with a smile, provides us with 'the namys of diverse maner houndis': 'First ther is a Grehownd. a Bastard. a Mengrell. a Mastyfe. a Lemor. a Spanyell. Rachys. Kenettys. Teroures. Bocheris houndes. Myddyng dogges. Tryndeltayles. and Prikherid curris. and smale ladies popis that beere away the flees.' We shall hear more of the greyhound, the mastiff, the 'lemor' or more properly lymer, the spaniel, the rache (an old name for the running-hound), the kenet, and the terrier. The 'bastard' is probably a greyhound cross, perhaps the rough-coated greyhound; it was also called a *veltre* in France and England, and a *zwickdarm* in Germany. The butcher's hound, the midden dog, the trundle-tail, the prick-eared cur and the small lap-dogs which relieve ladies of their fleas have no further place in this study.[2]

Leaving aside those dogs used mainly in falconry, which are described in Chapter 18, the principal breeds used in the classic medieval hunt were the greyhound, the alaunt, the mastiff and the running-hound proper or *chien courant* (see Fig. 14). These different breeds had their own specialized purposes, but certain types of hunting used them in varying combinations.

Greyhounds varied considerably in size and coat, and included very large animals resembling the Scottish deerhound; Gaston Phoebus recommends a greyhound of moderate size for a man of modest means, but suggests maintaining a range of sizes for different quarries if it is feasible. Both he and Gace de la Vigne reproduce versions of what is evidently a traditional medieval hunters' description of the ideal greyhound: 'Muzzle of wolf, haunch of lion, neck of swan, . . . eye of sparrowhawk, ear of snake . . .

> He had a shoulder like the roe's;
> His flank was like the woodland doe's;
> Loin of stag; tail of rat;
> Thigh of hare and foot of cat.'[3]

There are several versions of a similar description in medieval English manuscripts, including 'The Condyscyons of a grehounde ande of hys propyrteys. Thy grehounde moste be

> heddyd lyke a snake,
> ineckyd lyke a drake,
> ibrestyde lyke a lyon,
> isydyd lyke a noynon,
> ifotyde lyke a catte,
> italyd lyke a ratte.
> Thenne ys the grehounde welle ishapte.'[4]

The greyhound's value, of course, lay in its speed and willingness to seize and pull down a running quarry as soon as it reached it. The man in charge of a leash of greyhounds was the fewterer; his role was often to wait with his charges in a position to which game was then driven, and to release the greyhounds as it went past; sight of the hunted animal was essential for a greyhound. There should be a total contrast between its behaviour in and out of the hunting field: '. . . it should follow its master and do all his commands, being sweet, clean, joyous, willing and gracious in all its doings except towards the wild beasts, to whom it should be terrible, spiteful and hostile.'[5]

Phoebus alludes to greyhounds of 'Bretaigne'; it is not clear whether he means Brittany or Britain. Certainly Britain, particularly Scotland, was celebrated for the production of greyhounds in the Roman period and through the Middle Ages. The *Master of Game*, translated from Phoebus, alters the allusion to read: '. . . men clepyn greihoundes . . . of Scotland [and] of Bretayn',[6] and in the fourteenth century Sir John Froissart took back a fine white greyhound with him from Scotland to France.[7] Greyhounds were perhaps used less in Spain than elsewhere, at least in the hunting of larger game; Alfonso xi's *Libro de la montería*'s chapters on the breeding of hunting dogs concentrate on the alaunt and the running-hound, though a miniature of the King on his throne certainly shows a lean greyhound sniffing about, perhaps as a graceful presence rather than as a hunting dog.[8] John i of Portugal also concentrates on the alaunt and the running-hound.[9]

The role of the large alaunt, or alant, too, was to seize a running beast and bring it down, or so immobilize it as to enable the hunters to kill it. Phoebus states that in its general shape the alaunt should resemble the greyhound but that its head is broad and short (like a conger eel's, according to Alfonso xi[10]). In the medieval illustrations it is shown as substantially burlier than the greyhound, but smooth-coated and handsome. It had short, erect ears, which were sometimes trimmed to a point. The most favoured colour was white, with black patches around the ears or tail. Since it was used against large game such as bear, reckless savagery was more important than finesse, and an alaunt was often something of a handful:

> for he is bettir shaped and strenger for to do harme than eny other beest. Also comonly alauntz ben stordy [a mistranslation of the French source, *estourdiz*, 'dim-witted'] of here owyn nature, and have not so good witte as many other houndes have, for if a man prik [i.e. spur] an hors the alaunt wil gladly renne and bite the hors, also thei renne at oxen and at sheepe at swyne and to alle other beestis or to men or to other houndes, for men han seyn alauntz sle here maystire.[11]

Illustrations to the *Livre de chasse* show the alaunts muzzled and sometimes wearing heavy studded collars (Figs. 14, 16), and one of the Devonshire tapestries shows them equipped with a form of body armour, probably of leather, in a fight with a bear.[12] One of the *Hunts of Maximilian* in the Louvre shows an alaunt similarly protected in a boar-hunt,[13] and a sixteenth-century Flemish tapestry in Mellerstain Castle, Scotland, includes a large greyhound wearing quilted body armour. A Spanish miniature also shows alaunts strapped into red, green and blue body-coverings in a bear-hunt, but it is not clear whether these are for protection or show.[14] According to Phoebus, the finest alaunts came from Spain.[15] He recommends using greyhounds and alaunts together in hunting larger game such as the boar or bear, the greyhounds being swifter and seizing the animal first, the alaunts gripping more strongly ('better than any three of the finest greyhounds one could find') and pulling it down with their greater weight.

Mastiffs were sometimes used for the latter purpose, though their main role was to guard flocks against wolves and houses against malefactors. In the manuscript illustrations they show a distinct lack of refinement; huge, shaggy beasts of indeterminate shape and colour, with enormous teeth and spiked collars.[16] Visually unsuitable, clearly, to act as a royal or aristocratic accoutrement or gift as the greyhound and alaunt often did.

Speed from the greyhound, strength and tenacity from the mastiff, a combination of all three from the alaunt; characteristics necessary to bring a hunt to a rapid and bloody conclusion, to finish off a beast which had to be in sight for these abilities to be brought into play (hence the term 'gazehound', used to describe both greyhounds and alaunts). All three of these dogs lacked the ability necessary to initiate a hunt and to pursue it through its more complex phases: the power of scenting a quarry which characterized the *chien courant*, the running-hound, whose instincts were the foundation of the most ritualized and cerebral form of the medieval chase, hunting *par force de chiens*, 'by strengthe of houndes', the relic of which is modern fox- and stag-hunting. The appeal of *par force* hunting lay in its complication and subtlety, its duration, the music of the horn, and above all the craft of working hounds:

> Of all hounds, the finest sport one can have is with the running-hounds. . . . It is a fine thing to harbour a beast and to take it by strength of hounds and by craft, and to see the sense and knowledge which God gave to the good hounds. . . for with greyhounds and other dogs, good as they may be, a beast is taken or lost immediately, but the running-hound must hunt till the day's end, talking and crying in its own tongue, reviling the beast it pursues; so I prefer them to any other breed of dog, for they have more virtue in them, it seems to me, than any other animal.[17]

Most of the medieval illustrations show the running-hound as similar to the modern foxhound, but often rather burlier, less leggy and somewhat flatter in the face. There are dark, pale and piebald examples; according to Gaston Phoebus the commonest colour was a speckled black, but this may have applied only to his own area of south-west France. Alfonso XI mentions white, yellow, light brown, pure black and speckled black as acceptable colours; John I of Portugal, in order of preference, pure white and pure yellow, then mixed colours – all pure black dogs, he says, are bad. His reason lies in the medieval idea of the constitution of the body, and its combination of heat and cold, dryness and moisture: 'Dogs are warm and dry by their nature, and in black dogs it appears that this natural complexion is burned up, and turns to cold and moisture, in which lie all cowardice and evil.' The Spanish translation of the Arabic *Moamin*, in contrast, gives a recipe for a concoction to dye white or pied dogs black. In England, for Edward, Duke of York, 'the beest hewe of rennyng houndes and moost common for to be good is iclepid broun tawne.'[18]

As well as national differences in colour preference, there appears to have been geographical variation in physical and behavioural factors. Different manuscripts of the *Livre de chasse* and the *Livre du Roi Modus*, illustrated by artists who clearly have a consummate familiarity with the chase, reveal what may be regional differences of hound type (compare the relatively long-legged, rakish beasts of Fig. 5 with the dumpier, more beagle-like animals of Fig. 20). Some of the authors of classical antiquity go into detail about the hunting dogs used in different countries, but it is not clear whether their long lists of areas of origin indicate variants of running-hound or breeds widely differing in appearance and behaviour, though Xenophon and Oppian certainly describe hounds working by scent, in terms very similar to those used by the medieval authors in their depiction of the typical running-hound.[19]

Charles IX of France wrote his book *La Chasse royale* in the post-medieval period, but gives us some idea of the development of the French running-hound in earlier times. He mentions three basic strains, the black, the white and the grey. The black was of medium size, with tan patches over the eyes, and was thought by Charles to be descended from the line of hounds bred at the monastery of St Hubert in the Ardennes. He describes the black as not too strong, but with an extremely good nose and an ability to overcome the deer's 'ruses' (see p. 39) by following the scent back rather than by casting around. The white hound was also thought to have its origins at St Hubert, but Charles tells us little about it. He has more to say about the strain of hounds which he calls grey (although he likens their colour to a hare's): 'King Louis, when he went to conquer the Holy Land, . . . learning that there was a breed of hounds in Tartary which were excellent at hunting deer, had a pack brought back to France.' The grey was larger and leggier than the black and the white, with longer ears, somewhat wilder and less good at scenting. It was thought to be immune to rabies.[20]

Charles's favourite type of hound was the *blanc greffier*, the 'white secretary', a name derived from its original breeding, which involved a hound of the white St Hubert strain and a bitch belonging to the secretary of Louis XII. The first pup was white with a tan patch on the shoulder; it proved an outstanding hound, and its descendants shared its fine qualities. All other hounds, according to Charles, were crosses of these basic strains. The Norman hound, commonly called the Talbot after its importation into Britain after the Conquest, was probably larger than the modern hound, perhaps more akin to a modern bloodhound, and was probably bred down progressively in size, perhaps with greyhound crosses.[21]

In contrast to this view of France as the fountainhead of running-hound stock, however, we have Gace de la Vigne's description of the French king's pack as including hounds not only from *Bretaigne* (probably Brittany, in this case) but also from Germany and several other countries (ll. 7977–84).

The *Master of Game*, in a not entirely clear addition to Phoebus, distinguishes between the larger hart-hounds and the smaller and apparently more versatile kenets and harriers:

> There ben also rennyng houndes some lasse and some moor. And the lasse byn clepid kenettis and thes houndes rennen wel to al maner game and thei serven for al game, men clepin hem heirers and every hounde that hath that corage wil falle to be an heirere of nature with litel makyng, but there nedeth grete nature and makyng in yougth and greet travaille to make an hound renne boldely to a chase ther as is grete chaunge, or other chaces.

In modern hunting, harriers are normally used for the hare; this may have been so in the Middle Ages too, hence their name, though one of their roles, in hunting with bow and stable (see p. 65), was to clear the forest of 'rascal' (i.e. the smaller stags, hinds, roe, etc.) which might otherwise have distracted the larger hart-hounds, which would then be set to find the warier hart and hunt him to where the king's party waited with bows. There are references to the Keeper of the King's Harriers, which suggests that they may have been a distinct unit kept in separate kennels, and the *Master of Game*'s chapter on bow and stable hunting refers to 'the hondes that longyn to both the mutes', i.e. the hounds belonging to both the packs (French *meutes*): hart-hounds and harriers.[22]

In their hunting characteristics, some hounds ran very fast and close to the quarry at the start of the hunt, but ran out of energy through their haste and could end up too breathless and weary to take the beast. Gaston Phoebus, a conspicuous hispanophobe, says that this is typical of Gascon and Spanish hounds; good for the wild boar, with its lack of subtlety, but not for the wilier deer, with its twists and *malises*. Others were heavier and slower, scenting their quarry from well behind, and could hunt from dawn to dusk, patiently distinguishing the true scent from the false. Phoebus recommends a middle course between the two extremes. Such was the ill-favoured but effective British dog of the classical period, as described by Oppian:

> There is one valiant breed of tracking dogs, small indeed but as worthy as large dogs to be the theme of song; bred by the wild tribes of the painted Britons and called by the name of Agasseus. Their size is

like that of the weak and greedy domestic table dog: round, very lean, shaggy of hair, dull of eye, it has its feet armed with grievous claws and its mouth sharp with close-set venomous tusks. With its nose especially the Agassian dog is most excellent and in tracking it is the best of all; for it is very clever at finding the track of things that walk the earth but skilful too to mark the airy scent.[23]

A good hound should take a visible pleasure in its work, especially in its own success in finding a scent. Oppian, never one to call a spade a spade, employs lavish similes to convey the frenzy of the frustrated hound's questing and its joy on finding the scent:

Even as when a girl in the tenth lunar month, smitten by the birth-pangs of her first child, undoes her hair and undoes the drapery of her breasts and, poor girl, without tunic and without snood, roams everywhere about the house, and in her anguish now goes to the hall and anon rushes to her bed, and sometimes throws herself in the dust and mars her rosy cheeks; so the dog, distressed by devouring grief, rushes this way and that and searches every stone in turn and every knoll and every path and trees and garden vines and dykes and threshing-floors. And when at last he hits the airy trail, he gives tongue and whines for joy; even as the little calves leap about the uddered cows, so the dog rejoices exceedingly, and in haste he winds his way over the mazy fields; nor couldst thou lead him astray, even if thou shouldst then drive him very far, but he runs straight on, holding steadfastly to the sweet scent, until he reaches the end of his labour and to his goal.[24]

One needed to blend in one's pack hounds which hunted with their nose in the air and others which kept their nose to the ground; the former were good in cover and woodland, scenting the stag from the branches against which it had brushed; the latter came into their own in open ground and on tracks.[25]

Some writers stress the wisdom of restricting a pack to a single quarry species, a view summarized by the *Treatise of Englishe Dogges*:

Some for the Hare, some for the Foxe, some for the Wolfe, some for the Harte, some for the Bucke . . . Among these sundry sortes, there be some which are apt to hunt two divers beastes, as the Foxe otherwhiles, and otherwhiles the Hare, but they hunt not with such towardnesse and goode luck after them, as they doe that whereunto nature hath formed and framed them, . . . for they swerve some-times, and doo otherwise than they should.[26]

King Modus, nevertheless, recommends hare-hunting as a good way of both training stag-hounds and keeping them in trim in the close season, and Alfonso XI's only praise of deer-hunting is that it is a way of training young hounds for the nobler task of hunting the boar and bear. He started them on the hart, then used them against the boar and finally the bear; to reverse this order would have been to ruin them.[27]

There was a special term in France, *chien baut*, to describe the running-hound which united all the desirable characteristics: beauty, assiduity, strength, obedience, refusal to change to a different scent, and the ability to give tongue informatively rather than merely excitedly. The cries of the ideal hound should be steady and regular when following a clear scent, should cease when it was trying to overcome a problem, such as that set by a hart which had gone back on its tracks as a ruse and then leapt sideways to deceive the hounds, and should be redoubled when it found the true scent again. Some hounds in this situation cast about indiscriminately in circles to find the new course, which was a good enough trait, but might lead them to 'change', to pick up and pursue the scent of a different beast. The true *chien baut* could run with its nose in the air or to the ground as the terrain dictated, and was willing to work a long way up and down a riverbank to rediscover the scent of a stag which had used the water as a way of throwing off pursuit. 'The *chien baut* must not give up on its beast, not for rain nor wind nor heat nor any other weather, . . . and it must hunt its beast all day without the aid of man, just as if man were with it always.'[28] Phoebus, with all his experience, had known only three hounds deserving the title of *chien baut*.

The most famous *chien baut* was Souillart, who was presented to Louis XI of France as a pup, and ended his days with Jacques de Brézé, Grand Seneschal of Normandy. De Brézé wrote a poem, *Les Dits du bon chien Souillard*, in which the hound reflects in old age on the exploits of his youth, claiming:

> I have been a true *chien baut*, like those praised by Phoebus,
> And after my death no others will remain
> Except my children, of whom I have twenty-two.
> . . .
> In the days when I reigned, Baude was in her strength,
> That fine red bitch, full of good knowledge.
> Oise, the bonny and the true; Clerault and Jonbart
> Bore me company in many a wild place.
> Good little Mirault, and Mesgret and Marteau
> Gave me great help over land and water . . .[29]

Five of the hounds named here, in addition to Souillart himself, are mentioned in the list of two dozen who take part in the hunt in de Brézé's longer and presumably earlier poem, *La Chasse*. Most of these are mentioned individually in the hunters' exhortations, but the leaders are clearly the two experienced bitches, Baude and Oise.[30] One manuscript of *Les Dits du bon chien Souillard* gives the following list of hound names as a separate item:

> Blonde et Blondeau, Rose et Roseau, Mirre et Mirau, Huielle et Huiiau, Ride et Rideau, Ribe et Ribau, Clincque et Cliquau [sic], Berte et Berteau, Blesse et Blessiau, Oyse et Oyseau, Bride et Brideau, House et Houseau, Marte et Marteau, Clerre et Clerrau, Megre et Megret, Ribanie et Ribon, Bonniau, Beliau, Brifault, Bloquiau, Soullart, Roquart, Rapeau, Nonau, Mande, Gloute, Brunne, Lerre, Filong, Noise, Lose, Bauderon, Roussiau, Loquebaut, Ravault, Clabaut, Lieffart, Jombart, Fleau, Louvau, Loenne, Moeuse, Broeuse, Ostine, Fillette, Sade, Losette, Baudellete[31]

William Twiti, Edward II's huntsman, mentions only Richer and Beaumon as hounds' names; the *Master of Game* gives Bett (textually questionable), Loiere, Bailemond, Latymere and Bemond.[32] Alfonso XI gives many names in his accounts of specific hunts: Natural, Abadín ('Little Abbot'), Frontero ('Frontiersman'), Vaquero ('Cowherd'), Vasallo, Laguna, Fragoso, Preciado ('Precious One'), Barbada ('Bearded Lady'), Barbado, Guerrero ('Warrior'), Bustera, Ermitaño ('Hermit'), Ferreruelo ('Little Blacksmith'), Judía ('Jewess'), Tudela, Viado . . . These are mostly three-syllable names, in contrast to the one- and two-syllable names which dominate in de Brézé. Both Oppian and Xenophon recommend giving hounds 'names that are short and swiftly spoken, that they may hear a command swiftly'.[33] Xenophon recommends the following, mostly indicating colour, strength or behaviour (some of them survived into the modern era in the packs of the English shires): 'Psyche, Thymus, Porpax, Styrax, Lonché, Lochus, Phrura, Phylax, Taxis, Xiphon, Phonax, Phlegon, Alcé, Teuchon, Hyleus, Medas, Porthon, Sperchon, Orgé, Bremon, Hybris, Thallon, Rhomé, Antheus, Hebe, Getheus, Chara, Leusson, Augo, Polys, Bia, Stichon, Spudé, Bryas, Oenas, Sterrus, Craugé, Caenon, Tyrbas, Sthenon, Aether, Actis, Aechmé, Noës, Gnomé, Stibon, Hormé'.[34] The choice and listing of the names of the hounds making up the pack become something of a literary topos in the late medieval period, lending themselves to allegorical adaptation in French and especially German narrative poetry and tapestries (see pp. 80–81).

According to King Modus, a pack of hounds should consist of at least twelve running-hounds and a lymer,[35] a proportion which is borne out by medieval documentary sources. The size of a pack, however, was often considerably larger: the royal hunt in Gace de la Vigne's poem has fifty hounds (l. 8036). The French royal hunting accounts for the 1390s give the total canine establishment for each year: the numbers fluctuate somewhat, though the general ratio of running-hounds to lymers to greyhounds remains more or less constant. The accounts of different years show the purchase of bread, for example, for ninety-eight running-hounds, eight lymers and thirty-two greyhounds; ninety running-hounds, eight lymers and twenty-four greyhounds; ninety-six running-hounds, ten lymers and thirty-two greyhounds, etc. Sometimes simple global totals such as these are given; in other entries the figures are broken down into the king's own hounds and dogs borrowed (often with their huntsmen) from elsewhere: 'Item, for our Lord the King's twenty-four running-hounds, with six lymers and twelve greyhounds for hunting the boar, together with forty-eight running-hounds with thirty-six mastiffs and forty-one greyhounds borrowed, and several huntsmen borrowed for these dogs, to enable our Lord the King to hunt the boar in the present season . . .' The royal kennels appear not to have maintained many mastiffs, but to have borrowed them in large numbers when necessary, and I have found no reference in the French accounts to spaniels or terriers, or to harriers as a separate group.[36]

For writers of imaginative literature, such as Sir Thomas Malory, thirty couple of hounds appears to have been a normal complement for a royal or supernatural pack (see p. 75). At times two packs were brought together as a joint establishment for a hunting season. Gervaisot de la Chambre, Clerk of Venery to the French royal hunt, makes payments for bread, etc. for the maintenance not only of the usual royal pack, but also of '.xxx. hounds and greyhounds of Monsieur de Bourbon, being kept at common expense with the hounds of our said Lord the King, all together at St Eloy for the hart-hunting for sixteen days from the second to the eighteenth day of May'. At a lower social level, hounds were pooled as a way of enabling men of limited means to meet the economic strains. Alfonso xi of Spain mentions hunts in which two or three *escuderos* (squires) hunt in company, pooling resources of hounds and men. Gace de la Vigne is quite explicit about the fiscal consequences of hunting beyond one's means:

> It often happens that sensible men, with only modest rents, don't keep twenty or thirty hounds. I shall tell you what they do, on small revenues: if they love hounds, they work together, and one keeps three, another four, and they take their pleasure jointly. A relative, a neighbour . . . and they take hares and rabbits, badgers, wildcats, foxes and otters which damage warrens and fishponds. In this way they find their pleasure without coming to penury. Even lords with estates, if they have a large pack of hounds, should consider carefully

where the money will come from, for a man who lets his expenses increase beyond his income from his rents sets himself on the road to ruin. (ll. 10751–78)

A cautionary, Trollopean note in a poem otherwise imbued with an obsessive love of the hunt.

The illustrations of kennels in the various manuscripts of Phoebus's *Livre de chasse* show running-hounds and probably, in one case, a lymer (though the lymers were normally kept apart). The greyhounds were probably housed separately; they certainly had their own handlers, distinguished in the hunt accounts as *varlet de lévriers* or *page de lévriers* as opposed to *varlet* or *page de chiens*, and perhaps looked on as a lower social order; it was possible, though relatively rare, for a huntsman to be moved from greyhound duties to running-hound duties, or vice versa (see pp. 172–74). Edward I of England's huntsmen had charge of sixty-six hounds and five lymers, and Richard III's Master of the Hart-hounds received a feeding allowance for forty dogs and three lymers (see p. 27). The lymer (French *limier*, German *leit-hunt*, Spanish *can de traella*) had a special role in detecting the whereabouts of a hart on the morning of a hunt, when the huntsman in charge of the lymer went out with it on a leash in order to report back to the assembly. It was vital to locate the hart as precisely as possible without disturbing it; the essential qualities of a lymer, therefore, were strong scenting abilities and silence. It was often housed apart from the other hounds, sometimes in the huntsman's own accommodation, and received the special reward of the stag's head at the *curée* (Fig. 7).

Alfonso XI gives detailed instructions about training a lymer. The young dog should be taken on a quest (the initial search) with the most experienced lymer available, and when the time came to move the quarry the older hound should be in the lead until the last few moments, then the younger one should be allowed to go ahead on the strong scent, move the quarry, and then be made much of and fed with a titbit on the bed which the game had left. After the kill it should have more special titbits, the heart or liver, and this process should be gone through five or six times, but always in country where the possibility of error was minimal.

To curb a tendency to barking, the first resource was a beating; muzzling, holding the hound by the skin of the neck during the quest, or putting the leash around between its front legs to shorten its breath might also be tried. In serious cases one might take the lymer to an area of harsh terrain, full of game, and work it continually, putting up one animal after another, so that the hound grew weary of barking. Whenever it showed a tendency to improvement, it should be made much of. It is likely, however, that continual breeding was much more important in producing strains of silent hounds suitable for use as lymers. The thirteenth-century Latin treatise *De Arte Bersandi*, attributed to the German Guicennas, is much more detailed in its instructions for training the lone scenting-hound, though in this case the dog may have been a brachet rather than a lymer (see p. 47). The dog was put in the charge of a huntsman on foot, who took him to woods where stags had been, but not too recently, and encouraged with sweet words to follow their scent. He was dissuaded from following roe-deer, but it was important not to get angry with him at this stage. If he left the scent of the stag, he should not be dragged back to it, but left to return to it in his own time, and then caressed and rewarded with a lump of cheese. This went on for two weeks, a little longer each day. In the third week he was taken hunting, loose, with the running-hounds, after hares and foxes, to get him used to their 'ruses'. After a week's rest, he was put to questing in a real hunt. As well as carrying out the initial quest, a lymer or brachet also had to seek wounded deer. Guicennas recommends that, if a deer was wounded badly enough to die without running far, the new hound should not be used for it; he suggests trying to wound another less seriously in order to give the hound a long scent to follow.[37]

Medieval French miniatures show the lymer as larger than the other hounds, with a heavy, jowled head, large ears, and an intelligent though lugubrious expression (Figs. 1, 2, 4, 7); it was perhaps very close genetically to the original *chien de St Hubert*, and probably the forerunner of the modern bloodhound, which was certainly established as a breed by the sixteenth century.[38] The tapestries of the *Hunts of Maximilian* show the lymer as a sad-visaged, long-eared beast very similar to the bloodhound. The distinct role of the lymer was already established in the eighth century: the *Lex Alamannorum*, laying down fines for the theft of hounds, specifies a penalty of six *solidos* for stealing the leading hound of a pack, three for a secondary hound, and twelve for a *leit-hunt*, i.e. a lymer.[39] There is some doubt about the existence of a distinct breed of *leit-hunt* in medieval Germany, and in Portugal and Spain the lymer seems to have been simply a hound selected from a good scenting strain within the pack at an early age, and trained specially.[40]

While awaiting release, hounds were tied to each other by the neck in 'couples' (ten hounds are still referred to as five couple, eleven as five and a half couple, etc.). The couple itself might be spun by the huntsmen (recommended by the *Master of Game*, which states that they 'shuld be made of the here of an hors taille or of a mares taile for thei ben best and lasten better than if thei were of hempe or of wolle'[41]), or might be made simply from purchased cord, payments for which appear regularly in the French royal accounts: 'To Guillaume Cordelette, for forty-eight *toises* of cord bought from him to make couples and leads for the hounds, .viii.

sous'; 'To Perrin le Cordier of Senlis for sixty *toises* of cord from which were made couples, leads and hardes for the running-hounds, lymers and mastiffs, .x. sous'.[42] According to Edward, Duke of York, 'the houndes couples shuld be of a length bitwen the houndes a foot, and the rope of the limer .iii. fadom and a half [about twenty-one feet] and be he never so wise a lymer it suffiseth, the which rope shulde be maked of leder of an hors skyn wel itawed.'[43] In the French royal kennels ordinary cow's leather was used; a payment 'to Robin le Coudre for . . . cowhide bought to make six liams for the King's lymers' is typical. For a hound whose role was cosmetic rather than practical, the leash and the collar were sometimes extremely splendid: 'a lyame of white silk with collar of white vellat embrawdered with perles, the swivell of silver'; dog collars 'of crymson vellat with .vi. lyhams of white leather'; 'a lieme of grene and white silke'; 'three lyames and colors with tirrett of silver and quilt'.[44] Greyhound collars, too, could be splendid: 'le tissue white and green with letters and silver turrets'; 'soy [silk] chekerey vert et noir avec le tret, letters and bells of silver gilt'.[45] The leash and the couple also lent themselves to literary symbolism; for narrative usages of these motifs, see pp. 72, 80, 81.

Two, three or four couple of hounds, such as those waiting as a 'relay' (i.e. as fresh hounds ready to take over the chase from those who started it), might be 'hardled' together, sometimes with a rope – the 'harde' – passed through the rings of the couples, sometimes, as recommended by Modus, with a thin switch of juniper or other pliable wood doubled round the couples.[46]

Favourite hounds were objects of great affection and pride. Alfonso XI loves to record the devotion and tenacity of particular hounds along with those of the huntsmen whose exploits they outshone; indeed, the most striking note which emerges from his *Libro de la montería* is that of companionship and shared purpose existing between master, men and hounds. One or two dogs appear repeatedly in his accounts: Vaquero is the hero of several hunts, persisting on the scent when the others fall away, or kept in reserve for the most demanding phase of the hunt; in one particularly prolonged and difficult chase he is carried on a mule to save his strength, and takes over from the bitch Barbada in the final stages.[47]

The bitch Bustera was another to distinguish herself endearingly:

> In this forest [of Cañamares] a stag was brought to bay, and Fernán Gómez's hound Bustera, being heavy with pups, came to her time, and as each pup was born she picked it up in her mouth and took it away to a safe place, and went back to bay the stag. She did this with four or five pups, and after giving birth to them all, she still went back to bay the stag. Fernán Gómez and the other huntsmen saw it all.

When the stag was dead, they could not catch her, and off she went to the place where she had taken her pups.[48]

A few select favourites, sometimes fine specimens received as gifts,[49] were part of the household. Souillart, in his old age, slept in his master's chamber, near the fire.[50] Alfonso XI recommends keeping alaunts in the palace, to make them tamer and more biddable.[51] The large and handsome alaunt was a suitable reinforcement to the dignity of kings; Chaucer's Ligurge of Thrace, for example:

About his char ther wenten whyte alaunts,
Twenty and mo, as grete as any stere,
To hunten at the leoun or the deer,
And folwed him, with mosel faste y-bounde.[52]

The fifteenth-century Prince John of Portugal had two alaunts 'which he loved so much that he took them into his bed at night, and slept between them; one was called Bravor, a gift from his brother, . . . the other Rabez, which was sent to him by Fernam Peres d'Andrade'. These two were not simply coddled pets; the chronicle account goes on to relate how the Prince, pursuing a huge boar and failing to kill it by nightfall, lay down to sleep in the open country. His page, with Bravor and Rabez on their leashes, was overcome by weariness, tied one leash around his waist and the other to his leg, and fell asleep. In the night the boar emerged, and the impetuous Rabez pursued it, dragging the page and the other dog through the thicket after him. The Prince, enraged at the escape of the boar, raced after them and slashed through the leashes; the two alaunts brought the boar to bay, and the Prince killed it 'with the most splendid spear-thrust ever seen among huntsmen'.[53]

The accounts of the French royal hunt include such phrasing as 'Expenses for .cviii. running-hounds, .viii. lymers and .xxiiii. greyhounds, with .xx. greyhounds of the chamber of the said lord our King'; 'The cost of three valets looking after the .xx. greyhounds of the chamber, lodged with the hart-hounds from 27 May to 2 June'. One may infer a distinction between the greyhounds kept permanently in the hunt kennels and those kept in the palace as decorative display, which nevertheless accompanied the king when he went to Fontainebleau or Senlis for the hunting season. Whether the greyhounds of the chamber took an active part in the hunting is not clear; twenty seems an excessive number if their role was purely cosmetic.

The death of a favourite hound was a sorrowful affair. A miniature in Alfonso's *Libro de la montería* shows three of the King's huntsmen kneeling dolefully before him and stroking a dead or wounded hound which lies across their laps; the body of the culprit, a rather diminutive boar, lies in the foreground, black, bristly and very much alone (Fig. 17).

For a hound to be carried in the course of a hunt may have been relatively rare, but they were certainly transported to distant areas in preparation for royal hunts. The hound Vaquero mentioned above is involved in hunts in the mountains of provinces as far apart as Avila and Seville. Horse-litters conveyed the English royal hounds on long journeys; Thomas de Condovere and Robert le Sanser, huntsmen of the hart- and buck-hounds, were paid for a horse-litter for fifty-nine days for the transport of sixty-six hounds and five lymers, and the Scottish Lord High Treasurer's accounts often mention the 'tursing' of dogs in cages or baskets: 'For ane creil to turs twa doggis and for tursing of them to Linlithgow, .vi. s. .ii. d.'; 'To Jacob Edmonstoun to turs hame the doggis, .xviii. s.'.[54] The late fourteenth-century French royal hunting accounts include repeated and substantial expenses for carting, but these are normally for transporting equipment or food rather than hounds: eighteen sous to Jehan de Bosne for carters and horses to bring the equipment for the boar-hunts to the Forest of Halatte; four sous to Perrin de la Mare for carrying the hounds' bread from Senlis to St Christophe.[55]

A major consideration, and a constant source of concern when away from the main kennels, was the supply of dog food. James IV's treasurer uses a great deal of ink recording transactions in this connection: 'Item, in Strivelin, to Blak, to keip the Kingis doggis and feed thaim, .xv. s. .vi. d.'; 'To Jacob Edmonstoun to the keeping of the doggis, .xxxvi. s.'; 'Payit for the doggis met fra the tyme the King passit to Tayn quhill he come agayn, .xxiii. s.'.[56] Here 'met' (meat) may not be used in its modern restricted sense, but simply to mean food; the French royal accounts regularly show large bills for bread; to have the hounds in the vicinity was a godsend for a baker and, to a lesser extent, a butcher. Michel de Soissons, of Senlis in the royal forest, receives sixteen livres after one gathering 'for bread supplied by him . . . for the running-hounds, lymers, greyhounds and mastiffs, both the King's and those borrowed, being all gathered at St Christophe for the King to hunt the boar in the forest'. (Gaston Phoebus recommends feeding the hounds only on bread when they are not hunting, so that they will associate meat only with the *curée*, and hunt the more keenly. For the same reason the *curée* should always be given to them in the field, after the kill, and never in the kennels, lest they break off, wearied and hungry in a hard chase, to return home for food.) The royal hounds also received offal or blood, sometimes in the form of *potage*, especially if they were ill or *descouragés* (disheartened): 'For eight sheeps' plucks bought from Jehan le Masqueur, butcher, to give to several disheartened hounds who will not eat bread, four *deniers* each'; 'For four tripes bought in the market to give to several sick hounds . . .'; 'To Jehan, butcher, for eight pints of pig's blood to prepare the *potage* for the hounds . . .'; 'To Adam Maigollet . . . for four tripes for the *potage* of the hounds . . .'.[57] Sick hounds were also given bean broth (see Appendix I, p. 256).

The early fifteenth-century *Boke of Curtasye* specifies a daily subsistence allowance of one halfpenny per hound; it too mentions bread, supplemented by bones:

De venatore et suis canibus

A halpeny tho hunter takes on the day
For every hounde, tho sothe to say.
Tho vewter [fewterer], two cast of brede he tase,
Two lesshe of grehoundes yf that he hase.
To yche a bone, that is to telle,
If I to zou the sothe shalle spelle;
Bysyde hys vantage that may befalle
Of skynnes and other thynges withalle,
That hunteres can telle better than I.[58]

In 1407, however, we find an allowance of three farthings per day for each of the English royal hart-hounds, a halfpenny a day for a greyhound. Under Edward I a halfpenny a day is the allowance for the fox- and otter-hounds, a halfpenny or three farthings for a greyhound. Under Richard III the Master of the Hart-hounds was allowed 3s. 3d. per day 'for the mete of forty dogs and twelve greyhounds and threepence for three limers', which seems to support the view that the lymers were a separate and larger breed of hound in England.[59] The English royal hounds were sometimes fed on meat; King John commanded William Pratell and the Bailiffs of Falke de Breaut in the Isle of Ely to let the royal hounds 'hunt sometimes in the Bishop's chase for the flesh upon which they are fed'.[60] As well as being paid for from royal funds, the king's hounds in England were also supported by the revenues of various counties, and many were kept by individuals who held land from the Crown in return for keeping a stated number of hounds for royal use. A medieval king who travelled widely through his realm might keep establishments of hounds at his various castles and palaces (we find James IV of Scotland paying fourteen shillings 'to the man that kepis the doggis in Strivelin [Stirling] to by him clathis'), as well as drawing on the resources of the kennels of his noblemen. James IV kept greyhounds at Aberlednoch, near Comrie; Lord Drummond kept forty running-hounds for him at the Mill of Millnab in Strathearn, William Stewart kept six at Balquhidder, and hounds were also kept by John Murray of Hangingshaw in the Ettrick Forest and probably by Sir William Murray of Tullibardine.[61]

Recommendations on the selective breeding of hounds go back to the classics. Xenophon suggests relieving the bitches of work in the winter so as to strengthen them for producing their litters in the early spring, taking them hunting just occasionally as they near their time.[62] Grattius is more detailed on crossing hounds from different sources: '. . . an Umbrian mother will give to the unskilled Gallic pups a smart disposition; puppies of a Gelonian mother have drawn spirit from a Hircanian sire; and Calydonia, good only at pointless barking, will lose the defect when improved by a sire from Molossis.'[63]

Gaston Phoebus recommends spaying bitches unless one specially wanted to breed from them, 'for a spayed bitch will last in her worth and her hunting half again or twice as long as an unspayed bitch'. To bring the unspayed bitches through heat quickly, he suggests bathing them twice a day in the river; he also gives a recipe for aborting an unwanted litter, involving making the bitch fast for a day and then giving her fat mixed with the juice of the plant titimal (*Euphorbius Cyparissias*).[64]

When the pups ceased suckling, they were fed on bread and milk until they lost their milk teeth at about six months old, then weaned onto hard bread, with only water to drink.[65] Alfonso XI usually left his bitches only two or three pups, four at most. To select the best, one could arrange for the bitch to reveal her own opinions: 'Before they are nine days old . . . put them in a yard, and make a circle of straw around them, and set fire to the straw (not letting the heat go too near them). Let the mother go; the one she takes in her mouth and rescues first will be the best, and the one she takes next, second best, and so forth.' This is an ancient method; it appears in the Arabic *Book of Moamin* and in the *Cynegetica* of Nemesianus.[66]

Phoebus forbids taking a hound hunting below the age of a year; Alfonso suggests the same for the bitches, but says that the initiation of the males should be delayed for a further six months, and that alaunts should be a year and a half or two years old before they are taken hunting. A hound was unlikely to be worked after the age of nine years, or to live beyond twelve.[67] By eight he was a 'lick-ladle', hanging around the kitchens; by nine only fit to be a cart-saddle, according to the *Boke of St Albans*, his best years being around four and five:

> The first yere he most lerne to fede;
> The secund yere to felde hym lede;
> The .iii. yere he is felow-lyke;
> The .iiii. yere ther is noon syke;
> The .v. yere he is good ynough;
> The .vi. yere he shall holde the plough;
> The .vii. yere he will avayle
> Grete bikkys [bitches] for to assayle.

The .viii. yere likladill;
The .ix. yere cartsadyll.
And when he is commyn to that yere,
Have hym to the tanner,
For the best hownde that ever bikke hade [68]
At .ix. yere he is full badde.[69]

The medieval treatises are much taken up with veterinary matters. A huntsman had to be both apothecary and surgeon. A little magic might be helpful on occasion: to keep the hounds tranquil and content one could take a piece of hollow cane as long as a hound's tail, shave off the hairs of the tail and put them inside the cane, and place it in the roof of the kennels.[70] The main resources, however, were the needle and thread and a range of chemical and herbal medicaments. Surgical needles are a recurring item of expense in the royal French hunting accounts, especially during the boar season, when hounds suffered considerable wounding; in one example eight dozen are bought at a time specifically for this purpose.[71] As far back as Grattius we find references to the stitching of 'the martial wounds suffered in the fight . . . Above stands Fate; the insatiable Death-God devours everything and echoes round the world on sable wings.' He recommends sealing the open veins with the acid urine taken from the bladder of the dead quarry before sewing together the lips of the wound.[72]

The constant threat of rabies pervades both classical and medieval treatises.[73] None of them suggests any possibility of curing a hound which has developed the symptoms; Phoebus and the *Master of Game* recognize nine varieties of the disease, all fatal, and the number nine consequently has a role in prognosis and treatment: if 'eny hounde is wood [mad] of eny of the .ix. woodnesse he shal nevere be hool, and hure woodnesse may nouzt làst but .ix. daies that thei ne shal never be hool but dede'.[74] A prophylactic operation described by Grattius comes down via *Modus* and Phoebus to the *Master of Game*:

And some men seyn that it commeth to hem of a worme that thei have under the tunge . . . and that if that worm were take from hem thei shuld never wax woode, but therof make I noon affirmacioun. Nathelees it is good to take it from hem. . . . Take the hounde when he is passed half a yeere and hoolde fast his fowre feet, and put a staf over wherte is mouthe bicause that he shuld not bite, and after take the tounge and ye shall fynde the worme undir the tounge. Than shul ye slitte the tounge undirnethe and put a nedel with threde bytwix the worme and the tounge and knyt it and draw the worme out with the threde or ellis with a smal pynne of tre. And not withstondyng . . . it is but a grete veyn that houndes haven undir the tounge.[75]

For a hound or a man bitten by a rabid dog, there was some hope; one treatment was to take the victim to the sea and let nine waves wash over him (perhaps with the nine varieties of the disease in mind), 'and that is but a litel helpe,' says Edward, Duke of York.[76] King Edward I seems to have had some faith in sea bathing, however; he paid John le Berner ('berner' meant 'huntsman' or 'kennelman') 3s. 6d. for 'going to Dover to bathe six braches [hounds] by the King's order and for staying there twenty-one days'.[77] Other treatments were more painful or downright hilarious: plasters of rue; goose or pork fat; goat-dung and red wine mixed to a paste. For Phoebus, the best remedy is cupping the bite to draw out the poison before it reaches the heart, and applying, twice a day for three days, a mixture of chopped leeks, garlic, rue and nettles, boiled in olive oil and vinegar, as hot as it could be borne.[78]

More picturesquely, 'some taken an olde cok and pullen al the fetheres from alle about his eris [arse], and hongeth him by the legges and by the wenges, and setteth the cokkes eres upon the hool [hole] of the bityng and stroketh along the cok by the neke and by the shuldres bicause that the cockes eris shul soke the vemyn [suck the poison] of the biteng . . . and if the woundes be to litel thei must be made wydder with a barbouris launcet.' Even if this failed as a cure, it was taken as an aid to diagnosis: 'And many men seyn . . . that if the hounde were woode [rabid] the cok shuld swelle and deye, and he that was bitte with the hounde shall be hool, and if the cok ne dye not it is a tokenyng that the hounde was not woode.'[79] It must have given the cock, at best, a certain loss of his barnyard dignity and a jaundiced view of the ways of mankind.

It was generally recognized, however, that to escape rabies one needed divine rather than human aid. Grattius speaks scornfully of 'some whose prescription has been to fasten cocks' combs [an ancient link with the *Master of Game*'s treatment?] upon the dog-collar made from the light-shunning badger, or they twine necklets around, strung of sacred shells, and the stone of living fire and coral from Malta and herbs aided by magic incantations. And so the peace of the gods won by the protective amulet is found to banish baleful influences.'[80]

In medieval France, divine help was sought by different, though kindred, means: the French royal hunting accounts show, every year, payments such as this one to Perron le Parquier, *varlet des chiens*, 'to take all the hounds of the King to the Church of St Menier les Moret, and to have a mass sung in the presence of the said hounds, and to offer candles in their sight, for fear of the *mal de rage*, the disease of rabies, on the twenty-fourth of November: .xiiii. s. .viii. d.'[81]

A few medieval sources refer to hunting-leopards. I know of no description of their use; some of them were probably ornamental, and the miniatures and paintings suggest that the animals used were cheetahs. A cheetah hunts by stalking animals which it has in sight in open country and then outrunning them; it would be useless in woodland areas and could not provide anything beyond a superior variety of coursing. Cheetahs appear to have been used primarily in Italy: a manuscript of several hunting treatises in the Musée Condé, Chantilly, which has margins decorated with superb miniatures of hounds, hawks and an occasional cheetah with collar and leash, is of Italian provenance; a sketchbook in the Biblioteca Civica, Bergamo, includes a similarly collared cheetah; and the procession of the Magi in Gozzoli's painting in the Riccardi Palace in Florence is accompanied by cheetahs. There is a fine drawing of a hunting-cheetah by Pisanello in the Louvre.[82]

The use of the cheetah in Italy may well have been stimulated by the interest taken in Muslim culture and hunting usages by the Emperor Frederick II (see p. 220). Leopards are mentioned in his hunting correspondence (which includes an order to make coats for them), and in his entry into Ravenna in 1231 he was accompanied by a Moorish bodyguard and various exotic animals including elephants, camels and cheetahs.[83]

2

The Hart

The hart, inevitably, first; and for many reasons. In most countries it was the largest animal hunted; it was the noblest in appearance; it was an animal combining innocence with guile in a way which drew the best out of hounds and hunter and made the chase a cerebral as well as a physical exercise. Its solitary nature in the hunting season made the selection of an individual quarry a possibility; its venison, often salted, was a staple in the royal or aristocratic larder. In the final stages of a hunt, or in its time of rut, it could kill a man, yet it was thought to be so timid that it bore in its heart a bone (so-called, but really a mass of gristle) which alone prevented it from dying of fear, and which was given to pregnant women, or to young children, as an amulet.[1] It is the principal bridge linking hunting to imaginative literature, to the Scriptures, to the sainthood and to art; a beast into which man himself, in medieval legend, is repeatedly transformed; a magical animal, part of whose magic – unlike that of gryphon, mantichor and basilisk – challenged the everyday craft of the huntsman.

A manuscript in the Bodleian Library, Oxford, contains a full-page miniature showing six different stages of development of the antlers of a male red deer, captioned 'broket', 'stagard', 'stagge', 'harte of x', 'harte of xii' and 'harte of xvi'.[2] The text of the *Master of Game* amplifies this information and explains its relevance to the hunt: 'The first yere that thei ben calfed thei ben called a Calf, the seconde yeer a bullocke and that yere and so forth go to Rutte, the .iii. yere a broket, the .iiii. yere a staggard, the .v. yere a stag, the .vi. yere an hert of .x., and than . . . is he schaceable, for alway bifore he shal be called but rascayle or foly.'[3]

A well-grown, well-antlered, five-year-old stag, then, would not do; he was classified simply as 'rascal' or 'folly'. To be hunted in the classical manner, *par force de chiens*, 'by strength of hounds', the male deer had to be at least a 'hart of ten' – that is to say, he had to have at least ten tines on his antlers, more properly called his 'head'. The first three tines on the antlers at each side were the 'aunteler', the 'real' and the 'surreal'. These lower tines (now called the brow, bez and trez tines) were together termed the hart's 'rights', and every warrantable beast was supposed to possess them. The main stem was the 'beam' or 'perche'. The upper tines, the 'troches', were the ones which really qualified him for the chase, and it was customary to refer to the total number of tines only with even numbers. A hart with two tines at the top of each antler was said to bear a head of 'ten of the less' (French *dis des meindres*), the minimum qualification for a *par force* hunt. With two on one side and three on the other the head was 'ten of the greater' (*dis des greindres*); with three on each side, 'twelve of the less'; with three and four, 'twelve of the greater'. It was thought that a head of four and four was so abnormal as not to need a formal term; four and five was 'sixteen of the less' or 'sixteen of defaunte'; five and five 'sixteen of the greater' or 'sixteen atte fulle', etc.; 'and so it gothe forthe encresyng til it be of .xxxii., and then is he cleped *cerf resigne* and schall *go areyriere* [i.e. he will begin to dwindle]'.[4] 'And yf any man saye he hath seen a hart of more Branches, thinck he was not in this land.'[5]

The hart-hunting season varied from country to country, but coincided broadly with the 'time of grease' (Latin *tempus pinguedinis*), in which the rich feeding of spring and summer fattened the deer and developed their antlers. According to the *Boke of St Albans*

> Tyme of grece begynnyth at mydsomer day
> And tyll holi Roode day lastyth as I you say,[6]

which is to say from 24 June to 14 September. King Modus specifies the season as running between the two feasts of the Holy Cross, 3 May and 14 September, and both he and Phoebus say that the best of the hunting is around the feast of Mary Magdalene, 22 July, when the harts have lost their antler velvet and come into high condition, retaining some of their early-season speed and not having put on all the weight which prepares them for the rut and the winter.[7] Here and elsewhere there is a balance to be struck between the requirements of the chase and the larder.

Hunting the hart *par force de chiens* fell into several clearly defined stages: the 'quest' or 'harbouring' of the heart; the 'assembly' or 'gathering'; the 'moving,' 'finding' or 'unharbouring'; the chase itself; the 'baying' or 'abay' and 'death'; the 'unmaking', 'breaking' or 'undoing' of the hart; and the *curée*. Several of these stages combined practicality with ritual; some involved only a minority of key participants.

The quest

Ideally, a hunting party sought more than simply a hart of ten; it sought the finest hart available in the area. This involved preliminary investigation by several expert huntsmen (varlets or *aides* in France; see p. 176), each accompanied by a lymer. Instructions for the quest alone in Gaston Phoebus's *Livre de chasse* extend over ten chapters (nine for the hart and one for the boar).[8] The aim was to gather evidence as to both the location and suitability for hunting of several harts, so that a decision could be made as to where to begin the hunt.

A questing huntsman, according to Phoebus, had several things to help him. Most importantly, his lymer, a hound with highly-developed scenting abilities, trained to work silently on a leash and to pick up and follow the scent of a hart. At this stage it was important not to alarm the quarry, and when the huntsman judged from the lymer's reactions to the strengthening scent that they were close to the hart, he stopped and put down a *brisée* or brashing, a small branch broken from a tree, as a marker. Sometimes a branch was simply broken half-through and left hanging. The huntsman might then take a cast around the particular thicket in which he thought the hart was, to make sure, with the lymer's assistance, that it had not emerged in some other direction, putting down further markers as he did so.

During all this he would be alert to the possibility of other evidence or 'tokens'. These might include tracks (*pies, fues* or *foyes* in French), the hart's bed, frayings (*froyeis*) of bark where it had rubbed the velvet from its antlers, the level of the leaves and twigs disturbed by the antlers as the beast went through the wood, and even the flattened grasses where its feet had rested. The most helpful tokens were the droppings, called 'fumes', 'fumays' or 'femays' (*fumées* in French). Some or all of these factors would indicate whether or not the beast was a hart of ten.

The huntsman was trained at the varlet stage to distinguish between the tracks of the male and female deer; size and depth of the slots indicated degree of maturity. The relative position of the fore feet and the rear feet also helped in assessing size and condition: if the prints showed that the animal had placed its rear foot onto or in advance of the mark already made by the fore foot, it meant that it was a lean beast, since flesh on the ribs and flanks would prevent this. German hunters made the examination of tracks an exact and subtle science, in which depth, breadth, crispness, relative position, presence of specific ridges or balls of earth, etc., all played a part in indicating not only whether a beast was chaseable, but the age of the tracks and the pace and state of mind of the animal (Fig. 10).[9]

The length and breadth of the bed could be assessed, as could the amount of weight on the hart's feet and knees as it rose from the bed, making shallow or deep impressions in the ground. Frayings and broken twigs showed the approximate height of the antlers; flattened grass could be measured as so many fingers in width to show the breadth of the foot.

The crucially informative *fumées* of the red deer varied in size, shape and consistency, according to sex, the age of the beast and the season of the year. Up to mid-June the hart's excreta formed a single flattened unit, similar to cow-dung; only the overall volume was of use in assessing the age of the hart. From mid-June onwards the excreta hardened and took on an elongated form, the size and thickness of which indicated the age of the beast. From early July until mid-August the droppings took on the form of oval pellets, still adhering together at first in an elongated mass, but then separating as the season advanced (Fig. 11). If the individual pellets were sufficiently fat, long and black, with rounded ends, they indicated a hart of ten, except at fraying time, when this token was less reliable. Light or slimy *fumées* or pointed ends were a bad sign. If otherwise satisfactory *fumées* were slimier than normal, it indicated a hart of ten which had suffered some ordeal such as pursuit by wolves, and which therefore might not provide such a good hunt.

If possible the questing huntsman viewed the hart, perhaps by tying up his lymer and climbing a tree (Fig. 2). He then returned to make his crucial contribution to the assembly, carrying some of the hart's *fumées* 'the whiche hym ought to put in the grete ende of his horn and stoppe it with gras for fallyng out'.[10] He sometimes carried them in the folded hem of his tunic instead.

The assembly

This was a combination of social gathering and planning meeting, and is described in lyrical terms by Phoebus and the *Master of Game* (see my Introduction, p. 6). Fig. 3 shows the hunters at breakfast in the *locus amoenus* specified as desirable in the manuals. Like other miniatures with the same subject, it reflects the late-medieval tendency towards taking the rough edges off hunting; the water is taken not from a wild stream, but from a fountain whose architecture would not be out of place in a Renaissance garden, or in the domestic deer-parks described in the next chapter. The most important element for our study of the hunt is the group around the table, where the huntsmen returning from their quests have spread out the *fumées* among the breakfast dishes and each is arguing the case for hunting his own hart. The lord, or the Master of Game, or both together decided on the basis of the *fumées* and the huntsmen's verbal reports which animal to hunt.

The narrative poem *La Chasse*, by Jacques de Brézé, Grand Seneschal of Normandy, is a description of a hunt led by Princess Anne de Beaujeu, daughter of Louis XI. De Brézé was a member of a family celebrated for its devotion to hunting; his grandfather, Jehan de Brézé, is mentioned in Hardouin de Fontaines-Guérin's *Trésor de Vénerie* as one of the finest hunters of his era. To judge by de Brézé's poem, written in the 1480s, the practice of *par force* hunting in northern France in the late fifteenth century differed little from that of Gaston de Foix in the south-west a century earlier. The hunt he describes must have been the first of the season; the poem begins with de Brézé questing with his lymer on the eve of the Holy Cross in May (actually a day before King Modus's recommended opening date for the season). As recommended by Gaston Phoebus, he examines the area grazed by the hart, its tracks, and especially its *fumées*. Having left his *brisées* as markers, he carries some of the *fumées* back to the assembly, where he finds the other hunters at table. He does not state how many quests have taken place, but does say that there is a large number of *fumées* on the table, from different places.[11]

In contrast to these French sources, the English fifteenth-century method seems to have been to select and 'harbour' a single beast, using the local knowledge of the forester or parker (see p. 59) and his reconnaissance of the area in advance. From Edward, Duke of York's *Master of Game*, largely a translation of Phoebus's *Livre de chasse*, we learn that terminology differed: 'The woord *quest* is a terme of hert hunters by younde the see, and is as mooch as to say as when an hunter goth to fynde of an hert and to *herborowe* him.'[12] In describing this harbouring, Edward abandons his source's account of *par force* hart-hunting, evidently because of contrasting practice. The fundamentals, however, differ very little.

Edward[13] recommends a preliminary meeting on the eve of the hunt between the Master of Game, the Sergeant, the Yeoman Berners at Horse (see p. 266) and the Lymner (i.e. the 'lymerer' or handler of the lymer), 'and than he must ordeyne which of hem thre shal go for to harborowe the hert, and . . . he must charge the sergeant . . . for to warne all the yemen and gromys of the office to be at metyng at the sonne ryseng, and that the yemen berners on foot . . . bryng with hem the hert howndis, and this don axe the wyne [i.e. order the wine for the assembly]'. The man who is to harbour the hart should 'accorde with the foster [forester] of the baly that thei seke hym withinne where thei shuld mete in the greye daunynge'.

This small band of experts should, if possible, view and select a suitable hart on the evening of their meeting, 'to wete the more redely where to seke and harborow hym on the morow'. On the morning of the hunt, even if a beast had not been selected on the previous evening, much time was saved in comparison with the dispersed quests prescribed by Gaston Phoebus by calling on the local knowledge of the forester, 'that wil ought to knowe of his grete deeres hauntes', and 'shalle lede the hunter and the lymner thidere as he beest hopeth to se hym or fynde of hym wythout noyse, and if thei may se hym and thei be in the wynde thei ought to withdrawe [from] hym in the softest maner that thei kone for drede of frayeng hym out of his haunt, . . . til he drawe to his Covert, and to his liggyng'.

The huntsman with the lymer still had an important role to play in 'setting the covert', i.e. going round the area of woodland which the hart had been seen entering, and checking by observation and by the lymer's scenting that the hart had not left it. The lymerer also sought tracks and *fumées* as recommended by Phoebus. An additional element suggested by the *Master of Game* is that he should cut a scantilon, a piece of stick of a length exactly fitting into the track left by the hart's foot as it entered the covert. The scantilon (compare the modern carpenter's 'scantlings') should be left in the track, 'and that doon he shuld hewe a bowe of grene levys and lay it there . . . and kitte another scantelon theraftir to take to the huntere, that he may take it to the lord or to the mayster of the game at the metyng'. This done, in the assurance that the hart was safely harboured, the English huntsmen, like their French counterparts, returned with their verbal and material evidence to the assembly, which they called the 'gathering'.

The relays

In both France and England, the next stage after the decision as to which hart to hunt was the posting of relays. The whole pack of hounds was not simply led to the vicinity of the hart and released; on the basis of the lie of the land and previous experience small groups of hounds were stationed in positions past which the hart, once unharboured, was expected to run. Phoebus does not go into great detail on relays. A huntsman stationed with a relay of hounds ('.ii. couple of houndes or .iii. at the most'[14]) did not uncouple them immediately on seeing the hart; he normally waited until at least half the hounds pursuing it had gone past, and then released his own to join them, so adding fresh vigour to the possibly failing strength of the hounds which had begun the chase. To release a relay before the hart had passed was called to 'vauntlay'. It was crucial for a huntsman to make sure that the relay took up the scent in pursuit of the hart and not in the opposite direction (*à contreongle*), which caused total confusion.

The *Master of Game* gives much more importance to the details of the craft of relaying than does Phoebus: 'It were good to assyn som of the horsmen among the relaies to helpe the more redely the houndes if thei falle upon stinte [i.e. if they 'check', or take a false scent] . . . and to assign the relaies bi avice of hem that knowen the contre and the flight of the deer; and ther as moost daunger is, ther sette the rediest hunters and the best forsters and the boldest houndes.' A lymer should be stationed with one of the later relays, 'and the moor daunger the elder and the redier and the most tendir nosed hounde'. By 'daunger' he means the risk of the hart entering the area where there are many other stags, hinds or rascal, thus confusing the scent and necessitating the renewed use of the lymer.

The medieval sources give little indication of the timing of all these procedures. The quest itself must have taken a considerable time, beginning in 'the greye daunynge', when the king and his nobles were snug among their goose-feathers. All the employed huntsmen and the hounds had to be at the meeting 'at the sonne ryseng'. The royal and aristocratic hunters probably assembled some time later, to enable the quest and harbouring to be completed. The illustrations suggest that the hunt breakfast was well under way or complete when the reports were made (Fig. 3). By the time a decision had been reached and relays posted, the morning must have been well advanced; the relays were in the charge of huntsmen on foot, some of whom would have to travel a matter of miles to take up their position before the next stage in the hunt.

The moving or unharbouring

This was sometimes called simply the 'fynding'. The lymerer who had harboured the hart selected for the chase led the lord, the Master of Game, or whichever senior huntsman was in charge on the day, together with the other hunters and those hounds not sent off as relays, to the place where he had left his *brisées* marking the hart's entry to the covert in which it had its 'lyggyng' (Fig. 4). In the unharbouring the lymer continued to play a central role in assuring that the running-hounds took up the scent of the selected beast, and not some other lesser stag or rascal. The lymerer encouraged his hound to take up the scent from the entry point of the covert in order to find the hart's resting-place. It was important to keep the lymer's nose to the ground, with conventional words of endearment, lest it pick up the airborne scent of another beast. Even in the English *Master of Game*, French words are recommended: 'Ho moy, ho moy!'; 'Cy va, cy va!'; 'The lymner ay . . . shal speke to hym callyng his name, [be it] Loiere or Bailemonde or Latymere or Bemond.'[15] As they went, the lymerer left more *brisées* to guide the huntsmen who led the coupled running-hounds, some distance to the rear, and kept his eye open for tracks and droppings which would confirm that he was still on the scent of the original beast.

If he came to the bed of the hart, he felt it with his face or hand for warmth; if it was cold, it was not the true bed, but some earlier resting-place. If it was warm, and the lymer showed excitement, the hart had only recently left it. If the tracks leading away from the bed were deep and the slots widely spread and in a particular pattern, it showed that the hart was running away in fear, and the lymerer would blow his horn for the running-hounds to be brought up and uncoupled; otherwise he would continue until he had firmly established the route of the hart's departure, when he would tie his lymer to a tree and blow for the uncoupling. Some harts had a younger stag in their company, called their 'squire' (French *escuier*), and it was important not to let the hounds pursue the younger animal; there was a belief that the wily hart would deliberately cross his scent with that of his companion, leap to one side and run off in a different direction, leaving the hounds deceived and pursuing the squire.

With regard to the unharbouring, the *Master of Game* differs from Phoebus only in recommending that 'the yeman beerner the which is ordeyned to be fynder folow the lymner or be as nygh hym as he myght with the racches that he ledeth', and in mentioning the possibility of letting some of the running-hounds move the hart themselves if the lymer was taking a long time to find him, 'to have hym the sonner founde, but this trewly no skylful hunter oweth to do,' unless, that is, the day is so far advanced 'that the sonne hath dryed up the fues, and that thei have lytel day inowe to renne to hym and hunt hym with strength'.

With the hart moved, and hounds in full cry after him (Fig. 5), 'than shuld the lymner take up his hounde and folow after and foot it in the best wise that he can, and the beerner also, and every horsman go that go may, . . . and as oft as eny man see hym [the hart] or mete hym he shuld go to the fues and blowe a moot and rechace, and than halowe to the houndes to come forth with alle'.

The chase

The success of the hunt now depended on the ability of the hounds, guided by the perception of the hunters of their behaviour and reactions, to run the *droit* or 'perfect', i.e. to remain on the scent and not to 'change' to that of one of the numerous other deer in the forest or to be misled by the hart's efforts to deceive by interrupting its line of scent. Important among these were the 'ruse', in which the hart ran back some distance along its own track, intensifying the scent, then bounded to one side and made off in another direction, and the use it made of running water, which it entered at one point and left at a point well up or down stream.

The pursuit was essentially a joint effort of men and hounds, with much merry noise and reciprocal encouragement. The frequency and vigour of the cry of the hounds, and of the most experienced and reliable hounds in particular, were informative as well as invigorating: 'And if the hunters here that the houndes renne wel and putte it lustely forthe, they should route and jopey [shout encouragingly] to hem lustely and oft, and rechace also. And if ther be but oon hounde that undertaketh it lustely, thei shuld hue and jopeie to hym.'[16]

The horn played an important part, not simply by increasing general euphoria and encouraging hounds, but by conveying information about the progress of the hunt, the distance between hart and hounds, the hart's taking to water, and other things. The huntsmen at the relays, for example, blew a 'mote' and 'recheat' (or 'rechace') when they had released their hounds, for the information of others and particularly of the Master of Game or whoever else was 'hunting the menée' (working the main pack of hounds). Every relay was supposed to let the hart pass before releasing hounds, except the most distant, the 'back relays';

> for if thei atte bak see bi spredyng to fore of his clees [claws] and bi settyng fast and depe his argus ['ergots', dew claws] in the erthe, and if thei se hym have also cast his chaule [dropped his jaw?], than thei aught unlay ['vauntlay', or uncouple their hounds as the hart runs towards them] for avauntage of the houndes, for so shal thei the sonner have hym at abay, and fro then he nys but dede, if the hunters serve arigt the houndis.[17]

A pleasant phrase, this last one; the obligations are reciprocal; the hounds will do their honest best, and fallible man must try to live up to them.

The death

The crescendo of the *Master of Game*'s description of the hunt reaches a peak as the hart's physical resources ebb away, its faith in flight is replaced by desperate confrontation and it turns 'at bay', a beast of magnificent qualities of speed, strength and elusiveness, worn down only by the combined abilities of multiple opponents, and seen by some of the latter as undergoing the turmoil of despairing emotions which they would feel themselves if similarly harried: 'And he hath be so wel ronne to and enchased and entreved, and so oft relayed and vannlaied to, and that he seeth that bi betyng up the Ryvers or brokes, nor foillyng hem doun, ne goyng soile, nor rusyng to and fro upon hymself, whiche is to say in his owne fues, ne may not helpe hym, than turne he his hede and standeth at a bay.'[18]

When the hart turned at bay, surrounded by the hounds, the hunters who were up with the pack all blew a mote and recheat together, to inform the rest; any huntsmen in earshot in charge of relays uncoupled their hounds and let them join the rest, and all gathered together. The 'bay' or 'abay' was prolonged, if possible, until the arrival of the lord, but it was not allowed to continue too long; it was quite possible for the hart to kill or maim one of the excited hounds, and when 'hym thougt that the abay hath lastid long ynowe, than shuld who so were moost maistir ther bidde some of the hunters go spay hym [i.e. kill him with a sword] even behinde the shulder forthward to the hert'.[19] Some authorities recommend 'hamstringing' the hart to reduce the danger to the huntsman and to facilitate the final stroke: the huntsman approached the animal from the rear as it concentrated its attention on the hounds, and severed the main tendon of one of the rear legs. When the hart lay on its side, dead, the hunters all blew the death.

The unmaking

There was a recognized way of doing everything: formulaic cries, commands and horn-calls; ritualized ceremonies. The most striking imposition of ceremonial on activities essentially practical came after the death, in the flaying and butchering ('unmaking' or 'undoing' or 'breaking') of the animal and in the *curée*, the formal rewarding of the hounds.

The meticulous, almost religious, precision with which the dead hart was reduced to joints of meat and pieces of offal was a tribute to the qualities of the animal; it was not simply handed over to a butcher for dismembering, but was dissected in a ritual sequence, often by the king or the most distinguished person present, his sleeves turned back to the elbows to keep them out of the blood (see Figs. 6, 9). In *La Chasse* Princess Anne de Beaujeu asks Jacques de Brézé, the Seneschal, to perform the unmaking for her.[20] Special hunting cutlery was carried for the purpose: sets of narrow-bladed knives for cutting out the finer muscles, broader-bladed knives for severing bone, and dainty forks for the handling of delicacies. They were often finely inlaid with gold or precious stones, sometimes as a royal gift, and were carried in a special scabbard as a *garniture* (Fig. 29).

In fifteenth-century England the rituals following the death of the hart began with the bay or abay:[21] the hart was turned on its back with antlers in the earth, the skin of the throat was slit up the length of the neck, and then downwards at each end, forming two flaps or 'labelles' which hung down over the head, and cuts were made through the flesh down to the neck bone. Then the hunters stood back and blew the death as the hounds bayed the dead hart, from which they were kept back with short staffs 'to make the bettir noyse and make the houndes the better to knowe the hornys and the abay'. The hounds were then allowed to run in and briefly to tear at the flesh of the neck before being coupled up, after which the lymers were similarly rewarded. All this, of course, like the true *curée* which came a little later, was to reinforce the hunting instincts of the hounds with a proof that their efforts were dietarily worthwhile, and to establish in their minds the knowledge that the hart was their true quarry, and all other beasts should be regarded as rascal or folly.

After the abay, or as recommended by the French authorities, immediately after the death, began the unmaking. The first step was the cutting of the *fourchée*, a stick about the length of a shepherd's crook, forked at the top, with one prong longer than the other; this was set upright in the earth beside the carcass to receive certain specific organs and titbits. With the carcass on its back, the scrotum and testicles were removed and hung on the *fourchée*. The skin was split from throat to vent, down the inside of each upper leg, around the joints of the legs and around the neck behind the ears, to enable it to be completely peeled away towards the spine, leaving the flayed carcass lying free in the middle of the hide, the edges of which were supported with sticks to retain the blood.

The joints or individual muscles were then cut from the carcass; the hunter worked, broadly speaking, from the head backwards, starting with the tongue, continuing with the smaller muscles of the neck and shoulders, the shoulders themselves, and the internal organs. The pelvis, with the hind legs, and then the head and neck were severed from the chine; the hind legs were detached from the pelvis; the head and neck were separated, and the sides cut away from the chine. During all this titbits were gathering on the *fourchée*, each pierced with a small knife-slit to enable them to be hung there: testicles, tongue, the large intestine, sundry internal oddments, and certain small and tender muscles including one called in French *fol l'i laisse*, 'madman leaves it'. 'The morsels on the *fourchée* are the finest eating on the hart, and they are put there for the mouth of the lord,' says Phoebus.[22]

The bone of the pelvis, having no useful flesh attached to it, was called the *os courbin* in France, and was thrown to the crows. In England, however, the offering to the crows appears to have been different: 'There is a little gristle which is upon the spoone of the brysket which we call the Ravens bone, bycause it is cast up to the Crowes or Ravens whiche attende hunters. And I have seene in some places, a Raven so wont and accustomed to it, that she would never fayle to croake and crye for it, all the while you were in breaking up of the Deare, and would not depart untill she had it.'[23] The *Boke of St Albans* calls this the 'corbyn bone' or 'corbyn's fee' (compare the Scots *corbie*, 'carrion crow').[24]

The unmaking and *curée* were not always done immediately in the field; Anne de Beaujeu, in *La Chasse*, has the hart taken back to her hunting lodge, where she retires to her chamber to change her clothes before the unmaking.[25] Gaston Phoebus, while he concedes that occasionally to reward the hounds at the hunting lodge may be helpful in inducing them to return home willingly after a long hunt, maintains that the normal procedure should be to unmake the hart and reward the hounds where the kill is made, for otherwise they might give up in a long chase and return on their own to the kennel in the hope of finding food.[26]

The dainty unmaking of the hart was evidently more ritualized in France, at least initially, than elsewhere. The *Master of Game* is much more matter-of-fact about it, saying simply that the lord may wish to break the carcass himself, but that he will more probably delegate the task to someone else, and that the man performing it

> shuld undo hym the most wodmanly and clenly that he can; and be wondred ye not that I say woodmanly, for it is a poynt that longeth to a woodmannys craft, and though it be wel sittyng to an hunter for to cun don it [know how to do it] . . . it longeth moor to wodemannys craft than to hunders, and therfore as of the maner how he shuld be undo I passe over lithly, for ther nys no woodman ne good hunter in Engelond that thei ne can do it wel inow and wel better than I can telle hem.[27]

There is an implied criticism of Phoebus here: what the Duke of York is thinking, but doesn't say, is that there is no need of any of that Frenchified nonsense to butcher a carcass efficiently.

The elaborate French method of unmaking the hart is made to serve an important literary purpose in Gottfried's *Tristan*. This work includes a very full and elaborate description of the unmaking of a hart, not for instructional purposes, but to underline the foreignness of the young hero, Tristan, who performs it, showing his greater courtliness and sophistication in comparison with his down-to-earth Cornish hosts, whose attitude seems closer to the pragmatic view expressed by the *Master of Game* and who watch his performance and learn his specialized vocabulary with wonder. The details of the passage also serve to accentuate the contrast between Tristan as hunter and his later hunted state.[28] It is on the basis of this and related texts that the tradition of Tristan as a master of hunting lore is founded; it survives into the *Boke of St Albans*, which begins its hunting section with the injunction.

> Wheresoevere ye fare, by fryth or by fell,
> My dere chylde take hede how Tristram dooth you tell
> How many maner beestys of venery ther were . . .[29]

The *présent* of the hart's head on the top of a pole or spear is shown in certain medieval miniatures. The margins of the Taymouth *Horae*, possibly made for Queen Joan of Scotland in the fourteenth century, include numerous illustrations of hunting scenes involving, unrealistically, only ladies; one miniature shows the hart's head on a spear, another the boar's head carried similarly.[30] A similar scene in the Smithfield Decretals shows a king blowing his horn and a huntsman bearing a hart's head on a spear before an appreciative lady.[31]

The curée

The *curée* (the source of the English word 'quarry') was the ritual rewarding of the hounds.[32] This took various forms, but normally involved briefly feeding the hounds in such a way as to ensure that they associated the reward, visually and by scent, with the head and skin of the hart. Pieces of bread were mixed with the blood lying in the hide, usually supplemented with the paunch and the small intestines, emptied and washed in running water and then chopped up; sometimes, too, with the heart, lungs and liver. If the hounds were thin, or if they had hunted especially well, or if the pack was larger than usual, meat from the neck and shoulders might be added (though this was often the *droit* or reward of the employed huntsmen). The manuals do not indicate how the bread was brought to the *curée*, but the French royal accounts mention a payment to 'Jehan le Roy of Fontainebleau for the use of his horse to carry the bread for the hounds to the *curée* of a hart taken at Soisy sur Ecole' (Appendix I, p. 255).

When the mixture was ready, the hounds were encouraged to bay the hart again, kept back by the huntsmen's staffs, and then allowed to run forward and eat, to the accompaniment of hunting cries (Fig. 7). Variations on this basic pattern included making the *curée* in the emptied body cavity of the deer before the unmaking (Fig. 9); taking the cleaned intestines some distance away and interrupting the hounds halfway through their eating of the blood-soaked bread to drive them with hunting cries to the man holding the intestines, who then threw them among the hounds;[33] and, in England, an almost theatrical presentation and a prolonged baying by the hounds.

The *Master of Game* recommends that the hunters should 'loke where a smooth [area] of grene is, and thider bere alle this [i.e. the bread and chopped intestines] upon the skynn with as much blood as may be saved, and ther lay it and sprede the skynne theruppon, the heere [hair] side upward [a difference from Phoebus, presumably intended to increase the realism for the hounds], and lay the hede the visage forthward atte skynnes end of the neke.' All the unmounted berners, the grooms of hounds and the lymerers waited with their hounds in the green shade of the trees. Then the lord and the Master of Game took up the head by the antlers, one on each side, and the berners brought up the coupled hounds and stood with them facing the head. The Sergeant of Hounds cried 'Dedow!', and all the hunters blew the death together, and those without horns hallooed, as the hounds bayed before the hart until the lord let go his side of the antlers, the Master of Game pulled away the head, another man drew away the hide from the rear, and the hounds rushed in to take their reward; the blowing of the death continued until they had consumed it.[34]

The lymer was rewarded separately, usually by being allowed to gnaw some of the flesh from the hart's head (see Fig. 7), sometimes with an extra titbit such as the heart.[35] King Modus recommends that the head should be taken to the lymer, some distance from the other hounds, and that the lymer should be made to pull at his leash as he tries to reach it, encouraged with the same cries of 'Par cy! Par cy! Ve le sci aler!' as were used during the quest, before being allowed a good gnaw at the flesh of the cheeks.[36]

To suggest that Gottfried's use of the incident of the unmaking and *curée* proves that German hunting practice was less formalized than that of the French is dangerous. The mere availability to Gottfried of the specialized vocabulary argues otherwise, and Tristan is, after all, represented as impressing Cornishmen rather than Germans. In the Latin allegorical poem *Neptalym cervus emissus*, which explicitly describes Germanic procedures, there is a *curée*, the hounds receive the blood, the titbits are placed on a *cluppen* (forked stick) for the lord's table, other items are distributed to the huntsmen, and the master huntsman has, *de iure*, 'as his right', the head, neck and some smaller items.[37]

Some hunts carried the ritual on as long as possible. In the miniature reproduced in Fig. 6 a pack-horse appears to be waiting to take the venison home, and in de Brézé's *La Chasse* the carcass is taken away on a cart, but in *Tristan* even the journey home involves formality: the various sections of the hart are borne in the same positions relative to one another as they had occupied in the living animal, with the head at the front, followed by the shoulders on either side, and so on, to the accompaniment of horns.[38] There is ceremonial horn-blowing on arrival at the hall door or castle gate in the *Master of Game*'s account, and in the *Boke of St Albans*.[39]

This, then, was the classic form of the medieval hunt: the selection and pursuit of a single beast to its death in whatever place its strength, speed and wiliness enabled it to reach before they were outlasted and outwitted by those of hound and man. This pure form of hunting 'by strength of hounds' was evidently too strenuous for some. Gaston Phoebus introduces into his description certain elements alien to the true *par force* hunt: *défenses*, lines of men to prevent the hart from going in an unwanted direction; leashes of greyhounds grouped into a pattern into which the hart was driven by the running-hounds.

Phoebus stresses that these adulterations are for the benefit of those who see hunting more as a spectator sport, 'to provide a fine hunting spectacle for ladies, or for foreign gentlemen who have come without any urge to ride, and to give them their pleasure sooner'.[40] The greyhounds were set in leashes of two or, preferably, three, in a pattern of three or four ranks; the fewterers (huntsmen attending greyhounds) in the first two stations, with the swifter and lighter dogs, were concealed and allowed the hart to pass before unleashing; those in the third station unleashed their hounds when the hart was level with them; those in the last, with the heaviest but slowest dogs, the 'receivers', let them slip as the hart ran towards them, so that the beast was assailed from all sides. This involvement of greyhounds is not to Phoebus's taste; it reduces the importance of his beloved running-hounds, and results in a form of hunting which is a hybrid between the *par force* chase and the bow and stable hunt which is the subject of my next chapter.

3

Bow and Stable

We now step briefly backwards in time. The early Latin treatise *De Arte Bersandi*,[1] a brief and no-nonsense work on deer-hunting attributed to a German knight, Guicennas, lists the abilities necessary in a hunter. Many of them are irrelevant to the practices described in the previous chapter:

> He must know how to shoot well with the bow, *bene menare bestias* and many other things: to train his scenting-hound to follow a trail of blood; to stand properly by his tree; to remember the placements of the archers, which is the most important thing of all in this form of hunting; to observe the wind, by which he may know the direction the beasts will take and where he should place his archers; to cut arrow-shafts; to be handy with the crossbow; to make a bow-string if necessary; to skin and cut up a hart; to direct his scenting-hound well, which needs much experience; to sound a horn in all the ways a hunter needs.[2]

The word in the original Latin translated here as scenting-hound is *brachetus* (cf. medieval English brachet; German *bracke*); references to the trail and the lyam and Guicennas's description of the training of the *brachetus* (see p. 23) make it clear that he is writing of a scenting-hound used in a similar way to the lymer. Various German literary sources, particularly some in which the *bracke* is a pet rather than a hunting-hound, suggest that it was quite a small dog with pendulous ears, perhaps only spaniel-sized, and often white with patches of red or black.[3] In other particulars the hunt described by Guicennas (*domina omnium venationum*, 'the queen of all other forms of hunting') is clearly radically distinct from hunting *par force de chiens*: the quarry is plural; there are no running-hounds; the hound follows a trail of blood; above all, archers are involved.

Bene menare bestias: 'to guide the beasts well'. It is evident from the rest of the treatise that *bestias* means red or fallow deer; the author sometimes calls them *cervos*, and the brachet is discouraged from seeking *capriollos*, roe-deer. The translation of *menare* by a single word is difficult: 'guide' and 'lead' suggest a going before; 'drive' has an air of thrust about it which, as we shall see, is alien to the subtle process involved.

In *par force* hunting the future place of death was unknown; previous experience of a forest might provide a huntsman with a sound basis for speculation as to where a pursued animal might run, but even if it took that predicted route the place where it died would depend on its stamina, its ruses and the efficiency of the hounds. The operation covered large tracts of country. The agents of death were the hounds, or hounds and man together, and hue and cry were part of the delight.

The art of hunting described by Guicennas is altogether more subtle and microcosmic: a single hound, a small band of men who moved through the trees as softly as foot can fall; stealth, patience, one's own heartbeat in the hush of the woods. The place of death was planned; the instrument was the arrow or crossbow-bolt, flickering out of the dappled boughs of the clearings.

Six men, ideally: three archers and three horsemen (though four or even two men could do it). The archers were dressed in green tunic, hat and hood, to merge with the trees. If one had not previously located the deer, one let the brachet range freely; if one had located deer, he should be leashed. When the deer were in sight, the role of the horses became crucial; the procedure took advantage of the fact that the deer had less distrust of a four-legged animal than a two-legged one. The horsemen rode 'across the face of the deer', downwind from them; the brachet was carried on the crupper of one of the horses. The archers walked alongside, concealed from the deer by the horses, and stopped one by one to position themselves behind trees in a V-formation into which it was planned to guide the deer. The riders then circled round the deer to get upwind of them, moving by fits and starts, pausing while their horses took a mouthful of grass; this initial manoeuvring therefore involved virtually a complete circle, hence the French term for this type of hunting, *metre les bestes autour*.[4]

Once upwind, the horsemen edged closer to the deer, with the occasional snap of the fingers or click of the tongue, until that moment when one of the beasts froze and stared, and, moved perhaps by a whiff of human scent and by that half-doubt which any man who has hunted other animals has seen enter the mind of his quarry, walked a little way down the wind with head turned and eyes alert, to be followed in dribs and drabs by his fellows, nudged and gentled through the green wood towards the green-clad men who waited breathless with their arrows notched and their bowstrings half-tightened.

One had to create a delicate and fluctuating balance in the state of mind of the deer between their trust of other four-legged grazing beasts and their instinctive fear of the scent and the small sounds of man. If the latter took over too strongly, they might run away to one side before they reached the ambush, or race through it at a speed which made shooting difficult. If they really panicked, the day was probably lost; if they simply trotted away and disappeared, one put one's brachet on the ground again and the procedure was repeated. The brachet's other role was in locating the wounded deer. It was impossible for the most skilled archer to guarantee killing a deer outright, especially a moving one, but a trail of blood provided a good scent for the hound, which would track the wounded beast to the place where it had died, or harry it until its strength gave out.

In essence, this technique is probably very old; inducing animals to move to a point where they are vulnerable to the attack of waiting hunters is suitable for tribal hunting, requires small resources, and has as its aim the provision of meat rather than spectacle. Even on a much larger scale, and as a royal or aristocratic entertainment, the fundamentals of this method antedate *par force* hunting, in some areas at least. On the scale described by Guicennas, it is a much more productive method in relation to the input of men and hounds: *par force* hunting involved dozens of each and produced one deer; Guicennas's six men might easily go home with three deer, and in its most developed form, the bow and stable hunting of the late Middle Ages and Renaissance, a deer drive might end with the carcasses lined up in rows for counting.

Guicennas's classically stated method survives in use until the fourteenth century at least. King Modus suggests using only two horsemen with a good, well-trained brachet, an unstated number of archers, and unarmed men to fill any gaps in the line; these last should be positioned slightly more conspicuously than the archers, and should show themselves and cough when the deer approach, so as to direct them towards the bowmen.[5] Phoebus, too, recommends two horses, and says that the riders should be in green, with a circlet of green twigs around their heads to camouflage the face; there should be as many archers as can hide behind the horses, and not only their clothing but even their bows should be green; two *chiens pour le sang* (literally 'blood hounds', but not necessarily the modern breed of that name) should be kept some distance away and whistled up when needed.[6]

King Modus's mention of men other than the riders and bowmen is a step away from the silent purity of Guicennas towards true bow and stable hunting. Both Modus and Phoebus relegate the driving of deer to bowmen to a rather low position in their sequence of chapters, not far ahead of stalking, netting and snaring, whereas in Germany, Spain, England, Scotland and the Low Countries the ancient method of driving animals to fixed positions was preserved and developed, either in its original or some hybrid form. There are, for example, no unequivocal allusions to *par force* hunting in Scotland in any medieval source.[7] The method reaches its apogee in the royal hunts of the Renaissance depicted in the teeming panoramas of Lucas Cranach.[8]

In some Germanic sources the practice of *birsen* is condemned as unsportsmanlike, especially by Hadamar von Laber, who wishes to put out the eyes of anyone waiting in hiding to shoot at game; in others, however, it is seen as a pastime for the nobility and even the Emperor.[9] In Heinrich von Veldeke's *Eneit*, Ascanius hunts with a procedure not far removed from that of Guicennas, except that he takes twenty men with him, and several brachets:

> Ascanius rode out to that place
> With his hunting companions.
> He commanded the bows to be placed
> Near where they had found the game.
> Those who could shoot
> Went to their stand by the trees.
> Ascanius the Trojan
> Remained standing by a tree
> And ordered the game to be driven
> . . .
> Then there came towards him
> That deer which was tame,
> And when it came close to him
> And he thought he could shoot it,
> He hit it in the side.
> The game scattered widely,
> Fleeing in terror.
>
> . . .
> When he had wounded the deer
> He immediately slipped the hounds
> And set them after it . . . [10]

The twenty men taken by Ascanius may not all have been archers. King Modus has mentioned unarmed but stationary auxiliaries; some of Ascanius's men may have made up something slightly more formal, the 'stable'. This word is taken by some to be synonymous with the line of waiting archers;[11] it is clear in some sources, however, that the stable was a line of unarmed men whose job it was to guide the game along the desired route with noise and waving, often flanking a wood in which the archers waited at one end as the game was driven towards them, not by two or three restrained men on horses as in Guicennas, but by a clamorous line of beaters, a pack of hounds, or both. In France the stables were the *défenses*, in Spain the *vocerías*, 'shoutings'. A stable was not necessarily stationary; it could be moved along or pulled in for particular exigencies of terrain. In the *Craft of Venery* it is called the 'wanlace', composed of the 'wanlasours', some of whom apparently had greyhounds with them.[12]

Before the arrival of the Normans the drive was the standard method in Britain. The exaggerated exploits described in Gaelic heroic poems are sometimes based on it: the hunt around Cruachan in one twelfth-century poem, *The Magic Pig*, involves large numbers of men who drive the deer towards the stationary Fian; in another, *The Enchanted Stag*, 120 of the Fian, assisted by a thousand hounds, a thousand men and a hundred women, kill a hundred hinds and a hundred stags.[13] These obviously fictionalized numbers nevertheless indicate how the large-scale deer drive could be used as a literary means of demonstrating dominance and resources of manpower, just as bow and stable hunting continued to be used factually as a display of conspicuous royal resources until the end of the Middle Ages. The assistants mustered for a hunt could be numbered in hundreds: James IV of Scotland's treasurer pays out five pounds two shillings 'to Malcum Drummond to gif to .iii^{c}vi. [306] men that wes at hunting with the King', presumably not part of the regular hunting establishment, but mustered from the population of the area for a particular driven hunt.[14] This payment, divided up, gives fourpence to each man. The supply of beaters was evidently a routine obligation of Anglo-Saxon and later land-tenure; one finds references to it or to concessionary exemption from it in both England and Scotland.[15]

For the king and the nobleman bow and stable hunting could be a sedentary affair. Malcolm III of Scotland is described by Aelred as gathering with his noblemen and their dogs at dawn in a clearing in the woods; they then take up their individual hunting positions, *secundum legem venandi quam vulgus tristam vocat*, 'following the system of hunting which is commonly called the *tryst*'.[16] In England the archer's station, or sometimes the whole line of archers, was also called a 'set' (German *säze*),[17] a word also applied to the section of forest to be covered by a drive. The individual station was also called a 'stand' or 'standing'. There were normally dogs with, or within easy call of, each archer. Wyntoun, in the fifteenth century, describes King Duncan preparing himself with a bow and a brachet.[18] The brachet was used to track wounded deer; it was common, too, to have gazehounds at the trysts as adjuncts to the bows; they were normally large greyhounds, but sometimes (in Spain, particularly, where deer were a less favoured quarry than boar and bear) alaunts were used. The greyhounds or alaunts were slipped as the quarry ran past, wounded or missed, to pull it down immediately rather than to trail it. In England the tryst appears to have been specifically the place where the fewterers stood with the leashed greyhounds, probably some little distance back from the bowmen. The arrangement is quite clear in one of the paintings of Lucas Cranach.[19]

A good description of a drive is included in the story of the foundation of Holyrood Abbey, Edinburgh, as recorded in the Abbey's *Ritual Book*: 'At that time Scotland was well wooded, and the large Forest of Drumselth lay close to the east side of Edinburgh, full of large numbers of red and fallow deer, roe, wolves and wild boar. After Mass on the day of the Exaltation of the Holy Cross . . . the young noblemen of the court asked King David to go hunting.' Despite the protestations of Alwin, an English monk, the King agreed, and

> after breakfast mounted his horse and rode eastward through the valley called Abergare . . . between two hills, to the place where he thought the beasts would be most likely to flee from the hounds. The huntsmen went into the forest with their hounds, so as to drive out the beasts from the depths of the woods by their craft and the cry of the hounds, and soon the music of the hounds and the shouting of the huntsmen . . . filled the whole air with melody. The King waited silently, not far from the foot of Salisbury Crags, facing north under a leafy tree, with his nobles dispersed around with their dogs, hidden from the game after the manner of hunters. The King suddenly saw . . . a beautiful hart with huge antlers, rushing towards him.[20]

The rest of the account tells how the hart attacked the King's horse, and as the King fell he seized, by chance, a cross between the hart's antlers, which came away in his hand. The cross was worshipped in thanks for his deliverance, and the Abbey founded on that spot.

Phoebus's instructions for bow and stable hunting[21] include a description of the bow, which he says is called the English or Turkish bow: it should be of yew or boxwood, twenty hands (about 6 feet 6 inches) from end to end, with a silken bowstring. The bow should not be overstrong: one should be able to draw it easily without shifting one's position and to hold it unwaveringly after drawing it to enable an oncoming deer to reach the best position for the shot without being put off by the archer's movement. The arrow should be eight hands long (about 2 feet 6 inches); the arrowhead as long as the breadth of four fingers to the end of the barbs, five fingers overall. The archers and crossbowmen, dressed again in green, should be stationed downwind, a stone's throw apart if the wood was open, closer if it was not. They should have their back to a tree rather than hide behind it (hence the importance of being able to draw one's bow in advance and then remain motionless). Next, one placed one's stable along the flanks, as close as numbers permitted, went upwind, and began the drive with one's hounds.

From the bowman's point of view, there were certain precepts about when and how to shoot. A deer coming head on was best shot in the middle of the chest from as close as possible, though if one delayed one's shot too long the deer could run past on the right, which was undesirable, because to shoot to the right one had to swing one's whole body. If the deer was making to one's left, one let it come and shot it in the side (but aiming well in front to allow for its movement). Shooting straight to one's left or right had two related drawbacks: the beast was moving at its fastest in relation to the flight of the arrow, and one might miss it and shoot the neighbouring archer instead ('I saw Sir Geoffrey Harcourt shot in the arm like that,' says Phoebus, without any great note of emotion). It was safest to treat the passing deer as a safe grouse-shooter takes a low bird: either shoot it at an angle in front, or let it through the line and shoot it going away behind.

A deer did not always drop dead when struck. In Phoebus's mode of bow and stable hunting, if one saw one's arrow strike, and the beast ran on, one blew one's horn or whistled to summon the scenting-hounds, which were stationed at each end of the line of archers. This suggests that he did not employ greyhounds. He calls the scenting-hounds lymers, and gives no indication that they were any different from the lymers used at the start of a *par force* hunt. Retrieving and examining the arrow gave an indication of the ease with which a deer might be found: one could judge the depth of penetration, and if the blood was thick and sticky it meant that the beast was probably hit *entre les quatre membres*, between front legs and back, probably mortally, and would not run far. Clear, bright blood meant less likelihood that the wound was deadly, and more work for the lymers. If the arrow bore traces of the contents of the belly, the wound was mortal, but death would not come as swiftly as when the deer was hit in the ribcage.

Phoebus clearly has plenty of experience of bow and stable hunting, and for him any form of hunting is better than fretting indoors, a prey to evil thoughts, but it is not really his cup of tea. He sums up his chapter on it engagingly and slightly dismissively by acknowledging that the true masters of the sport are elsewhere: 'I know little of hunting with the bow; if you want to know more, you had best go to England, where it is a way of life. In anything to do with hunting, I can only tell you what little I know. So, hunting with the bow you take the beasts without really working the hounds: you set your stables, you put in your men to beat and make a noise through the wood, and the deer void the wood and come to the bowmen.' *Et voilà, c'est tout*, he almost adds.

And so to England. The hunting of the deer by Sir Bertilak in the fourteenth-century poem *Sir Gawain and the Green Knight* is not only splendidly vivid and atmospheric; it is a consummate description, by a knowledgeable hunter, of the technicalities of bow and stable hunting. All

the elements which I have already described are included: the line of
archers; the stable; the running-hounds, initially in couples, then ranging
free; the beaters; the fewterers and their greyhounds; the noise of horn,
hound and voice. Moreover, this extract from an imaginative work clarifies
for us certain things which in the practical treatises should have been made
clear, but are not.

The scene is Sir Bertilak's castle; the time is the early morning. No ladies
are involved in the hunt; the quarry of the predatory Lady Bertilak this day
will be Gawain, still sleeping. In the grey dawning, then:

> . . . the high lord of that land was not the last
> Arrayed for that riding, with rank on rank of men.
> When he had heard Mass, and taken a hasty mouthful,
> He hurried with his horn, hot for the hunting-field.
> Before the first beam of the sunshine brightened the earth
> He and his knights were in saddle, high on their horses.
> Then the handy huntsmen coupled up their hounds,
> Cast open the door of the kennel and called them out;
> Blew loud on their bugles, three plain blasts;
> Brachets bayed at the horns, and gave their brave cries;
> Those which chased off were chivvied back and chastised;
> A hundred hunters, as I have heard tell,
> > Of the finest.
> > Fewterers joined those at the trysts;
> > Huntsmen uncoupled their hounds.
> > The forest was woken and stirred
> > By the echoing notes of the horn.

The wild beasts quivered at the cry of the questing hounds;
Deer ran though the dale, distracted by fear,
Hastened up the high slopes, but hotly were met
By the stout cries of the stable, staying their flight.
They let through the antlered harts, with their handsome heads,
And the brave bucks too, with their branching palms,
For this fine lord had forbidden, in fermisoun[22] time
That any man should molest the male of the deer.
The hinds were held in the valley with hey! and ware!,
The does driven with din to the depth of the dale.
Then the shimmering arrows slipped from the bowstring, and
    slanted,
Winging their way from every tree in the wood.
Their broad heads pierced the bonny flanks of brown;
The deer brayed and bled, as on the banks they died.

The hurrying hounds still chased them, and harried them still;
Hunters came after with high hue of the horn,
Cleaving the cliffs with the clear noise of their cry.
The beasts which ran on and broke through the ranks of the bowmen
Died at the resayt, seized and dragged down by the dogs;
They were harried from the slopes and teased down to the streams,
So skilled were those who stood down at the sets,
And the greyhounds so great and so swift to grip them
And to fling them down, faster than one could follow
    With the flick of an eye.
  The lord, in high good humour,
  Now galloping, now on foot,
  Saw the merry day wear on
  Till the fall of night.[23]

Notice how the terrain governs the positioning of archers, stable and fewterers: the drive is down a wooded valley, so that the flight of the deer is confined and channelled to the archers; the deer try to escape up the sides of the valley, and are turned back into it by the shouting of the stable, stationed in a line along the upper slopes on each side; the hounds, mounted hunters and beaters drive the deer between the two parallel lines of stable, and the archers do their work; deer which run on behind the archers again try to take refuge by climbing the slopes; 'teazers' are sent up by the fewterers to chivvy them out, they come down to the water, a desperate deer's last refuge, and are caught by the larger greyhounds, the receivers, waiting at the receiving-station, the 'resayt'.[24]

Two new aspects, which I think are inter-related. Firstly, only the hinds and does are killed; the red stags and fallow bucks go free. Secondly, Sir Bertilak, despite his eminence, is not a member of the line of archers, but rides with his hounds to move the deer.

The stags and bucks go free because it is, explicitly, 'fermisoun', the close season. The word occurs in medieval legal documents: Richard II made an annual grant to the Abbess of Wherwell, in Hampshire, of two bucks 'de grees' (i.e. in time of grease) and two does 'de firmeson'.[25] Sir Bertilak works his pack of hounds in preference to standing with a bow in his hand because he prefers it (and because, for literary purposes, he is quintessentially a man of action, in contrast to the misguidedly, and temporarily, inert Gawain). We have heard Gaston Phoebus, another man of energy, wax lyrical about *par force* hunting and speak rather dismissively of bow and stable. Sir Bertilak knows all about *par force* hunting, and is a master of it (despite his Englishness): later in the poem he hunts both the boar and the fox *par force de chiens*. The essence of *par force* hunting was the harbouring and pursuit of a single selected animal: stag, boar, bear or fox. Hinds and does did not lend themselves to it because they are usually in a herd, though single hinds were sometimes hunted *par force* by heartless men in the summer when they had their calves with them and were isolated.[26]

So if Sir Bertilak is to hunt deer at all, in the close season for the hart and the buck, it has to be the hinds, whose season, according to Phoebus, begins when that of the hart ends and continues until Lent,[27] and the hinds were hunted with bow and stable. But he, and, one imagines, Phoebus, would rather be in company with the hounds, dismounting, directing, planning, sounding the horn, than standing with a bow, performing a role which any late-medieval aristocratic lady was expected to be able to cope with. If they can't have *par force* hunting, they prefer that part of bow and stable hunting which most resembles it.

The question of seasons, then, is crucial. One cannot claim that the hart and buck were never hunted with bow and stable; there is clear evidence that they were (see Fig. 8), and in its ultimate refinement bow and stable hunting fell into two stages, the hart being reserved by special techniques for the second. However, it appears likely that the true devotee of *par force* hunting would prefer to use that method whenever the hart and buck were chaseable. He would fall back on bow and stable during the season of the hinds and does, or when he had a large and/or mixed company to entertain, and he would take an active rather than a static role, as master of hounds rather than the most favoured archer.

Sir Bertilak's three quarries are the boar, the fox and the deer. According to the *Boke of St Albans* the boar is in season from the Nativity of Our Lady (8 September) to the Purification (2 February); the fox from the Nativity of Our Lady to the Annunciation (25 March); the hart from Midsummer Day (24 June) to Holy Roode Day (the Exaltation of the Cross, 14 September). The hunts in *Gawain* are part of the Christmas festivities, and the author knows as well as Sir Bertilak that the hart is out of season.

Before examining bow and stable hunting in its fully developed form in fifteenth-century England, something must be said about enclosed hunting areas and deer-parks. The stable's role was to guide the fleeing deer along a predetermined route. This could also be achieved by inanimate means. At the most primitive level, hunters in prehistory and on through the Middle Ages must have drawn on accumulated experience to drive game in a particular way in relation to the terrain so as to use the lie of the land, river valleys, defiles in the rocks and other natural features to guide the quarry to the waiting hunters, or into snares or traps. These regularly used routes have left traces in modern place-names. In Scotland, for example, the Gaelic word *elrick*, used to describe the place where the stationary hunters waited, survives as a common place-name. In some cases rudimentary fieldwork makes the reason quite clear; the farm of Elrick in Kincardineshire, for instance, in the old royal hunting forest of Cowie, overlooks the Burn of Muchalls at a point where the valley deepens and narrows, and the hill of Carn Elrick, in the Grampians, is close to a defile at the mouth of Glen Einich.

Later, the hunter evolved artificial means. These included 'hayes' or long nets, set on poles, and used either as a means of capture (as they are still, by poachers after rabbits, hares or even partridges) or as a way of preventing a beast from escaping sideways so that it could only run towards the hunters waiting in ambush. In the Middle Ages there also evolved, with the decrease in wilderness and the increasing role of hunting as a viewable entertainment, the more rigid structure of the fence, pale or deer-dyke. This was typically a ditch and an earthen bank with a wattle fence or oak paling on the top, and was probably created originally as an adjunct to the natural terrain, to stop up a repeatedly used escape route or to narrow a point of passage. It evolved into a complete enclosure, sometimes with deer-leaps which allowed entry but not escape, gates (which in the later period became fanciful follies), and its own legal status: the enclosed game-reserve or deer-park (Fig. 26).

Permanent enclosures constructed to restrict the movement of game probably existed at least as early as the ninth century. A document of Charlemagne of the year 812 requires 'our woods and forest to be well kept. The *Judex* [estate steward] . . . to preserve well our beasts of chase in the forests, and to protect hawks' nests . . . The *Judex* is to take great care of the fences of our parks, mending them from time to time, not waiting until a complete new fence is needed.'[28] In late-medieval France, however, the word *parc* was used to mean not just a game-park, but any area enclosed by a fence (as is 'park' in Scotland still); Phoebus describes a method of catching wolves alive involving two concentric *parcs*, which in the miniatures are enclosures of wattle woven around stakes, and are only a few yards in diameter.[29]

The *Domesday Book* mentions two different kinds of restrictive enclosure: the park and the haye. The park had a fixed and complete barrier around it; the exact nature of the haye is not clear, but since the word is used in other contexts to mean both 'hedge' and 'long-net', it was probably of a flimsier nature, and may have been simply a series of palisades or hurdles designed to guide driven game towards waiting archers or nets in what was otherwise an open wood, or to act as a pen for the capture of wild deer which might be transferred to a permanent park, as the 'hay yard' was used at Falkland in Fife (see p. 60). The latter possibility may be supported by the phrasing of the entries: *.iii. haiae capreolis capiendis*, 'three hayes for the taking of roe-deer', but *capiendis* need not rule out killing, and in one place *stabilituras*, 'stands', are mentioned, which implies the involvement of archers. In only one case, the haye of Donnelie in Warwickshire, does the *Domesday Book* indicate the size: half a mile long and the same across. Hayes are mentioned chiefly in the descriptions of the counties of Worcestershire, Herefordshire, Shropshire and Cheshire, usually in groups of from two to seven.[30]

In contrast to the allusions to over seventy hayes, *Domesday* mentions only thirty-one parks, mostly in the South of England. The most northerly are in Shropshire and Norfolk. Eight belonged to the king, most of the rest to members of the aristocracy, a few to prelates or ecclesiastical bodies (the Bishop of Bayeux had three in Kent, the Bishop of Winchester one at Waltham, the churches of Pershore and St Albans one each).[31] In the later Middle Ages and the Tudor period the number of parks increased enormously; the right of 'imparking' could be granted or purchased, and so formed a source of royal revenue. Harrison, in his first edition of Holinshed's *Chronicles*, was able to complain (with exaggeration, but no doubt reflecting a general impression) that

> the twentieth part of the realme is employed upon Deere and Conies
> . . . I would gladly have set downe the just number of these inclosures
> to bee founde in every countye, but sith I cannot so doe, it shal suffice
> to say, that in Kent and Essex only are to the number of a hundred . . .
> the circuite of these inclosures . . . containe oft times a walke of foure
> or five myles, and sometimes more or lesse, whereby it is to be seene
> what store of grounde is employed upon that vayne commoditie
> which bringeth no manner of gaine or profit to the owner.[32]

In 1512 the great house of Percy, Earls of Northumberland, had a total of 5571 deer in twenty-one parks in Northumberland, Cumberland and Yorkshire alone, and also owned parks in the South of England.[33]

The park was normally conveniently close to the palace or castle; sometimes immediately adjacent to it or surrounding it, so that hunting might be viewed even from the battlements. In Scotland, such parks were in being certainly from the twelfth century onwards, and were created not only by kings but by their landed subjects.[34] Sometimes a nobleman or religious foundation needed royal permission: Robert the Bruce allowed Robert de Crosby *ad habendum liberum parcum*, 'to have a free park'; Arbroath Abbey was allowed by Robert I in 1319 to create parks and deer-leaps in Dunbarrow and Conan.[35] In both Scotland and England, however, baronial parks seem sometimes to have been created without special licence.

The institution of the park was not simply a matter of the hunter's convenience; it involved a radically different and rather saddening concept of the relationship between man and the animals of the wild. A deer was *res nullius*. While it was in a man's woods it was his to catch if he could; as soon as it left his boundaries it was someone else's. To enclose one's woodland, therefore, and to enable deer to enter it without being able to escape, was to acquire permanent possession of creatures formerly free-ranging and without a fixed owner.

Royal parks had an appointed parker or keeper (an administrator, not a gamekeeper). In Scotland, where considerable evidence for the details of park management is available in the Exchequer Rolls and the Lord Treasurer's Accounts, he might be a prominent ecclesiastic, such as the Bishop of St Andrews, Keeper of the Park of Collessie in 1450–51, or the Abbot of Lindores, appointed Keeper of Linlithgow in 1498.[36] Appointments were sometimes hereditary, such as that of the Frasers to Cowie in 1327 and that of Thomas Home to Duns Park in 1452.[37]

The following is a document of Queen Margaret of Anjou specifying the obligations of one of the royal park-keepers:

By the Queene. To the Keeper of Our Park of Apechild [Apchild, or Abfield, in Essex], or his Depute there: Wel beloved, we wol and expressly charge you that, for certain considerations moving us, our game within our parc of Apechild, wherof ye have the saufe garde and keping, ye do, with all diligence, to be cherishsed, favered and kept, without suffryng eny person, of what degre, estat, or condicion that he be, to hunte there, or have course, shot, or other disporte, in amentising [possibly amortising, i.e. alienating] our game above said, to th'extent that, at what tyme it shall please us to resorte thedor, your trew acquital may be founden for the good keping and replenishing therof, to th'accomlissement of our intencion in this partie. And that in no wise ye obeie ne serve eny other warrant, but if hit be under our signet, and signed with our owne hande. And if eny personne presume t'attempte to the contrarie of the premisses, ye do certiffie us of their names: and that ye faill not herof, as ye will eschew our displeasure at your perill, and upon forfeiture of the kepyng of our said park. Yeven at Plasshe [Pleshey, in Essex], the .xxviii. day of August the yere [1449].[38]

Some parks were very large; the construction of the earthen bank was a considerable labour, and the wattle fence needed constant maintenance; labour for the purpose was required by the king from his tenants. A deer-park might have internal divisions to facilitate the organization of drives, or simply as the result of extension. This can be seen in the case of the surviving earthwork of the Kincardine Deer Dyke in the eastern Grampian Mountains, adjacent to the site of Kincardine Castle near Fettercairn. The area of the park is about two miles wide and (if it originally extended to the castle) about three miles long. There is an internal division, and there are gaps in the pale where it crosses valley bottoms; these may have been closed off with a wooden fence which could be removed, either to use such a place as an elrick or to drive the wild deer into the park from the open forest for restocking.[39]

James IV's treasurer's accounts and the Exchequer Rolls provide considerable information on the procedures and problems of the park system, especially for the royal parks adjoining Stirling Castle and Falkland Palace, where the distinction between wild and domesticated deer becomes blurred. We find deer in the parks being fed on hay or oats in hard winters,[40] and domestic cows being bought to suckle and foster deer calves.[41] Deer which escaped were apparently not particularly difficult to recapture; James pays 3s. 6d. 'to ane man kepit the deir that brak furth of the park of Strivelin'.[42] Artificial stocking is common; deer are moved from one park to another, perhaps to introduce new blood. Some allusions to the carting or 'tursing' of deer are ambiguous, and could well refer to carcasses: 'To ane man that brocht tua hertis to the King fra the Hunthall [of Glenfinglas], .vi. s.'; others certainly relate to live deer: 'To ane man of the Lard of Wemes that brocht thre quyte deir to put in the park, .xxviii. s.'.[43] White deer were no doubt welcome as a decorative feature, perhaps reinforced by an awareness of the magical role of the white hart in literature. In another unambiguous allusion to stocking with live deer, Lord Willoughby is allowed by the Duke of Norfolk to kill does during a hunting visit to Framlingham Park on condition that 'for as many doys as he kyllyd heere he schulde put quyke [live] doys in Hersham [probably Horsham, Sussex] park' (see Appendix II, p. 262).

For the Scottish parks, however, the main source of new stock was the wild, with Falkland an important source of supply for Stirling. In addition to (and probably inside) the main park pale, James created a temporary enclosure at Falkland, the hay yard, 'hay' being a variant of the word 'haye' or 'haie', meaning net. There are references to the 'winding' of the hay yard, which probably means that it was of woven wattle hurdles. From the accounts it appears that at restocking time part of the park pale was opened up, the hay yard constructed within it, and the deer driven down from the open country, probably the Lomond Hills to the west, by huntsmen with dogs ('rache' is from the same source as English 'brachet', and was the normal Scots word for a scenting-hound[44]), and by men employed specially on the day. Once in the hay yard some of the deer were probably netted for easier handling and sent to royal parks elsewhere; the rest would be allowed to enter the main park: 'To him he gaif John Balfour passand with raches in the cuntree to drif the deir to the park, and for wyndyng of the hay zard for deir taking, .xiii. s.'; 'laid down to .xxxii. men divers dayis with Maister Levisay at the deir taking; ilk man on the day .viii. d.'; 'To the werkmen that tuke the deir in the fald, in drinksilver, .v. s.'; 'For deir nettis quilk zeid [which went] to Faukland, .vi. l. .xviii. s.'.[45]

Deer were transported to Stirling from Falkland in litters, constructed at the same time as the deer-taking: 'For making of .ii. littaris for carying of deir, .iiii. s.';[46] four men made the journey repeatedly, taking three days each time, except when delayed by floods: 'To Andro Matheson for the littar passand this winter bipast .xvi. tymes to Strivelin with deir, to foure men passand tharwith . . . ilk man on the day .viii. d., furth ilk tyme thre dayis, and ane tyme foure dayis, for the wateris stoppit thaim.' They were paid for at least six other journeys earlier.[47] The Master Levisay involved in the deer-taking, who was English, also appears in the treasurer's account taking deer alive within the park,[48] and in 1503, for the King's wedding, three men worked for twelve days in the park catching deer and other game.[49]

The interplay between the unenclosed forest and the park may also be observed in a hunting agreement drawn up in 1247 between Roger de Quincy, Earl of Winton, and Roger de Somery, Baron of Dudley, about rights of hunting in and around Bradgate Park, one of several parks bordering Charnwood Forest, Leicestershire. The right of hunting in the park is reserved by de Quincy for himself; de Somery is allowed to hunt in the forest with nine bows and six hounds. The archers are to use not barbed arrows, but *sagittas pilettas*, arrows with rounded knobs on the shafts to prevent over-penetration. If a wounded beast enters Bradgate Park by one of the deer-leaps, de Somery is allowed to send in up to two men after it, without bows (but presumably with a hound), but must abandon the search at sunset. A brace of does and a brace of bucks from the park are to be given to de Somery every year.

Any owner of game rights with a grain of sense and a close knowledge of his ground devises his leases to improve his own sport while ceding some of it to his tenant, and the above arrangement was probably carefully shaped to benefit Roger de Quincy; whatever de Somery's men killed, it is likely that their hunting would drive not only wounded but also unwounded deer from the open forest into the Earl's park, and that even the wounded deer which entered would in some cases be stricken sufficiently lightly, because of the special arrows specified, as to elude the men sent after them and subsequently to recover. The same may have been true of his agreement with the priors of Ulverscroft, who were permitted to hunt in Charnwood Forest *usque ad saltum*, 'as far as the deer-leap' of the parks of Bradgate, Groby and Loughborough.[50]

Bradgate was fenced with vertical pales of oak. Accounts still exist concerning the 'perambulator' and the 'palemaker' of the park, and the rents raised from non-hunting activities such as herbage (pasturing) and pannage (the grazing of pigs, especially on acorns). Indiscriminate timber-cutting evolved into a system of 'coppice under standards', i.e. large trees, mostly oak, with an 'underwood' of coppiced hazel or sweet chestnut, the cyclical cutting of which produced further income.[51]

Predators caused problems. Steps were taken to kill foxes in the park at Falkland with 'ane stalp [trap] and the irn graith [equipment] to the samyn, be the Kingis command',[52] and men were appointed to keep down wolves at Stirling.[53] Phoebus, in contrast, informs us that it is possible to take wolves alive in the wild by 'diverse engines', release them into a game-park and then hunt them *par force*.[54]

Such were the game-parks, then. The smaller baronial ones, with their enclosing barrier and perhaps not over-wild inhabitants, served as the setting for the genteel and undemanding hunts with which the late-medieval aristocracy entertained themselves and their guests, and for which a special lady's crossbow (called in German *damenschnepper*) was developed; such hunts were a source of chauvinistic pride to the English herald in the *Débat des héraulx d'armes*: 'The kingdom of England is adorned with fine hunting, for there is such abundance of parks, full of venison: fine red, roe and fallow deer, and when the ladies resort there for entertainment they take singular joy in shooting with the bow and killing these beasts.'[55]

In the much larger royal deer-parks, the scale was big enough for the deer to retain much of their wildness, but nevertheless the institution of the park must have had a marked effect on that feeling of aspiring quest and unpredictable outcome in the mind of the hunter, who now knew that, in whatever direction his quarry might run, or his hound lead him astray, not only the beast he pursued but he himself would be brought up short by the park pale in a couple of miles. In confining the beasts, he confined his own imagination.

The game-roll of Richard Chambyr, the keeper or parker of Framlingham (see Appendix II), gives a good impression of the scale of hunting in a large park of fallow deer in the late Middle Ages and the early Tudor period, and of its carefully supervised nature. Framlingham belonged to the Duke of Norfolk. The game-roll shows that the Duke used venison to cement social relationships and to give voluntary and institutionalized gifts to the Church: he disposes of carcasses to fellow aristocrats, to abbeys and priories, to the local parson as his tithe, and to towns and villages such as Ipswich, Woodbridge and Harlaxton. The parker's problems include marauding dogs, poachers (including a parish priest, found stalking deer with a bow and arrow on the Eve of Holy Rood) and considerable losses through diseases called the wyppes, the garget and the rotte. It is likely that the incidence of disease was much greater in a well-stocked park than in the open forest because of a build-up of parasites. There were also very substantial losses of deer in winter, especially of fawns. One receives the impression of a system under which the numbers and condition of the deer in the park were closely monitored.

A redeeming veterinary feature of the park system was that a dominant stag, exhausted after the rut, was normally killed by the other males, 'for in parkes . . . ther shal be no seson that the greet hert ne shal be slayne with the othere, nat while he is at the Rutte but whea he is withdraw and is poor of love'. This annual renewal of the blood did not always occur in the forest: 'In the woodes thei not so oft slee eche other as thei done in the playne cuntre. And also there is dyverse Ruttes in the forest, and in the parke may noon be but with inne the parke.'[56]

In fifteenth-century England, Edward, Duke of York, who translated Gaston Phoebus's treatise and called his version the *Master of Game*, made certain significant alterations to the content of his source. The most notable is the space given to bow and stable hunting. Edward retains Phoebus's chapters on *par force* hunting, and indeed achieves a lyrical beauty in his translation of them, but adds a long and detailed chapter of information on 'the maner of hundyng whan the kyng wil hunte in foreste or in parke for the hert with bowes greyhoundes and stable'.[57] It has the air of being written not for the instruction of hunters generally, but almost as a set of regulations for the organization of the English royal hunts, and for the guidance of future Masters of Game.

The operation revolves around the arrival and positioning of the king and queen. Much has to be done in advance of their coming. Men and transport are ordered, and their mustering organized by the local sheriff at the behest of the forester or parker:

> The maister of the game shuld be accorded with the maistir forster or Parker wheder that it be where the Kyng shal huntt soche a day, and if the sette be wide [i.e. if a large area is to be hunted] the forsid forster

> or parker shuld warne the shiref of the shire that the huntyng shuld be inne, for to ordeyne stable suffisaunt and cartis eke, for to brynge the deer that shuld be slayn to the place where as quyrreis [i.e. *curées*] at huntyngges have ben acustomed to be, and than he shuld warne the hunters and feutreres whider thei shuld commen.

Everyone except the royal shooting party had to arrive early, the sets or standings for the archers were decided on, and the men of the stable and the fewterers were put in position, as were the Yeomen of the King's Bow and the grooms responsible for his dogs:

> And if the huntyng shal be in a park alle men shuld abide atte park gate, sauf the stable that oweth to be sette or [i.e. before] the kyng come and thei shuld be sett bi the parkers or forsters, And the mornyng erly the mayster of the game shuld be at wode to se that alle be redy, and he or his lieuetenaunte or which of the hunters that hym lust, oweth to sette the greihound and ho so be tesours to the kyng or to the quene . . . And than the maister forstere or parker oweth to shewe hym the kyngges stond, and if the kyng wold stonde with his bowe and where al the remenaunt of the bowes shuld stond and the yemen for the kynges bowe owen to be ther to kepe and make the kynges stondyng and abide ther without noyse to the kyng come. And the gromys that kepen the kynges dogges and chastised greihoundes shuld be ther with hym.

When all was ready the Master of Game had to ride to meet the king 'and brynge hym to his stondyng, and telle hym what game is with inne the sett and how the greihoundes ben sett, and eke the stable and also to tell hym wheder he be better to stond with his bow or with the greihoundes'. An additional duty of the fewterers at the royal standing was to build bowers, 'faire logges of grene bowes at her trestes for to kepe the kyng and the quene and the ladies and gentil women and eke the greyhoundes fro the sonne, and fro evil wedir'.

When the king and queen were installed, and the other archers at their sets, the Master of Game blew three long motes on his horn for the uncoupling of the hounds. At this point we see another difference from previous descriptions, this time a practical refinement rather than a social one:

> Than shuld the sergeant of the mute [i.e. pack; French *meute*] of the hert houndes if ther be moch rascaile with inne the sette make alle hem of the office . . . hardle her houndes, and in every hardel suffisen .ii. or .iii. couple of houndes atte the moost, and than to stond abrod in the wode for relaies and than blow .iii. moot to the uncouplyng.

And than shuld the eirere [harrier] uncouple his houndes and blow .iii. moot, and seke forth saying loude and longely *ho sto ho sto moun amy ho sto.*

Here the procedure is complicated by the fact that there are two completely distinct packs (or 'mutes') of hounds, with different roles. Hart-hounds were specialized creatures, trained to hunt the hart; harriers would bustle about shifting all and sundry, but lacked that specific training and narrowing of their vocation. The harriers were used to clear the wood of rascal, the younger red and fallow deer, and perhaps also the roe, before the hart-hounds took over from them.

The part played by the harriers, then, was by way of an overture. The hart-hounds were spread about the wood in groups of two or three couples, but were hardled (see p. 24). When they were in position, the Sergeant of the Hart-hounds blew for the uncoupling, but this signal was to the Master of the Harriers, himself referred to in the passage quoted above as the 'eirere', who then worked his hounds busily through the 'sette' (here meaning the area to be hunted) quarter by quarter. The company knew by the notes of his horn what progress he was making: 'and as oft as he passeth with inne the sette from oon quarter to an other he shuld blow drawyng, and whan he is passid the partyng of the quarter and entred in to a newe quarter he shuld blow .iii. moot, and seke forth . . .'

The rascal, young and inexperienced, left (or 'voided') the wood much more willingly than the harts, to be shot by the archers or brought down by the greyhounds. If the harriers did move a hart, they were allowed to pursue it, and the hart-hounds joined in as relays, and if it came to the bows or the greyhounds and was killed the Master of Harriers blew the death, rewarded his hounds a little, and went back to his lowlier work with the rascal.

It was then the turn of the hart-hounds, and their more specialized noses:

And after that the eirers han wel ronne and wel made the rascaille to voide, than shuld the sergaunt and beerners of the hert houndes blowe .iii. moot ech after other and uncouple ther as thei suppose the best liggingis [hiding-place, lying-place] for an hert. . . . And whan the rascaile is thus voided than ben the hert houndes uncoupled and thei fynde the grete olde wily deer that wil not lightly voide and thei enchase hem wel and lustely, and make hem voide both to bowes and to greihoundes, so that thei do here devoire [their duty] at fulle.

We see, then, the point of the two packs of hounds. An additional factor is the importance of *par force* hunting, in which the same hart-hounds were probably employed. It would not do to let them chase about after rascal; they were for the classic duty of seeking only the hart, and no other idea should be allowed to enter their noble heads.

As the arrows flew, and the frantic deer were dragged down by the greyhounds, and the queen and her ladies sat in their green bower and clapped their hands, or perhaps talked of how the Italian minstrels had performed on the previous evening, men who simply looked forward to the day's ending jolted through the trees on carts, loaded and unloaded the warm and bleeding carcasses, and lined them up for the final ceremonies:

> And alle the while that the huntyng lasteth shal cartis go about fro place to place to bryng the deer to the quyrre and ther lay it on a rewe all the hedes oo way and every deres fete to other bak. And the hertes shuld be laide on a rowe or .ii. or .iii. after that thei be many or fewe, and the rascaile in the same wise bi hemself, and thei shuld kepe that no man come with inne the quyrre to the kyng come save the maister of the game.

Edward gives a complex instruction about the horn-calls with which the hunting is brought to a close: the king or the Master of Game blows an initial note, and the call is taken up and partially repeated, possibly individually, by any hunter who has been successful, 'and therbi may a man wit [know] as thei here men strake homward wher thei han wel spedde or none'. The Master of Game then leads the king to inspect the assembled carcasses, and the king gives instructions as to their disposal: venison is given to the local gentry, the Church and the hunters.

The *curée* of the deer after a royal bow and stable hunt was a massive task. The hart-hounds were rewarded as after a *par force* hunt: the carcasses selected for the king's larder were undone by the huntsmen and fewterers of the royal kennels, the offal from the deer was spread on the hide of the finest hart, whose head the hounds ceremonially bayed (another way of fixing their minds on that quarry alone) before receiving their reward. The harriers and sometimes the greyhounds were similarly rewarded, but with less ceremony. The huntsmen were also rewarded with a complicated distribution of hides and venison (see p. 181). What the recipients did with the hides is not clear; used them, cured, for household purposes, presumably, or sold them to the tanners. What they did with the venison is not in doubt; they did the same as any sensible Englishman; the same as the belligerent and patriotic Andrewe Borde, for example:

I have gone rounde about Chrystendome, and overthwarte Chrystendome, and a thousande or two and moore myles out of Chrystendome, Yet there is not so moche pleasure for Harte and Hynde, Bucke and Doe, and for Roo-Bucke and Doe, as is in Englande lande: and although the flesshe be dispraysed in physicke, I praye God to sende me parte of the flesshe to eate, physicke notwithstanding . . . All physicions sayth that Venson . . . doth ingendre colorycke humours; and of trueth it doth so: Wherefore let them take the skynne, and let me have the flesshe. I am sure it is a Lordes dysshe, and I am sure it is good for an Englysheman, for it doth anymate hym to be as he is: whiche is stronge and hardy. But I do advertyse every man, for all my wordes, not to kyll and so to eate of it, excepte it be lawfully, for it is a meate for great men. And great men do not set so moche by the meate, as they doth by the pastyme of kyllynge of it.[58]

4

The Symbolism of the Deer

In the *Livre du Roy Modus* Queen Ratio (Reason), the consort of Modus (Practice), intervenes periodically to provide the hunter with food for contemplative thought. Under the influence, perhaps, of the Book of Job, which tells us 'Ask now the beasts, and they shall teach thee; and the fowls of the air, and they shall tell thee' (XII, 7), she uses the behavioural characteristics and physical features of the quarry species as the basis for moral and religious comparisons which are fully meaningful only to the hunter. Her most elaborately worked homilies are based on the hart and the boar, polarized examples of virtue and vice, timidity and reckless rage, the divine and the devilish. She contrives to make the hart symbolic of Christ's Nativity and Passion, the Ten Commandments, the temptations of the world, and man's means of escape from them.[1]

The 'bone' in the heart of the stag, which gives it courage and endurance when it would otherwise die of fear before the hounds, reminds Ratio of the entry of God into the womb of the Virgin, which provided spiritual comfort for man and saved him from the fear of damnation. The principal hunting miracle, St Eustace's vision of a crucifix between the antlers of a hart, to which I shall return, reminds the hunter of the death of Christ. God has furnished man's brain with the Ten Commandments to enable him to prolong his life and defend himself against his enemies; he has provided the hart with ten branches on its antlers which have the same function on a physical level. The mode of the hart's flight from the hounds, in which it uses the hard and stony ways to obscure its trail, and takes to water to destroy its scent, is recommended as an example to man in his flight from the devil: he must take the hard road of penitence and abstinence, and be bathed in holy water.

Queen Ratio's comparison continues with a correlation between the enemies of man – the world, the flesh and the devil – and those of the hart, for which the devils are the wolves which hunt and devour it, the flesh is its irresistible urge to seek the females in the rutting period, which leaves it so weakened as to be an easy prey to the wolves, and the world is represented by the men who hunt it for their pleasure and to sate their gluttony.

The hart also furnishes a symbol of man's potential for eternal life through purgatory:

> God gave to the hart the ability to regain its youth and to live so long that it is the longest-lived of all beasts, and when it is so old that it cannot grow older, it goes by its nature to seek an ant-hill, below which there is a white snake. The hart scatters the ant-hill, kills the snake and swallows it; then it goes off into a deserted place and becomes as if dead, and throws off its flesh and its hide, and becomes young again, as if it were four or five years old.

Point by point, Ratio relates this legend to man: the ant-hill is the riches he accumulated in life, which he must scatter and give to the poor in his old age; the snake is avarice, which he must tread underfoot and swallow; the flight to the desert is the renunciation of the world, and the casting off of the flesh is the soul's abandonment of the body as it passes into purgatory and on to eternal life (with a permanent age of thirty-two, according to Ratio: the age at which Christ died).[2]

Much of this is peculiar to Queen Ratio, who is a great concocter of similes, but incorporated in her instruction are several more widely known elements. The legend of the conversion of St Eustace was popular in the Middle Ages, and was a common subject of medieval and Renaissance painters, including Pisanello (Fig. 31) and Albrecht Dürer. Eustace was originally named Placidas; in Aelfric's version of the legend he was a virtuous Roman who gave alms to the poor. Hunting with his soldiers one day, he became separated from them in the pursuit of a beautiful hart, which eventually took refuge on a rocky ledge. As Placidas gazed at it, 'between the antlers of the hart shone the image of Christ's holy cross, brighter than the rays of the sun, and the likeness of Our Lord, Christ the Redeemer; and He put the speech of men into the hart, and spoke to Placidas, calling, "Ah Placidas, why do you persecute me? It is for your sake that I have come now, to reveal myself to you through this animal. I am the Christ whom you worship unwittingly; the alms which you give to the poor lie before me." '[3] Placidas was converted, baptized as Eustace with his family, and underwent various ordeals and eventually martyrdom.[4]

The miraculous vision of the Crucifix was associated later with St Hubert, who became the patron saint of hunters and of the monastery which is thought to have developed the famous strain of hunting-dogs which bore his name. Hubert, too, appears in medieval paintings, such as the late fifteenth-century depiction by the Master of Werden in the National Gallery, London.[5] St Hubert's Day is 3 November; St Eustace's, 20 September.

Queen Ratio's juxtaposition of the reference to Eustace and her comparison of the Commandments with the hart's antlers prompted an illustrator of the *Livre du Roy Modus* to fuse the two in an effective miniature which was copied in several other manuscripts. Stags appearing in the margins of manuscripts of non-hunting works also occasionally bear a crucifix between their antlers.[6]

The longevity of the hart is an ancient commonplace, repeated by various classical and medieval authors, prominent in the bestiaries, and fostered by the eager misinterpretation of ambiguous incident. Both this idea and that of the renewal of its life with the aid of the snake were known to practical huntsmen, and were included, with reservations, in such treatises as Phoebus's *Livre de chasse*[7] and the Duke of York's *Master of Game*:

> An hert lyvoth lengest of eny beest, for he may wel lyve an .c. yere, and the eldere he is, the fairere he is of body an of heed and more lecherous, but he is not so swift ne so ligt ne so myghty. And yit mony men seyne, but I make none affirmacioun upon that, whan he is ryght olde he hetyth a serpent with his foote til she be wrothe, and than he oteth hure and than gooth drynk, and than he rennethe hidere and thidere to the watir and venyin (i.e. the venom) be medled togydere and maketh hym cast al his evel humours that he had in his body, and maketh his flesshe come al newe.[8]

In the *Bestiaire divin* of Guillaume le Clerc this belief serves as the basis for a religious comparison: the hart is Christ himself, the serpent Satan.[9]

A celebrated incident which was taken as reinforcing the popular idea of the longevity of the hart occurred when one was taken in the French royal forest of Senlis during the reign of Charles v (1364–80) wearing a gilded collar with the inscription *Hoc me Caesar donavit*, which was interpreted as meaning that Julius Caesar had put it on the hart. A possible explanation is that the collar had been put on the animal not many years earlier by one of the German emperors, who called themselves *Caesar* in their Latin documents. If the Senlis incident did occur, it was either the origin or a reinforcement of a recurring element of hunting folklore: Nicholas Upton, a fifteenth-century canon of Salisbury and Wells, mentions that stags

> were caught a hundred years after Alexander's death, which he himself had ringed with signed golden necklaces. And I have often heard tell of a stag that was killed in the forest of Windsor near a

certain stone called *Besanteston*, near *Bageshott*, that wore a golden collar with the legend:

> *Julius Cesar quant jeo fu petis*
> *Ceste coler sur mon col ad mys.*
> [Julius Caesar put this collar
> round my neck when I was small.][10]

Thirty would be a considerable age for a stag in the wild; much less than the 1400 years attributed to it by Oppian.[11]

In the above quotation from the *Master of Game* concerning the serpent, water is important in the hart's rejuvenation; it is important, too, in the animal's behaviour in the chase, as a source of refreshment and a means of evasion. The thirsting hart of Psalm XLI. 1 ('As the hart panteth after the water brooks, so panteth my soul after thee, O God') is the basis for medieval commentaries and allusions relating the hart to penitent man, thirsting for spiritual refreshment, or to the soul thirsting for God, and harried through life by the devil. In Chaucer's *Parson's Tale* 'the feend seith, "I wole chace and pursue the man by wikked suggestion, and I wole hente him by moevynge or stiringe of sinne."' There are even, perhaps, oblique allusions to the harbouring, the *prise* and the unmaking: '"I wol departe my pryse or my praye by deliberacion, and my lust shal been accompliced in delyt: I wol drawe my swerd in consentinge": for certes, right as a swerd departeth a thing in two peces, right so consentinge departeth god fro man: "and thanne wol I sleen him with myn hand in dede of sinne": thus seith the feend.'[12]

For Hugh of St Victor the hind (more defenceless than the hart) represents the soul, the hunters are devils, their arrows are man's desires and their nets his senses.[13] Examples of the hart as the hunted soul continue to occur in the Renaissance: in one tapestry set the hunter Nature moves the hart with the help of the lymer Youth; the chase is continued by hunters such as Vanity, Sickness and Old Age with the hounds Pride, Sorrow, etc., until the final stroke is delivered by Death.[14] A lively Austrian woodcut shows mounted devils pursuing a variety of animals (possibly representing different aspects of man's nature) which run hither and thither through a wood enclosed by long-nets (Fig. 33).

The harried, and especially the wounded, deer also furnishes the basis for allegories of the Passion of Christ, who joined man on earth and fell victim to the forces of evil. The most elaborate of these is *Neptalym cervus emissus*, a fourteenth-century Latin work, akin to a sermon, which survives in the library of the University of Graz.[15] It takes as its starting-point the enigmatic text of Genesis XLIX. 21: 'Naphtali is a hind let loose: he giveth goodly words,' though the harried animal is masculine throughout, *cervus*.

The opening lines state that every Christian should follow Christ like a hunting dog; he has shed his blood to make the pursuit easier. This, however, is not the principal image, which is the harrying of Christ by the Jews and the forces of evil. The work is written by a man with a detailed knowledge both of hunting procedures and vocabulary and of the Scriptures.

After a passage justifying the identification of Naphtali with Christ, the author describes the course of a real hunt, explaining specialized German vocabulary such as *anheczen*, 'to hunt with hounds'; *laithunt* and *schayder*, 'lymer'; *ruorhunt*, 'running-hound'; *iegermayster*, 'master huntsman'; *cluppen, fourchée*; etc. The deer's use of water is mentioned, and it is killed with bows and arrows, swords, spears and nets.

Reverting to his religious theme, the author summarizes his argument: that Christ was similarly hunted and killed by *infernalis canibus et dyabolo, infernali venatore*, 'the hounds of hell and the infernal huntsman, the devil'. With allusions to Biblical animal and hunting imagery (e.g. Ecclesiastes VII. 27; Psalm LXXIV. 11) he begins a series of comparisons remarkable for the depth of knowledge which they reveal of the two fields juxtaposed. He even sees potential flaws in his allegory and forestalls criticism from hunters: 'It may be asked, "Why then was Christ not taken in September [i.e. like the hart in the height of the 'time of grease']?" I answered that the hunter, that is to say the devil . . . could not take him until he shed his antlers, for Christ did this at the same time as the stags, who shed their antlers in March.' Christ's antlers were his divine power, which he shed, 'saying . . . "Not my will, but thine, be done"' (Luke XXII. 42).

The lymer in the comparison is Judas; the devil, of course, had him on a leash, which subsequently hanged him (unwanted or offending dogs appear to have been hanged in the Middle Ages as a normal means of disposal; see Appendix II). Judas, like the lymer in the quest, identified the quarry, Christ, among his fellows; Judas and the Jews fell to the ground (cf. John XVIII. 4–6) as huntsmen do when they wish to confirm the trail of the hart. The devil's hounds, the Jews, chased Christ into a net, the house of Ananias, and tried to ensnare him with accusations, but he tore the net apart with his reply to their question. In the house of Caiaphas they tried to pierce him with the sharp swords of their charges, and, having failed, used the arrows of Pontius Pilate.

The ending of this self-explanatory allegory is missing. Since the author included in his factual description of a hunt details of the unmaking and the *curée*, it seems evident that he intended to extend his comparisons to cover the Crucifixion. One can only speculate as to the details. The reward of blood to the hounds as the giving of Christ's blood to unthinking mankind? Some specific allusion to the wound in the side, or to the four limbs? The

Cross as *cluppen* or *fourchée* conveying the crucified Christ to the Lord?

Sir Thomas Malory's imagery of the hart, at one point, relates to the Immaculate Conception and the Resurrection, and is based partly on the idea that the animal can renew its own life. In the quest for the Holy Grail, Sir Galahad, Sir Bors and Sir Perceval follow a white hart, accompanied by four lions, which leads them into a hermitage. As the hermit sings the mass, the three knights

> saw the herte becom a man, which mervayled hem, and sette hym uppon the awter, . . . and saw the four lyons were chaunged: one to the fourme of man, and another to the fourme of a lyon, and the thirde to an egle, and the fourth was changed to an oxe. Than toke they her sege [seat] where the harte sate, and wente out thorow a glasse wyndow, and there was nothynge perisshed nother brokyn. And they harde a voyce say: 'In such maner entred the Sonne of God into the wombe of Maydyn Mary, whos virginité ne was perisshed, ne hurte.'

The nature of the hart is explained to the knights by the hermit: 'And well ought oure Lorde be signifyed to an harte. For the harte whan he ys olde, he waxith yonge agayne in his whyght skynne. Ryght so commyth agayne oure Lorde frome deth to lyff, for He lost ertheiy fleysshe, that was the dedly fleyssh whych He had takyn in the wombe of the Blyssed Virgyne Mary. And for that cause appered oure Lord as a whyghte harte withoute spot.'[16] The four lions are the Evangelists. Implicit in this, in the Arthurian context, is the mutually enriching association in Malory's mind between Christ, the Hart, and the alluring white beasts of his own and other medieval narratives.

In the legend of St Eustace, the relationship of Christ to the animal is more complex: after using the hart to lure Placidas, the hunter, away from his companions, Christ firstly becomes identified with it when the Crucifix appears between the antlers, and then becomes the hunter himself: 'I come in order to reveal myself to you through this hart, and to hunt you and capture you with the nets of my mercy.'[17]

The concept of Christ, God or the Church as hunter of errant souls is explicit in certain medieval didactic works. Again, there is a scriptural basis for it: 'Behold, I will send for many fishers, saith the Lord, and they shall fish them: and after will I send for many hunters, and they shall hunt them from every mountain, and from every hill, and out of the holes of the rocks' (Jeremiah xvi. 16). In an Anglo-Saxon work called the *Ormulum* the Apostles are told 'to hunt after souls . . . to turn them to Christendom . . . All this was openly revealed by Bethsayda, for it means "hunter's house", and so they have to hunt, not deer with hounds, but men with the gospel.'[18] In one case (see p. 142) the father confessor is represented as a hunter of souls, and the Archangel Gabriel is commonly represented as a hunter, especially in tapestries of the hunt of the unicorn, which he pursues it allegorically named hounds (see pp. 154–55, 158).

For the medieval writer of narrative literature, the principal appeal of the hunt, and especially the hunting of the hart, is that it detaches a man (I am afraid I know of no medieval heroines to whom this applies) from his normal environment and, frequently, his companions, and takes him into unfamiliar territory. In medieval fiction this new territory is not merely topographical, but emotional and sometimes moral. In the Arthurian romance, particularly, detachment from one's environment is synonymous with immersion in that misty landscape in which sudden and unexplained demands are made on the resilience and prowess of a hero who is weary and disorientated, and who, in many cases, has been stripped of those accoutrements which marked his position in a secure social framework – his hawk and his hounds.

This solitary departure into the unknown often occurs accidentally: the knight is simply out hunting, gives chase to an animal, fails to kill it and finds himself lost. Many Spanish oral ballads begin in this formulaic manner; the hunt is simply a prelude, though commonly the failure of the hunt presages a larger calamity, even an encounter with death.[19] In other ballads and romances a solitary hunt may be proposed by a malevolent enemy, who knows that it will pit the hero against a magic or invincible quarry. Such is a Spanish ballad of Lancelot,[20] which is incomprehensible except in the context of the Arthurian idea of the adventure and especially the quest as a proof of the hero's courtliness: as Lancelot takes his ease among the ladies of the court, one of them asks him to deliver to her a white-footed hart which, unknown to Lancelot, is really a prince transformed by a curse. It is ravaging the countryside, accompanied by seven lions and a lioness (a distant link, possibly, with the lions/Evangelists in Malory), killing many knights and, in a modern oral version,[21] living by eating their hands as its sole diet. Lancelot, flower of chivalry, mounts up and sets off unquestioningly with his hounds. This ballad, enigmatically truncated in the Spanish version, is related to the more explicit French *Lai de Tyolet*.[22]

The magical element of whiteness is extended to the whole animal in an early episode of Malory's account of Arthur's Round Table: a threefold quest in which Sir Gawain, Sir Torre and King Pellinore are tested and proven.[23] After the ceremony of Arthur's marriage to Guinevere, Merlin tells all the knights to be still, 'for ye shall se a straunge and a mervailous adventure'. In the ensuing hush, there com rennynge inne a whyght herte into the hall, and a whyght brachet nexte hym, and thirty couple of blacke rennynge houndis com afftir with a grete cry. And the herte went aboute the Rounde Table, and as he wente by the sydebourdis the brachet ever boote hym by the buttocke and pulde on a pece, wherethorow the herte lope a grete lepe and overthrew a knyght that sate at the sydebourde. And therewith the knyght arose and toke up the brachet, and so wente forthe oute of the halle and toke hys horse and rode hys way with the brachett.

Ryght so com in the lady on a whyght palferey and cryed alowde unto kynge Arthure and seyd, 'Sir, suffir me nat to have thys despite, for the brachet ys myne that the knyght hath ladde away.'

'I may nat do therewith,' seyde the kynge.

So with thys there com a knyght rydyng all armed on a grete horse, and toke the lady away with forse wyth hym, and ever she cryed and made grete dole. So whan she was gone the kynge was gladde, for she made such a noyse.

Merlin, however, does not accept that the incident is closed, 'for thes adventures muste be brought to an ende, other ellis hit woll be disworshyp to you and to youre feste'. On his advice Arthur sends off Sir Gawain to hunt the white hart, Sir Torre to bring back the brachet and King Pellinore to seek the lady and her abductor. The three set off on their separate quests and, of course, run into situations more demanding than retrieving a hart or a hound. First Gawain

folowed his queste. And as he folowed the herte by the cry of the howndis, evyn before hym there was a grete ryver, and the herte swam over. And as Sir Gawayn wold a folowed afftir there stood a knyght on the othir syde and seyde, 'Sir knyght, com nat over aftir thys harte but if thou wolt juste with me.'

'I woll nat fayle as for that,' seyde sir Gawayne, 'to folow the queste that I am inne.' And so he made hys horse swymme over the watir. And anone they . . . ran togydirs fulle harde.

Gawain kills this knight, and he and his brother 'folowed afftir the whyte herte, and lete slyppe at the herte thre couple of greyhoundes. And so they chace the herte into a castel, and in the chyef place of the castel they slew the hert. Ryght soo there came a knyght oute of a chambir with a swerde drawyn in his honde and slew two of the grayhoundes.' This knight is the owner of the white hart, a gift from his lady; his enmity towards Gawain is reciprocated by the hero, who shows a hunter's love of his hounds in his incredulous question, 'Why have ye slayne my howndys? For they dyd but their kynde, and I wolde that ye had wrokyn youre angir uppon me rather than uppon a dome beste.'

The knight is defeated and forced to return to Arthur's court to tell of Gawain's triumph; he carries one of Gawain's greyhounds on his saddle before him and another behind. Meanwhile, Sir Torre has set off in search of the knight with the brachet. Like many of his literary contemporaries, 'he mette with a dwarfe suddeynly, that smote hys horse on the hede with a staff, that he reled bakwarde hys spere lengthe.' The dwarf, having led Sir Torre to joust with two hostile knights whom he defeats, enters his service and conducts him to a white pavilion, in which a lady sleeps; beside her is the white brachet. Sir Torre removes the hound and rides with it towards Camelot, but is challenged on the way by Sir Abelleus, 'the moste outerageous knyght that lyvith, and the grettist murtherer'; Sir Torre kills him and returns to Camelot to be rewarded for his 'queste of armys' with an earldom.

Similarly, after sore trials, King Pellinore completes his quest by slaying the abducting knight and returning with the lady, who is then presumably reunited with the brachet, though this is not stated; in the Arthurian mode details which appear crucial as a starting-point tend to become lost in the evolution of the plot. The thirty couple of black running-hounds, for example, fade leaderless out of the story as if swallowed in the dark background of a forest painted by Uccello.

This triple quest in search of hart, hound and lady, conducted at a key point in the establishment of Arthur's moral leadership, is used by him as the basis of a manifesto of the ideals of the Round Table; a creed, especially, of manly behaviour towards women:

> Thus whan the queste was done of the whyght herte . . . the kynge stablysshed all the knyghtes and gaff them richesse and londys; and charged them never to do outerage nothir morthir, and allwayes to fle treson, and to gyff mercy unto hym that askith mercy, . . . and allwayes to do ladyes, damesels, and jantilwomen and wydowes socour: strengthe hem in hir ryghtes, and never to enforce them, uppon payne of dethe. Also, that no man take no batayles in a wrongeful quarell for no love ne for no worldis goodis. So unto thys were all knyghtis sworne of the Table Rounde, both olde and yonge, and every yere were they sworne at the hygh feste of Pentecoste.

In an earlier hunting episode[24] King Arthur himself spurs after a great hart for so long that his horse falls dead; this brings him into fleeting contact with the most enigmatic quarry in medieval literature, the Questing Beast, which looms out of the woods, indeterminate of feature, but preceded by 'the noyse in the bestes bealy lyke unto the questyng of thirty couple houndes'. It pauses briefly before him to drink; while it drinks the noise stops, to restart as the Beast makes off into the forest, a weird amalgam of quarry and pack, obligingly providing its own hunting music as the only assistance to the footsore King Pellinore, who has pursued it for a year without any stated reason. Arthur offers to take over the chase, and receives an indignant rejection: '"A, foole," seyd the kynge unto Arthure, "hit ys in vayne thy desire, for it shall never be encheved but by me other by my nexte kynne," . . . and soo passed on his weye.' Later this family vocation devolves on Sir Palomides, but nobody succeeds in slaying the Beast. It would have provided a fascinating *curée*.

With its pell-mell, clamorous chase and bloody ending, the hunt lends itself to literary imagery portraying the warfare for which, in real life, it was a preparation. One of the finest examples is the ballad *Chevy Chase*,[25] which describes an incident in the festering hostilities between the Scottish Earl Douglas and the Earl of Northumberland, Henry Percy, in the Scottish border country. The title, *Chevy Chase*, leads us to expect an account of hunting; *Chevy* refers to the Cheviot Hills. At the start of the poem a large hunting party sets out from Percy's castle:

> The Percy out of Banborowe came,
> With him a mighty meinye,
> With fifteen hundred archers bold
> Chosen out of shirés three.

The 'meinye' (the stress is probably on the second syllable, to judge by the rhyme) is the mounted hunting party (French *menée*; see p. 40). We are given a lively account of the hunting, with certain revealing details. Percy's intention is to hunt with bow and stable; he seeks venison as much as sport, and his success is considerable:

> The drivers through the woodés went,
> All for to raise the deer,
> Bowmen bicker'd upon the bent [grass]
> With their broad arrows clear.
>
> Then the wild [deer] thoro' the woodés went
> On every sidé shear;
> Grayhounds thoro' the grevés glent [darted]
> For to kill their deer.
>
> This began on Cheviot the hills abune
> Early on a Monenday;
> By that it drew to the hour of noon
> A hundred fat harts dead there lay.

77

So far, then, a poem about hunting, which continues with the unmaking (here the 'brittling') of the deer. This is interrupted, however, by the arrival of Earl Douglas. The transition from hunting to warfare is both eased and accentuated by the poem's semantic resources:

> At the last a squire of Northumberland
> Looked at his hand full nigh;
> He was ware o' the doughty Douglas coming,
> With him a great meinye.

Douglas's *menée* is bound, not on hunting, but on revenge. The merry scene of the brittling is replaced by the clamour of battle; swords and spears reddened with the blood of the deer are turned against men, and the lines of dead deer are paralleled by a list of slain aristocrats. Douglas is killed by the arrow of one of Percy's hunters; Percy himself by a spear-thrust. In the ruefully ironic final stanza, the mirroring of the beginning in the ending of this double carnage is reinforced by the poem's allusion to its title:

> Jesu Christ! our balés bete [relieve our woes],
> And to the bliss us bring!
> This was the Hunting of the Cheviot:
> God send us all good ending!

The medieval courtly writer, enjoying hunting, or at least finding himself regularly in the company of persons who did, and constrained by literary fashion to devote his creative efforts largely to the theme of courtly love, not surprisingly looked to the conventions and rituals of the one to enliven his expression of the other. The social and emotional aspects of the hunt; the restraints of civilized hunting behaviour; its range of specialized vocabulary; the obsessiveness with which it was pursued; the effort to overcome the twists and turns of an elusive quarry; the quest for an animal exceeding others in beauty and quality; the self-imposed difficulties and postponement of final success in order that the pursuit itself may be better relished; all these parallel similar factors in the code of courtly love. The physical aspects, especially the killing of the beast with sword, spear or arrow, and the disposal of its flesh and blood to hunter and hounds, provide ready evocations of the consummation which lurks in the mind of the courtly lover, but is normally sublimated.

Thus the female lover is often symbolized by a hind or doe. In one case, *Aucassin and Nicolette*, she makes the comparison herself: the shepherd boys tell Aucassin:

> A maiden came here, the most beautiful thing in the world, so that we
> believed her to be a fairy, and this whole wood was bright with her.
> And . . . we made covenant with her, if you came here, to tell you that

you should go hunting in this forest, where there is a beast which, if you could take it, you would not part with one of its limbs for five hundred marks of silver, nor for any price; for the beast holds such a medicine that if you can catch it you will be cured of your wound. . . . Now hunt it if you will.[26]

We are here on that quivering tightrope between chastity and sexuality which provided the enduring tension sustaining courtly love. In some instances the sexuality looms larger: an example is the dream of the jealous and rejected lover in Boccaccio's *Decameron* who sees his lady hunted by a knight whose hounds tear her to pieces and are given her heart as their reward.[27] One critic has suggested that the tension generated by the usual courtly love triangle (lady, knight/lover and husband/feudal overlord) may underlie the practice of the *présent*, the presentation by the hunters of the severed head of the hart to their lord; the suggestion being that the head represents that of the lord himself, and the *présent* is a sublimation of the desire to slay him as an obstructive rival, or at the least to put the horns of cuckoldry on his head.[28]

Because of the enforced chastity of the lady in the courtly love tradition there is much reciprocal influence between the love code and the literary presentations of the Virgin Mary, whose perfection assists the idealization of the beloved, and who is herself sometimes alluded to in terms similar to those of courtly love poetry. The Virgin, too, in the allegory *Neptalym cervus emissus*, is the *gratissima cerva*, the most blessed hind, who brought down Christ, the hart, from the mountains to the lowlands of our terrestrial life.[29]

The symbolic hunt may also have morality or some specific virtue as its quarry. The courtly hunter who sounds his horn in the Burrell Collection's tapestry (Fig. 32) and the dainty lady who clings so closely to him as they gallop through the wood are in pursuit of the stag Fidelity – an elusive quarry, but one which appears to be running into their net. The legend on the scroll reads:

> I hunt for Fidelity;
> If I find that,
> A more pleasant time
> I will never have lived.

In the late Middle Ages the imagery of the hunt is developed by courtly love poets into full-scale allegory. The minutiae of hunting procedures lend themselves well to a theme which is itself characterized, even when treated literally, by formality and gradation. The treatment of love as a campaign governed by rules of behaviour goes back as far as Ovid, and is continued in the Middle Ages in codes of amatory procedure and even in the juridical format of the Courts of Love. The formal patterning of the lover's allies and enemies, the moral qualities hindering or assisting his efforts, the varying reactions of the woman pursued, the stages in his success; all these find expression in images drawn from the hunting field: symbolic woods and thickets, the quest as the search for a lady, the moving as the tentative approach, allegorically named hounds, the ruses of the hart as the lady's indifference or heartlessness, rivers and other natural features as the obstacles to love's progress, the death as the consummation or at least as the reciprocation of feeling.

A relatively simple example is a thirteenth-century French poem, *Li dis dou cerf amoureus*, 'The Enamoured Hart'.[30] The author begins by describing the hunting of a hart, and proceeds to relate it to the pursuit of a woman. The huntsman in this allegory is *Amour*, Love; the hart is the woman (an illustration in the manuscript depicts the running hart as having a woman's face; it is pursued by a mounted figure with angelic wings[31]). The hart is moved by the lymer, *Boine Amours* (Courtly Love), and the running-hounds which pursue it (i.e. the factors, in this case in the woman herself, which work to incline her to accept the idea of love) are, in couples, *Pensers* and *Souvenirs* (Thoughts and Memories) and *Volentés* and *Désirs* (Wishes and Desires).

Moved from the thicket of *Orgueil* (Pride), the hart is harried by Thoughts and Memories (of the lover's merits), and subsequently assailed by Wishes. When all four of the running-hounds join forces against it, the hart tries to lose them by taking to water (i.e. the lady, disturbed by her own growing ardour and fearing the gossips and slanderers who plague courtly lovers, seeks to draw back from the relationship). The hunter calls on his relay of hounds, *Pitiés* and *Humilités* (Pity and Gracious Mercy), and this finally turns the scale in the hunter's favour. After the death the hounds drink the blood. In other examples of the hunt of love, this might be taken to express the sexual success of the male lover, but here the hounds are the lady's own qualities, and the *curée* represents rather her own fulfilment in the consummation of the affair; the mental and emotional is nourished by the physical.[32]

The list of allegorically named hounds becomes a conventional element in later hunting allegories, particularly in German poetry. The hounds normally represent characteristics or resources of the male lover, himself the hunter in most examples. In *L'amoureuse prise*[33] they include (in a total of twenty-eight) Beauty, Kindness, Simplicity, Courtesy, Sweet Talk, etc.; in *Die Jagd*, by Hadamar von Laber,[34] who develops the hound allegory in greater detail than anyone else, Joy, Bliss, Delight, Perseverance, Spirit, Longing, Moderation, Daring and some forty more. Allegorically named hounds also appear in tapestries of the Hunt of the Unicorn (see p. 155).

Marcelle Thiébaux has made the point that whereas the French allegories of the hunt of love are characterized by success, the death of the hart and the consummation of the relationship, in their German counterparts the prolonged and agonizing aspiration of the hunter normally remains unrewarded, and the paradox of courtly love, that success both lowers the moral status (and hence the attractiveness) of the woman and deprives the man of the benefits conferred on him by his persistence in an unsuccessful cause, is preserved. *Die Jagd* is a splendid example of this: the hunter, here the lover himself, pursues his hart/lady with his allegorical hounds, through a series of minor advances and discouraging setbacks, in search of a success infinitely postponed; he changes from youthful vigour to grey-haired doggedness in the course of the poem. His lymer is *Herz* (Heart); his relays *Lust* (Delight) and *Genäde* (Grace). Hadamar makes great play with specific elements such as the lyam or leash which restrains Herz, the calling into the chase of new hounds when the previous ones fail, the track of the hart as love's path, the stream of *Leckerïe* (here probably frivolous, teasing flirtation), where hounds may be delayed or drown, and the advice of other, less scrupulous, huntsmen/lovers whose attitudes are distorted by lust for the kill and indiscriminate willingness to take any quarry available.[35] Such associations of the hunt with the erotic must have been reinforced in some medieval minds by the dual meaning of the word 'venery' (derived in one sense from the Latin *venari*, 'to hunt'; in the other from *venereus*, 'pertaining to Venus'). Spenser employs the homonymic resources effectively when he describes Thyamis going to the woods 'to seeke her spouse, that from her still does fly and follows other game and venery'.[36]

In Hadamar sexual fulfilment is postponed indefinitely; the hart, though once brought to bay, is never taken. The sexuality of the stag, nevertheless, was well-known to the hunter, 'and the eldere he is, the fairere he is of body and of heed, and more lecherous'.[37] Renaissance paintings often include the stag motif with this aspect in mind. In one painting of *Susannah and the Elders*, a stag sniffs at Susannah's discarded garments as the Elders approach through the garden and a hare, another animal associated with sexuality, is stirred from rest by their approach.[38] In Rubens's *The Three Graces* the triangle of pink bodies in the foreground is echoed by three stags in the distance.[39]

At the popular level, too, in a reversal of the symbolism of the hunted hind as the woman, the male lover may be represented by the stag in poems in which the woman's viewpoint is expressed. This is the case in many Galician-Portuguese traditional lyrics, in which the stag is commonly associated with running water and the pretty girl:

Her lover passed by,
Who loved her truly;
The stag of the forest
Was stirring the water.
   Joy of lovers;
   Lovers' joy[40].

'Tell me, my daughter, my bonny daughter,
Why did you linger by the cold stream?'

'I lingered, mother, by the cold stream;
The stags from the hill were stirring the water.'

'You lie, my daughter, you lie for your lover.
I never saw a stag stirring the water.'[41]

One interpretation of the annual Horn Dance of Abbots Bromley, Staffordshire, is that it began as a medieval ceremony of fertility; six of the dancers carry sets of ancient reindeer antlers (carbon-dated around 1000–1100), which normally hang in the village church. The other characters in the dance are the Fool, the Hobby-Horse and Maid Marian. One stage of the dance involves two lines of three dancers, the antlers dipping in a feigned combat reminiscent of the rut of the red deer. The dance now happens in September, but a seventeenth-century source describes it as 'a sort of sport . . . celebrated at Christmas (on New Year and Twelf-day) call'd the Hobby-horse dance, from a person that carryed the image of a horse between his leggs . . . and in his hand a bow and arrow [with] which he made a snapping noise as he drew it too and fro, keeping time with the Musick; with this man danced 6 others, carrying on their shoulders as many Raindeer heads 3 of them painted white and 3 red . . .'[42]

The symbolic ambivalence of the hart is sufficiently established by the Renaissance period to enable Lucas Cranach, as well as creating the most lively hunting panoramas ever produced,[43] to include it in a range of roles in his numerous paintings of the Garden of Eden and the Fall of Man. In some, the hart and its accompanying hind or hinds are simply an aspect of the peaceful Earthly Paradise which precedes the Fall, one species among several. In some of the scenes of the plucking of the Apple, however, the impressively antlered hart lurks close behind the Tree, its rough-coated sexuality contrasting with the smooth body of Eve, and also, in one case, with the gentle roebuck, symbol of abstinence (see p. 89). In several paintings the massive, curling antlers encircle Eve's hips as she offers Adam the fruit; in another the upper tines of the antlers are carefully positioned near Adam's fig-leaf to suggest a phallic connotation, reinforcing the associations of procreation conveyed by the pair of partridges in the foreground.

The hart's presence in Cranach's paintings of Venus[44] and of Diana, who rests naked on a kneeling hart as Actaeon draws his bow before her, hints at similar associations, though there is an allusion, naturally, to Diana the Huntress. In another work we see the lustful Actaeon transformed into a hart and torn to pieces by his own hounds. But the Adam and Eve paintings have a rich, ambivalent shorthand. The hart remains a symbol of Christ: in the painting in which its sexual associations are closest to being explicit, we see behind it, framed in its antlers where St Eustace saw the Crucifix, the unassuming but redeeming lamb.[45]

5

The Buck, The Roe, and Three Fringe Activities

The buck

The fallow buck, except in one respect, was held in markedly lower esteem than the hart, was less generally hunted, and yet was sufficiently similar in habits, size and appearance to engender no folklore or symbolism peculiar to itself. Gaston Phoebus assumes that many of his readers will never have seen one, and feels obliged to give a physical description; in the south-west of France, at least, they must have been a rarity.[1] Fallow deer came into their own with the increased number of deer-parks in the later Middle Ages; the Framlingham accounts, for example, relate exclusively to fallow deer (see Appendix II).

The buck was a fine beast for the kitchen; it was smaller than the hart, but was a good converter of food and carried more venison in proportion to its stature than its nobler rival. Both Phoebus and the *Master of Game* comment on its excellent eating qualities: 'The buckes flesshe is more savery than is that of the herte or of the Roo bucke. The venyson of hem is ryght good, and ykept and salted as that of the hert.'[2]

In France, the fallow deer were normally born around May; their rutting period was later than that of the red deer by about a fortnight. The males of different ages had their specialized names, again differing from those of the hart:

And ye speke of the Bucke, the fyrst yere he is
A fawne sowkyng on his dam, say as I yow wis.
The secunde yere a preket, the third yere a sowrell,
A sowre at the .iiii. yere, the trowthe I yow tell.

The .v. yere call hym a Bucke of the fyrst hede;
The .vi. yere call hym a Bucke, and do as I you rede.[3]

Another source gives 'sowre' for the third year and 'grete sowre' for the fourth.[4] 'Sowre' and 'sowrell' are descriptive of colour, like the term 'sore hawk' used to describe a bird in a particular state of plumage in falconry (see p. 196). Most medieval sources are much vaguer about the desirable form of the buck's antlers or 'head' than about the hart's. King Modus, for instance, says unrevealingly that: 'the one with the highest head and the longest and broadest palm is held to be the greatest.'[5] The *Boke of St Albans*, however, gives a more detailed description:

The hornys of a grete Bucke or he so be
Most be summyd as I say; herkenyth to me.
Too braunchis first pawmyd he most have,
And .iiii. avauncers, the soth iff ye will save;
And .xxiiii. espelers, and then ye may hym call,
Where so ye be, a grete Bucke, I tell yow all.[6]

This description is of the two sides in total; each has a 'branch', the main stem, with two tines or 'advancers', above which the branch flattens and broadens into the 'palm', from the front edge of which grow several tines (a dozen in a great buck), the 'espellers'. Among other semantic differences from the hart were the words to describe the noise made by the buck ('An hert *belowys* and a bucke *gronys* [groans]') and its action in going to covert ('An hert *herbourghith*; a Bucke *lodgith*')[7].

Buck-hunting was at its best from mid-June to mid-September.[8] Several authorities, both French and English, place the hart and the buck in fundamentally distinct venatorial categories. For the *Boke of St Albans* the distinction is between the 'beasts of venery' and the 'beasts of the chase':

Bestys of venery

. . . Fowre maner beestys of venery there are:
The first of theym is the *hert*; the secunde is the *hare*;
The *boore* is oon of tho; the *Wolff* and not oon moo.

Bestys of the Chace

And where that ye cum, in pleyne or in place,
I shall yow tell which be beestys of enchace.
Oon of theym is the *Bucke*, another is the *Doo*;
The *Fox* and the *Martron* and the wilde *Roo*.[9]

The *Boke* gives no explanation, but William Twiti expands a little (although he contradicts the wording of the *Boke* in applying 'enchase' to the group which includes the hart):

> 'He [the hare] is *enchased*, and so is the hart, and the wolf and the boar.'
> 'And, sir Hunter, tell me which beasts are *aquilled*.'
> 'The buck and the doe and the fox and the vixen and all other vermin.'
> 'Now I would learn how many beasts are moved with the lymer, and how many are sought with running-hounds.'
> 'Sire, all those which are enchased are moved with the lymer, and all those which are enquilled are sought with running-hounds.'[10]

For Twiti, then, the distinction between these two categories, and therefore between the hart and the buck, was that hunting the former involved a quest with the lymer, whereas the pursuit of the latter was begun simply by allowing running-hounds to find the scent themselves.[11] By this definition, however, the hare should not be classed with the hart and boar, since it was sought with running-hounds (see pp. 112–15), and matters are complicated further by another passage in the *Boke of St Albans*:

> My dere sonnys echeon, now will I yow lere
> How many maner beestys as with the lymere
> Shall be upreryde in fryth or in felde:
> *Booth the hert and the bucke* and the boore so wilde,
> And all other beestys that huntid shall be
> Shall be sought and founde with Ratchis so fre.[12]

This difference between Twiti and the *Boke of St Albans* appears irreconcilable, unless 'bucke' in this last passage is due to a scribal misinterpretation of 'wulfe'.[13] When one turns one's attention from semantics to practice, however, one finds unequivocal statements from Gaston Phoebus which contradict the last quotation: 'One does not follow the buck at all with the lymer; one does not go on quest as one does for the hart; the buck's *fumées* play no part as tokens, and he is judged solely by his tracks and his head.'[14] It may be that in late fifteenth-century England the practice had developed of seeking the buck with the lymer, but I have no evidence to support the statement in the *Boke of St Albans*. Earlier in the century the royal buck-hounds were not accompanied by lymers when they were sent off on tour to replenish the royal larders; there is sometimes a mention of a bercelet, but this hound was almost certainly intended to track down deer wounded by the archers in bow and stable hunting rather than to raise individual bucks at the start of the hunt (see p. 183).

On the morning of *par force* buck-hunting, therefore, the huntsmen of a kennel of buck-hounds perhaps had longer in their beds than their counterparts in an establishment of hart-hounds, the assembly had only a social role, and the subtleties of selective judgement were markedly less. King Modus excludes even the tracks of the bucks from the judgement, which he limits solely to an observation of the head.[15] The opening stage of the hunt was the finding of the scent left by the buck at its early-morning feeding-grounds or between there and its lodging in the woods. For this the hunter used four or at most six of his best running-hounds, keeping the rest coupled. According to Phoebus,[16] when they found the scent (stronger than that of the hart, according to *Modus*[17]) the hunter dismounted to make sure that his hounds were following the scent in the right direction. It is difficult to see how he could do this without a close scrutiny of the tracks. The rest of the pack was then uncoupled, and from then onwards the chase was, in essence, like *par force* hart-hunting.

Phoebus does not mention relays, and *Modus* clearly states that they were not used.[18] This may have been because the buck had less stamina than the hart, perhaps because of its greater proportion of flesh to bone; it did not give as long a chase as the hart.[19] The buck was more willing, or at least more likely, to pause in its flight, so that hunting it at the 'forloyne' (i.e. from a long way behind it) was less necessary and the hounds found the scent fresher and were encouraged.[20] It was also thought less wily, though it did use water as a resource of escape.

Fallow deer did not mix readily with red deer. If the two species were in adjacent areas, the bucks could cause additional problems for the master of a pack of hart-hounds, especially if his hounds had previously been used in buck-hunting: if the hart crossed the scent of a buck, the hounds' memory of the tastier flesh of the buck, reinforced by its stronger scent, would make them change from following the scent of the hart to pursue that of the buck.[21]

The unmaking and *curée* were the same for the buck as for the hart. Fallow deer lent themselves well to life in the enclosed park; as the Middle Ages drew to their end, although the distinction was far from being hard and fast,[22] there was probably an increasing identification of the buck and doe with bow and stable hunting in the parks, and of the hart with *par force* hunting in the open forest.

The roebuck

The roe, dainty and spare, though it no doubt fell prey to the snare or arrow of many a plebeian poacher, was not an important item in the feeding of the royal or aristocratic household, and it was classed as rascal by the hart-

or buck-hunter. It was healthy eating, even medicinal, the 'moost holsom to ete of eny othere wilde beestes flesshe; they lyven with good herbes and withe other wodes, with vynes, with breres [briars] and with hawthorns, withe leeves and with al wexyng of yonge trees'.[23] However, the roebuck appealed more to the hunter's eye and brain than to his stomach; it is described with a greater approximation to affection than any other beast, a wry, amused admiration that an animal so graceful, so small, should deceive and elude man so resourcefully, as if not only the beauty but also the wiliness of the hart were quintessentially distilled within it.

The habits and hunting of the roe were sufficiently differentiated from those of the larger deer for the animal to have its own associated vocabulary. This is most amply explained in the *Boke of St Albans*: the cry of the male, for example ('. . . iche Roobucke, certayne, *bellis* [bells] by kynde'); the collective names for a herd of roe (six made up a 'bevy', ten a 'middle bevy', twelve a 'great bevy'). To conform with custom one spoke not of a 'great' roebuck, but of a 'fair' roebuck, and the animal had its own changing terminology of age:

> The first yere he is a kyde, soukyng on his dame;
> The secunde yere he is a gerle, and so be siche all;
> The thirde yere an hemule loke ye hym call.
> Robucke of the first hede he is at the .iiii. yere;
> The .v. yere a Roobucke hym call I yow lere.[24]

The most characteristic of these names are 'gerle' and 'hemule'. In another source these are given as 'gryll' and 'henull'.[25] In the *Master of Game* there is an unequivocal use of 'emel' meaning female, doe.[26] It is tempting, therefore, to assume that in the *Boke of St Albans* the two words mean 'girl' and 'female' and allude to the delicacy and grace of the immature male; the *Boke* uses 'roo' to allude to the doe.

For the *Master of Game* (here closely following Phoebus), 'The Roo bucke hath no seson to be hunted', by which he means that they may be hunted at any time. Both authorities, however, recommend leaving the does alone when they are heavy in kid, 'for here kydes, that shuld be lost, unto the tyme that thei have kyded, and that the kyddes can fede hemself and lif by hemself with owte here dame'.[27] This voluntary restraint is formalized into specific seasons by the *Boke of St Albans*, which rigorously separates the seasons for the roebuck and the doe, with a close season for both between 2 February and Easter, probably with the same aim of protecting the kids:

> Seson of the Robucke at Ester shall begynne,
> And till mychelmas lastith nygh or she blynne [i.e. before it ends].
> The seson of the Roo begynnyth at Michelmas,
> And hit shall endure and last untill Candilmas.[28]

The idea that the roebuck may be hunted at any time persists in the *Noble Arte of Venerie* (1576), but this may be simply due to Turbervile's slavish adherence to his source, Jacques du Fouilloux's *La Vénerie*, the fifth edition of which was amplified with material from Phoebus.[29] Medieval ideas on the mating of the roe were confused by the phenomenon of the false rut. Roe mate in July or August, as the *Boke of St Albans* correctly states (St James's Day is 25 July);

> At saynt Jamys day where so he go
> Then shall the Roobucke gendre with the Roo;
> And so boldely ther as ye durne,
> Then is he calde a Roobucke goyng in his turne.[30]

There is also, however, a false rut in the autumn, when the bucks return to the trodden circles around which they chased the does in summer:

> Also the Robucke, as hit is weele kyde,
> At holyrode day he gooth to Ryde,
> And usith the bit: When he may gete hit.[31]

This phenomenon underlies the mistaken opinion of Gaston Phoebus that 'they go to their lovemaking in October, and the rut lasts about a fortnight.'[32] Another belief expressed by the *Boke of St Albans* is that the roe disposes carefully of its cast antlers:

> At saynt andrew day his hornys he will cast;
> In moore or in moos he hidyth hem fast,
> So that no man may hem sone fynde;
> Ellys in certayn he dos not his kynde.[33]

In contrast to the stag and the fallow buck, the roebuck was celebrated among hunters for its monogamy and fidelity, and for the maternal devotion of the doe:

> The roebuck never ruts with more than a single female, and the buck and doe will stay together the whole season, as birds do, until the doe is due to give birth, when she will leave the male and go off to produce the kid, for the buck would kill it if he found it. And when the kid is old enough to feed itself, the doe rejoins the male, and they will always be together. . . . And if you separate them and hunt one of them far from the other, they will rejoin each other as soon as they can, and will seek each other until they are reunited.[34]

This devotion is the basis of the use of the roe as a symbol of chastity or abstinence in late-medieval art. The roebuck is prominent, for example, in two paintings by Lucas Cranach of the most celebrated abstainer of all, St

89

Jerome.[35] In one the roebuck is inside the saint's study; in the other, an exterior, it stands beside his desk. In another painting by the same artist, one of his many versions of the Fall of Man, the roebuck acts as a symbolic counterpoint to the stag (see p. 82).

The best-known depiction of roebuck hunting is Paolo Uccello's *The Hunt* in Oxford's Ashmolean Museum, in which it is difficult to perceive any order other than that imposed by the artist's compositional skill.[36] Unless Italian custom differed markedly from that of France and Britain, the activity in this marvellously atmospheric painting is largely the result of Uccello's imagination, though it has been suggested that the work may be based on a scene in some *novella*.[37] In an open forest, darkening to blackness in the background, a party of about thirty huntsmen, largely clad in scarlet, some on foot and armed with fragile-looking spears, others mounted, with short swords unlike normal hunting-swords, have some- how virtually surrounded a group of at least seven roe deer, all (unrealistic- ally) bucks, which are being harried hither and thither at the centre of this human and equine stockade by over two dozen greyhounds. One deer has been killed and is being carried by a hunter across the front of his saddle. No scenting-hounds are in sight. Some of the greyhounds have not yet been unleashed.

The only procedure which I could suggest as having this situation as its culmination is that hunters have completely surrounded an area known to contain roe and, keeping their greyhounds leashed, have converged on the centre, containing the deer in a shrinking area and eventually letting slip the greyhounds. This could only work with a larger force of helpers than appears in the painting; in the course of a modern pheasant shoot a roe- deer will commonly run back between beaters moving in line only a few yards apart. Uccello's painting is more theatrical than realistic, and the descriptions of roe-hunting in the medieval manuals are markedly different from his representation, as is the illustration in the Italian *Tacuinum Sanitatis*.[38] Greyhounds were certainly used against the roe, but the hunter's principal ally was again, as we shall see, the running-hound.

The roe was not normally judged by any tokens except its antlers; its tracks and droppings were of little use in distinguishing male from female or the mature from the immature buck.[39] The lymer played no part in the hunt;[40] the scent was found by two or three of the running-hounds, and then taken up by the pack, which was normally less numerous than those used for the red and fallow deer. Phoebus[41] recommends a solitary, early- morning quest by one of the huntsmen, unaccompanied by a lymer, to view a suitable beast at its feeding-ground or on its way back to the wood and to leave his *brisées* as markers from which the hounds may take up the scent. Phoebus is very appreciative in all he says about the roebuck, whose small size is its only drawback as a quarry; this opinion is readily reproduced by the *Master of Game* (an indication of the popularity of the roebuck in England which is later manifested in the generous attention given to the animal by the *Boke of St Albans*): 'And zif the Roo buk were as faire a beest [i.e. as large and heavy with venison] as the hert, I hold that it were a fairer huntyng than of the hert, for it lasteth al the yere and it is a good huntyng and of greet maystre, for thei rennen ryght longe and gynnously.'[42]

This long and ingenious running made it desirable to post relays, and to be always well up in touch with one's hounds, since 'the roebuck stops and starts more often . . . than the hart, so that the hunter must hunt it more craftily and subtly than he does the hart, for it is a most wily little beast, and very strong. And the hunter will find himself casting about after losing the scent of a roebuck thirty times more often than that of a hart.'[43] The roebuck tried to remain in its covert as long as it could, and greyhounds were used to make it 'void' and run in more open country. The *Boke of St Albans* gives two special words to describe the crisscrossing and rusing of the roe:

When ye hunt at the Roo then shall ye say thoore
He crossies and tresones yowre howndys byfoore.[44]

The roe's increasing weariness became manifest in the reduction of its initially bounding flight to a simple run (the French saying, *le chevrel a perdu ses saux*, 'the roebuck has lost its leaps,' meant something akin to 'having one's wings clipped'), and in the changed appearance of its hide and hindquarters: early in the chase the hair was bristly and the white of the hindquarters prominent, but in the latter stages the hair appeared smoother and the white rump less evident.

After the death the treatment of the carcass varied considerably. *Modus* says baldly that the roebuck was skinned and unmade exactly like a hart, but does not specify what the hounds received.[45] Phoebus flatly contradicts this, saying explicitly that 'one must not skin it or unmake it as one does a hart.'[46] He recommends that the hounds receive a reward of blood-soaked bread, perhaps with the addition of cooked meat or cheese, and also the whole or the bulk of the flesh of the roebuck, chopped and mixed with the bread on a bed of straw; he did, however, retain the haunches occasionally for the kitchen. He appears to have used roebuck-hunting, in particular, as a way of gaining the affection and demonstrating the obedience of his hounds: after spreading out their reward he would keep back the hounds, and indicate with his finger which hunter's order they were to await before rushing forward, and afterwards he would call them to him individually and give them each a bone from the carcass, with verbal endearments.

In England the roebuck seems to have been more frequently carried home as a whole carcass for the kitchen. William Twiti recommends rewarding the hounds only with the feet, and leaving the skin on the carcass.[47] The *Master of Game*, here only partly following Phoebus, states that 'he is hardeled but not undone as an hert, for he hathe no venyson that men shuld ley in salt, and some time he is zeven al to the houndes, or al or partie.'[48] The *Boke of St Albans* repeats Twiti's mention of the feet as part of the reward and explains the method of 'hardelling' the dead beast, i.e. converting it into an easily portable bundle by entwining its four legs and head (though the instructions would be barely comprehensible except to someone who already knew how to do it):

> With the bowellis and with the bloode
> Rewarde ye yowre howndis, my sonnys so goode;
> And eche foote ye shall cutte in .iiii., I yow kenne.
> Take the bowellis and the bloode and do all togedre then.
> Yevyth hit then to yowre howndys so,
> And moche the glaadder then thay will go.
>
> . . .
>
> The Roo shall be herdeled by veneri, I weene:
> The .ii. forther [fore] legges the hede layde bytwene,
> And take oon ender [hind] legge up, I yow pray,
> And that oder forder legge right as I yow say
> Uppon the oder forder legge booth ye hem pytte,
> And with that other forther legge up ye hem knytte.
> Oon thys maner thus, when you have wroght,
> All hoole to the kechen then hit shall be broght,
> Save that yowre howndes eete: the bowellis and the fete.[49]

The reindeer

The reindeer enters French and English hunting literature of the Middle Ages simply because of a desire for comprehensiveness on the part of Gaston de Foix, who calls it the *rangier* and includes in his *Livre de chasse* a short chapter on the nature of the beast and another, even shorter, on how to hunt it.[50] He claims to have seen reindeer in Norway and Sweden, and to judge by the graphic nature of his description he took part in reindeer-hunting himself.

I have mentioned the importance to the hunter of antler development in the hart and, to a lesser extent, the buck; the reindeer was a source of fascination to Phoebus because of the size and complex pattern of its antlers. They were the only aspect of reindeer-hunting which made it more difficult than hart-hunting, since when the animal was at bay even large alaunts and greyhounds were dissuaded from attacking it by the enveloping rampart of its horns. The miniaturist who painted the illustration in the best manuscript of Phoebus depicted the reindeer as a normal hart, but with enormous, many-branched antlers extending backwards beyond its own rump.[51] In some of the other manuscripts the exotic nature of the beast gave the illustrators free rein to depict it as an unathletic, wool-bearing creature, something between a hat-rack and a merino sheep.

In Scandinavia, if we may believe Phoebus, the reindeer was hunted with bow and arrow, nets, fall-traps 'and other engines'. No quest was made with the lymer; when hunted with hounds the reindeer gave poor sport, hindered in flight by the weight and spread of its antlers, 'and since there is in its hunting no skill to speak of, either of hounds or of huntsmen, I shall say no more, for I have already said enough'.[52]

The ibex

The best description of medieval ibex-hunting is given, again, by Gaston Phoebus. He obviously hunted ibex himself, but only *faute de mieux*, and he of course was a fanatic; there is no indication that many other persons of his social level did the same, and the creature was in any case unavailable in most areas, including the civilized lowlands of England and northern France. There are scenes of ibex-hunting in the *Fischereibuch* of the Emperor Maximilian, but Alfonso XI of Castile, who must have been aware of the existence of the ibex, makes no mention of it as a quarry species.

It emerges from Phoebus that the animal was a regular quarry of the Pyrenean peasantry, who relied on its skin as a waterproof material for clothing and shoes, 'and in my mountains more people are dressed in that than in scarlet' (by scarlet he means a variety of cloth rather than a colour).[53] The animal was very common in the Pyrenees in the fourteenth century; Phoebus writes of having seen over five hundred at once in winter, when they descended to escape the snows and find feeding.[54] He despises them as food, saying that their flesh gives rise to fevers and is eaten only by folk who have nothing better. It was, however, salted for winter. The ibex's impressive horns are never shed, and it was thought that each ring on the horns represented a year of life. After the rutting period, which lasted a month from the Feast of All Saints, males and females came down to the foothills and remained in herds until Easter, when the males went back to the high ground and took up residence in ones and twos, like the hart, in individual woodland territories, and the females remained down near the streams to give birth.

The solitariness of the male ibex from Easter to the late summer made it possible to adapt the procedures of *par force* hart-hunting to this more localized quarry. Phoebus[55] recommends a week spent in advance reconnaissance and preparation, observing the lie of the land and especially stopping with hayes and nets the routes of access to some of the high places where the ibex might try to take refuge. If it was impossible to do this with nets, men were stationed in large numbers on the crags, either to kill the animals with crossbows (a specialized version of bow and stable hunting) or to dissuade them from climbing up by throwing stones.

The hunters spent the night before the hunt high in the mountains, in the shepherds' huts. In the morning a quest was carried out with a lymer and the animal's *fumées* were observed, as in the case of the hart. The pack consisted of ten or a dozen hounds, plus relays, which were essential: four at least, each of four hounds, some stationed well up towards the tops of the peaks to take over from the hounds exhausted by the climb in the summer heat, others by the streams. They should more properly be called vauntlays, since they were released as the ibex came towards them.

Phoebus describes with awe, and perhaps some overstatement, the marvellous agility of the animals, especially their astonishing downward leaps: 'I have seen one jump down ten *toises* [about sixty feet] in one leap, and not harm itself; . . . they are as steady on the top of a rock as a horse on the ground. Sometimes they jump from so high that their legs give way, and they let their head take the blow on the rocks and so save themselves, . . . but sometimes they break their necks.' Their massive horns and strong neck made them a formidable adversary at close quarters; Phoebus describes them breaking the arms and legs of men trapped against a tree, and 'the strongest man in the world, hitting them on the back with an iron bar, would not bring them to their knees.'[56]

Such close-quarter encounters, however, were rare. The ibex often provided a prolonged hunt, since its home territory was a landscape which made it difficult for running-hounds to keep up with it, and usually impossible for a hunter on foot or horseback to remain in touch with his hounds and to be present at the kill; and for these reasons even the energetic Gaston de Foix has no great appetite for the sport.[57]

The chamois

Phoebus considers the Pyrenean chamois and the ibex together; he is fully aware that they are different species, but makes no distinction between the two for hunting purposes, though his methods were probably applied to the ibex more often than to the chamois. In the Alps, however, the chamois as a separate quarry was hunted by two methods not described by Phoebus. Our main source of information is the hunting literature produced by or under the aegis of the Emperor Maximilian I.[58]

Maximilian's dedication to hunting is celebrated in the tapestry series *The Hunts of Maximilian* in the Louvre. His craggy profile appears, too, in one of the hunting panoramas of Lucas Cranach, *The Stag Hunt of the Elector Frederic the Wise*,[59] and one of the finest examples of the cutler's craft, a set of gold-inlaid hunting swords and knives presented to Maximilian, is preserved in the Waffensammlung in Vienna.[60]

One's choice between the alternative forms of Alpine chamois-hunting depended on whether one's aim was to fill the larder or to reveal one's prowess against an individual animal. Large drives were organized, using the peasantry as beaters, with the aim of driving the chamois into a lake, where they were killed from boats.[61] This largely Germanic practice was used, too, in deer-hunts. Cranach's paintings show the crossbowmen waiting behind the trees along the bank of a river or lake into which the deer are being driven; in one picture spectators watch from a boat; in another boatmen are retrieving the dead deer from the water.[62]

For Maximilian, however, the cream of chamois-hunting was an arduous individual sport in which the hunter put himself in some personal danger with no assistance even from hounds. It involved clambering alone up the Alpine rock-faces, where the animals were so nimbly at home, and either shooting them with a crossbow or killing them with a specially developed javelin. The hunter wore six-spiked crampons, and a skullcap to protect him from falling stones, and carried an alpenstock. Maximilian was famous for his skill with the crossbow; it was said that he could shoot ducks in the air with it and that he once killed twenty-six hares without one miss.[63] For the chamois, however, he preferred the javelin. Either weapon must have been a heavy encumbrance to a hunter toiling up the rocks towards a quarry whose shyness and agility could take it out of range so suddenly and frustratingly. The javelins were eight or nine feet long, with a double-edged iron point, some seven inches long and two inches broad. An example is preserved in the Waffensammlung in Vienna. The weapons were very carefully kept, and were hung up in special boxes to keep the shafts straight, sometimes in the organ-lofts of churches.[64]

The Boar

Medieval man saw the stag and the boar as polarized extremes. This antithesis is richly productive at the literary and symbolic levels; the practical hunter perceived it vividly, visually and pragmatically. In contrast to the timid, elegant, wily deer, thought to have a special bone in its heart which alone saved it from dying of fear,[1] the boar is massive and ugly, black in appearance and character, the archetype of unrelenting ferocity. Completely fearless, unmoved by pain, it is capable of killing dog, horse or man. In imaginative literature it is the quarry of the epic hero; less subtle and evasive than the stag (the usual quarry in the sophisticated courtly romance of a broadly later era), less resourceful in malice and ruses, 'he tresteth not wel myche on his rennyng, but only on his defence and his despitous dedes.'[2] The boar is able to draw on extremes of bravery and pride or *orgueil* in its own nature, and demands a like response from the hunter in the single combat in which its pursuit ends.

For Gaston Phoebus the boar is the most dangerous animal in the world:

> the animal . . . which will kill a man or a beast most quickly, for a lion or a leopard will not kill a man or a beast with one blow, as he does, for they can kill only by raking with their claws or biting, whereas the boar kills with a single stroke, as one might with a knife. He is a fierce beast, proud and perilous, for . . . I have seen him strike a man and split him from knee to chest, so that he fell dead without a word; . . . he has often brought me to the ground, horse and man together, and killed my horse.[3]

The terrifying aspect of the boar as a malign solitary is amplified in the manuscript miniatures (see Figs 16, 18, 20, 21): it is depicted as huge, as big as a horse; its eyes are wide and malevolent; the horrific mouth bristles with teeth; most awful are the curved, gleaming tusks graphically described by Phoebus: 'He uses the top tusks for no other purpose than to make the lower ones sharp and cutting; these lower ones are called his *weapons* or his *files*, and with these he wreaks his evil. When he is at bay, he sharpens them constantly by clashing them together to make them keener.'[4] The foaming mouth is a further grisly element.

The boar was hunted with varying degrees of dedication over most of Europe, but to judge by the surviving manuals and by its role in imaginative literature it was most valued in the Iberian peninsula and in Germany. The fourteenth-century *Libro de la montería* of Alfonso XI of Castile is concerned largely with the boar and the bear. Although he acknowledges the superior craftiness of the stag, he describes its hunting briefly and without enthusiasm, as if under an obligation to do so: 'Although it is less important than hunting the bear or the boar, it is one of the three kinds of chase, and therefore we must describe it.' For Alfonso, stag-hunting is useful principally 'for the good which comes of it in making dogs for hunting the boar and the bear'.[5] Legal penalties for poaching offences in the hunting reserves of the kings of Portugal suggest a similarly lower valuation of the deer; the *Red Book* of King Alfonso V specifies: 'Item. Whoever kills a boar or a sow or a piglet shall pay two thousand *reis* for each beast. Item. Whoever kills a stag or a hind or a fawn shall pay one thousand *reis* for each beast.'[6] The *Livro da montaria* of John I of Portugal is concerned almost exclusively with the boar.

In the *Débat des héraulx d'armes*, of about 1460, the French herald, addressing his English counterpart, boasts: 'We have all the wild animals which you have, but we have many more, for we have *sangliers*, which are wild black pigs, and wolves and lynxes, and you have none of them. And know ye that these are cruel beasts, and that it needs people of high mettle to defeat them.'[7] However, the Englishman in John Coke's rejoinder to this, the *Debate betwene the Heraldes*, refutes this criticism heartily: 'Item, we have almaner of bestes salvages that you have, and more plente of them to chase; as hartes, hyndes, buckes, does, robuckes *and wylde bores*. And as touchynge wolves, wherof you have plentie, God be thanked, we have none. In lyeu wherof we have foxes, hayres, conys and otters, in moste habundaunce.'[8]

In the classic French treatises the boar season is said to run from the Feast of the Holy Cross (14 September), or from Michaelmas, when they were high in flesh, to St Andrew's Day (30 November), when they joined the sows for mating. The *Boke of St Albans* extends the season considerably, linking it with the feasts of the Nativity (8 September) and Purification (2 February, Candlemas) of the Virgin Mary.[9] The boar could be hunted from the time when he left the herd after his third year and became solitary. The *Craft of Venery* deduces the etymology of the French word *sanglier* from his unsociable nature: ' "Why clepe ye borre *symguler*?" "For he is the furst yere a *pigge*, the while he sokythe his dame, and when his dame hathe left him, then is he called at that yere *suklyng*, the whiche is called yn ffrenche *sorayne*. The III^de yere they ben called *hogastrys*, and when he is of age of IIII yere, he schall departyn out of companye by kynde of age and schal gone alone. And when he is alone, he schall then be called *synguler* for the causes fore seid." '[10]

The boar was hunted *par force* in much the same way as the stag, but behaved differently. He could be singled out for the hunt by his large tracks, the size of his bed, or the height of the mud which he rubbed off his back onto the trees on emerging from his wallow. In the early season he might be found gleaning the pea or cereal fields, later seeking apples in the orchards, and in the advanced autumn in the oak-woods looking for acorns. The variety of his diet and the continued availability of elements of it well into winter are the *Boke of St Albans'* justification for prolonging the season:

> For at the Nativyte of owre lady swete
> He may fynde where he goth under his feete
> Booth in wodys and feldis corne and oder frute,
> When he after foode makyth any sute.
> Crabbys and acornys and nottis ther thay grow;
> Hawys and heeppes and other thyng ynow,
> That till the Purificacion lastys as ye se,
> And makyth the Boore in seson to be,
> For while that frute may last, his time is never past.[11]

He had a tendency to sulk in thick cover at the least sign of danger:

> A boor hereth wondire wel and cleerly, and whan he is hunted and commeth out of the forest or of the bussh . . . he putteth his head out of the woode, or he putteth out his body, and than he abydeth there and harkeneth and loketh about, and taketh the wynde in every side, and if that tyme seeth ony thyng the whiche myghte lette [hinder] hym of his way that he wold goo, than he turneth hym agane into the wode, and than wil he never more come out, tho al the hornes and al the halowyng of the world were there.[12]

He was sought initially with the lymers, and report was made to the assembly. The huntsman whose boar was chosen led the rest back to his markers, found the boar's bed, felt it with his hand, and, if it was warm, blew for the release of the hounds. Even at this early stage, scorning the evasive crafts of the stag, the boar might face the hounds and attack them, and later in his flight he might do this repeatedly and then run on with striking stamina, 'and flee from the sonne rysing to the sonne goyng doun, if he be a yonge boor of III yere old'.[13] The *Gawain* poet has seen it all:

> Then they beat on the bushes, and bade him uprise,
> And out he came, bringing peril to those in his path;
> Dreadful in size as he drove out towards them,
> An ancient beast, long separated from the herd.
> Savage he came, the hugest of his kind,
> Fierce in his grunting. Many were in fear,
> For three were felled to the earth in his first charge,
> Then away he raced, leaving the rest unharmed.
> They hallooed with all their lungs, 'Sohow! Sohow!';
> Put their horns to their mouths, and blew the rechase.
> Merry was the hue and cry of the hunters and hounds
> In quest of this boar, to quell him with clamour and noise.
>> Full often he turns at bay
>> And maims the jostling pack.
>> He wounds the hounds, and they
>> Howl and squeal most sorely.
>
> . . . But the lord on his swift horse spurred after him,
> Blowing his horn like a bold warrior in the field.
> He blew the rechase, rode on through the rank thickets,
> Seeking this wild swine till the shafting sunset.[14]

The difficulty of bringing the boar finally to bay made it essential to organize one's relays of hounds, 'for a boar will run far, and also he kills and injures many hounds. If there were no fresh hounds he could well escape, so have two or three relays posted.'[15]

As soon as one came anywhere near a boar enraged by a pack of hounds, one was in peril, even on horseback; much more so when on foot. Several of the medieval writers dwell on the boar's sinister eyes, but to a hunter who could prevent his bowels from turning to water and retain his presence of mind the eyes were a very practical help in diagnosing the animal's state of mind and foreseeing its actions. John I of Portugal gives precise details of how its appearance indicated an impending attack: 'If the hunter sees that the boar at bay has his snout low to the ground and his ears flat on his head, and is clashing his tusks to sharpen them, that boar is keen to see the hunter closing with him. The hunter had best look to himself, for there will be no avoiding a joust with him.' The immediate indicator of the boar's assault, however, was the movement of the eyes; John I imbues this with an anthropomorphic frenzy of vengefulness:

> As soon as the hunter sees the boar and it sees him, it pricks its ears, and rolls its eyes like a thing stirred by a burning rage. I use the word

rage [*ardimento*] because rage and valour are very different things: rage describes a man whose heart is moved by anger, who, beyond the bounds of reason and self-awareness, forgets all danger to body, honour and reputation, and seeks only to put an end to the thing which angers him, in order to venge his spite.[16]

After this, the hunter's time was short, quick reflexes and calmness essential. 'The eyes roll in rage, and it takes two or three steps towards him, ears pricked. As soon as the hunter sees this, he must prepare himself, for let him be sure that the boar will come so quickly that it will seem that not an instant elapses between the beginning of his charge and his arrival on the spear; or, if the hunter misses his aim, on the man himself.'[17] John I devotes several detailed chapters to the exact techniques for receiving the onrush of a boar in varying circumstances: straight ahead, downhill, crossing, etc. If one was on foot, falling down or letting the boar between one's legs could lead to maiming or death. In normal circumstances one stood with one foot forward, the other back and directly behind the front foot, and one hand forward on the spear, which had to be at waist height. The other hand, further back on the spear, played the crucial role in aiming. One leaned slightly towards the boar, and at the moment of impact one leaned further into the blow and thrust with the hands, not aiming at 180° to the animal's course, but with the rear hand holding the shaft at a very slight angle so that in the event of missing the boar's head and shoulders there was still a chance of hitting it further back.[18]

Gaston Phoebus is very specific about the hunter's grip on the spear:

His spear should be crossed [i.e. with a crosspiece a little way back from the point; this could be a detachable bar bound on with a thong, or could be forged as part of the blade or riveted to it], sharp and keen; he must hold the shaft in the middle, with as much in front of him as behind, for if he held it too short in front, when he struck the boar, which has a long head, the snout would reach him, for the spear would go deep and the boar . . . could wound or kill him. So as to be able to put more force into the blow and to move his hand wherever necessary, he must never grip the spear in his armpit, but after the impact he should put it there and thrust hard. And if the boar is stronger than him, he must jump about retaining his hold, and push and push until God gives him aid or help arrives.[19]

In thick cover one might have to approach the boar on all fours (John of Portugal tells us: 'In our country the huntsmen do this all the time'[20]) and adopt a special half-kneeling technique: one put one knee forward as a support to the front hand on the spear-shaft, and the rear foot back so that again one was leaning into the impact; a style also used by the Romans against lions (Fig. 16).[21]

In *Gawain*, somewhat unusually for a hunter on foot, to judge by the manuals, Sir Bertilak uses a sword to meet the direct attack of the boar:

Sprightly he dismounted, left his horse,
Brandished his bright blade, and boldly stepped forward,
Strode through the ford to where his foe waited.
The beast watched him come with weapon in hand,
And raised up his hair, snorting so fiercely
That many feared for the knight, lest he come off the worse.
The swine made his rush, driving direct for the man,
And brave man and boar were both entangled together
In the whitest of the water. The beast came off worse,
For the man marked him well at their first meeting,
Set the sword-point in the slot of the neck,
And pierced him to the hilt, sundering the heart.
Snarling he succumbed, and was rolled by the rush of the river.
    A hundred hounds caught him,
    Biting him bravely;
    Men brought him to the bank
    and the dogs did away with him.[22]

Such killing in water was not unusual; John I devotes a whole chapter to the technique. Whereas the *Gawain* poet is keen to maximize the danger and glory, the practical hunter tries to exploit the simple advantage of having longer legs than the enemy: 'The hunter should try to prevent the boar reaching the bank . . . when he sees the boar swimming, he should get into water so deep that it reaches his chest (for then he knows that the boar cannot touch the bottom) and wait for him, for the boar cannot strike him in this situation.' Again, after the blow, one had to hang on and keep the spear in the boar, so that he could be brought to the bank and would not be lost downriver.[23]

Gaston Phoebus shows similar pragmatism, surprising in a knightly age, in his recommendation against dismounting to kill the boar: 'It is perilous indeed to put oneself at risk of death or maiming to gain so little honour or profit, for I have seen good knights, squires and servants die by doing so.'[24] When the running-hounds were accompanied by alaunts, mastiffs or large greyhounds which could attack and hold the boar, the hunter could dismount and kill it more surely with a spear on foot, as shown in the Devonshire tapestries. An impressive kill from horseback, however, had its own dangers and was more highly praised, not least because of its knightly associations and military relevance:

for hunting is a training for all types of fighting met with in war: against a foe crossing in front, in a head-on encounter or in a pursuit; in an awkward situation or a sounder one. For every kind of military encounter, hunting is a better training than jousting. If the tourney teaches a man how to strike with a sword on a helmet, how much better he will learn by striking down a boar when his only chance of saving himself is by a good thrust with the spear.[25]

Just like the hunter on foot, the mounted man faced the bayed boar and incited it to charge ('*Avant, maistre! Avant! Or sa, sa!*' in Gaston Phoebus). He stood up in the stirrups with his horse at the trot, and met the onrush with a downward thrust of the sword, blunt on one or both edges of the upper part of the blade in case the onward momentum of the boar carried it against the hunter's thigh (see Figs. 5, 18, 55). In the south-west of France anyone who killed a boar with a sword, without assistance from the great dogs, was rewarded with the *umbles* or *nombles* (usually the kidneys, with the flesh and fat from the inside of the back).[26] The sword could also be used to kill a fleeing boar as the horse overtook it, and the spear, too, was used, either like a lance in jousting (John I calls this method *justar*) or thrown from a moving horse. The latter method involved the danger of the spear missing and sticking in the ground and the horse impaling itself on the shaft; to avoid this Gaston Phoebus recommends pulling the horse's head sharply to the right immediately after the throw.[27]

Success in this form of hunting depended greatly on the quality of one's horse. Those in the medieval miniatures (Figs. 5, 13, 18, 19, etc.) usually look smaller than a modern hunter, clean-legged and somewhat broad in body and chest. They had to be responsive to the bit, to avoid the dangers of tree- branches and rocks, in any form of *par force* hunting, but in the boar-hunt, where accuracy of aim might be a matter of life and death, the great essential was a serene temperament. 'Hunters must have nothing to do with a nervous horse, for this is one of the worst faults that a hunting-horse can have, . . . for we would have been ten or a dozen times in danger of death had we been on a nervous horse, and we advise all hunters never to put themselves astride one'; so says John of Portugal.[28]

Even in *par force* hunting, archers or crossbowmen were sometimes involved in finishing off the boar.[29] In some areas, especially Spain and Portugal, the boar was driven towards lines of hunters waiting at *armadas* with bows, crossbows or spears, and additional dogs. Alfonso XI of Castile, in his exhaustive listing of the hunting grounds of northern Spain, is meticulous in setting down the right positions for hunters, beaters and relays. A typical entry is:

Dosante, Val de Guida, Val del Orrio and Val de Bodino all go together. The lines of beaters [*vocerías*, literally 'shoutings'] are as follows: one from the peak above the hill of Santa María along the ridge to the hill of Santa María, and from there along the road to the hill called Sotiello, and to Peña del Arzón; another from Hozeja to Ingueros; another from La Muñeca to Caveñes de Yeres, and from there to Los Torales; another from there to the right of Cestiérnaga, beyond the river and to the right of San Helices. And there should be a relay of dogs above Val de Guida. The *armadas* [the lines of waiting hunters] should be one at the hill of Sotiello and the others in Val Severo.[30]

Daunting logistics in rough country, requiring a substantial force of men.

To kill a boar with the thrown spear as one stood in an *armada* needed special skills. The hunter had to allow for the surprising speed of the animal rushing past him (as opposed to at him), just as a modern shooter swings his gun-barrels ahead of a pheasant before pulling the trigger. 'Never throw at any part of his body, but only at the point of the head, or even further in front; . . . consider the boar's speed: if he is going very fast, aim a little in front of him; if not so fast, aim for the head. If you aim at the shoulders or flank, the spear can easily miss altogether.'[31] If the boar was only wounded, dogs stationed with the *armada* were released to pursue him.

Modus also gives details of taking boar by driving them into nets with the hounds, a procedure whose name, the *déduit réal*, suggests that it was held in quite high esteem. It was done in November, between All Saints' and St Andrew's Day, when the seasons for boars and sows overlapped. It involved a large input of men, nets and dogs, but had compensating rewards in the exhilarating tumult of hounds, horns and beaters and in the large bags obtained; *Modus* tells us: 'When the wood is well- stocked, one can take them in plenty. I saw King Charles, son of the good King Philip, hunting in a wood called the Boulaie Guérardet in the forest of Berteuil, where he took twenty-six wild pigs in a day, not counting those which escaped from the nets.'[32] The sows were generally less dangerous than the boars, and less prone to turn at bay when pursued, but when enraged they could charge like a boar. Lacking tusks, they remained over a fallen man longer than a boar, trying to savage him with their teeth, but rarely killed him. They too were hunted *par force*, often by mistake when the hounds took up their scent instead of that of the selected boar, and could run for enormous distances (for two whole days, according to *Modus*).[33]

The death of the boar was followed by the unmaking, or cutting-up of the body, and by the 'reward' or *fouail*, a ceremonial sharing of the benefits with the dogs, corresponding to the *curée* of the stag (Fig. 20).[34] A fire was important for two purposes. The head was severed, the blood reserved and the feet removed. Two crossbars were placed through holes cut in the skin of the front and back legs, with a pole lengthways under them. With this the carcass was supported over the fire, and the bristles were burned and beaten off (although Twiti recommends cutting up the boar *tut velu*, 'all hairy'[35]). With the carcass on its back, the testicles were cut out, then the shoulders and hams were removed in succession and placed against the flanks as supports. The belly skin was cut open and all the internal organs taken out; the carcass was turned over and the chine removed with knife and axe, leaving the two sides separate, and the chine and sides were jointed. The *Craft of Venery* is precise about the proper number of edible items resulting from a decently butchered boar: 'If he be undo as it is rygt, he schall have XXXII *hasteletts*' (cf. the modern 'haslet'). Judging from Twiti and the *Boke of St Albans*, these were the head, the collar, the heart, the lungs, two shoulders, two 'pestles', two 'gambons', two fillets, two haunches, four legs, four feet, four pieces of the chine, and six of the sides.[36]

Of the various organs, the stomach, spleen, liver and testicles (see also below, p. 108) were sometimes reserved for the kitchen, but in the view of Gaston Phoebus these, the intestines, and everything else from within the boar (except sometimes the kidneys and the adjacent fat and flesh) were rightly the due of the dogs. These items were broiled on the fire, and great rounds of bread soaked in the boar's blood were roasted on the embers, no doubt making many a hunter's mouth water after a gruelling autumn or winter day. The offal and bread were then cut up and mixed together, and the dogs were encouraged to devour them by the cries of the company. Again we see the hunter's concern for his dog's health; the main reason for cooking their portion is the weather:

> Firstly, the flesh of the boar is less pleasant to the dogs than that of the deer; cooked, it is tastier and they eat it more gladly. Also it does them more good cooked and hot, for one hunts the boar in hard weather, and perhaps the dogs have come through water or rain, so the fire is good for them on their return ... and the reward benefits them greatly, being cooked, and warms all their body within. The *curée* of the deer should be done where it is killed, if the hour is not too late; but the reward of the boar should be done on returning to the hunting lodge.[37] (See Fig. 20)

We have seen the encounter between man and boar described in terms recalling encounters between human adversaries; also that the boar combines traits which are in some cases enviable (power, courage, stamina) and in others antipathetic (pride, anger, vindictiveness, physical menace). It is not surprising that the moral and literary symbolism of the boar is mixed, and that in the progress from the Dark Ages to the early Renaissance one can perceive the stress shifting from its desirable to its undesirable aspects as European society becomes more civilized and Christianized. In the pagan era, especially in Germany, the boar was a cult animal. Oaths were sworn on the sacrificial boar, and he was sacred to the god Freyr, the protector and ancestor of certain tribes. The association of the boar's head with Christmas may be a survival of this ancient role, perhaps reinforced by the belief, common in primitive societies, that one acquires the strength of one's enemy by consuming him, and especially those parts of him in which his nature is most manifest. Some of the late-medieval boar's-head carols associate the head merely with celebration:

> The boris hed in hondes I brynge,
> With garlondes gay and byrdes syngynge;
> I pray you all, helpe me to synge,
>> Qui estis in convivio.

Others link it very deliberately with the Nativity:

> This borys hede that we brynge here
> Betokeneth a Prince withowte pere
> Ys born this day to bye us dere.
>> Nowell!, Nowelle!

> This borys hede we bryng with song
> In worship of hym that thus sprong
> Of a virgine to redresse all wrong.
>> Nowell!, Nowelle![38]

There was also a belief among hunters in France that the boar's flesh had medicinal properties in the spring; the *Master of Game* tells us, rather reservedly, that 'in Maii some good hunters of byonde the see seyne that in that tyme thei bere medecyne for the good heerbes and the good floures that thei ete but theruppon I make non affirmacion.'[39] In *Beowulf* the boar is the device of the heroic Geats, and its image is used as a piece of defensive magic: 'The shining helmet . . . was adorned with gold, encircled with lordly bands, as in the past days the weapon-smith had wrought it; formed it wondrously, and set it round with boar-images, so that after that no sword or battle-knife could ever cut through it.'[40]

This identification with individual and tribal defence and prowess leads to the boar's being linked symbolically or as a supporting motif with the hero in epic poetry and the early romance, especially in Germanic areas. This may take the form of a mere simile, or the boar may be the hero's heraldic device.[41] The bad side of the boar, however, often enables him to represent the enemy. The Arthurian legends associate him sometimes with villain, sometimes with hero. In the *Mabinogion* the black boar Twrch Trwyth is really a wicked king, transformed by God in punishment, and is pursued into the sea by Arthur. In the romance *Robert of Gloucester*, however, and in Geoffrey of Monmouth's *Historia Regum Britanniae*, Arthur himself is described as the Boar of Cornwall.[42] In her prophetic dream in the thirteenth-century version of the *Nibelungenlied*, Kriemhild sees the hero, Siegfried, pursued through a field of red flowers by two boars; subsequently, after excelling in the hunting field, Siegfried falls victim to the plotting of Hagen and Gunther, and dies among the blood-drenched flowers, his heart transfixed by Hagen's hunting-spear.[43] Even here there is ambivalence: in the later stages of the poem Hagen's boar-like energy and thrust become heroic.

The pre-Christian worship of the boar combines with his blackness and implacability to set him up as an antithesis of those virtues and associations embodied by the stag, and specifically to make him a symbol of paganism. In several versions of the story of the battle of Roncevaux the massacre of the Christian French by the Moors is foretold in symbolic dreams. The Emperor Charlemagne dreams 'that he was in France, in his chapel in Aix, and an evil boar bit his right arm,' the right arm being, of course, Roland, who dies in the battle. In the *Roman de Roncevaux* Roland's betrothed, Aude, dreams that Roland and Oliver are surrounded by hostile boars, and in the fourteenth-century *Bastars de Buillons* 'the Christians are lions, the Saracens are boars.'[44]

Like the deer or the lost hawk, the boar can lead a hero into an alien environment where, separated from his companions, his hounds lost or slain, he is vulnerable to adventure or to death. In the case of the boar, this is not always a casual flight. The foundation legends of certain monasteries in Germanic areas (e.g. Kremsmünster) or areas influenced by Germanic tradition (e.g. San Pedro de Arlanza in Spain) involve a boar-hunt. In other cases the chase is based on wicked intent on the animal's part, so that the boar comes to be seen as an assistant or symbol of the devil. This may arise partly out of early commentaries on Psalm LXXX, which construe the boar as the devil or his agent, or from an association with the Gadarene swine into which Christ directed the legion of devils conjured out of the man with the unclean spirit in, for example, Mark, Chapter V. There was a belief among practical hunters that a boar could take away more than a man's life: John I of Portugal tells us that 'some men say that a man who dies of wounds inflicted by a boar will lose his soul.' He decries this belief, but nevertheless devotes a whole chaper to refuting it.[45] The link with the devil, and the 'talk of the devil' principle, may underlie the replacement of the normal word for boars, *sangliers*, in *Modus* by the circumlocution *les noires bestes*, 'the black beasts' (just as the words for weasel, snake and fox are replaced by euphemisms in certain rural cultures for reasons of taboo), though at this remove it is hard to know whether this usage is euphemistic or is intended to stress the boar's villainy. The prosaic royal French hunting accounts also allude to the 'black beasts'.[46]

In certain respects the boar in literature shares the characteristics of the dragon: he sometimes has a lair, strewn with the bones of his victims, and a further link, his supposedly fiery mouth, goes back at least to the Greek writer Oppian:

> There is a tale touching the Wild Boar that his white tusk has within it a secret devouring fiery force . . . for when a great thronging crowd of hunters with their dogs lay the beast low upon the ground, overcoming him with long spear on spear, then if one take a thin hair from the neck and approach it to the tusk of the still gasping beast, straightway the hair takes fire and curls up. And on either side of the dogs themselves, where the fierce tusks of the swine's jaws have touched them, marks of burning are traced on the hide.[47]

The boar's repulsive mouth enables him to symbolize the slanderer or intrusive gossip in the literature of courtly love. As the boar may slay the hunter, so the slanderer destroys the lover's relationship with his lady, and threatens her reputation. In *La Chace aux mesdisants* he is hunted down with allegorical hounds such as Joy, Kindness, Beauty and Pity, and after the kill his evil tongue is pierced with a sword.[48] Some imagery of the boar has a strongly sexual aspect. The brilliant miniaturist who embellished the Paris Manuscript 619 of Gaston Phoebus's *Livre de chasse* with detailed depictions of all the different game animals and dogs shows only the boar engaged in copulation, and in other miniatures the boar's genitals are prominent (Fig. 21). Sexuality figures overpoweringly in Oppian's description centuries earlier:

> Unceasingly he roams in pursuit of the female and is greatly excited by the frenzy of desire. On his neck the hair bristles erect, like the crest of a great-plumed helmet. He drops foam upon the ground and gnashes the white hedge of his teeth, panting hotly; and there is much more rage about his mating than modesty. If the female abides his advances, she quenches all his rage and lulls to rest his passion. But if she refuses intercourse and flees, straightway stirred by the hot and fiery goad of desire he either overcomes her and mates with her by force or he attacks her with his jaws and lays her dead in the dust.[49]

Small wonder that some hunters looked on the boar's testicles as a prized addition to their diet and removed them as the first act after the kill.[50]

Elements of Oppian's vision of the boar, especially the importance of the mouth as expressive of sexual vigour, recur in certain medieval revelatory dreams. In Chaucer's *Troilus and Criseyde* the hero dreams of

> . . . a boor with tuskes grete,
> That sleep ayein the bright sonnes hete.
> And by this boor, faste in his armes folde,
> Lay kissing ay his lady bright Criseyde,

and is quick to conclude that his love is unfaithful to him. Boccaccio's version is sexually more vivid: Troilo dreams that Criseida is receiving the thrusts of the boar's mouth, and apparently taking pleasure from it.[51] In Gottfried von Strassburg's *Tristan* the fact that the hero's heraldic device is the boar, together with the explicit imagery of the tossing head and foaming mouth, renders unequivocal Majadoc's dream of Tristan's seduction of Isolde, the wife of King Mark: 'The Steward saw in his dream as he slept a boar, fearsome and dreadful, that ran out of the forest. Up to the King's court he came, foaming at the mouth and whetting his tusks, and charging everything in his path. . . . Arriving at Mark's chamber he broke in through the doors, tossed the King's appointed bed in all directions, and fouled the royal linen with his foam.'[52]

Less frequently, the boar symbolizes keenness of ear. In Longthorpe Tower, in the barony of Peterborough, the fourteenth-century artist who devised the mural of the Wheel of the Five Senses depicts Hearing as a boar with its ears pricked.[53] Queen Ratio's moral and religious interpretation of the symbolism of the stag (see above, p. 68) is paralleled by her stern exposition of the evil nature of the boar, in which she brings together many of the above associations and adds a few more prosaic ones. He is black and ugly, and thus represents those who have lost spiritual light and live in the darkness of worldliness. He exemplifies human sins: anger, like those wrathful men who lack charity and humility; pride, in that he disdains flight and faces the hounds and is destroyed, as the man who scorns confession and salvation awaits the assault of devils and spiritual death. His two tusks are like the daggers wielded by drunken men emerging from the tavern. He keeps his head close to the earth, as do contemporary men whose thoughts never rise above the worldly. He pushes his face into the soil, and so symbolizes those who seek the delights of the flesh and the stomach. He wallows in mud as the rich wallow in the filth and ordure of the Antichrist. His toes are twisted and crossed, like those of the folk who wear ludicrous shoes for fashion's sake, deforming their feet to resemble those of the devil whose disciples they are. His bed makes a great hole in the ground; so too will the grave of those who give themselves to the delight and vanity of this world, devoting their soul to the devil's glory and thereby gaining damnation. Even the sow, swollen up by her seven piglets, recalls man puffed up by the Seven Deadly Sins.

Ratio's ringing condemnation of the boar is accompanied in *Modus* by a list of the devil's commandments. The text says that these 'emerge from the boar's mouth, as you may see in the illustration', but the accompanying miniature shows the boar biting the foot of a tree in which sits the devil, his face now half-erased by fearful or pious readers; the commandments ('Displease God', 'Despise the poor', 'Believe in sorcery', etc.) emerge on scrolls from the branches. Ratio's words, however, are also reflected in a marvellous miniature showing the Mouth of Hell as the jaws of a boar.[54]

7

The Hare

'Nowe we will begynne at the hare.'
'And wherefore at the hare rather then at eny other best?'
'For why it is the most merveylous beste that is in this lond.'[1]

Why so marvellous? The *Boke of St Albans* provides some rather opaque answers:

That beast kyng shall be calde of all venery . . .
For he fymaes and crotis and roungeth evermoore
And berith talow and gres: and above teeth hath he foore.
And other while he is male: and so ye shall hym fynde,
And other while female and kyndelis by kynde.[2]

For the late-medieval hunter, obsessed with classification and semantic snobbery, the hare was a challenging anomaly, falling neatly neither into the category of animals like the deer and other ruminants, which were 'flayed', whose fat was 'tallow', whose droppings were 'fumes' (verb: to 'femayen' or 'fumay'), and whose hide was called 'skin', nor into the group of smaller beasts such as the fox which were 'stripped',[3] whose fat was 'grease' (also applied more generally, however, especially in the term 'time of grease'), whose hide was called 'piles' (French *peau*) and whose droppings were 'fients'. As a ruminant (i.e. which 'roungeth'[4]), the hare had a right to the terms 'femayen' and 'tallow,' but he was not 'flayed':

All that bere skynne and talow and Rounge, leve me,
Shall be flayne, safe the hare, for he shall stripte be.[5]

The idea that the hare was hermaphroditic, or changed sex from time to time, was ancient and persists today among countrymen. 'The common sort of people suppose that they are one year male, and another female . . . the Hunters object that there be some which are only females and no more,

110

but no male that is not also a female, and so they make him an Hermaphrodite. Niphus affirmeth so much, for he saw a Hare which had stones and a yard [i.e. male genitalia], and yet was great with young.'[6] Even the knowledgeable Gaston Phoebus seems uncertain as to whether to call the hare 'him' or 'her', changing the gender of his pronouns in a random manner (sometimes *il* and *le*, sometimes *elle* and *la*).[7]

There is, of course, no substance to the idea, which arose from the ambiguous appearance of the hare's genitals. The *Boke of St Albans* is on firmer ground in another statement about this wondrous beast:

> . . . when he is female and kyndelis hym within,
> In .iii. degrees he hem berith or he with hem twyn:
> Too Rough and .ii. smooth, who will hem se,
> And .ii. knottis also that kyndelis will be.[8]

This phenomenon of superfoetation in the hare was known to Xenophon and Oppian.[9] The pregnant hare may 'kindle' or conceive again before delivering her first leverets. The second foetuses, smooth-skinned, are usually aborted at the same time as the first, fully-formed litter. It is even possible for a third conception to take place, and for the hare to bear the embryos (the 'knottis' mentioned by the *Boke of St Albans*) at the same time as the fully-formed and half-formed litters.

A creature of some distinction, then; but the hare was 'kyng of venery' not because of its physiological oddities, but because hunting it *par force* was a microcosm of the most complex and subtle aspects of the medieval chase, and so furnished ample scope for the display of that catechistic repertoire of word and phrase which distinguished the socially accomplished hunter; the other principal method of taking the hare, by coursing with grey-hounds, provided a dazzling and physically less demanding aristocratic spectator sport.

It was in England that the hunting of the hare *par force* was most appreciated. Edward, Duke of York's *Master of Game* alters Phoebus's chapter order to put the hare first, the deer second, 'for al blowyng and the faire termys of huntyng commen of the sechyng and fyndyng of the hare'.[10]

Even for Phoebus, however, who had a range of larger game readily available to him, the hare is a *moult bonne bestelette*, a splendid little beast. He shows the true hunter's spirit, in that the harder an animal is to outwit or outrun, the more highly he rates it. The hare's appeal lay in a dislike of travelling in straight lines, which the hunter saw as evidence of malice aforethought.

> Whenever she goes to rest, whether it be near her grazing or far away,

she goes so subtly and craftily that no man in the world would say that a hound could unravel her path to find her. She will go a bowshot or more in one direction, then retrace her steps and go off in another, and do this ten or twenty times; then she will enter some piece of rough and pretend to rest there, and crisscross ten or a dozen times and make her ruses there [i.e. leap sideways like a deer], then she will take some difficult path and make off into the distance.[11]

King Modus suggests that the best time to hunt the hare is in March and April, because then they are pregnant, full of easily acquired spring grazing, and less complex in their movements because they have less need to travel for food.[12] The growing corn was a reliable place to find them in the spring:

The hares abiden in sondry contre, al after the sesoun of the yere, somtyme thei sitten in the feerne, somtyme in the hethe, and in the corn and in growyng wedis and somtyme in the wodes. In Averyll and in May, when the corn is so long that thei mowe hide hemself therinne, gladly thei will sitte therynne. And whan men bygynne to repe the corne thei wil sitte in the vynes and in other stronge hethes, and in busshes and in hegges, and alway comynly in the covert undir the wynde, and in covert of the Reyne.[13]

The hare seems to have been given little respite in much of the Middle Ages; Phoebus says that it is the only beast with no closed season; for Twiti, too 'the hare is alwey in seson to be chasyd.'[14] For Dame Juliana, however,

At Michelmas begynnyth huntyng of the hare
And lastith till mydsomer.[15]

Another welcome aspect of the hare was that it could be hunted in the morning, after it had returned to its form, or the evening, when it had travelled to its feeding ground (sometimes over half a league away). In summer, Phoebus recommends one to hunt from matins to the hour of prime, then to feed and water oneself and the hounds, and rest in the shade or indoors until the heat abates around the hour of nones, when the hares have gone to feed, and to hunt again until night.[16]

The hunter's delight lay in watching the hounds unravel the hare's deceitful course by following its scent. This was already a visual joy in the classical period; the hare is the prime quarry described by Xenophon, and although he appears to have driven the hares into fixed nets, the initial stage of the hunt was the merry questing of the scenting hounds:

They will go forward full of joy and ardour, disentangling the various tracks, double or triple – springing forward now beside, now across the same ones – tracks interlaced or circular, straight or crooked, close or scattered, clear or obscure, running past one another with tails wagging, ears dropped and eyes flashing. As soon as they are near the hare they will let the hunter know by the quivering of the whole body as well as the tail, by making fierce rushes, by racing past one another, by scampering along together persistently, massing quickly, breaking up and again rushing forward. At length they will reach the hare's form and will go for her.[17]

Phoebus mentions several factors indicating merit in a hare. Tracks and droppings, so crucial in the assessment of the hart and the boar, played no role in hare-hunting; nor did the lymer. A hare which remained in its muse or form until spotted with the naked eye was thought to be confident in its own strength and bound to run well; so was a beast which, once moving, put up its tail like a rabbit. A running hare's ears were thought to indicate its state of mind: with both ears up it was thought to be confident of escape; with one down on its neck, it still felt strong; when both went down it was weakening.[18]

Xenophon stresses the importance of verbally encouraging the hounds; this remains an important feature in the late-medieval hare-hunts described by William Twiti and Dame Juliana Berners, in which the hue and cry of the hunters (*huer* in French is 'to shout when hunting') is reinforced by the music of the horn. The fifteenth-century *Craft of Venery* uses as its prime source Twiti's *Vénerie* of around 1330. There are English and French versions of Twiti, the French being the older; the English translation presérves the French of the cries and exclamations recommended for hare-hunting. These snippets of French are also preserved in the *Craft of Venery*, the *Master of Game* and the *Boke of St Albans*, which in this respect are all derived from the same source; a good example of the primacy of the sophisticated French in the hunting practices of the late Middle Ages (compare the wonder of Tristan's foreign hosts at his knowledge of the complicated *curée* of the hart in Chapter 2).

Instructions in the *Craft of Venery* are precise:

> Ye schall blown at the furst III mots [notes of the horn], and aftirward y schall let myn houndes out of coupall and y schall sey to hem *avaunt. sire, avaunt!* and aftirwards III tymes *so howe!* . . . and I schall blow alwey III mots bytwyx myn speking tyl the hare be mevyd, and aftirward y schall sey *cha, cha, sy avaunt, a ha ha, sy, dons, sy!* And yf ye sen that youre houndes hav luste and grete wille for to aloyne [distance] hem from you, ye schall sey thus: *howze, amy, howze, venes y, moun amy, venes y!* And yf ye sen that any hounde fynde alonlyche of hyr and he hathe a name, as *Recher* or *Bemound*, ye schall sey thus:

oyez a Bemound le vaylaunt, qui quide trouver le couard ou le court coue! ['Hark to Beaumont the brave, who thinks he has found the coward or the short-tail!'], and so for to draw all the other houndez to hym. . . . Yf it be in grene corne, or it be in pasture, then schalt sey *la dons, la il est venuz pur ly pestre!* ['There, then, there is where he came to graze!'] and *sohowe!* alwey at the last of youre wordez . . . And yf he come more forthe on pleyn feld or arabill land and youre houndez sechen of hur, ye schall seyn *la, dans, la il est venuz pur luy secher!* and *sohowze!*[19]

This is all a cheerful enough business for hound and hunter; for the local peasantry the merry music of the horn and the sight of the romping hounds must have been as welcome as the arrival of the tax-collectors. Their crops were damaged, and perhaps not all hunters were as ready to recompense them as James IV of Scotland, whose treasurer paid out forty-two shillings 'to the puir folkis hed thair corn etin in Strethern at the hunting'.[20] Hare-hunting caused particular problems, being carried out largely on arable or grazing land, and often involving young hounds, difficult to control, which had not learned adequately to distinguish a hare from the more domestic quadrupeds.

> They become transported by their strength and youth, and run ever forward paying no heed to anything, and when one forhues them [calls them back] to the sager hounds, they will not return, and sometimes they chase sheep and cattle. So the mounted hunters should spur on to beat them with their long staffs, and, if they have seized sheep or other beasts, to thrash them well and put fear into them. And thus, chasing the hare through the open country, one develops the hounds' wind and brings the young ones into shape.[21]

The *Master of Game* describes the same problems, and recommends having horsemen with long rods 'for to kepe that none hownde folowe to sheep, ne to other beestis, and if they do, to ascrie hem sore and alight and take hem up and bilaissh hem wel saying *Ware, ware, ha ha, ware*, and laysh hem forth to her felawes'.[22]

There were other frustrations for the hare-hunter. The biased author of the *Treatyse of Fysshynge with an Angle* saw no pleasure in it whatsoever:

> for huntynge as to myn entent is to laboryous. For the hunter must alwaye renne and folowe his houndes, traveyllynge and swetynge full sore. He blowyth tyll his lyppes blyster, and when he wenyth it be an hare full oft it is an hegge hogge. Thus he chasyth and wote not what. He comyth home at evyn, rayn beten, pryckyd, and his clothes torne, wete shode, all myry; some hounde lost . . . such greves and

many other happyth unto the hunter, whyche for displeysaunce of theym that love it I dare not reporte.[23]

The medieval treatises have little to say about coursing the hare with greyhounds; Phoebus alludes to it briefly as an alternative to *par force* hunting, but appears to think it so comparatively unsubtle as to need no explanation. There are sufficient allusions to it elsewhere to make it clear that the method was both common and highly regarded as a spectacle, and the greyhound's French name, *lévrier*, is based on this particular quarry, the *lièvre*. Even in coursing, scenting-hounds had a role to play, finding and raising the hare which was then pursued by the greyhounds (Fig. 24).

The *Master of Game* dwells principally on *par force* hunting, but also describes a combination of this with the use of greyhounds, rather like a miniature version of bow and stable deer-hunting: the hare was hunted in covert with the running-hounds (here called *racches*, 'ratches'), but greyhounds were also stationed around, held on a leash, probably in couples, by the fewterers: 'And if the hare happe to come out to the greihoundes aforn the racches, and be dede, the fewtrer that lette renne shuld blowe the dethe and kepe hur as hoole as he may to the hunters be come, and than shuld thei rewarde the houndes.'[24]

The early writers are imprecise about the type of scenting-hounds used in hunting the hare, and it seems likely that the basic hound was used indiscriminately for hart, boar and hare. *Modus* certainly mentions the use of hart-hounds to hunt the hare to keep them in trim in the closed season for deer (see p. 18). *Harriers* and *kenets* (from the French *chienets*, 'little dogs') are mentioned, but again in connection specifically with the deer (see p. 65). There is no medieval mention of the beagle, which appears to have evolved later through a process of breeding down for size by crossing the larger hounds with perhaps whippets or terriers.[25]

The death of the hare, as befits a worthy quarry, was followed by a brief ceremonial, sometimes called the 'hallow': the hunter who was nearest took the dead hare from the milling hounds, held it aloft, and blew the death, 'that men may gader thider'. The hare was stripped (i.e. its skin was removed, except from the head), the gall bladder and paunch thrown away, and the body was 'choppid also smale as it myghte be so that it hange togedire'. It was then held high, the master of the hounds blew the death again, and all the hunters hallooed, with the hounds baying around the hare, which the berner 'shuld . . . pulle as hye as he may every pece from other and cast to every hound his reward'.[26]

In the fourteenth century Gaston Phoebus employed a different procedure: he recommends that the dead hare be placed on the ground, and the hounds encouraged to bark at it, kept back some distance by the huntsmen's staffs. He rewarded his hounds by soaking bread in the hare's blood and spreading it on a bed of straw, sometimes adding fragments of cooked meat and cheese, still keeping the hounds back until the order to them to fall on it. The hare's flesh, he says, is disagreeable to hounds and makes them vomit, and therefore reduces their willingness to hunt the hare. He does, however, allow the kidneys, heart and tongue to be included in the reward.[27] The *Noble Art of Venery* also recommends giving the hounds fragments of cheese and bread.[28]

Dame Juliana repeats the general instructions of the *Master of Game*, but also has a mind to furnishing the larder:

> The hunter shall rewarde hem with the hede,
> With the shulderis and the sides and with the bowellis all,
> And all thyng within the wombe save onli the gall;
> The paunche also, yeve hem noon of thoo.
>
> . . .
>
> Then the loynes of the hare loke ye not forgete,
> Bot bryng hem to the kechyn for the lordis meete.[29]

When I was a child, my grandmother, like many another, used to remind me to say 'Hares, hares, hares!' when I went to bed on the last night of a month. She was a woman of urban background, who might well not have recognized a hare had one presented itself. To omit the incantation was said to invite bad luck. Was I warding off the evil influence of the hare, or invoking its protection? The original association was probably between the hare and the lunar month, the cycle of the moon. It is well-known that if one is touched by moonlight while sleeping, one goes mad, and the hare, as well as being mainly nocturnal or crepuscular in habits, is well-known for madness, especially in its springtime period of apparently deranged dancing, boxing and racing around, oblivious of human presence.

The animal is one of the great mythological archetypes, like the fox, the snake and the lion, and is characterized by ambiguity. It is celebrated for craftiness, but can sometimes show contrasting foolishness. It is thought to transform itself from male to female, and has weird reproductive characteristics. It has a witch-like ability to appear out of nowhere, and to disappear as mysteriously. The wailing of a wounded hare is unnervingly like that of a child, so much so as to make men reluctant to shoot it for fear of hearing its cries. It is on these characteristics of canniness, uncanniness and transformation that the popular beliefs and legends about the hare are based.

In the seventeenth-century Scottish witch trials, it emerged that the witches' ceremonies included making a ritual change into an animal by incantation, and that a favoured transformation was into a hare:

I sall goe intill ane haire,
With sorrow, and sych, and meikle caire,
And I sall goe in the Divellis nam'
Ay whill I com hom again.[30]

The hare-witch still plays a role in traditional folk-tales, especially in the Celtic areas,[31] and remarkable behaviour or an apparently magical escape from death by a hare may be explained by the conclusion that it is a witch transformed. Hares are feared by Scottish fishermen; the sight of a hare is as fearful an omen as sailing on a Friday or seeing the minister, and even the mention of the hare is taboo; the word must be replaced by a circumlocution.[32]

In many cultures, the hare is an envied trickster, defeating more powerful beasts by native wit. That arch-survivor Brer Rabbit is really a hare, ultimately lonely in his triumphs. The Tortoise's placid victory is enhanced by the general invincibility of his opponent, a trickster tricked. In the marginal illustrations of medieval manuscripts, the hare is perhaps the commonest animal, often as trickster or in scenes on the theme of 'the world upside-down': chasing a hound; astride a hound and hunting a man; as a falconer, hawking with an owl; aiming a crossbow at a man in a tree (Fig. 25); riding a lion; attacking a castle; playing the bagpipes or the organ; as knight, cleric or judge. In the French *Roman de Renard* (1203) the hero, Reynard the Fox, meets the hare, Couard (i.e. Coward; compare the huntsman's cry in the *Craft of Venery*, quoted previously), carrying a peasant dangling from a stake over his shoulder (compare Fig. 24). A misericord in Manchester Cathedral shows a group of hares roasting a hunter on a spit.[33]

These sundry threads (admiration, dazzlement, scorn, affection, fear, taboo) are interwoven with the keen natural observation of a hunter, who finally reveals a hunter's appetite, in a Middle English incantatory poem:

The Names of the Hare

Whene'er a man a hare shall meet,
That beast shall by him ne'er be beat
Unless he set down on the land
The thing he carries in his hand
(Be it staff or be it bow),
And bless him with his elbow, so;
And with right hearty veneration
He shall utter this rogation
In worship of that very hare,
And afterwards shall better fare:

'The hare, the scotart,[34]
Big-fellow, Bouchart,[35]
Harekin, frisker,
Turpin, traveller,
Path-beater, white-spot,
Go-by-dyke, shit-maker,
Deceiver, cowardly one,[36]
Steal-away, nibbler,
Evil-met, faint-heart,
White-tail, beast in the dew,
Grass-biter, Goibert,[37]
Late-to-home, traitor,
Lack-friend, cat-of-the-wood,
Wide-eye, cat-in-the broom,
Purblind, cat-in-the-gorse,
Skulker, west-looker,[38]
Wall-eye, side-watcher,
Player in the hedgerow,
Hart-of-the-stubbles, long-ears,
Beast-of-the-straw, quick-springer,
Wild one, leaper,
Low one, lurker,
Wind-swift, skulker,
Shag-mad, squat-in-the-hedge,
Dew-kicker, dew-hopper,
Sit-still, grasshopper,
Fiddle-foot, ground-clinger,
Light-foot, bracken-sitter,
Cabbage-stag, herb-grazer,
Go-by-ground, sit-you-still,
Pintail, turn-to-hill,[39]
Start-up-quickly, shiver-maker,
White-belly, run-with-lambs,
Brainless, nibbler,
Little one, scaredy-puss,
Frightener, word-breaker,
Snuffler, cropped-head
(His chief name is Villain),
Hart-with-the-leather-horn,
Beast-that-dwells-in-the-corn,
Beast-that-all-men-defame,
Beast-that-no-man-dare-name.'

When these words have all been said,
Then is the hare's power allayed.
Then you may wend you forth
East and West and South and North,
Wheresoever a man will,
If that man has any skill.

Good-day to you now, Sir Hare!
May God let you so well fare
As to come before me dead,
Either in civet, or in bread!

Amen.[40]

'In bread' means in a pastry case; a 'civet' is a stew (cf. modern French *civet de lièvre*). The *Tacuinum Sanitatis* has reservations about the hare as food: 'Quality: warm and dry in the second degree. Preferable: younger animals which have been caught by hounds. Utility: good for people suffering from corpulence. Harm: causes sleeplessness ... produces melancholy humours. Suitable for people with a cold constitution, in winter and in cold regions.'[41] For stout and cheerful men in northern climates, then, here is one medieval version of the civet:

Harys in cyveye

Take Harys, and Fle hem,[42] and make hem clene an hacke hem in gobettys, and sethe hem in Watere and salt a lytylle; than take Pepyr, an Safroun, an Brede, y-grounde y-fere, and temper it wyth Ale. Than take Oynonys and Percely y-mynced smal togederys, and sethe hem be hem self, and afterward take and do ther-to a porcyon of vynegre, and dresse in.[43]

8

The Bear

Two of the Victoria and Albert Museum's Devonshire hunting tapestries include scenes of bear-hunting. In one, *The Boar and Bear Hunt*, the appearance and garb of the participants are similar to those seen in other areas of the tapestries, but in the bear-hunting scene which occupies a third of the *The Otter and Swan Hunt* the hunters are moustachioed or bearded; some wear turbans; two are mounted on camels.[1] This reinforces a view which emerges from a study of the late-medieval manuals: for the sophisticated societies of northern France, Britain and the Low Countries, with their shrinking areas of wilderness and increasingly refined and schematized hunting practices, the bear must have been a remote quarry, almost as exotic as the lions which medieval townsmen saw in depictions of Roman hunting such as the one on the sarcophagus which serves as the basin of the fountain in the square in Spoleto; the subject of travellers' tales rather than the stuff of personal recollection; the equivalent of the tiger in the consciousness of nineteenth-century Europe. The bear finds no place in Queen Ratio's neat classification of the sweet and stinking beasts, nor has King Modus anything to say about hunting it.[2]

Surprisingly, even in Germany relatively little practical attention appears to have been given to bear-hunting in the latter part of the Middle Ages. There are a few literary allusions in, for example, the *Nibelungenlied*, Hartmann's *Erec* and Gottfried's *Tristan*, but the bear is insignificant in the symbolism and – to judge from the practical manuals – the organized hunting pursuits of medieval Germany, though there is a little material on bear-tracks in a manuscript in the Hohenlohe archives.[3]

Further south, however, in the Pyrenees, the bear remains an important and demanding quarry, familiar to Gaston Phoebus in his hunting excursions from Foix (he begins his chapter on the bear[4] by telling us that most people have seen one, so that a description of them is superfluous, whereas the English *Master of Game*, largely a translation from Phoebus, omits his chapter on the bear completely). In Iberia its importance is very considerable, and the bear and the boar are ranked together, much higher than the deer, as beasts worthy of the attention of royal hunters by Alfonso XI of Castile and John I of Portugal. Alfonso's bear-hunts, in particular, retain qualities of primeval obsession and epic endurance of man, hound and quarry through the bitter, snowy wilderness of the Castilian sierras, in comparison with which the deer-hunting of Northern Europe appears dilettante and effete. Bears were protected for hunting by the king throughout the whole of Portugal, anyone killing one without royal permission being fined a thousand *libras*.

Phoebus, at least, observed a close season, hunting the bears only between May and their mating in December, whereas Alfonso appears to have been prepared to hunt the females with their cubs in the early spring, and even to harry them out of hibernation. Bears have an endearing and anthropomorphic quality, apparent to the medieval illustrator: the miniature of bears in Phoebus shows them rolling about cheerily with their cubs, and in the Devonshire tapestries the only hint of a feeling for animal rights is the perplexed bear-cub pausing in its escape into the undergrowth to look back, distressed, at its dying mother.[5] Alfonso, however, while ungrudging in his admiration for the animal, remains unaffected by sentiment.

After mating in December the bears spent around forty days, i.e. the whole of January and part of February, hibernating in caves. The cubs were born in March; dead, according to Phoebus, until their mother had licked them into shape and life. According to Oppian this was because

> they are much given to venery and that not orderly. For evermore by day and night the females lust for mating and themselves pursue the males, seldom intermitting the pleasures of union; . . . ere the season of birth, ere the appointed day arrives, she puts pressure on her womb and does violence to the goddesses of birth, so great her lechery, so great her haste for love. She brings forth her children half-formed and not articulate, shapeless flesh, and unjointed and mysterious to behold . . . And she licks with her tongue her dear offspring, even as cattle lick one another . . . So doth the she-bear shape her children by licking.[6]

Phoebus adds the quaint touch that 'when the bear has his way with the she-bear, they do it like man and woman, one stretched on top of the other.'[7]

The bear's diet varied seasonally: fruit, green plants, honey, acorns, grapes, wild and domestic animals including sheep, pigs, goats and even cattle. In its sense of smell it was thought to be exceeded only by the boar; it could smell acorns in a forest from six leagues away, according to Phoebus. Its flesh was not much eaten, being considered unhealthy; only the paws were looked on as reasonable eating, but its fur was no doubt useful, and its grease was a cure for gout and hardening of the sinews. A bear was 'in grease' from May to December.

It was not normally too difficult for hounds to follow a bear in average terrain, since its pace was not much faster than a man's and it had none of the ruses of the stag, but the bear-hunt presented particular problems which for Alfonso XI made it the finest hunting of all.[8] One was that the terrain was not normally average, but harsh and mountainous. Another was that of finding the bear at the start of the hunt. It travelled a long way between its eating place and its lair, and its tracks were less obvious than those of the deer and the boar. Alfonso appears to have sent his *buscas* (groups of several huntsmen with hounds) to range over a wide area as the first stage of each hunt, and to have had reserve resources of men and hounds in nearby villages to cope with future contingencies.

Once raised, the bear had immense endurance, often necessitating several relays of fresh hounds, and the closing stages were more awkward than in the case of the boar. The bear's strength made it advisable to have alaunts and mastiffs as well as the running-hounds, which caused logistical problems, and it would not rush out of a tight corner to its own death like the boar; the huntsman had to approach it, placing himself in danger of being hugged or bitten to death. 'Their arms are wondrously strong, and they squeeze a man so hard as to destroy him. If they have a man by the head, they will break it open to the brain and kill him. If they have a man's arm or leg in their teeth and paws, they will break it in two, and if wounded they will sunder any spear-shaft in their paws.'[9] There is a fine represent- ation of a huntsman being hugged to death in Lucas Cranach's painting in the Prado of the hunting of Charles v.[10]

We see the strength of the paws in an anecdote about Prince John of Portugal, who, faced with a large bear,

> rode so close to it to strike it that the bear reared up on its hind legs to pull him from the saddle. The Prince . . . raised himself so much in the saddle that he was right over the pommel, and the bear, stretching out his claws to seize him, caught the rear part of the saddle and tore away the cantle completely, with a large part of the horse's rump. The Prince, undaunted, with no cantle and his horse wounded, wheeled round and renewed the attack, and would not leave the bear until other hunters arrived to help with spears.

King Denis of Portugal was saved from death at the hands of a bear only by a timely prayer to the Virgin, and a statue of a bear was placed on his tomb in a monastery in Odivellas.[11] It is not surprising that when the author of the *Nibelungenlied* needs a supreme example of Siegfried's animal strength and prowess he makes him defeat a bear. The manner of his triumph is noteworthy: he is clothed in animal pelts himself, scorns weapons, tackles the bear in single combat and subdues and binds it by simple strength. The episode, which terminates with a comic/heroic scene in which the bear runs amok through the camp to be finally killed by Siegfried, is followed soon afterwards by the killing of Siegfried himself (see p. 106). Marcelle Thiébaux has studied the structural relationship of the incidents; she also mentions Aelfric's *Colloquy*, in which face-to-face confrontation with a bear is used to exemplify the simple manliness and heroic nature of hunting: '"How did you dare to kill the bear?" "I stood opposing him and slew him with a sudden blow." "You were so brave!" "A huntsman shouldn't be fearful."'[12]

For one man to kill a bear must have been a rarity, and Phoebus strongly advises against trying it, but two men with spears could do it relatively easily if they worked in concert, 'for his way is such that he wishes to take revenge on whoever strikes him. When one man strikes him, he runs to him, and when the other strikes, he runs to him, so that they may strike him as often as they wish, provided they keep their wits about them and remain calm.'[13] Phoebus also mentions the use of nets in bear-hunting, an ancient practice described by Oppian, who explains the process of finding a bear in a thicket with scenting-hounds, setting nets around it, driving the bear out and guiding it into the nets with a rope hung with vulture and stork feathers.[14]

Like the boar, the bear was found in different areas at different seasons, depending on the food available: cereal crops, grapes, acorns, beech-nuts. He was hunted *par force*, like the hart and boar. His tracks and other tokens were not the subject of an exact science like those of the deer. His droppings were of no help in identifying his age and size, since their shape and consistency depended largely on his diet. The tracks of a male, especially those of the rear paws, were rounder and shorter than those of the female, and Alfonso mentions that if a bear had urinated close to its droppings it was a female.[15]

Because of the long journeys made by the bear to its feeding-places from its lair, especially in the spring after it emerged hungry from hibernation, Alfonso XI's practice was to adopt a procedure of multiple searches or *buscas*, each party normally taking four to six hounds, including one really good scenting-hound, and to retain at least ten hounds himself, so that when he heard by the call of the horn that a *busca* had found a bear he could hurry to join his own hounds to those of the *busca* to start the chase with an initial pack of fourteen or sixteen. This is his ideal way of proceeding; in actual fact, as we shall see, rapidly formed *ad hoc* plans were often necessary. Good places to look for a bear in the early season were the green areas along the streams, where the bears went in search of watercress, young grass and herbs. An early-season bear, once found, was easier to kill than a late-season one, because of the tenderness of its paws in the rocky terrain; both Alfonso and Phoebus say that the bear in hibernation sucks its paws to give solace to its empty stomach, and thus softens them.[16]

Because of the bear's stamina a hunt often continued until nightfall, to be resumed the following day; indeed, many of Alfonso's hunts continued through several days. If a bear had been brought to bay or pursued into some identified covert by the hounds in the late evening, it was important to prevent it from moving away under cover of night. A few hounds were left to continue baying near the bear, and a line of fires might be lit to prevent the beast from escaping to the area where it was thought to want to go. If the hounds seemed to weaken, they were encouraged by voice and horn, but the huntsmen remained some distance away, taking their sleep by turns. If a hound gave up, it was fed and another replaced it, though it was important to reserve some fresh hounds for the morning, especially one good scenting-hound.[17]

If a she-bear was found with cubs, the cubs were killed as soon as possible so as to concentrate the attention of the hounds on the single major quarry, but this was looked on as undesirable compared with hunting the male bear.[18] Alfonso had no scruples, however, about hunting bears from their hibernation quarters; parties of eight hounds were sent to cover the surrounding caves where the bear might take refuge, and twelve or fifteen to where the bear was thought to be lying, on the evidence of tracks, broken branches, debarked tree-trunks, etc.

For the killing of the bear, Phoebus recommends crossbows, bows and arrows, and spears for the huntsmen on foot, and the thrown spear for the mounted hunter. If one tried to thrust the spear into him, or to kill him with a sword-thrust like the boar, 'he would embrace you, and kiss you none too graciously.'[19]

To perceive the essence of medieval bear-hunting, one can do no better than to read Alfonso XI's detailed accounts of his own experiences. Here are his descriptions, pragmatic and unembroidered, of the course of two hunts in the sierras near the junction of the modern provinces of Avila, Toledo and Madrid, in western Spain. It is in his organization of men and hounds that we see hunting coming closest to tactical war, as opposed to mere pursuit and battle, and his recollections exemplify to the highest degree that obsessive, almost religious, compulsion with which medieval and pre-medieval hunters, having raised a quarry, drew on the deepest reserves of their own and their hounds' physical and mental resilience in order to pursue it to its end.

El Rencón and the hill-face above Escarabajosa and El Castrejón and the gorge of Escarabajosa are all one forest, and it is good for bear in winter. The *vocerías* [beaters' lines] are one from the hilltop above Escarabajosa to the hill of Frades, and from there across the summit to the hill of Don Yagüe; another from the hill of Don Yagüe to the hill of La Samoza; another from the hill of Don Santa María across the summit to the hill of La Samoza. The *armadas* [lines of stationary hunters, usually with relays of hounds and perhaps alaunts and mastiffs] are on the road from Cadahalso to El Adrada: one to the right of Cabeza Pinosa, another to the Arroyo del Fresno, and two more on the road itself, between the Arroyo del Fresno and Escarabajosa.

It happened one Monday that we raised two bears there at the hour of terce, and the manner of it was this: all the *buscas* had returned from the hill and the gathering had been blown, but Martín Gil had continued in his search with about six hounds, and he moved the larger of the bears. He put his hounds after it, and they followed it from the wood of El Castrejón, where it was found, to the gorge of Escarabajosa, and there it turned at bay. Pero Carrillo and Pedro de Mendoza set off to this first bear with another six hounds as relays, and on the way they ran into a second bear and put their six hounds after him. The bear which Martín Gil had moved, the larger of the two, ran on and went through our *armada* against the forest of Manjavacas before we could get there, but as he went through they put another six hounds after him, making twelve in all. When I reached the *armada* he had gone through, and I could not overtake him before the forest of Manjavacas.

Yñigo López and García Ruiz, the *alguazil*, went with us, and we followed him close through the forest, and could not hit him with anything until the fall of night, when he was wounded by a thrown spear. We were short of hounds and huntsmen that day, because all the rest had stayed with the other bear in the gorge of Escarabajosa until they killed him, well into the night. Seeing ourselves overtaken by darkness, we sent Yñigo López and García Ruiz with another four huntsmen on foot to station themselves between the bear and the Sierra de Cenicientos, and to make fires to prevent him from escaping that way, and to encourage the hounds not to give up. We and the other huntsmen did the same to cut him off from the Sierra de Guisando . . .

And from the first sleep onwards, the hounds gave up one by one, and only Fragoso and Preciado stayed with him. When he saw that only two hounds were left he set off along the road from El Adrada to Las Rozas, and on the road Fragoso gave in, and only Preciado kept up with him to the foot of the Sierra de Guisando. By this time it was midnight, and when we saw that Preciado too had given up we decided that it was poor huntsmanship to pursue the bear any more that night, so we gathered our hounds and went to the village of Las Rozas to sleep. And I sent word to my people in El Adrada to come to my aid with hounds, and especially good scenting-hounds, and they brought me Barbada and Vaquero.

On the following morning, Tuesday, I sent out five *buscas*, a pair of huntsmen in each, to cast about to find his track, and to ask the shepherds at what hour they had heard a hound with a high-pitched cry, so as to be able to make their search at the place where the hound had given up. Two of these huntsmen came on his trail and blew to the scent, and we joined them. We ordered them to take Barbada and set off after him, and to carry Vaquero on the mule to save his strength, and we followed the trail with the hound on the leash from Guisando to the River Alberche. When we came down to the river, Diego Bravo and Pero Ferrández blew to the scent on the other side; we had sent them there the previous night to see if they could find where the bear had crossed. We forded the river to where they were blowing, and found that they were on his trail.

So we ordered Barbada and Vaquero to be put on his trail with the other hounds, and after a while they came on a bed made by the bear, around the hour of matins; they went on along his fresh trail, and when we knew from the hounds' behaviour that we were nearing the place where he was lying they took the leash off Vaquero and he went to bay the bear on top of the Hill of Villa Alba, looking to El Quejigar. When they saw that he was at bay, they unleashed all the hounds, and they came up on him and pursued him until noon, when he was killed on the road from El Quejigar to El Helipar, about a third of a league from the inn at El Quejigar.

To be sure that he was the one we had followed on the previous day, we looked to see if he was wounded, and sure enough we found in him the head of the spear with which he was struck the day before. And with such a hunt as this we prove that when a good quarry is raised and pursued with determination, if the hounds are good, one may be sure of killing him.[20]

Las Cabreras de Navaluenga is a fine forest for bear, winter and summer. The *vocería* is high on the sierra and downwards along the ridge to La Pedriza de Pero Sancho; the *armada* is at El Horno de Varrialejo.

Once in this forest we left Santa María del Tiemblo on a Tuesday and put up a bear, and they did not succeed in putting hounds after him until he reached Las Cabreras above Navaluenga, at the hour of vespers. They found him in Las Cabreras, and saw him going away through the snow, and put eight hounds after him, and were close after him until his first sleep. Then they saw that night would prevent them from troubling him, and the huntsmen were likely to perish from cold, so they came down from the sierra to a house which they found in the middle of the forest.

Alfonso Martínez and Pero Peláez lay all night where the bear was lying, and gathered all the hounds around midnight, and when the moon rose that night Yñigo López and Pero Carrillo left the house with all the huntsmen and joined Alfonso Martínez and Pero Peláez, and they took up the bear's trail. On the Wednesday morning, at the hour of terce, they put eight hounds on his trail, including Martín Gil's hound Moral, who led them a good two and a half leagues on the scent until he brought them to the bed of the bear. Pero Martínez de Oyarve said that they dared not kill him then, but should wait for our arrival, which they expected.

When they saw that we were not coming . . . they put twelve hounds to him and moved him again, and they say that they would have liked to kill him then, but he refused to do battle, so they put another thirteen hounds after him, twenty-five in all, and pursued him over the pass of El Fondo, where only three hounds were still after him, Natural, Abadín and Frontero, all the rest having given up. And that night Alfonso Ferrández, Martín González, Benito and Gómez slept close to the bear all night, high in the sierra, with these three hounds.

On the following day, Thursday, they went after him again, and followed him back to Las Cabreras de Navaluenga, where he was first found, and he did not stop to rest once in the whole day. That Thursday, at the hour of nones, they set four hounds on his trail, and Pero Martínez de Oyarve went with them after the bear to the top of the pass, and at nightfall two hounds gave up and were brought back down, and the others slept near the bear all night, and the huntsmen slept in Navaluenga.

At first light on Friday they took up the scent on the top of the pass, and followed the bear three leagues through the snow. When they left the snow behind, our huntsmen Diego Bravo and Martín Gil followed the trail for two leagues along a track, which the bear never left until he turned off and went into a little piece of woodland which would not have held a roebuck, and they put twelve hounds onto him at noon. Then he went twice through our *armada* on the hill where we were waiting on the day we left Santa María, and he turned at bay in the vineyards of Santa María del Tiemblo. Alfonso Martínez de Bavia said that there was nobody there to kill him, as they could have done, for the huntsmen were some distance away, and very weary.

That night all the hounds left him but the good Natural and Vaquero. Martín Gil, Diego Bravo, Pero Martínez, Martín González, Alfonso Martínez and Pero Peláez went with them after the bear until the first sleep to find out which way he was heading, so as to find his trail again on the following day, Saturday. That night the huntsmen returned to Santa María del Tiemblo to sleep, and sent word to the ones who had stayed in El Adrada to rise early, which they did. At dawn on the Saturday Martín Gil and Diego Bravo took up the hunt again and followed the bear from the River Alberche to the top of Las Cabreras del Quejigar, where he got up the other time that he went over to Peña Ocaña, and by then not one hound was interested, through sheer weariness, and the huntsmen were following the bear by sight, though the hounds' interest revived when they came near his resting-place.

Then they set ten hounds after him, and they followed him until midday, and were forced to give up through exhaustion, all but Natural, Vasallo, Laguna and another piebald dog, of which huntsman I am unsure. Then, the huntsmen being all exhausted, they put relays of many hounds after him, which had remained behind, and these brought him to his death. He died that Saturday at the hour of nones, between Cabeza Osera and La Sarnosa, in a place called La Yecla, near Las Cabreras.

So the hunting of this bear went on through five days and four nights, and hounds were with him all day, and at night some were with him until midnight and others right through until dawn; and since this hunt was so stubbornly pursued, we set it down to show that when some unusually fine quarry is put up, and it is not killed that day, if one pursues it with determination it will be killed on the second, or the third, if the huntsmen do their work like huntsmen.[21]

Small wonder, perhaps, that the flower and exemplar of all medieval huntsmen, Gaston Phoebus, should have died after a bear-hunt. On Tuesday, 1 August 1391, accompanied by his bastard son Yvain, he set off from the castle of Orthez in the Pyrenees. A peasant had come to the castle on the preceding evening to tell him of the presence of bears in the neighbouring forest. The hounds pursued a huge bear which took refuge in the forest of Sauveterre, on the road to Pamplona. Its fate is unknown, unlike that of Gaston III. After the hunt he returned to Orthez, where the hunt supper was prepared in the hall of the hospice. He asked for a basin of water to wash his hands, two squires came forward, one with the water and the other with a hand-towel. As he wet his long fingers he turned pale, his legs gave way and he fell backwards crying 'Je suis mort!' He died within half an hour, probably of cerebral congestion. His son Yvain was urged to hurry to the castle of Orthez to take possession of it and his father's treasure; he was given Phoebus's ring and hunting knife to identify himself to the porter, who had been ordered to open to nobody without such identification. The body of Gaston Phoebus lay in a candlelit chapel until 12 October, when it was buried in the Church of the Cordeliers.[22]

An amalgam of art and life: the bear that got away

I have mentioned the epic tone of Alfonso XI's bear-hunts. One four-teenth-century Spaniard, possibly the ghost writer or some subsequent reviser of the King's *Libro de la montería*, wrote the following letter in response to a letter he, or perhaps the King himself, had received from Alvar García. Its humorous allusions are to the romance rather than to the epic; it is a rare early example of Spanish Arthurianism. Despite its burlesque tone, it supports the theory that hunters could have literary ideals and precedents in mind, or at least that their attitudes to hunting were conditioned by their being members of a society in which the ritualized testing of heroism was a recurring artistic feature.

From the content of the letter, one deduces that Alvar García had been hunting, that he had uncoupled his hounds to pursue what he thought was a boar, and that either the boar turned out to be a bear or the hounds switched their attention to a bear. This is not explicit, but the similarity between the course of the hunt and the bear-hunts already described in this chapter, and particularly the mention of the snow, the mountain-tops and the pursuit through the night, strongly suggest that the animal was a bear, as does the extravagant name given to it. Obviously Alvar García had written in hyperbolic terms of the size of the animal, the weariness of his hounds and the harshness of the weather to justify his abandonment of the chase. He is here being good-humouredly chided by his fellow huntsmen; of the saintly Evangelists whose censure is being passed on, two, Juan de Fuenteovejuna and Pero Peláez, are mentioned in the hunt descriptions in the *Libro de la montería*.[23]

The Arthurian tone emerges in the name of the beast (one is reminded of the sinister Questing Beast in Malory, which ranged around, unexplained, pursued by the dogged Sir Pellinore, making a noise inside its belly 'lyke unto the questyng of thirty coupyl of houndes'.[24] It may be purely coincidental, or due to the use of some common French original, that when Sir Pellinore returned to Camelot 'he was made to swere uppon the four Evangelistes to telle the trouthe of hys queste frome the one ende to that other.'[25] Other links with medieval romance are the description of the encounter as a battle between a man and an enchanted beast; the partially invented setting and the nebulous wasteland where the beast dwells; the motifs of penance and the uncomplaining acceptance of hardship (one thinks again of Gawain, going out through the drifting snows on a bitter New Year's Day, bright in his freshly burnished armour, to face his ordeal at the Green Chapel); and most especially the concept of the hunt as an *adventure*, in the restricted Arthurian sense of a demanding but potentially fulfilling opportunity granted to one in order that one may be truly revealed to oneself and to others. Alvar García, poor man, missed his chance and let himself down in the eyes of a band of brothers, the royal huntsmen of Castile.

> From the Captain-General of all huntsmen from the Rising to the Setting Sun, and from the Orient to the Occident
>
> To you, Alvar García, Marshal of the Welsh March.[26]
>
> We have read the account which you sent us in which you say that while passing through the mountains populated by the Welsh, at a place called St Peter Between the Waters, you uncoupled your hounds after a boar, and that without noticing it you had found the Black Dragon of the Enchanted Wool (which you call more simply 'This Damned Animal'[27]). If it was as you described it, then the first name is certainly the correct one, and not 'This Damned Animal', as you put in your letter.
>
> You also say that although you knew that it was not the quarry you were seeking, you could not refrain, for greed, from putting hounds after it, and they followed it all day until nightfall, and pushed it through the *armada* two or three times, and it received two rather insignificant wounds. On this point we reply that you have our sympathy as a hunter, for we know the trials you must have undergone. We are pleased that the beast is alive, and we pray God that its wounds may be indeed slight, so that it may not die a sudden death in the far-off wilderness which is its home, without hearing the voices of terrestrial angels, *Amen*. You say that hounds and huntsmen were with it until the first sleep, and that from then onwards they gave up one by one, except for two brave and stubborn hounds which

continued alone. As for the huntsmen, men of Extremadura and Galicia alike, to whom you sent word that they should go out through the snow across a sierra with the beast: poor fellows! Even from here I feel pain for them, so harried and shelterless, and for their sighs and groans, and the curses they must have called down on those who had brought them there. And you, wretched Alvar García, heard them unmoved.

. . . But let us suppose that all this happened; what did you and the huntsmen do that night? Or the following day? It appears that from that point onwards you did nothing, even though you say that there was snow on the ground and you had with you men who knew the area well. If you failed because of some non-hunting matters which you had to attend to in the service of the King or the Count, his son, I am sure that spending two days on pursuing such an adventure as this, even unsuccessfully, would have displeased the King less than abandoning it for some other cause, and his son the Count too.

If you abandoned it for lack of hounds, we believe that an adventure such as this could be achieved with the few which you had. Even if they were weary, if the huntsmen had followed the trail by sight and taken the hounds with them until they were near the place where the Beast lay, there was nothing to stop the hounds getting on his trail, especially with snow on the ground. If you say that you gave it up through stress of weather, because you could not find the resolution of true huntsmen, that is the only true reason you can offer. If that is how it was, you should write to me to tell me how you could have the heart to pursue it and then to be dissuaded by bad weather, lest I think you a poor huntsman, since you had found such an adventure and undertaken it.

But even in reply to this reason, which is the real one, the Evangelists Santo Domingo Pascual, San Juan de Fuenteovejuna, San Antón de Valdeiglesias and San Pero Pelay say that you should have waited on the weather two or three days in order to achieve such an adventure as this, with the persistence of true huntsmen. *Et qui vivit et regnat Deus per omnia saecula saeculorum. Amen.*

And may God grant it to us some November to be in that land where walks that great monster which we have dubbed the Black Dragon of the Enchanted Wool, so that we may redeem something of your failure, and give you some recompense for the penance you underwent on that harsh day and evil night when you did battle with it.[28]

9

The Uneatable (I): The Wolf and the Fox

The wolf

In medieval descriptions of the wolf one finds a clarity of antipathy which is missing from the mind of the hunter in his relationship with the animals so far dealt with. It would be difficult to hate a hart, even were attitudes to it not conditioned by hagiological legend, Biblical imagery, moral analogy and its literary role as transformed hero; the female deer is a symbol of feminine grace in cultured and popular poetry; the bear is endearingly human in its ability to walk on two legs, its sexual manners and its love of honey and sleep; the hare, while weird, is both admired and pitied. Even the horrendous boar excites admiration, sexual awe and the appreciation of the gourmet.

The wolf kills, and consumes its victims. It was a threat to rural economy: according to Gaston Phoebus the medieval wolf ('which most people have seen'[1]) killed animals up to the size of a cow or a horse, and even with a sheep or goat in its mouth could easily run away from a shepherd unless the man had mastiffs with him. It would sometimes kill every sheep in an unattended flock before eating one of them. It was a threat to other game, killing roe-deer, wild pig and even stags. Worst, it was a threat to human life; the only animal mentioned in the medieval treatises as using man as a regular food source. Country children were often taken, according to Phoebus, by old wolves which were losing their teeth and speed.

Younger wolves, too, acquired a taste for human flesh, and, in French, the special name *loup garou*, from their activities, usually nocturnal, on the fringes of medieval war. Wolf packs tended to follow armies, disturbing the night, but sometimes performing a useful function: 'Thei folowyn comonliche after men of Armes for the carayns [carrion] of the beestis or of the dede horses or other thinggis. They howlen as the hounds, and if thei be

132

but .ii. thei make such a noyse as if there a route of .vii or .viii., and that is be nyght, whan the weder is cleer and brygte.'[2] They did not confine themselves to the dead war-horses, however: 'Ther ben some that eten children or men . . . and thei ben cleped *werwolfes*, for men shuld be ware of hem:

> Whan they acharneth [feed] in a contre of warre, ther as batels han be ther, thei ete of dede men and of men that ben hanged that thei may areche herto, oither whan thei fall from the galows; and mannys flessh is so savery and so plesaunt that whane thei han taken to mannys fleissh thei wold nevere ete flessh of other beest, thof that thei shuld dye for hunger; for many men han seyn whan thei han lost the sheepe thei have take and ete the shepherde.[3]

The wolf was thought to be so subtle in its hunting that men attacked by it had no inkling of its approach. It carried rabies, and its bite was in any case thought to be sometimes poisonous because it ate toads and other venomous creatures.[4] Even its sexual habits were seen as reprehensible – a reflection of the secretive lechery, misdirected favour and jealous rage which guilty medieval men saw in their own, slightly redeemed for Phoebus by the parallel with the *service amoureux* of the courtly love code. When the she-wolf is in season, he tells us:

> all the males pursue her like dogs following a bitch, but only one will couple with her. She will lead the wolves around for six to eight days without eating or drinking or sleeping, for they lust so much after her that they think of none of these things. And when they are wearied, she lets them rest until they are asleep, and then she goes to the one which she thinks has loved her most and worked hardest to get her and scratches him with her paw to wake him, and she goes off and couples with him. That is why, when a woman misbehaves herself, we say that she is like a she-wolf, because she takes the ugliest and worst, as the she-wolf does. Because he has suffered and starved more than the rest he is poorer and thinner and more wretched.[5]

The favoured suitor's triumph could be short-lived, however: 'Some folk say that no wolf ever saw its father, and there is some truth in this, because it sometimes happens that when . . . the other wolves wake up, they follow the female's tracks, and when they find her and the wolf together, all the rest attack the wolf and kill him.'[6] If the male escaped the jealousy of his frustrated fellows, the pair might stay together up to and after the birth of the cubs. The female, at least, revealed loyal behaviour as a mother, whereas Phoebus dwells at length on the self-centred greed of the father in a developing war of the sexes:

> The male wolf always eats his fill first, then takes what is left to the

133

cubs. The she-wolf is different: before she eats she takes the food to the cubs, and she eats with them. If the male is still hungry, he takes the prey from her and the cubs and eats his fill and leaves the remains, if there are any; if not, they may die of hunger if they choose and it will not worry him, if his own belly is full. When the female sees this, she is cunning and crafty enough to leave the food well away from the cubs, and come to see if the male is there. If he is, she waits until he has gone and then brings the food to the cubs. But the male is cunning too, and when he sees her coming without any food, he goes and sniffs her mouth, and if he smells that she has been carrying something he takes her in his teeth and punishes her until she has to show him where she has left her prey. So the she-wolf, next time she comes back to the cubs, creeps up and does not show herself until she sees whether the male is there or not. If he is, she hides until his own hunger makes him go off to look for prey, and then she brings the food to her cubs. This is the honest truth. There are people who say that she bathes her body and head when she returns, so that the male will not smell that she has been carrying anything, but of this I am not sure.[7]

One can infer from Phoebus and the *Master of Game* that efforts were made to domesticate wolves, perhaps by hunters or shepherds who acquired cubs after killing their mother, and saw them as a potentially superior replacement to the mastiff. The efforts were unsuccessful because of the animal's ineradicable tendency to evil. In this passage we see the medieval hunter's leaning to anthropomorphism taken to extremes: not only is the wolf inherently a bad character, it also has an introspective ability which makes it aware of its own incapacity for self-improvement and of the justice of man's implacable hostility towards it:

Men may not norsshe a wolf thoo he were take never so yong, and chastised and bete and I hold under disciplyne that he ne shal do harm if he have tyme and space for to do it; as nevere shal he be so prive [tame] if men leve hym out that he ne shal loke hider and thider for to loke if he may do eny harme, or he loketh if eny man wil do hym eny harme, for he knoweth wel and woteth wel that he doth evel, and therefore men ascriethe and hunteth and scleeth, and yit for al that he may not leve his evel nature.[8]

A dead wolf provided little of material use to the man who killed it. There were beliefs that its right forefoot could be used to cure pain in the breast, or the inflammation occurring in the jaws of domestic boars when their tusks were broken to make them more easily handled, and that its liver, dried and powdered, could cure liver complaints in humans, but Phoebus is wary of accepting them, 'for I am loth to include in my book anything but the strict truth'. The pelt was a source of warm mittens and cloaks, but it needed careful treatment if it was to lose the stink of wolf.[9]

Queen Ratio uses the character of the wolf as a basis for an attack on the fourteenth-century clergy, especially the parish priests, who should be like shepherds guarding their flock, but instead are wolves preying on it. They are full of secular vices which are imitated by the innocent villagers, to the detriment of their souls; in particular, they seize the ewes which are their female parishioners, do their will with them and kill their souls by leading them into mortal sin. Wolves, 'after wandering about all day doing evil, gather at vespers to howl together, and their howling is ugly, horrible and spine-chilling'; this is comparable to the dissolute priests, who have spent the day in the tavern and other disreputable places, staggering to the church to howl the service of vespers. The unoriginal nature of Ratio's comparison is redeemed by her final reference to the Eucharist: 'Nothing could be worse than to see a man, so favoured among others that he is allowed to bless and to handle the sacred body of Jesus Christ, behaving like a wolf and deserving its name. When the Lamb is in the clutches of wolves, we are in danger.'[10]

With apparently so little to commend it to man's favour, this ravenous, venomous, evil-smelling, man-eating, immoral and inedible creature is included by the *Boke of St Albans* in its select list of the four *bestys of venery*, along with the hart, the hare and the boar.[11] King Modus places it in his list of the beasts to be taken *par force*, though as one of the five black beasts, the others being the boar, sow, fox and otter.[12] Phoebus devotes almost twice as many folios to the wolf as to the hare; six times as many as to the fox; six times as many as to the fallow buck.

The reasons for the hunter's appreciation of the wolf were its power, speed, strong scent and a self-confident and economic use of its abilities which made hunting it teasing and interesting. It is difficult to understand why the wolf should have been given any seasonal respite, but according to the *Boke of St Albans*

> The seson of the wolfe is in iche cuntre
> At the seson of the fox, and evermore shall be,[13]

that is to say from the Nativity of Our Lady (8 September) to the Annunciation (25 March). According to the *Forest Laws*,[14] the season for both was shorter still, beginning at Christmas (though this may be due to a misinterpretation of the Nativity of the Virgin as the Nativity of Christ). The fox, as we shall see, was hunted principally in January, February and March, and this may have been so of the wolf too, though Phoebus[15] says that the wolves are busy mating in February; this would make his own method, which we shall come to shortly, ineffective. These winter months were when pelts were thickest and most useful, and when the wolves from the high ground had followed the shepherds' flocks down to areas of human habitation. A further reason may have been that other woodland game was unavailable. The hart was out of season; the seasons for boar and roe ended at Candlemas. The hare was never out of season, but was essentially a creature of the open ground rather than the forest. The fox, everywhere, and the wolf, in those still extensive areas where it survived, were resourceful beasts, capable of fully taxing the abilities of hounds and providing interest and exercise for the hunter. The allotting to them of a season, therefore, may have been simply a reflection of practice; it was not that that was the only period when wolves and foxes were worth hunting, but rather that it was the time when other forms of chase were dwindling or forbidden; when, in short, the hunter had nothing better to do.

Why, then, stop in March? Firstly, this probably applied in practice only to *par force* hunting; there is evidence of foxes and wolves being killed by other methods outside the season specified by the *Boke of St Albans*. Secondly, there is the question of the breeding season of other woodland species. By late March the hinds and does were heavy in calf; they gave birth, according to Phoebus, in May,[16] and the calves were dependent on their mothers for some time afterwards. Going by the dates given in the *Boke of St Albans*, there was no *par force* hunting in woodland between 25 March and 24 June; I have found no medieval source which states explicitly that this was to allow the hinds and does peace for calving and rearing, but it seems likely. The closest to a pronouncement on these lines is Gaston Phoebus's recommendation about roe-deer: he differs from the *Boke of St Albans* in saying that roe may be hunted at any time, but says that the does should be left in peace 'from conception until the fawns are weaned',[17] though he himself evidently broke this rule. There is, in any case, some conflict about the opening date of the hart-hunting (see p. 33).

Another element mentioned by *Modus* as limiting the fox (and presumably wolf) season is the summer diet; it included poisonous reptiles which made the fox's bite venomous. The hounds, sagacious beasts, were aware of this, and therefore reluctant to tackle it. In many areas the wolf, from April onwards, would be going back to the higher ground as the snows receded, and in the summer would be less evident as a problem except to the upland shepherds.

The wolf was evidently much hunted *par force* in France; both Phoebus and King Modus devote considerable space to it. Elsewhere it seems to have been more the victim of traps, snares and other engines of death. There were certainly abundant wolves in the Iberian peninsula, but neither Alfonso xi of Castile nor John i of Portugal suggests them as suitable quarry for a royal pack of hounds. The German treatises, too, though they include paragraphs on the wolf,[18] appear to have regarded the killing of it as a matter of practicality rather than entertainment. There were certainly full-time wolf-trappers in Germany; the *Tresslerbuch* of Marienburg mentions the local *wolffenger* in 1408 and 1409, in one case after the purchase of a pair of shoes for him.[19] There is one German literary reference to hunting the wolf with hounds, in *Reinhart Fuchs*,[20] but it was probably not a widespread aristocratic practice in medieval Germany.

Wolves were still widely distributed in Britain in the Middle Ages. In Saxon times the Welsh, excused certain other taxes, were required to provide the king with 300 wolf-skins per year, and in 1281 Edward I ordered Peter Corbet to organize the destruction of wolves in the counties of Gloucester, Worcester, Hereford, Shropshire and Staffordshire.[21] They were evidently less common in England by the fifteenth century; they are not mentioned by Twiti or in the *Craft of Venery*, and Edward, Duke of York, though he translates Gaston Phoebus's chapter on the nature of the wolf, alters the first sentence with three telling words: 'A wolf is a common beest inow and therfore me nedeth not to tell of his makyng, for fewe men be *byyonde the see* the whiche ne have seie some of hem';[22] he repeats the phrase twice later in the chapter, and leaves out altogether Phoebus's chapter on the practicalities of hunting the wolf, which probably indicates that *par force* wolf-hunting was not current English practice.

In Scotland wolves continued to be a substantial problem, even quite close to towns, throughout the fifteenth century, as is evident from the royal decrees regarding them and the rewards offered for killing them, but there is little to suggest that they were hunted *par force*. Bishop Lesley's *History*[23] describes the wolf as 'a greater beast', though whether he means to rank it as a superior quarry is doubtful; otherwise, the wolf is an animal to be put down by trappers such as the one appointed in Stirling in 1288,[24] or harried by gatherings of countrymen as required by the Act of 1427 which makes every baron responsible for organizing his tenants to take part in four wolf-hunts in the spring, with a two-shilling reward to anyone who killed a wolf.[25] James II decreed in 1457 that, for the destruction of wolves, local magistrates 'sall gader the countrie folk three tymis in the yere betwix Saint Merks Day and Lammas for that is the tyme of the quhelpis [cubs]'.[26] Anyone killing a wolf was to have a penny from each householder in the parish.

Other rewards for killing wolves include five shillings given to Gilbert Home for killing ten wolves in Cockburnspath in 1458, a penny for every five houses in the parish for anyone bringing a wolf's head to the Sheriff of Inverness, and five shillings 'til a fallow brocht the King [James IV] .ii.

wolfis in Lythgow'.[27] The monks of Melrose, granted lands by Robert of Avenel in the twelfth century, were prohibited from taking large game, which Robert reserved for himself, but explicitly permitted to trap wolves, which certainly suggests that the animal was seen as a pest rather than a hunting resource.[28]

No matter what method, sporting or pragmatic, was used against the wolf, its tracks and other tokens were of interest to those seeking to kill it. *Modus* gives tracking details: the wolf's prints are bigger and rounder than a dog's; the ends of its toes are rounder, and it has a bigger pad and bigger, less pointed claws. Its droppings are normally full of fur, because it eats its prey fur and all. The she-wolf leaves smaller tracks, but her pad, toes and claws are still broader than a dog's. She leaves her droppings in the middle of a track; the male leaves his to one side. A young wolf has tracks like the she-wolf, except that the claws are longer and more pointed.[29]

Knowing the age of the wolf was important: a mature wolf was confident in his strength and would run in a leisurely manner, sometimes stopping to wait for the hounds; the hounds sensed his confidence and did not relish tackling him, and so needed to be constantly urged on. A young wolf fled in fear, and this raised the hounds' spirits. Two or three greyhounds were sometimes allowed to run with the pack, and they would be the dogs to finally overtake and kill the wolf. The wolf did not usually turn at bay, but, apart from voluntary rests when he was confident, simply ran until he was caught.[30]

King Modus makes the wolf-hunt *par force* sound a very straightforward affair, though the kill must have been very dangerous for the hounds. Phoebus is quite willing to hunt the older wolves, but recommends limiting the hounds to young wolves until they are trained to the business, and gain enough confidence to overcome their natural fear. Phoebus's wolf-hunts are complex in their organization; they involve advance preparation and an economic insouciance beyond the possibilities of the average yeoman.[31]

One had to get the wolves into the right place by exploiting their appetite for carrion. The right place was a wood separated by about a league and a half from larger areas of forest. One killed a horse or ox and cut off the four legs, and four huntsmen carried (not dragged) the limbs to the forests, on all four sides of the target wood if possible. The rest of the carcass was left in the target wood. The huntsmen then dragged the limbs around behind their horses in the forest, and back across the open ground to the carcass. If the idea worked, the wolves followed the scent during the night and ate their fill on the carcass. An alternative was to leave an immobilized live animal in the wood and lay drag trails in the same way.

On the following morning a huntsman went cautiously to the wood, perhaps climbing a tree downwind, to see if the wolves were still there. He might also take a lymer to find out if the wolves had emerged from the wood, and if so, how many had been there. Another way of finding out if the wolves were there was to imitate their call and wait for the reply. If the huntsman thought the wolves had left the wood, he could examine the bait and assess how many had been feeding, but it was essential to proceed cautiously, for the wolf is a *merveilleusement malicieuse beste*.

This could continue for several nights, to bring the wolves into a state of confidence, the whole aim of the procedure being to persuade the wolves to remain in the target wood after daybreak. If they still refused to do this, the huntsman's courage was put to a considerable test in order to delay their feeding time: on the evening before the hunt he had to hang the carcass up in a tree, out of the wolves' reach, and strew a few bones in the wood, presumably at some distance from the carcass. The wolves arrived as usual, found nothing in reach but bones, and stayed to gnaw them. An hour before the dawn, when, as we know, it is always darkest, the huntsman had to creep into the wood with his mind full of the knowledge that he had spent several days luring into it hungry wolves from which he had now withdrawn what had become their regular diet. No doubt he trod warily through the midwinter night; if there was snow to muffle his footsteps it was of small comfort, since it conferred the same benefit on the wolves. He cut down the carcass and crept away. The wolves eventually found the carcass and settled to gorging themselves on it; when they had eaten their fill, it was after daybreak, too late for them to return to the main forest under cover of darkness; they stayed where they were.

Ideally, the lord for whose benefit all this nocturnal craft was being employed should then arrive and begin the hunt. Lords being what they are, 'since occasionally they do not rise at the crack of dawn,'[32] it was sometimes necessary to ensure that the wolves stayed in the wood by lighting a line of ten or a dozen fires, with one or two men beside each to sing and talk, a stone's throw apart and a couple of bowshots from the wood, until the lord arrived.

And so to the hunt proper. For a man completely dedicated to *par force* hunting, it would follow the normal course of moving the wolf and hunting it with the running-hounds to its death, perhaps aided in the later stages by large greyhounds, alaunts or mastiffs. Phoebus's method, however, tilts the balance away from the sporting towards the practical; it is in fact like bow and stable hunting without the archers. The direction of the wind was important: one stationed fewterers with three or four leashes of greyhounds on the edge of the forest, downwind from the wolves. If this was in the direction in which they habitually returned to the forest, so much the better, but the essential thing was to keep the scent of the fewterers and greyhounds from the wolves.

One also posted stables: 'One should have ordered all the people under one's control one or two days in advance, and asked all one's neighbours, to come and help . . . and they will gladly do it because of the damage the wolves do to their cattle.'[33] The lines of stable were posted along each side of the wood, two thirds of the running-hounds were positioned strategically about the wood to act as relays, and one then entered the wood with a lymer and the rest of the pack to drive the wolf, wary by now, towards the waiting greyhounds. Phoebus does not clarify whether the aim was to move one selected wolf, and it is hard to see how this could be achieved, unless the hunters were aware that only one wolf was using the wood.

Plenty of encouragement to the hounds; plenty of horn-blowing to keep them to their work, since some of them would be wary of tackling a wolf. The greyhounds and fewterers should be well camouflaged with branches, and in a staggered, possibly diamond, formation: the first leash was to let the wolf pass; the second and third leashes waited until the wolf was level with them; the last fewterer released his greyhounds to stop the wolf's course as it ran towards him, and the others converged on it. *Et ainsi le devront ilz prendre*, 'and so they should take him'.

Subtlety; bravery; planning; attention to the terrain and the weather; knowledge of one's quarry and one's hounds. Nothing for the larder; little glory; the gratitude of one's neighbours; a hound or two maimed. If the hounds were to retain any appetite for hunting the wolf, they had to be deceived at the end of the hunt by an apparently unceremonious *curée*: the wolf was gutted and its belly washed out, and one put inside it a mixture of chopped mutton or goat's meat and bread for the hounds. It was especially important to reward the greyhounds, 'for they will take any beast more gladly than they will take a wolf'.[34]

King Modus describes a rather more functional method than Phoebus's: the luring of the wolves was done in a similar way, but the greyhounds were replaced by hanging nets, set quietly by two men in the baited wood before the start of the drive. A stone's throw from the nets, in the direction of the wolves, men were posted in hiding, each armed with a sword and two sticks, one with a forked end. The sides of the wood were flanked with stables, as in Phoebus's technique. When a wolf ran towards the nets, the men in hiding let it pass their tree, then threw their plain stick after it to make it run, startled, into the nets; while it was entangled they ran after it, held it down by the neck with their forked stick and killed it with the sword.[35]

Wolves were also taken alive by divers stratagems (see pp. 239–41), and sometimes released into a park, where they were then hunted, probably *par force*.[36] In France, wolf-hunting *par force* continued to be an aristocratic sport well after the medieval period. In 1566 Jean de Clamorgan wrote a book, *La Chasse du loup*, devoted exclusively to the sport, and dedicated it to Charles IX; it ran to over a hundred editions, including several in other languages.[37]

The fox

The wolf was feared and hated; it emerged from dense forest or rocky hills to kill, but otherwise its environment and man's were broadly separate. The fox's depredations were on a more domestic level: it took, not the sheep on the mountain or the corpse on the battlefield, but the dithering hen; it was a great nuisance, but nobody was afraid of it, and the grudging admiration which surrounds the fox in medieval fable and universal folklore arises out of the small countryman's constant battle to outwit it, to protect innocence against guile; a battle which somehow draws him close to the animal, makes him more guileful himself, and gives the fox, alone among the hunted animals, an international personal name: Reynard.

That most hunting in twentieth-century England should be directed against the fox is due largely to the resilience of the species, its ability to thrive in changing and even urban conditions. Already in the Middle Ages its activities were centred on the habitations of man: 'He lyveth of al vermyn and of alle kareyns and other fowle wormes; his best mete that he moost loveth is hennys, capones, dokes, young gees and other wilde fooules whan he may gete hem, and also botirflies, gressopes [grasshoppers], milk and buttyr. They done grete harme in wareyns of conynges [rabbits].'[38] Vineyards were a favourite resort of the fox when the grapes were ripening. Phoebus's illustration of the fox shows one creeping through the grass, wide-eyed and ears pricked, towards a pair of unsuspecting domestic geese, whose splayed, ungainly feet somehow accentuate their defenceless innocence. The same contrast is the basis of numerous misericords and other carvings in English cathedrals and churches; many of these are based on specific episodes in the French *Roman de Renard*.[39]

Queen Ratio's comments on the fox are predictable: 'His nature is deceitful, malicious, crafty, covetous, rapacious, perfect in all villainy.' One of the commonest folk beliefs about the fox, with some basis in fact, is that he feigns death to attract birds close enough for him to seize them.[40] In the *Bestiary* of Philippe de Thaun he therefore symbolizes the devil: 'To people living carnally he shows pretence of death, till they are entered into evil. Then he takes them by a jump and devours them, as the fox does the bird when he has allured it.'[41] The idea of the devil snaring the unwary also lies behind a carving in Bristol Cathedral: the upper section shows St George slaying the dragon; the lower part is clearly meant to be antithetical, and shows a fox seizing a goose.[42]

In medieval illustration, and especially in church carvings, one of the commonest representations of the fox is as preacher, priest, friar or bishop, usually with a congregation of dim-witted ducks or geese.[43] Ratio includes churchmen among the disciples of Reynard, for 'he has lectured to all three estates, and clerics, noblemen and labourers are learned in his docrine; advocates of canon and civil law are adept in his skills.' She has already employed the symbolism of the deceitful preacher in her attack on the wolf, however; her only precise comparison involving the fox has to do with his feigning death, which she uses to criticize men who go among the congregation in a crowded church and fall down with their tongue hanging out as if stricken by epilepsy, the sufferers from which were thought to be holy, in order to extract money from the gullible.[44]

The familiar stink of the fox and the nature of its den are important in an allegory of sin and confession contained in Henry of Lancaster's *Livre des seyntz medicines*.[45] This takes as its starting-point the conventional idea that idleness is the root of vice. *Peresce*, Sloth, is the vixen; she mates with *Orgueil*, Pride, in the heart of man, which is one corner of the foxes' den, the body. The several entrances to the den, from which the stench of fox emerges, are likened to the bodily orifices. The cubs produced by Sloth and Pride are the other five Deadly Sins, and emerge with their parents under cover of darkness to do evil. The hunter or forester who kills them, driving them out of their den, the body, is the priest who hears a man's confession: 'Just as a forester or parker keeps his ground to the best of his power and destroys all the vermin, so the good man does all he can to keep me to the path of virtue and to hunt down evil vices.'[46]

When the foxes/sins have been driven into the open and killed, the confessor has them skinned, and their pelts are displayed in the castle hall, 'so that the lord and everyone else may see them, . . . and so a man should do with his sins: retain their outward skin, and keep it always as if hanging in the hall before his eyes; that is to say in the open, where the eyes of his heart may see it, . . . and he should want his sins to be seen and recognized by everyone, like the fox's pelt'.[47]

If the fox was near its earth, it was difficult to take: this was so of the pregnant vixens, which would be down a hole at the first note of a horn. Otherwise, however, this *moult malicieuse et fausse beste* provided excellent hunting, running close to the hounds and giving a strong scent: 'The huntynge for the fox is faire for the good crie of the houndis that folowen hym so nye and with so good a wille; alway thei senter of hym for he fleth by thik spoies and also for he stinketh evermore.'[48] For the hunter whose chief pleasure lay in watching and hearing hounds working on a scent, therefore, this small, guileful and, in the culinary context, useless creature could provide a hunt as interesting as that of the hart. Phoebus mentions its pelt as of some use, as an inferior and rather smelly fur, and its fat and marrow as a cure for hardening of the sinews.[49]

The season specified by William Twiti, the *Craft of Venery* and the *Boke of St Albans* is

> . . . fro the Nativyte
> Tyll the annunciation of owre lady fre.[50]

However, given the nature of the fox, this was certainly not universally observed. Even the normally punctilious hunter questioned in the *Craft of Venery* is willing to turn a blind eye and hunt a fox found out of season by his hare-hounds, though without great ceremony: '"Sir hunter, yf youre houndez fynde of a fox oute of seson, woll ye rechasen apon youre houndez?" "Ye, Syre, yf my houndez have gret will renne, then y woll do it, but y will not wite that it is the fox but an hare and noght speke of his right but of the hare. And yf he be tak, y schall reward myn houndez with brede, but y schall make nou abay, ne the fox schalt noght come in to the hall."'[51] By 'make nou abay' he means that the ceremonial baying of the dead beast by the hounds will not be conducted. Twiti and the *Craft of Venery* are obsessed with etiquette; to hunt the fox out of season, and half by accident, as an agricultural pest, may be arguably a reasonable thing, but to conduct the related ceremonial out of season is unthinkable.

France and England were the strongholds of medieval fox-hunting *par force*; elsewhere the fox was kept down by traps, snares and poisons, or by driving it out of its earth with sulphurous smoke or by using terriers. The only German literary reference to a fox-chase appears to be in *Reinhart Fuchs*,[52] whereas there are numerous references to trapping and snaring. It is unlikely that a fox would do immense damage in a deer-park, except perhaps during the calving season, but efforts were clearly made to put them down in James IV of Scotland's park at Falkland (see p. 62).

Before starting a hunt it was important to deny the fox its underground refuges by stopping the earths during the previous night, when the foxes were abroad hunting. One went around midnight, put faggots in the entrances, and stamped earth down on them. As a visual deterrent one also peeled two sticks and placed them in the form of a cross before the entrance, 'and the fox will not approach them, for he will see the cross of peeled sticks and think it is some engine for his downfall' (see Fig. 27).[53]

The lymer had no role to play in a fox-hunt. The *Boke of St Albans*, at its most parental, is firm on this point: with the exception of the hart, buck and boar,

. . . all other beestys that huntid shall be
Shall be sought and founde with Ratchis so fre.
Say thus I yow tolde, my childer so bolde.[54]

So the fox was hunted 'with ratchis so fre', with a group of uncoupled running-hounds. Not with the whole pack: first one placed one's relays at strategic points, and often lined the edge of the wood with stables, especially to cut off the way to any attractive thickets. One then sought the fox within the wood with about a third of one's hounds (only three or four, according to King Modus), then as many more once they had found a scent.[55]

Practice differed; sometimes greyhounds were employed as well as the running-hounds. Phoebus says that greyhounds, even large ones accustomed to taking boar or wolf, were loth to tackle a fox, partly because of its habit of fouling them with excrement as a last resort. Nevertheless, he suggests stationing fewterers with greyhounds downwind of the fox.[56] The *curée* was done in the same way as for the wolf (see p. 140). In addition, one could boil the flesh of the fox and feed it to the hounds chopped on the skin, a practice highly recommended by Phoebus.[57] The refusal of the hunter in the *Craft of Venery* to allow the head of an out-of-season fox to be brought into the hall suggests that such a ceremony was observed, probably at supper, after a hunt in the open season.

The finest medieval description of a fox-chase is undoubtedly Sir Bertilak's third day's hunting in *Gawain*. Factually, it includes virtually everything mentioned by the practical treatises, including the greyhounds, though in the *Gawain* version it appears that these are posted in the stable rather than specifically downwind of the fox. Again, Sir Bertilak rises early:

Full fair were all the fields with clinging frost;
Over the wrack rose up the reddened sun
Bright and clear through heaven's cloudy coasts.
Hunters unhardled hounds beside the holt;
Rocks rang in the trees to the roar of horns.
Some hounds fell on the fewte left by the fox,
Using their craft to cross and cross again.
A kennet cries, the huntsman calls his name,
His fellow hounds, milling and snuffling, follow,
Romp on the track, racing on in a rabble.
The fox flees on before; they find him soon,
Settling to run as soon as he is in sight,
Crying his doom full clear with clamour and noise.
Many a thorny thicket he dodges through;
Loops back by many a bush, and lies to listen,

Leaping at last a hedge and little ditch
To steal out secretly beside a spinney;
Thinks him away from the wood and the hounds with his wiles;
But now, unaware, finds himself faced by a fewterer,
With three grim greyhounds, eager to grasp him.
       He sees,
    And starts away again,
    And, still strong, flees,
    Dismayed, but running yet
    To his stronghold in the trees.

Then would your heart have been high with the cry of hounds,
When all the pack came on him, and pressed in pursuit.
They cried the view, and called such a curse on his head
That all the towering tops of the cliffs might have tumbled.
Here he met a halloo, when the hunters came on him;
There he was sworn at, and swerved at a snarling word.
Here he was threatened; there he was damned for a thief,
Unable to tarry, his trackers still at his tail.
Whenever he raked away to the fields, he was run at,
And as often went back to the wood, the wily Reynard.
The lord and the hunters were led behind him like laggards,
Many a mile through the hills, till mid-afternoon.

Until, eventually, Sir Bertilak,

Foreseeing the path of this fox, now followed so long,
Springs across a spinney to spy the rogue,
As he hears the cry of the hounds that harry him on.
Through the rough of the thicket he sees Reynard come running:
The pack of hounds press panting on his heels.
The man, seeing the wild thing, watches and waits;
Draws his bright blade, and flings it at the beast,
Which shies from the sword; would start back if he could;
He hesitates – and the lead hound has him,
And the rest fall on him in front of the horse's feet,
Wild in their noise, and worry the wily one.
The lord alights from his horse, and lifts the fox,
Wrenching him roughly from the mouths of the raches;
Holds him high aloft and gives a halloo.
About him stands baying many a brave hound;
Hunters hurry to gather, each with his horn,

Still sounding the recheat until they see him.
When all the noble company has come,
All that there bear bugle blow at once,
And all the rest halloo, that have no horn;
The merriest music heard by ears of men
Was the song that there was raised for Reynard's soul.[58]

What these passages convey much better than the manuals is the hunted animal's twisting agility of mind and limb; the writer feels sympathy for both hunter and hunted. Both emerge with credit, the animal perhaps with slightly more, outnumbered as he is, with every hand and voice against him. Sir Bertilak triumphs, but the final fanfare is a tribute to the fox as well as to the hunter.

In the context of the poem, this dual identification is crucial: during this third hunt the indolent Gawain is in the castle, a human quarry, tested and ever harder pressed by the predatory Lady Bertilak. Like many an Arthurian hero, he attains stature, both in his bedchamber and eventually under the whistling axe of Sir Bertilak in the guise of the Green Knight, through being tried and tested. So too the creatures pursued by the medieval hunter: left unmolested, or simply trapped and snared, they would reveal only the most outward and inglorious aspects of their abilities and nature. Their behaviour in flight and in death is an exaltation, and furnishes for the hunter a revelation of the possibilities of an unsullied purity of courage and a truth to oneself to which he too may aspire, though hopelessly.

'The fox ne pleyneth hym nat whan men slee hym, but evere he defendeth hym at his pouer the while he may lyve.'[59] That is why there is a fanfare for Reynard's soul.

10

The Uneatable (II):
Otter, Lynx and Badger

The otter

In the Middle Ages the otter was certainly a more familiar sight than it is today (*assez commune beste*, according to Gaston Phoebus). As one of man's competitors for the food resources of the countryside it was regarded without affection or sentiment. It was seen as the aquatic counterpart of the fox: greedy, crafty, preying on the witless, not only in flowing water but, more destructively, in those fishponds which furnished an important supplement to the limited diet of aristocratic hall and monastery refectory. During Lent, particularly, a pair of marauding otters must have been a considerable dietary menace to a lordly or monastic table, 'for a couple of oters without moor shal wel destroy of fish a poons or a greet stangk, and therfore men hunteth hem. . . . She hath evel bityng and venomes, and of hure strength defendithe hure myghtely fro the houndes.'[1]

Queen Ratio[2] tells how the fox, wandering along the riverbank, found an otter's holt and, thinking it was the home of one of his relatives, went in. After a frank discussion of their wicked natures and modes of life (in medieval iconography the otter symbolizes the tyrant or despot[3]), fox and otter found themselves to be soulmates; being no threat to one another, they agreed that they would become *maistres des yaues et des fores*, 'masters of the waters and forests' (compare the title of the French royal Master Huntsman, p. 172), reigning jointly and without friction over the natural world. The otter explains that his principal source of food is the well-stocked 'stank' or fishpond, and his method is to swim around on the surface, beating the water with his tail and frightening the fish to the edges, so that he can then swim around the banks under the water and take the fish easily.

The French phrase meaning 'to swim underwater', *nâger entre deux eaux*, is the basis of Ratio's moral comparison between the otter and man. As an idiom, the phrase (literally, 'to swim between two waters') is the equivalent of the English 'to have a foot in both camps', or 'to run with the hare and hunt with the hounds'. This enables Ratio to digress into an attack on flatterers and self-seeking fence-squatters.

The otter is the last beast regularly hunted *par force de chiens* with which I have to deal, and is categorized by King Modus as one of the black beasts, in the wider application of the phrase. In and around fishponds it was snared and trapped, but in rivers, especially those of small width and depth, it provided a specialized variety of hunting with a pack, the hounds of which were probably, in general, limited to this particular quarry. Consequently otter-hunting acquired its own vocabulary: the droppings were called 'spraints' or 'tredles' (French *espreintes*), the tracks 'marks' (French *marches*). Both had a role in the preliminary assessment of a prospective quarry: the she-otter's droppings were darker than the male's, and her tracks in the sand or soft earth of the sloping riverbank were smaller and narrower, with thinner toe-marks.[4]

The otter-hunt was like a miniature, riverine version of the hart-hunt, with quest, assembly, unharbouring of the quarry, pursuit, death, and *curée*.[5] The best hunting, at least in France, was in March and September, when the rivers were moderately low and the weed-growth limited.[6] Specially trained lymers were used in the quest or quests. For a single river four huntsmen, ideally with a lymer each, were needed; two were on each bank, one to go upstream and one downstream. The lymers sought the scent; the huntsmen looked for the droppings near the water's edge and the prints left by the otter as it left or entered the river. It was important to decide whether the prints suggested that the animal was going up or down the river.

Locating an otter from these indications could take time; otters are not creatures of permanent residence, but move to new areas according to the availability of food, hence the need for the quest. Even when established in a new dwelling, the otter might travel a mile or two from its holt when hunting. It normally went upriver, attracted, according to the manuals, by the scent of fish in the water, and then digested its meal while floating down placidly with the current. The idea of a creature hunting by water-borne scent would be almost magical to a medieval hunter, used to the trick of the hart which took to water to destroy the scenting-line for the hounds; it probably reinforced the idea of the otter as an aquatic reflection of the wily fox.

After the quest the huntsmen returned to report to the assembly or gathering ('for if one goes on quest for something, one must also have an assembly,' says Phoebus), and the hounds were then led back to the selected point of the river. The hounds were uncoupled a bow-shot or two from where the otter was thought to be lying, so that they could get the high spirits out of their system before being put on the scent.

The lymer and other hounds, then, proceeded to move the otter, which invariably took to the water. Hunters were stationed up- and downriver from the hounds, at fords and shallows. They normally carried barbed tridents or two-pronged forks, but some miniatures show them with plain spears, and one illustration shows them with staffs with a sickle-shaped blade on the end.[7] These hunters tried to spear the otter as it swam past through the shallow water. If one missed one's aim one had to run along to the next shallow and gaze again into the stream, as the hounds, hunting among the tree-roots and under the banks, harried the otter along the green and murmuring tunnel of water and boughs. In a larger river this type of hunting was combined with the stretching of a large net, with a leaded bottom rope, across the width of the river.

One of the Devonshire tapestries, *The Otter and Swan Hunt*, shows the dead otter being held aloft, hanging by the lower jaw from the two-pronged fork of a finely-garbed hunter who is sounding his horn; the hounds mill around the hunter's feet as a company of aristocrats of both sexes looks on.[8] In the *curée* the hounds were usually given bread, cheese, and perhaps some cooked meat carried for the purpose. Both Phoebus and King Modus, however, suggest that they might sometimes be given meat from the otter itself, and that they will hunt the better for it.

The texts of the medieval manuals say nothing about a specific breed of otter-hound. In some of the manuscript miniatures the hounds look just like those used in *par force* hart-hunting, and Phoebus mentions the possibility of using otter-hounds in the hunting of the hart, to which they contributed a specialized willingness and scenting ability if the hart took to water. Some medieval miniatures, however, show otter-hounds as rough-coated, which suggests that in certain areas, at least, strains were already emerging which developed into the modern otter-hound (see Fig. 28). In *The Otter and Swan Hunt* the dogs are smooth-coated and short-eared, and appear to be some kind of small alaunt or alaunt–greyhound cross. Gace de la Vigne says that good hounds are wasted on the otter, and recommends spaniels and mastiffs, with greyhounds kept at hand to kill it if it should come onto dry land.[9]

The kings of England had otter-hounds as early as 1175, when a grant is made to Roger Follo, Henry II's otter-hunter. In the reign of King John the royal otter-hunters, Ralph and Godfrey, were despatched to the Sheriff of Somerset 'with two men, two horses and twelve hounds, for as long as they find employment in capturing otters in your shire. And as soon as they cannot capture any, you are to forthwith send them back to us, and any cost you may incur through them shall be accounted to you at the Exchequer'.[10] Allusions to the royal otter-hounds or their keepers recur throughout the Middle Ages. The establishment was modest: in both 1212 and 1485 there were just twelve hounds and a brace of greyhounds.[11]

Otter-skins were a commercial commodity. In Ireland, under Henry IV, rents were paid in otter-skins, and they were imported from the Continent into early fourteenth-century England.[12]

The lynx

The lynx was a very localized quarry. No hunting author except Gaston Phoebus, whose aim is a comprehensive survey, devotes any great attention to it.[13] The Master of Game translates Phoebus's chapter describing the animal, but not the one which describes the hunting of it. It was certainly hunted par force, rather unceremonially, in south-west France, but the Iberian manuals ignore it. There was puzzlement as to what the creature actually was, and this emerges in the range of French names for it: loup cervier, perhaps interpreted popularly as 'deer-wolf', from its habit of taking young deer for food or because of its prominent ear-tufts, like miniature antlers; chat loup, 'wolf-cat'; and Phoebus's own suggestion: chat leopard, 'leopard-cat'.[14]

Most lynx-hunting happened by accident when hounds were seeking something else, but having found a lynx hunters allowed the pack to pursue it, not simply as an act of pest-control but because it furnished an enjoyable par force hunt, running well and turning at bay every so often like a boar. If one was alerted to the presence of a lynx in the area, one took strong greyhounds and crossbowmen to assist in the kill. Phoebus does not mention any form of curée, and evidently looks on lynx-hunting as an occasional necessity, an enlivening but unelevating variation from the norm.

The same is true of the hunt of the common wildcat, which usually took to a tree as soon as it was hard-pressed, and was then unceremoniously shot by the bowmen. Medieval hunting men, in fact, with their love of the honest and open-hearted running-hound, have an unsurprising loathing of cats, summed up in the Master of Game's condemnation: 'as of comoun wylde cattes me nedes nat to speke myche of hem, for every hunter in Ingelond knowethe hem and her felnesse and malice wel inowe. But oone thing dare I wel say, that if eny beest hath the develis streynt in hym, wythoute doute it is the catt, and that both the wilde and the tame.'[15]

1 The quest, the first stage in the classic method of hunting *par force de chiens*. Several huntsmen, each accompanied by a lymer, disperse to find a suitable hart.

Cy deuise coument on doit aler en queste entre les champs et la forest

2 If possible the quality of the hart, especially of its antlers, is confirmed visually.

3 The assembly or
gathering: the merits
of the various beasts
located are assessed.
Notice the
droppings, spread
on the tablecloth for
examination.

Cy deuise comment lasseublee se doit faire en este et en yuer.

Cy deuise comment on doit mener les chiens a faire la suite.

4 The lymer leads
the coupled running-
hounds to the
selected hart.

5 The hart is
unharboured, the
hounds are
uncoupled and the
chase begins.

Cy deuise comment on doit aler laissier courir pour le cerf.

6 After the death the
ceremonial
unmaking begins.

7 The ritual rewarding of the hounds in the *curée*. The lymer is rewarded individually.

Ey druse commant on dort faire le droit a son limier et la cuvriee aur ch

Ey druse conut on puet traire aux bestes a larbaleste et a lair de main.

8 The other principal method of hunting deer: bow and stable.

9 A different form of *curée* in a Flemish tapestry: two greyhounds receive their reward in the belly cavity of the deer (here a hind or doe).

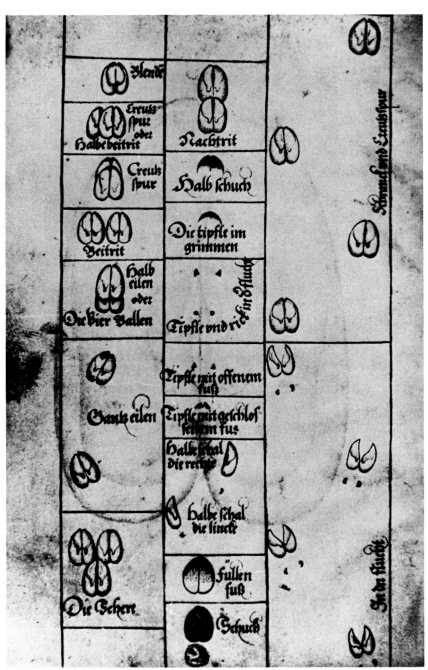

10 The study of deer-tracks: a fine art in Germany, exemplified in this diagram from the Hohenlohe archive in Neuenstein.

11 Seasonally varying forms of deer-droppings, drawn within an illuminated initial.

12 The hunting-horn and its baldric.

13 Female involvement in hunting. The man on the right is waiting with an alaunt for the last stage of the chase.

Cp apres deuise des manieres et conditions des chiens.

14 The main varieties of dog used in medieval hunting. Top: left, a large, rough-coated greyhound; centre, a running-hound; right, a slightly larger hound, possibly a lymer. Bottom: left, two alaunts, one muzzled; centre, two small, smooth-coated greyhounds, with a small running-hound (probably a harrier or kenet) in front; right, a mastiff wearing a spiked collar, and perhaps a greyhound-mastiff cross or bastard.

Cy deuise du chenil ou les chiens doiuent demourer z comment

15 The kennels.

16 Boar-hunting on foot. Notice the different spear-patterns, and the reckless alaunt.

17 Lament for a hound. Alfonso XI of Castile discusses a casualty after a boar-hunt, and receives priestly consolation.

18 Killing the boar from horseback.

Comment len doit couurir
lup au sanglir et le tuer ¶
Aprentis demande com
ment len doit tuer le sin

tlieu ¶Tmodus despont qt
tu aus mant piece chacie toy
sanglier et tu beoins giulseu
abape deuv ou .iij. sois sayss

19 An early fifteenth-century altarpiece showing the foundation legend of the monastery of Polling in southern Germany. Count Tassilo (top left) and his hunting party pursue a hind, which, ignoring hounds and hunters, scrapes the ground and reveals the Holy Cross (top right). Tassilo brings the bishop (bottom left), who blesses the Cross. The Count resolves to found the monastery of Polling on the site (bottom right).

20 The unmaking of the boar. Notice the fire, and the chilly hunters' appreciation of it.

Coment on doit deffere le sanglr.

21 Shooting a boar in its wallow. Notice the prominent testicles, the devilish feet, and the contrasting peace of the pastoral background.

22 Alfonso XI of Castile prepares for a bear-hunt. The bears wait unsuspecting in the distant sierra as several questing parties seek them out. Some of the hounds wear coloured body armour.

a garganta de stā marja q̃ es entre la hoz de escarabajosā z el monte dela vaqiriza z el pie de sancho velasco z roble do fesseros z dos fornillos z nuño oxo es todo vn mont te z es bueno de osso z de puercos enla otoñada z enel invierno z son las luzerias la vna por çima dela cabeza de stā marja fasta'l collado dela samora z donde abestueso malo z la otra desse bestueso malo fal

23 Medieval netting and snaring techniques.

Ci deuise a fere hayes por toutes bestes

24 Hare-hunting. In this fifteenth-century Italian example both scenting-hounds and greyhounds are used.

25 The world upside-down. Compare the hare on the right with the hunter on the left of the previous illustration.

E n babilone vont ⁊ mueuent amidi
Q uant il furent montes ⁊ des loges parti
L i escuier de lost ont tout ars ⁊ brui
A grant ioie cheuauchent les puis de ual garni

26 A deer-park: a stylized Franco-Flemish depiction of around 1500.

27 Earth-stopping before a fox-hunt.

qis conuient aler les loutreurs au   au dessous les loutreurs pour le
tresr et au dessous du giste et regar   gaitier a tout leur foene et ont
der au fons de haue se il verront   tous iours leueil au fons de la
passer. Et se leuoit il doit ferir de   ue. et quant bin deulx leuoit pas
sa foene et metre paine de tuer si   ser si fiert de la foene et le leue co
come il est figure ci desous.   tre mont et les chiens la baient

28 Otter-hunting.

30 The head of a hunting spear
(Italian, around 1430).

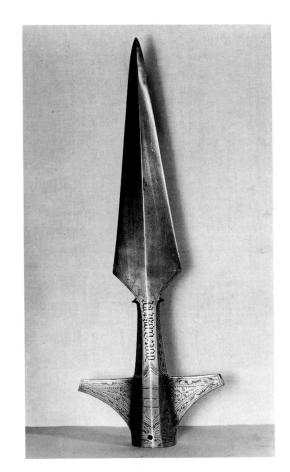

29 An Italian garniture of hunter's
cutlery of around 1430.

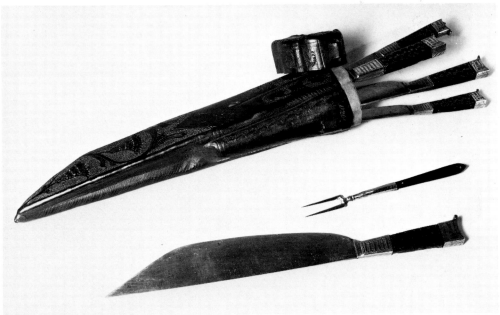

32 *The Pursuit of Fidelity*: a fifteenth-century tapestry from the Upper Rhineland.

31 The most famous hunting miracle: the conversion of St Eustace (Pisanello's version).

33 The Devil as hunter;
the animals are the
harried souls of men.

34 The hunters hunted:
death pursues Mary of
Burgundy in an
illustration in her own
Book of Hours; the
hunters' eyes look
heavenward, beyond
the Crucifix.

35 The taking of eyass hawks in a French manuscript of Frederick II's influential *De Arte Venandi*.

36 Falconers (left) about to take a hawk from the mews in order to trim its beak (right).

37 Falconers and the mews. The man on the left is about to give his falcon a bird's leg as a tiring. Notice the special falconer's knot, which can be tied and untied with one hand.

38 Training a hawk, still secured by a creance, to come to the swung lure.

39 Falconers in the mews.

40 A thirteenth-century personal miracle recounted in verse by King Alfonso the Wise of Castile. Top left, the King casts off his falcon after a heron; top right, the falcon strikes the heron, which falls into the water; middle left, the King tells a falconer to retrieve it; middle right, the swimming man disappears under the water; bottom right, prayers to the Virgin to save him are answered; bottom left, he emerges, gives the heron to the King, and all the company praise the Virgin.

41 A fifteenth-century Italian lady hunting partridges.

42 The knight as bird of prey in a German manuscript of around 1300.

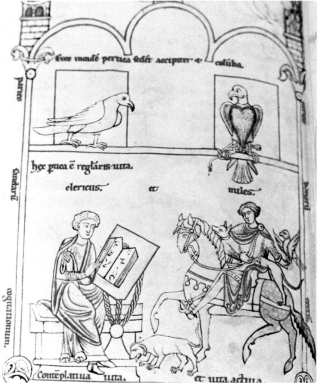

43 The bird of prey (a goshawk) symbolizing the knight (Austrian, around 1220).

44 A French or Italian miniature of hunting at the river. Notice the mixed company;
the spaniels putting up the birds, which include herons and mallard; the little drum
on the left; the greyhounds waiting to help the falcons in the kill if necessary.

45 The hawk and lovemaking: a German poet and his lady of around 1300.

46 Falconry as a seasonal symbol: an illustration of the month of May in a *Book of Hours*. The naked figures began as Gemini, the Twins, but are misinterpreted in some manuscripts as a pair of lovers.

47 An old falconer in a late fifteenth-century tapestry. Notice the lure at his belt, and the ornate collar of the greyhound.

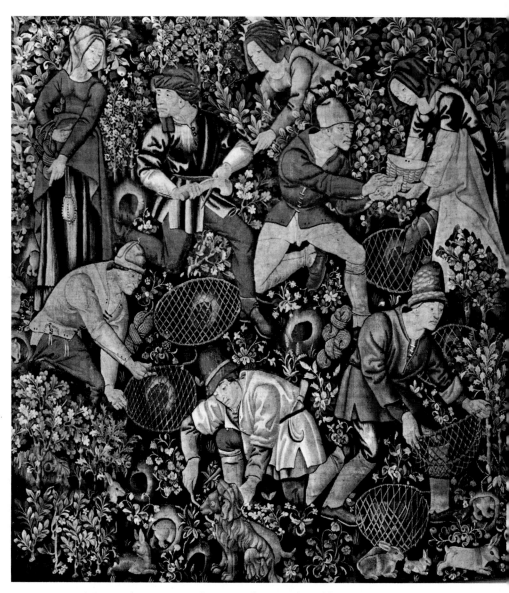

48 A Burgundian tapestry of peasants ferreting for rabbits.

49 Hunting woodcock *a la folletoere*.

50 A cock pheasant, lured by a trail of grain and then angered by its own image in a mirror, about to dislodge the sticks holding up a basket trap.

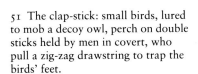

51 The clap-stick: small birds, lured to mob a decoy owl, perch on double sticks held by men in covert, who pull a zig-zag drawstring to trap the birds' feet.

52 The camouflaged cart.

53 The stalking-horse.

54 The hawk as social indicator: an Italian family of the late fifteenth century, grouped around the hawk on the father's fist. The tactile chain links child to mother, mother to father, father to the hawk whose presence seals their joint dignity.

55 Medieval practice continues, with refinements, into the Renaissance: Maximilian I kills a boar. Notice his specialized boar-sword with its thin shaft, broad point and twin tines to prevent over-penetration (compare Fig. 18).

The badger

The badger, too, was rather below the dignity of the serious hunter. Edward, Duke of York has little time for it: 'I take noon hede to speke myche of hym, for it is no beest that nedeth eny grete maystrie to devise of the huntyng of hym ne to hunt hym wyth strength.'[16] It was hunted with hounds, but, as the *Boke of St Albans* explains, slow hounds would do; the short-legged badger, if it could not trot back to its drey and vanish underground, preferred to take refuge in the thicket rather than try to outrun the hunt:

> What beest yit Mayster, I ax it for non yll,
> That moost hoole all houndes rennen untill,
> And also sone the slowyst shall hym over take
> As the swyftist shall do, what way so ever he take?
> That beest a Bausyn hight, a Brok or a Gray;
> Thes .iii. namys he hath, the sooth for to say,
> And this is cause therof: for he will by kynde
> Go thorugh thornys a way the thykest he may fynde.
> Ther as the swyftist houndes may no forther goo
> Than the slowest of foote, be he never so thro.[17]

'Thro' means 'eager'. The three names of the badger all relate to his colour: 'bausyn' means 'piebald' (Old French *bausen*); 'brok' means 'grey' (Old English *broc*).

Gaston Phoebus, whose main justification for hunting is that it keeps one from idleness, naturally has little time for the badger, which 'lives more on sleep than on anything else'.[18] It is unlikely that there was a recognized season for badger-hunting, though since its grease was useful the autumn would probably be the best time. A manuscript in the Bodleian Library states that:

> The ceson of the brok at Paskes [Easter] shal begyn,
> And til myssomer lastes ay er that hit blyn [i.e. ends].

However, this is probably a mistake for 'roebuck'.[19] The badger never strayed very far, and was principally nocturnal in habit. These factors shaped the hunting of it: at midnight on a moonlit night, when the badgers were abroad, the hunters fixed purse-nets in the entrances to the set; the mesh was large enough for the badger's head to pass through. In the early morning a small pack of hounds was put through the neighbouring thickets. The illustration in Phoebus's chapter shows two leashes of medium-sized greyhounds being used, which rather contradicts the *Boke of St Albans*. The badgers made for the set and either were taken in the nets or, if the dogs were fast enough, turned at bay and defended life bravely until they were killed. Purse-nets alone would take an unsuspecting badger; the size of the mesh was important because with his head through the net he could not gnaw his way free.

Badgers were probably a quarry of the peasantry rather than anyone else. The hunters in the manuscript miniatures are humbly clad and armed only with mattocks. King Modus's description of badger-hunting is given for the benefit of a poor man who wishes to make himself shoes of the animal's skin, which he says is very long-lasting. Phoebus also mentions its use as shoe-leather, and a belief that if a child's first shoes were of badger-skin he would have the lifelong power to cure horses of a disease called 'farcin' (glanders?) simply by getting on their back. The badger's abundant fat was used in human medicine.

11

The Unicorn

For the literate hunter of medieval England or northern France, an encounter with a unicorn, though beyond the common run of his experience, would have been hardly more incredible than running into some other exotic but authenticated quarry such as the reindeer, whose antlers, according to Gaston Phoebus, enclosed its entire body, or one of the bears which led Alfonso XI through the snows of Extremadura for days and nights on end. Everyone knew that there were unicorns: was their existence not attested to by classical authors, by the Bible, by the works of the Church Fathers and the reports of modern travellers alike? Were there not artefacts, cups, sword-hilts of unicorn ivory, and indeed whole horns, elaborately carved and set with jewels, in royal and cathedral treasuries?

Marco Polo's description of the unicorns he saw in Sumatra obviously refers to the rhinoceros: 'They have hair like that of a buffalo, feet like those of an elephant, and a horn in the middle of the forehead . . . the head resembles that of a wild boar . . . They delight in mire and mud. 'Tis a passing ugly beast to look upon, and is not in the least like that which stories tell us of as being caught in the lap of a virgin.'[1] The illustrator of the version of Marco Polo's account in an early fifteenth-century manuscript of the *Livre des merveilles*, however, ignored these details and depicted the unicorn as it appears in heraldry: a handsome, pony-like beast with a fine mane, a goat's beard, cloven hooves and a long, twisting horn.[2]

The painter Erhard Reuwich, who went on a pilgrimage to the Holy Land with a canon of Mainz Cathedral, Bernhard von Breyderbach, and supervised the printing of the canon's *Pilgrimages to Mount Sion* in 1486, included an engraving of a unicorn very similar to the miniatures in the *Livre des merveilles*. At the foot of the page in which the unicorn appears with the crocodile, camel, giraffe, salamander, etc., is the inscription (in Latin): 'These animals are depicted truly, just as we saw them in the Holy Land.'[3]

There is also considerable evidence for the existence of the unicorn in various Old Testament allusions,[4] and in pictorial representations of Old Testament scenes in which there is no textual authority for the involvement of the unicorn, the creature appears with other animals representing the scope of God's Creation. In the scene of the Creation in *Queen Mary's Psalter* the unicorn is directly before the throne of God, the animal closest to His feet, and in the scene of the flood it queues with the other beasts waiting to enter the Ark.[5] Paintings commonly show the unicorn as one of the smaller range of animals accompanying Adam and Eve in the Garden of Eden.[6] In certain versions of the temptation of Eve,[7] the presence of the unicorn hints at the Redemption, since it was used as a symbol of Christ from the early Church Fathers onwards. The Biblical passages allude to the animal's strength and invincibility; 'Who then is this unicorn but the only-begotten Son of God?' asks St Ambrose in his commentary on the Psalms.[8] St Basil interprets Job xxxix. 9–11 in a similar way.[9]

The main source for medieval writers on the unicorn was the collection of animal legends called the *Physiologus*, originally a Greek work compiled between the second and fourth centuries, which furnished much of the material for the bestiaries.[10] The *Physiologus* describes the unicorn as small but very fierce, and states that no hunter could capture him. The only means of capture (mentioned too in Marco Polo's account, above) was by leaving a virgin in the forest; the unicorn meekly laid his horn in her lap and the hunters were able to take him. In some versions the animal kisses the virgin's naked breast.

In the *Physiologus* and the bestiaries this surrender of the unicorn to the maiden is taken to symbolize the Incarnation of Christ: God, invincible, took on flesh in the womb of the Virgin Mary, and thus made himself vulnerable to the wiles of man, and specifically to capture and death at the hands of the Jews. The animal symbolizes both the invincibility and the humility of Christ.[11]

From the thirteenth century onwards this symbolism acquires a further hagiographical dimension through the addition of the Archangel Gabriel in the role of hunter. A thirteenth-century German poet calls Gabriel the *Himeljeger*, 'heavenly hunter',[12] and the image of Gabriel as hunter lives on in rural Britain, where some people still allude to the wild geese, passing on migration with their aerial music which carries for miles over the wintry woods and frozen stubbles, as Gabriel's hounds. In paintings and in tapestries the encounter between the unicorn and the maiden becomes an allegory of the Annunciation. This symbolism appears particularly frequent in Germanic areas. The Gelnhausen altar frontal is typical: the Virgin sits in a *hortus conclusus*, a fair garden with a fountain, enclosed by a wall with turrets and gates; the small, bearded, cloven-footed unicorn has his front feet in her lap, and she holds the horn with her right hand. Her identity is indicated partly by a halo, but principally by the legend *Ave gratia plena dominus tecum*, emerging on a scroll from the hunting-horn blown by Gabriel, who is entering from the left, as is normal in such depictions. He bears a spear and is accompanied by a couple of running-hounds on a leash.[13]

Other versions vary in their details. In one German tapestry Gabriel's hounds are named: Chastity, Justice and Humility, and a scroll floating over the unicorn's neck bears the word 'Virginity'. The *hortus conclusus* is of woven wattle fencing, and is strikingly similar to the medieval deer-parks (see Fig. 26); the gate of the enclosure is the *Porta Celi*, the Gate of Heaven. The two hounds which appear with Gabriel in the painting of the Annunciation in Erfurt Cathedral are also named, one being *Fides Spes*, the other *Caritas*, i.e. Faith, Hope and Charity. The unicorn in this depiction is a glorious thing of gold.[14]

Certain tapestries develop the allegory to include a greater range of Christian symbolism. In a Swiss altar frontal Gabriel's four hounds are Truth, Justice, Peace and Mercy; as the unicorn runs towards Mary, Adam pierces it with a crossed hunting-spear, saying, 'He is wounded because of our sins'; the blood falls into a chalice held by Eve, who says, 'By His blood we are saved.' Other Biblical elements, all identified with scrolls, include the Ark of the Covenant, the Star of David, the Burning Bush and Gideon's Fleece, and the garden contains plants symbolizing humility and charity, and a pelican reviving its young with its own blood, a symbol of the Resurrection.[15]

The cross-fertilization which enriches the two great medieval literary cults, worship of the Virgin and courtly devotion to one's beloved, is again apparent in the similarity of some of the examples described above to paintings and tapestries on the theme of courtly love. The association of the unicorn with the Virgin makes it a symbol of chastity; in depictions of the triumph of Chastity the chariot of this virtue, or of the woman whose chastity is being praised as exemplary, is drawn by unicorns; these representations include illustrations of Petrarch's *Trionfi* and Piero della Francesca's *Triumph of the Duchess of Urbino*.[16]

In certain versions, however, the relationship between the woman and the animal is ambiguous: she sometimes looks alluringly at the hunter; in one case, the *Rochester Bestiary*, she is naked, and the interplay between her body and the possible carnal implications of the horn suggests, at the least, a possible alternative to chastity.[17] The only person frequently depicted riding on a unicorn is the medieval wildman or 'wodewose', a leaf-clad embodiment of fertility and carnality.[18] The naming of the allegorical hounds is a further link with secular love-poetry (see pp. 80–81).

Human love, not necessarily carnal but at least worldly, is the theme of decoration on ivory boxes and panels and on the Swiss *Minnekästchen* or love-casket. The latter sometimes shows the lady and the unicorn, in certain cases with a pursuing hunter and a hound or hounds. In several French ivories the capture of the unicorn accompanies scenes depicting the loves of courtly heroes such as Lancelot and Tristan.[19] The unicorn's helpless subjection to the maiden serves as a parallel to the servitude of the courtly lover, most explicitly in this comparison by Richard de Fournival in his *Bestiary of Love*:

> Man has five senses: sight, hearing, smell, taste and touch . . . and I was captured through my sense of smell, as the unicorn falls asleep when it scents the sweet fragrance of virginity in the maiden. There is no beast so hard to capture, and it has a single horn in the middle of its forehead which no armour can withstand, and nobody dare attack it or await it except a virgin. For when it smells her fragrance, it kneels and humbles itself to her sweetly as if to serve her. And so wise hunters who know the beast's nature leave a virgin in its path, and it falls asleep in her lap, and then the hunters, who dare not attack it when it is awake, kill it. Just so did Love take vengeance on me; for I had been the proudest man of my age towards Love, and thought that I should never see a woman whom I should wish to possess . . . And Love, the wily hunter, put in my path a maiden whose fragrance lulled me to sleep, and I died the death suffered by lovers, which is desperation without hope of mercy.[20]

An auxiliary attribute of the unicorn, stated by the *Physiologus* and supported by travellers' tales, was its ability to purify water by dipping its horn into it.[21] It was also thought that a cup made from unicorn horn would protect the drinker from poison, and that a fragment of the horn could be used as an indicator of the presence of poison. Royal and aristocratic inventories include entries referring to such items, normally richly mounted with gold, silver or precious stones. In some cases they were evidently made from the ivory of the narwhal, a small Arctic whale, whose slender, twisting horn resembles that which the unicorn normally bears in medieval depictions.[22]

The most lavish representations of the hunt of the unicorn are in a series of tapestries in the Cloisters Museum, New York.[23] In the first we see a group of finely dressed aristocratic hunters, with more soberly clad huntsmen, setting out into the forest. They have all the usual accoutrements of the hunt: swords, spears (a slightly unusual design with a single prong instead of the more normal crossbar) and horns; they are accompanied by couples of frisking greyhounds and more earnest running-hounds. Another huntsman, probably a lymerer who has successfully completed his quest by locating the unicorn, beckons from a distance.

In the second tapestry we see the hunting party surrounding the pure-white unicorn as, apparently unaware of their approach, it dips its horn into a stream emerging from a formal, circular fountain in a *locus amoenus* shared with other animals and birds: rabbits, pheasants, goldfinches, a hart, and others out of keeping with the European tenor of the verdant landscape – two lions, a panther, a genet and a hyena. The third scene shows the unicorn crossing a river, harried by the running-hounds; greyhounds are being unleashed in what appears to be the final stage of the hunt, since the animal is surrounded by grim-faced huntsmen onto whose spears it appears to be running.

In the fourth tapestry, however, we see the unicorn defending itself with spirit. All the dogs except one have now been released; the unicorn is piercing the chest of one of them with its horn and kicking out with its hind feet at a huntsman. A richly garbed hunter in the left foreground blows a horn. The fifth scene, which survives in fragments, must have shown the taming of the beast by the maiden, of whom we see only the hand on its neck. They are inside a *hortus conclusus* with a paling fence through which roses twine. A running-hound and a greyhound are attacking the now docile unicorn; a second young woman looks alluringly at a huntsman who blows his horn outside the fence.

The sixth scene is a composite: we see the unicorn being pierced by the spears of the huntsmen as a companion blows the death; it is then carried on a horse to be examined by an aristocratic couple who have emerged, with other people, from a castle in the background. The dead animal wears around its neck a circlet of oak-twigs, bearing thorns and a single red berry. The seventh and last tapestry shows the unicorn restored to life, lying calm and content inside a small circular fenced enclosure. It is tethered to a tree by a chain running from the fine collar attached to its neck.

In most aspects, if one substituted a hart for the unicorn in the Cloisters tapestries, one would have in Scenes One, Three, Five and Six a realistic depiction of a medieval hunt, though the absence of horses, except the one beast of burden, is curious. It is clear, though, that the unicorn is intended to be not merely exotic, but symbolic. An immediate reaction to the final scene of the chained unicorn, content in its flowery enclosure, might be to assume that this hunt is that of courtly love, that the unicorn is the lover, captured by and subject to the lady, like Richard de Fournival. Such an interpretation might be supported by the intertwined initials A–E which appear in the tapestries (paired letters were commonly the initials of the partners in the marriage which inspired the creation of a tapestry[24]); by the alluring glance of the young woman in Scene Five; by the prominence of an evidently devoted couple in Scene Six, and perhaps too by the pair of pheasants in Scene Two.

Other elements, however, suggest a different interpretation (additional, rather than alternative, since in the medieval context, when a motif was as well-established in different and reciprocally influential roles as was the unicorn, one symbolic thread need not obliterate another). The scene in which the unicorn is first found has strong similarities to pictures of the Earthly Paradise: the fountain of divine love to which the unicorn contributes with the immersion of its purifying horn; the representative group of animals coexisting peacefully and unrealistically.[25] Even the pair of pheasants recalls such scenes.[26] The stream into which the fountain's water runs flows through the foreground of the next two scenes. The garland of oak-leaves on the dead unicorn might be looked on as a recognition of valour, were it not for the unrealistic thorns and the single berry, like the berry 'as red as any blood' (and specifically Christ's blood) in the old carol, *The Holly and the Ivy*. A pair of goldfinches, commonly a symbol of Christ through their associations with thistles and thorns,[27] appears in several of the tapestries, and the pheasants of the second scene are symbolic of the Redemption in certain contexts.[28] The unengaging features of many of the hunters, especially the one who wounds the unicorn with a spear-thrust to the chest, support the idea that an allusion to the Passion of Christ is intended, a view further bolstered by the pristine peace of the revivified unicorn in the final scene.

If the unicorn is Christ, then the maiden is the Virgin. The tree in the final scene bears pomegranates. With its abundance of seeds, the pomegranate symbolized fertility, and so would suit the interpretation of the tapestries as an allegory of human love, but the fruit was also variously likened to the Church, to Christ and to Mary, its fragrance and juice to the blood of the Redeemer or to the immeasurable bounty of the Virgin. The unicorn of the final scene, the risen Christ, appears to bear residual drops of blood on neck and sides, but on closer examination these are seen to be drops of juice from the pomegranates of the tree to which it is chained.

If we need further proof of the identity of the maiden, Scene Four provides it. The gentle face of one courtly hunter is in marked contrast to those of his brutish companions. On his scabbard we see the embroidered legend *Ave Regina C[oeli]*, a variation of the words of the Annunciation. His eyes gaze out of the scene of the hunt and anticipate the coming of the unicorn to the maiden's lap; the hunter is Gabriel, and the call he blows on his horn is to herald the coming of Christ.

Thus, while a literate medieval observer would be unlikely to study these tapestries without some sympathetic feeling for the hunted unicorn as symbolizing the courtly lover, they are principally a thoughtful and skilled amalgam of allusions to the Christian fundamentals of the Fall of Man, the Annunciation, the Nativity, and the Passion and Resurrection of Christ; the embodiment of these concepts in the form of a hunt is yet another example of the richly pervasive presence of hunting in the medieval courtly culture.

12

Hunting Music

John I of Portugal's justifications of hunting include the aural refreshment of the spirit. His imagery, having risen to the sublime, swoops to the anatomical:

> When one's hearing is blunted by listening to unpleasant things, it is refreshed by the pleasant things to be heard in the hunt; for it is a thing of beauty to hear the huntsman blow to the scent, and then to hear the cry of the hounds, as they find it, and are all running together; a beauty beyond all reckoning, for even Guillaume de Machaut [the French poet and composer] cannot create such harmonies and melody as do hounds when they are running true. Then there is the blowing of the horns, and the hue and cry of the huntsmen after the hounds, 'Eylo vay! Eylo vay!' All these are as effective in refreshing one's ears as rhubarb in restoring the liver![1]

Other authors, as we shall see, make similar comparisons between the sounds of the hunt and courtly music, and the imagery is well-chosen: the three elements of horn, hound and human voice form musical sections, sometimes playing separately and according a role to the individual soloist, sometimes joining in a spontaneous and joyful polyphony, crowned by a formal and triumphal coda.

The medieval hunting-horn was the principal tool and symbol of the huntsman's craft. It was carried by employed man and aristocratic hunter alike, and all were expected to be able to use it properly, since its role was to communicate not only euphoria but also information, and the blowing of a wrong call could crucially mislead and delay the other hunters. In medieval Wales a huntsman taking an oath did so on his hounds, his leashes and his horn.[2] In Castile an inefficient huntsman was cracked over the head with his horn as a symbolic dismissal (see p. 185). In literary battles representing the traditional rivalry between huntsmen and falconers, the huntsmen use their horns as weapons, the falconers their lures.[3] The horn, slung from its baldric and stopped with a bunch of grass, made a handy receptacle in which the lymerers conveyed the 'fewmets' to the gathering (see Fig. 3), and after the hunt it could swiftly be converted into a drinking vessel.

Manuscript illustrations and tapestries show horns varying in length, shape and diameter. In the fourteenth and fifteenth centuries England was famous for its hunting-horns: Thomas Vapol, an English merchant, sold 'an English horn with silver-gilt decoration' to the Duke of Burgundy in 1394; Henry Bolingbroke gave three large silver-gilt horns to Philip, Count of Vertus; and Louis of Orleans paid 117 francs for twenty-three hunting-horns sent from England.[4]

One of Edward, Duke of York's major alterations of his source, Gaston Phoebus's *Livre de chasse*, is his section on the horn. Phoebus gives a whole chapter to the horn, and a miniature shows the Count himself instructing his huntsmen in blowing,[5] but in the *Master of Game* Edward goes into much more detail on the varieties and construction of the horn:

> Ther byn divers maners of hornes, that is to say *vugles, grete abotes*, huntes hornes, *Ruettis*, smale forsters hornes, and mene hornes of .ii. maners. That oo manere is wexed with grene wex, and grettere of sum, and for [because] thei ben best for good hunters, therof will I devise how and of what fasson thei shuld be drive.
>
> First, a good hunters horn shul be dryve of .ii. span of lengthe, and nought moche more ne moch lasse; and nought to [too] crokyng neither to straught, but the *flewe* [the mouthpiece end] of .iii. or .iiii. fingers uppermore than the *hede*, that lowde [lewd, unlearned] hunters callen the *grete eende* of the horn; and also that it be as greet and holow dryven as it may be to length, and that it be shorter at side to the *bandrike* [baldric] ward than at the nether side; and that the hede be as wide as it may be, and ay ay dryve smallere and smallere to the flewe; and that it be wel wexed, thikker or thinner after as the hunter thenketh that it wil best soune, and that it be wexed the length of the horn from the flewe to the *byndyng*; and also that it be not to smal dryven from thick byndyng to the flue, for if it be the horn wil be to mene of soune.
>
> And of hornes for fewtrees [fewterers] and wodemen I speke not of, for every smale horn and other mene hornes unwexed ben good inow for hem.[6]

Edward's list probably includes horns not used in hunting. The 'vugle' was not like a modern bugle, but was a simple curved horn, originally perhaps that of the wild ox, also called 'bugle'.[7] The 'ruet' was probably a small horn of almost circular shape, most likely of metal (French *rouette*, 'little wheel'). The 'grete abote' was large, obviously, perhaps portly and euphonious but is otherwise a mystery. Foresters, fewterers and woodmen could manage with inferior horns; these were not waxed, whereas the true hunter's instrument, made from cattle horn, was waxed between its binding in the middle and the mouthpiece or 'flue'. Horns fitting Edward's description may be seen in Figs. 1, 9, 12, 19, 24, etc.

Most of the horns surviving from the medieval period are larger and more magnificent than the hunter's instrument described by Edward. The horns bought or given by royalty, such as the one mounted in gold and silver ordered by Louis of Orleans, or Charles v of France's own horn of ivory, slung on a silk baldric decorated with fleurs-de-lys and gold dolphins, may well have been used in the hunt, and roused literary echoes in King Mark's gift of a golden horn to Tristan when he equipped him as Master of his Hunting,[8] the hunter's horn of ivory bound with nine rings of gold described in *Garin de Loherain*,[9] and even Roland's 'olifant'. However, most of the more splendid horns, especially the magnificently carved olifants of elephant ivory and those thought to be made from unicorn horn, were for decoration or ceremonial, being too clumsy for practical use. The inventories of the Dukes of Burgundy include, among many other rich horns, one of gold encrusted with nine diamonds, nine rubies and eighteen pearls.[10]

The range of calls for the horn varied from country to country and author to author. The calls consisted of combinations of long and short notes (*mot* in French, 'mote' or 'moot' in English) and pauses. Pitch appears to have been uniform in the calls sounded by a single hunter, though there must have been a variety of pitch in different horns. Melodic horn music developed only in the post-medieval period, to be elaborated into a separate musical genre in France. Some writers simply list the calls; others use different methods to convey their syllabic pattern, some purely descriptive, some onomatopoeic, and one uses a specially devised notation. In the following list of calls the verbal descriptions are transcribed in linear form, and the onomatopoeic versions are reproduced unchanged.

Gaston Phoebus, *Livre de chasse*:[11]

1. 'To recall fellow-hunters from their quests to the assembly when one has found a great hart or boar': ———— ————.

2. *laisser courre*: 'to call up hounds for the unharbouring of the hart': ———— ———— ————.

3. *chace*: 'to be sounded by the huntsman who rides with the hounds as they run: ———— —— —— —— —— —— —— (*ad lib*).

4. 'When a beast leaves its own territory': —— —— — — — —
   —.

5. *requeste*: 'when the hounds take up the scent again after a check':
   —— — — — — —— — — — —.

6. *prise*: 'when the beast is dead': —— — — — — — — — *(ad lib)*; 'and if there are other horns, the ones should respond to the others, and at the end they should blow two long *mots* one after another'.

7. *retraite*: 'when one withdraws and returns to the hunting lodge':
   ——; —— ——; —— —— ——.

Gace de la Vigne:[12]

prise: 'For everyone together blows *prise*,
   Making such melody,
   With skilful *hockets*[13]
   and one long, final *mot*,
   That no man hearing them
   Could seek any other Paradise.'

Livre du Roy Modus:[14]

1. *corner pour chiens*: 'to call for hounds when one has found the hart with the lymer': ——; 'if hounds are far away and one needs them quickly': —— —.

2. *chasse*: 'when hounds are running': —— —; — —, — —, — —; —, — —, — —, — —; —, — —, — —, — —.

3. *queste*: 'when hounds are uncoupled in a wood to seek a beast not found with the lymer': —— — ——.

4. *retret*: 'to recover one's hounds when they have given up hunting and are scattered in the wood': —— — — — —; —— — — — —.

5. *prise*: 'after taking a hart *par force*': —— — — — — — — *(ad lib)*; —— ——; 'and all those with a horn should blow together, and it is sweet melody; and the same call should be blown from time to time on the way homeward'.

Alfonso XI of Castile, *Libro de la montería*:[15]

'All huntsmen, in order to blow the horn properly, should practise it with the more expert when they are at leisure in the villages, so as to know all the calls they must blow when they go hunting, namely:

163

1. 'Prepare to set out'.
2. *pregunta*: 'enquiry'.
3. *rastro*: 'scent'.
4. *poner canes*: 'uncouple hounds'.
5. *corredura*: 'hounds running'.
6. *ladradura*: 'bay'.
7. *vista*: 'view'.
8. *traspuesta*: 'change'.
9. *tornado es*: 'quarry rusing' [?].
10. *a so pie*: 'quarry very close' [?].
11. *ocisa*: 'death'.
12. *acogida*: 'final gathering'.
13. *senziella*: 'simple, when no game is found'.

William Twiti, *Art of Venery* (French version):[16]

1. *menée*: 'You must blow *menée* for three males and a female: the hart, the boar, the wolf and the she-wolf.'

2. 'When you have moved the hart with the lymer': ——— ———; 'and if the hounds do not come as quickly as you would wish': ——— ——— ——— ———.

3. *rechase*: 'when hounds are running': *trourourourout, trourourourout, trourourourout.*

4. *forloyng*: 'when the hounds have distanced themselves from you [in pursuit of the hart]': *trout, trout, trourourout; trout, trout, trourourout; trourourout, trourourout, trourourout.*

5. *parfet*: 'one long *mot* and then *trourourout, trout, trout; trourourout, trourourout, trourourourout; trout, trout, trourourout*; all repeated twice more, with a long *mot* to finish'.

6. *hors de bounde*: 'when hounds pursue the beast *hors de bounde* [out of bounds] in bow and stable hunting, that is to say when the beast runs through the line of archers and the hounds go after it: a *mot* followed by *trourourourout, trourourourout, trourourourout*'.

The English version of Twiti shows certain slight variations:[17]

1. *menée*: '"Syre hunter, for how many bestis shall a man blow the mene?" "... ffor III males and for one femalle, that is to say for an hert, the boor, the wolfh male, and alle so the wolfh female as wel as to here husbond."'

164

2. ' "How shall we blowe whan ye hav sen the hert [with the lymer]?" "I shall blowe after one mote II motes. And if myn howndes come not hastily to me as y wolde, I shall blow IIII motes and for to hast hem to me and for to warne the gentelys that the hert is sene." '

3. The rechace is mentioned ('Than shall y rechace on myn houndis III tymes'), but not described.

4. *forloyne*: 'When he is ferre from you, than shall y chase hym in thys maner: *trout trout tro ro rot, trout trout tro ro rot, trou ro rot, trou ro rot.*'

5. *perfygt*: 'Than ye shall begynne to blowe a long mote and aftirward II short motes in this maner *trout trout* and than *trout tro ro rot*, begynnyng with a long mote, ffor every man that is a bowte yow and can skylle of venery may knowe in what poynt ye be in yowre game be your horn.'

The *Craft of Venery*:[18]

1. 'When the hert is mevyd and stert and is out of youre sight': ———, ——— ———; 'and yf myn houndez com nought to my will as hastliche as I wold have them': ——— ——— ——— ———.

2. The rechace is mentioned ('And then shall y rechasyn apon myn houndez III tymes'), but not described.

3. *forloyne*: 'When he is fer fro me, y schall blow in other maner, and that is this: *trout trout trororout, trout trout trororout, trororororout*, V tymes this last mote.'

4. *parfit*: '*trororororout, trout trout trout trout trout trout trout, trororororout*. Thou schalt begyn with a long mote and end with a long, so that every man that is about yow may know what poynt ye been yn and youre parley by youre blowyng.'

In the *Master of Game* the Duke of York promises a chapter on horn-blowing,[19] but this is not included. From individual references one may glean the following:

1. When the lymerer moved the hart and saw it moving away, he was to blow a mote and rechase; if he moved it without seeing it, a rechase only.[20]

2. A man releasing relays, on seeing the hart pass, was to blow a mote and rechase.[21]

3. To call up the lymer to reestablish the correct line of scent, one blew a

mote. On establishing the line, the lymerer called *'Cy va! Cy va!'* and blew a rechase, which was repeated by the other hunters.[22]

4. If hounds had lost the scent, and a hunter saw what he thought was the hart, he was to blow a mote and rechase, and then two motes to summon the berner with the hounds. A berner or lymerer summoned by a horn call was to 'answere blowyng in this wise: *Trut Trut Trut'*.[23]

5. When the hart stood at bay, everyone was to halloo together and blow a mote and rechase.[24]

Also mentioned in the *Master of Game*, without any detail, are calls for the forloyne (which the Duke of York says was never to be used in park hunting), the perfit, the stynt, the death and the pryce.[25] The most detailed descriptions are of two joyous, celebratory fanfares, one played after the *curée* and the other on arriving home. When the hounds have gobbled up the blood-soaked bread and titbits,

> than shuld the lorde, if hym list, and ellis the Maister of the Game, or in his absence who so is grettest next hym, shuld strake in this wise, that is to say blow .iiii. *moot*, and stinte not half an Ave Maria while, and blowe other .iiii. *mootis* a litil lenger than the first .iiii. *moot*, . . . and than the gromys couple up the houndes and draw homward faire and soft. And alle the remenaunte of the hunters shuld strake in this wise: *trut trut trororow trororow*, and .iiii. *moot*, with al of one length, not to longe, not to short, and other wise shuld not the hert hunters strake fro then forth til thei go to bedde.

On arriving home, 'at the halle door or at celer dore', the *meene* or *menée* was to be blown:

> First the Maister or who so is grettest next hym shalle begynne, and blowe .iii. *mote* allone, and at the first *moot* the remenaunte . . . shuld blowe with hym, and be ware that noon blow lenger than other, and after the thre *moot*, even forthwith thei shuld blowe to *recopes* [to recouple hounds], as thus: *Trut Trut trorororot*, and that thei be avised that from that tyme that thei falle inne to blowe togedir, that none of hem begynne afore other ne ende after other.[26]

The *Master of Game* also mentions special calls for use in bow and stable hunting, involving combinations of the mote with the strake or stroke, the exact nature of which is not clear. The prise and the *menée* were only to be used after killing a hart *par force*, except in bow and stable hunting when the king was taking part and a beast was killed by the hart-hounds.[27]

The *Trésor de Vénerie*, a long poem by the fourteenth-century French aristocrat Hardouin de Fontaines-Guérin, is useful primarily because of the clarity of its descriptive and pictorial detail on the music of the horn. In Hardouin's slightly crude miniatures each illustration of a stage or incident in the hunt is accompanied by its particular call, represented in a system of musical notation involving groupings of black and white squares and oblongs, each representing a note (though variation of pitch is never alluded to and appears to play no part). These syllabic elements are grouped into six basic units or *mots*:

1. the *mot single*: one black square.

2. the *demi-double de chemin* (half-double for the road): two white squares joined.

3. the *mot double de chemin* (double for the road): four white squares.

4. the *mot double de chasse* (double for the chase): one black square and two white, all three joined.

5. the *mot long*: one black oblong, the length of three squares.

6. the *mot de chasse a un dapel*: a black square, two white squares, and a black oblong, all joined.[28]

These *mots*, in their turn, are varyingly grouped to form the following functional hunting calls:

1. *chemin* (road):

■■■ ■ □□□□ □□□□ □□□□ ▬ ▬ ▬
▬ ▬ ▬ □□□□ □□□□ □□□□ ■■■

2. *asemblée* (gathering)

▬ ▬ ▬ ▬

3. *queste* (quest):

□□ ■■■■
□□ ■■■■

4. *chasse* (hounds running):

□□ ■■■■■□□ ■□□ ■□□
■□□ ■□□ ■□□ ■□□ ■□□

5. *vehue* (view):

6. *mescroy* (change):

7. *requeste* (quest afresh when quarry returns to covert):

8. *leaue* (water):

9. *relaies* (relays):

10. *ayde* (bay, request for help):

11. *prise* (death):

This phrase is then played in turn by the other hunters, and followed by:

12. *retraite* (draw homeward):

13. *appel de chiens* (to call hounds together):

14. *appel de gens* (to call hunters together):

The *appel de gens* may also be done with the voice: *hou hou, hoouuuu.*[29]

As well as the verbal encouragements and admonishments given to hounds, in which French vocabulary lingered long in English usage (see pp. 113–14), some hunters used a small range of oral calls in situations normally requiring a horn-call. We see one example of this in Hardouin's description of the *appel de gens*. The French verb for this is *huer*, an onomatopoeic word suggesting that the calls were probably attempts to produce with the voice a noise approximating to that of the horn. The calls listed above as Numbers 1 and 2 in Phoebus's description are to be produced on the horn or orally. *Modus* prescribes oral calls as follows:

1. 'For the lymerer to call up hounds when he has found the hart: one long mote.'

2. 'When hounds are running: three long motes, one after another.'

3. 'To call one's companions together: two short motes and a long, long one.'[30]

Alfonso XI is, as far as I know, the only author who mentions another vehicle for communicating hunting information in the field: the smoke-signal. The scale of his hunting in the sierras was such that even a well-blown horn might not carry from the *buscas*, the parties of questing huntsmen, to the main party. He recommends that 'if they have found a good bear, they should make four *afumadas* (puffs of smoke); if an average bear, they should make three; if a good boar, two.'[31]

The music of horn and voice conveyed information and encouragement from man to man, and from man to hound. The medieval manuals, however, come closest to lyricism in their descriptions of the music of the hounds themselves, which was crucially informative to the hunter skilled in its interpretation and intimately aware of the notes of each individual hound. The most analytically technical account of the cry of hounds is that of Gaston Phoebus;[32] the most imaginative and vivid is Gace de la Vigne's:

Then there is heard a sound
Such that no living man
Ever heard so fine a melody.
No *response* or *alleluia*
In the fine chapel of the King
Ever gave such pleasure
As hearing such a hunt.
Some sing a *motet* as they go;
Others sing a *double hocket*.
The biggest sing the *tenor* part;
Others sing the *countertenor*;
Those with the sharper voice
Sing the *treble* with a will;
The smallest sing the *quadruplum*,
Making a fifth on the *duplum*.
Some sing a *minor semitone*;
Others a *major semitone*;
Diapente, diapason,
And the rest *diatessaron*.[33]

This passage is not simply a cobbling together of a jumble of musical terminology; Gace has in mind specific aspects of the cries produced, singly and jointly, by a pack of hounds, and expresses them in carefully chosen technical vocabulary, alluding to particularly relevant features of medieval polyphony. In horn-calls the pitch was constant; in hound music variety of pitch was a principal source of delight.

Gace's comparison with the responses and alleluias is a straightforward beginning. The point about the motet and double hocket is that both are polyphonic (i.e. they are performed by several voices singing different parts). The motet has three parts. The double hocket is a form, growing old-fashioned by Gace's day, in which, with the beat continuing normally, one singer takes a breath on the beat and another off the beat, giving alternating contributions to a single melodic line (this is the simplest variety; there are more complex forms). These comparisons, then, express very nicely the combination of different levels of pitch in the pack, and the pauses in the individual hound's cries which nevertheless leave the overall impression continuous.

The polyphonic complications increase: the tenor is the lowest part in medieval polyphony; in rising order of pitch we then have the counter-tenor, the treble, and the quadruplum, with apparently a fifth part in Gace's mind singing a fifth higher than the duplum (another name for the countertenor). In the last four lines we are into the field of melodic intervals: the major and minor semitones are straightforward; diapente is a perfect interval of a fifth; diapason is a whole octave; diatessaron is a fourth.

Gace is writing for the courtier. It is interesting that the passionate interest in hunting and falconry shown elsewhere in his poem did not preclude a sound knowledge of the more aesthetic aspects of medieval courtly life. Unless he is consciously wasting his time in this passage, his courtly public, too, must have combined the same interests.

13

The Huntsman

In the summer of the year 1393 Guillaume le Prouvencel was a *page des chiens* (page of hounds), the lowest ranked and lowest paid office in the hunting establishment of King Charles VI of France, with the exception of the 'two poor varlets who sleep with the hounds and receive no wages'. There were eight other pages of hounds. There were also three *pages des lévriers* (pages of greyhounds), who had the same wages as the pages of hounds, but who were probably somewhat looked down on. A *page* might sometimes change from looking after greyhounds to looking after running-hounds as he gained experience, but on the whole such transfers were a rarity. The *pages'* wages for one third of a year, paid on the term days of Candlemas, Ascension Day and All Saints, were six livres, fourteen sous and five deniers.

Another le Prouvencel, Philippot, perhaps an elder brother, perhaps the father of Guillaume, was a *varlet des chiens* (varlet of hounds), with a thrice-yearly wage of just over ten livres. This was one level above the page of hounds. There were also *varlets des lévriers* (varlets of greyhounds, fewterers, sometimes also called in French *veautriers*). The higher grades in the hunting rankings were the *aide de la vénerie* (assistant huntsman), who received a total of twenty-seven livres, three sous and four deniers per term, and the *veneur* (huntsman), who received forty-six livres, seventeen sous and four deniers. The whole establishment was under the direction of the *Maistre Veneur et Maistre des Eaues et des Forests* (Master Huntsman and Master of Waters and Forests), who received payments of just under ninety-five livres thrice yearly. On the same financial footing as the *aides* was a single *clerc de la vénerie* (clerk of the hunt); it is uncertain how far he participated actively in the hunt, but his main role was organizational and clerical.

These details are gleaned from the hunting accounts compiled, in triplicate, by the clerks of the hunt in the last few years of the fourteenth century. The accounts survive in several neatly written and immensely informative manuscripts in the French National Library.[1] One interesting aspect is the surnames of the huntsmen, which are linked with their office in some cases. The modern English *Hunter* and *Parker* have obvious derivations, but some of the huntsmen in the French accounts have more specific surnames which must have originated as nicknames: as well as the obvious Gillet Parquier, we find Jehan Corneprise, 'John Blow-the-death'; Jehan Huelievre, 'John Halloo-the-hare'; and Guillot le Mastinier, 'Guillot the Mastiff-man' (see Appendix I, p. 258). We may deduce that the profession of huntsman was one in which family tradition was strong. Guillaume and Philippot le Prouvencel are one of the many cases of the repetition of a surname: Guillaume and Louys de Cochet, both *veneurs*; Robert and Mahieu de Franconville, both *veneurs*; Perrin and Guillaume le Parquier, both *varlets des chiens*; Robin Rasson, *varlet des chiens*, and Adam Rasson, *varlet des lévriers*. Philippe de la Chambre, *clerc de la vénerie*, is succeeded in that office by his nephew, Gervaisot de la Chambre.

So, too, at the higher levels: the *Maistre Veneur* in the 1390s is Messire Philippe de Courguilleroy, described as a *chevalier* (knight); one of the *veneurs* is Jehan de Courguilleroy, *escuier* (squire). In the higher grades the profession of huntsman was compatible with nobility; the Franconvilles, too, are squires. Indeed, it appears that a huntsman not born into the nobility could aspire to become a squire and presumably, therefore, a knight. In the higher levels of the profession, and only in those levels, he was, as we shall see, mounted. While not synonymous with being a nobleman, enjoying the right to ride a horse was an important factor related to the concept of the *chevalier* in the Middle Ages.[2] In 1443 Alfonso v of Portugal includes among the beneficiaries of a specific tax, along with mounted and foot huntsmen, the *Escudeiros de El Rei* (King's Squires); he also recognizes that they fall under the control and are subject to the censure of the Master Huntsman.[3] They must have been either scions of the nobility who had entered service with the king's hunt, or mounted huntsmen who, with the king's favour, were making their way into the nobility.

The latter possibility is supported by John I of Portugal in his *Livro da montaria*. In a typically stern and moralizing chapter, after telling knights and squires not to become so obsessed with hunting as to estrange themselves from the rest of society, he writes that 'likewise the *moços do monte* [foot huntsmen] should always be considering how they may become *escudeiros*, or how they may make a good marriage . . . for they should avoid such things as may prevent them from achieving these aims.' Men progress in life by doing what is good and serving their master, he says, and 'not by being huntsmen and thinking that this means that they have to behave badly and frequent taverns and whorehouses'.[4]

The full royal French hunting establishment at the Feast of All Saints, 1393, consisted of the Master Huntsman, six *veneurs*, two *aides*, the Clerk of the Venery, eight varlets of hounds, three varlets of greyhounds, nine pages of hounds and three pages of greyhounds.[5] Five years later, in 1398, some had prospered more than others. Philippot and Guillaume le Prouvencel had both been promoted, the former to be an *aide* and the latter a *varlet*. Two of the *aides*, Gilles Brossart and Richart Potier, had risen to be *veneurs*. Jehan Huelievre, a lowly page of greyhounds in 1393, had become first a page of hounds and then a varlet of hounds, but Jehan Regnault and Guillaume de la Bourne were still pages of greyhounds. Gillet Parquier had just been promoted, halfway through the term, to be varlet of hounds on the death of Guillaume Gloret, and had himself been replaced by a new page, Robin Hennoquel.[6] The wage scale remained unchanged over these five years. A recurring item of expense is the purchase of clothes or shoes for the two poor men who slept with the hounds;[7] presumably they received some food as well, if only the bread which was given to the hounds.

Some of the other late-medieval European monarchs maintained similar establishments. Alfonso XI of Castile mentions over two dozen huntsmen by name in his descriptions of hunts in the *Libro de la montería*, though it is difficult to assess the period covered by his descriptions. Sometimes the huntsmen are accompanied by others, unnamed: 'Pero Carriello spent that night on the hill *con pieza de monteros* [with a band of huntsmen]'; 'We sent Yñigo López and García Ruiz with another four *monteros de pie* [unmounted huntsmen].'[8] The Emperor Ferdinand's registers of correspondence are another source of information, though it is often difficult to know in his case whether men named as, for example, taking greyhounds from one place to another are huntsmen or falconers; in those cases involving hunting-leopards they must have been huntsmen.[9]

We can produce no similarly comprehensive roll-call of names for English or Scottish royal hunting establishments, though references to named huntsmen may be found in, for example, the Treasurer's Accounts of James IV. Certainly to organize bow and stable hunting on the scale described in the *Master of Game*, with two distinct packs of hounds, a considerable stable and numerous fewterers, must have required resources similar to those of the French court. The debt of English hunting to the French does not appear to have extended to the adoption of the same stratified levels of employment; in his version of Phoebus's treatise Edward, Duke of York deletes all the allusions to the grades of *page*, *varlet*, *aide* and *veneur*, and simply describes the educational progress of the huntsman.

Gaston Phoebus's detailed instructions about the training of a huntsman and his progress through the grades correlate perfectly with the system reflected in the royal accounts.[10] A *page des chiens* should start, he tells us, at the age of seven. This may seem young, but 'everyone knows that a child of seven today knows more than a child of twelve when I was young.' *Plus ça change*. The *page*'s first job was to learn the names of all the hounds and bitches in the kennels and to recognize them by sight; for this purpose he was given a written list, which is interesting, in a period when by no means all of the European nobility, even, could read and write. He had to clean out the kennels every morning, replenish the water troughs twice a day, turn over the hounds' straw bedding every three days and replace it entirely once a week.

We can see the *pages* going about their duties in Fig. 15. The hunt kennel, for a large pack of hounds, was a single building about ten *toises* in length and five wide (about 60 feet by 30).[11] The hounds lived on the ground floor, but it was good to have an upper storey as well, as insulation against cold in winter and heat in summer, and an internal fireplace. The hounds slept on beds of oak wood (or, in the royal kennels, of hazel hurdles; see p. 256), raised a foot above the floor and covered by a deep layer of straw. Inside the kennel, but away from the beds, were half a dozen posts bound with straw against which they urinated; the urine was led away through one or two channels in the floor.

On one side of the kennel, preferably to the south, there was a run of the same dimensions as the kennel, walled or fenced. The kennel had doors front and back, and the one leading into the run was normally open. Some of the manuscript miniatures show the kennel as a charmingly designed, symmetrical building, rather like a nineteenth-century bandstand with dormer windows. Fig. 15 shows the ground floor with open sides, but this is probably simply to allow us to see the *pages des chiens* scattering the hounds' bedding inside; the run appears markedly larger than the kennel, in conflict with the instructions of Phoebus's text, but in medieval illustration one must treat proportions with reservation.

In Phoebus's kennels the *pages* had to spend their days and nights with the hounds, partly to prevent them fighting, though in the royal kennels, as we have seen, the night duty was given as a kind of charity to two poor men who *gisent avec les chiens*, literally 'lie with the hounds'. It was probably a cosy enough job on a winter's night, if one could bear the fleas; a few score of slumbering hounds must have worked up enough heat to make the inside of the kennel one of the warmer parts of the castle buildings.

The *pages* were taught to make nets, couples for the hounds and lyams for the lymers. They had to groom the hounds with a comb and rub them down with straw every morning, and take them out twice a day for exercise in an area where they could chew grass if they wanted it, to cure disorders of the canine belly. There was also instruction in the formal language of the hunt, and in horn music. A miniature in one manuscript of Phoebus shows the Count himself giving lessons in horn-blowing to a class of seven (perhaps a rough guide to the size of his hunting establishment, if one compares it to the dozen or so *pages* in the royal hunt accounts); a large white hound listens approvingly. They were also taught the rudiments of uncoupling hounds, and after a hunt it was the duty of the *pages* to find any hounds which were missing by tramping round the neighbouring villages.

It was important to maintain the hounds' feet in good order, especially out of the main hunting seasons. Walking them in stony places helped, but the *pages* also had to trim their claws with scissors. When the hounds' feet were sore after hunting through stony ground they were bathed with salt and water; if they were inflamed, a vinegar-and-soot mixture was used. Feeding the hounds was also the duty of the *pages*. They had to keep an eye open for any hound which was off its food, which would then be given soup and sometimes meat to restore it. It was also important to cut back on food the day before a hunt, but to give the hounds half a loaf of bread at the assembly to keep up their strength through the day.

At the age of fourteen the page was ready to become a *varlet des chiens*. The *varlet* was allowed to accompany a superior in the handling of a lymer, and was introduced to the skills of assessing a hart and a boar by their tracks, droppings, frayings of trees, etc. Tracking was taught with the severed feet of representative dead animals, the instructor making imprints in the soft ground to show the different tracks of the hart at the walk, the hart in flight, the hind, the boar, etc. The *varlet* also learned the hunter's catechism of the specialized vocabulary for describing the droppings, etc. of different animals, and the various states of a stag's antlers, and he was taught the virtue of combining keenness with quietude of bearing, 'that he be both at feelde and at woode delyvered and wel eyed and wel avised of his speche and of his termys, and ever glad to learne, and that he be no boostour ne jangelere'.[12]

The *varlet* also had to learn the ceremonial processes of the beginning and the end of the hunt: the quest, the report to the assembly, the moving of hart and boar, the proper unmaking of both animals, and the ritual of the *curée* (though the unmaking and *curée* after a *par force* hunt would normally be carried out by some noble member of the company, a *veneur*, or at the very least an *aide*).

The huntsman's next promotion was a double elevation: neither *page* nor *varlet des chiens* was mounted, but on promotion to *aide de la vénerie*, at about the age of twenty, one acquired a couple of horses. Phoebus's picture of an *aide* shows him rather grandly attired, with an air of noble maturity.[13]

He was expected to take part in the quest, but on horseback, with a *varlet* on foot handling the lymer under his direction. Both *varlets* and *aides* were expected to keep a lymer in their own quarters, according to Phoebus. The *aide* would dismount to check the *varlet*'s findings, and if the hart was selected for the hunt after the report to the assembly, the *aide* himself would handle the lymer in the moving of the hart, and supervise the uncoupling of the hounds. After that he had an active role in controlling the hounds from horseback, riding the *menée*, i.e. close behind them, driving them back to the scent if they tried to change, and blowing the relevant calls.

An *aide* who moved a hart had the right of unmaking it, according to Phoebus. On returning home, the *aide* was allowed a little snack and a drink or two, then he had to supervise the grooming and feeding of his horses by his *varlet* (it appears that an *aide* had his own *varlet* permanently assigned to him), report to his master, and then have supper and drink his wine at his master's expense, and go to his bed.

Phoebus gives no age at which an *aide* should become a *veneur*; no doubt it was a matter of waiting for dead men's shoes. The *veneur* was supplied with three horses, wore leather thigh-boots for protection against thorn and thicket, and rode with a sword and a knife at his belt for killing and unmaking the quarry. He wore green in the summer for the hart-hunting, grey in winter for the boar. He also carried a stick, about thirty inches long, the *estortouere*, partly as a mark of office, but also for its practical purposes: he used it to protect his face by deflecting branches, and to slap his boot to encourage the hounds. From the time when the stags lost their velvet until they cast their antlers, the stick was peeled; for the rest of the year it was not. Sympathetic magic?[14]

The *veneur* had to know everything connected with the practical organization of the hunt: harbouring, placing relays and greyhounds, riding *menée* and guiding the hunting of his hounds, killing the quarry and handling the unmaking and the *curée*. How free a hand he would have with all this would depend on whether he was single-handed or simply one of several *veneurs* under a Master Huntsman, and on how interested his master was in performing some or all of the functions of the huntsman.

At present, similar information on the huntsman's career is lacking for countries other than France. The *Master of Game* reproduces Phoebus's description of duties and training without major modifications, which suggests that English practice was not very different, though the four stages of the career are not specified with the same rigidity. In Spain, Alfonso XI[15] divides huntsmen simply into *monteros de pie* (foot-huntsmen) and *monteros de caballo* (mounted huntsmen). He says nothing about age or remuneration, but there does seem to have been a division of duties, the *montero de*

177

pie being concerned mainly with handling the lymer and tracking, the *montero de caballo* with the working of the whole pack of hounds. Both should be skilled in kennel management; both carried the same equipment: a horn, a weapon (usually a spear for the foot huntsman, a sword or throwing-spear for the horseman), a lyam, flint and steel, and a needle and thread for sewing up wounded hounds. The only difference was that the foot-huntsman also carried a loaf of bread to sustain the hounds if the hunt continued overnight. The Spanish foot-huntsman appears to have been expected to maintain a special relationship with one particular hound, like the French *varlet des chiens*. In Spain, horn-blowing techniques were picked up in spare moments.[16]

Early in their careers, Spanish huntsmen were introduced gradually via the less demanding hunting situations: a foot-huntsman's first serious responsibility might be tracking and moving a quarry when the tracks were obvious because of previous snow, or rain-softened ground; a mounted huntsman's might be to hunt a small forest in winter with a large *armada* and plenty of alaunts to compensate for his inexperience.

In fifteenth-century Portugal, too, the normal categories appear to have been the *Monteiro Moor* (Master Huntsman), the *monteiro de cavallo* (corresponding to both *veneur* and *aide* in France) and the *moço do monte* (corresponding to *varlet* and *page*). *Moço* is not a very complimentary word; it implies youth or inferior status. Certain Portuguese documents, however, also mention *monteiros da camara* (huntsmen of the Chamber) and *moços da camara que tevessem caães do Senhor Rey* (pages of the Chamber in charge of the king's dogs).[17] These were presumably permanent members of the king's retinue, as opposed to the huntsmen attached to a specific reserve such as Santarem. The dogs were probably alaunts, which Alfonso XI recommends keeping in the palace to make them more biddable (see pp. 14, 25), or greyhounds, which Phoebus says should not be kept together in kennels,[18] and which commonly appear in medieval miniatures as royal accoutrements.

John I of Portugal has something to say on hunting clothing.[19] For him colour was of no great importance, but practicality mattered to some degree: narrow sleeves, or leg-of-mutton sleeves, narrow from the elbow to the wrist ('provided this does not conflict too grossly with fashion'); the tunic should not come below the knee, even for the mounted huntsman; boots were essential. In one of the hunts described by Gace de la Vigne, in contrast,

> . . . the *veneurs* mounted up,
> . . . there were *aides*, pages, *varlets de chiens*;
> Everyone was dressed in green,
> For everyone there was to do with the hunt.[20]

In the medieval illustrations there is little consistency in the colouring of hunting garments. The suggestion by Phoebus that the huntsman should wear green in summer and grey in winter has some support in the miniatures of the many manuscripts of his book and of the *Livre du Roy Modus*, in which grey and green are the dominant colours, but it was obviously not a universally observed precept. The clothing of both mounted and foot-huntsmen varies in colour within a single manuscript, and the colours include others in addition to green and grey. The *varlet* handling the lymer in Fig. 1, for instance, has one stocking green and the other red. Some miniatures show a distinction in colour of livery between the mounted huntsmen and those on foot; a picture of the *curée* of a hart in a manuscript of the Arsénal Library, Paris, shows the mounted huntsman in blue and red and his subordinates in uniform green; in the same manuscript's illustrations of boar-hunting the rank and file are in uniform grey.[21]

For archers and fewterers waiting at the stands and trysts, green clothing would obviously be desirable, and is specified in some descriptions of bow and stable hunting (see pp. 49–52). The gorgeous company in the Devonshire tapestries, however, are dressed in all the colours of the rainbow. In the paintings of Lucas Cranach and in the Grimani Breviary, too, while the employed huntsmen and some of the noble archers are suitably dressed in green, some of the aristocrats taking part, especially the ladies, are using the occasion for a display of colourful fashion.

As well as their wages (sevenpence halfpenny a day to William Twiti, Edward II's huntsman in 1322; ninepence a day in 1323 and 1326; twelve pence a day to the Master of the Hart-hounds in the early fifteenth century) huntsmen received perquisites and had certain rights and protections. In fourteenth-century Spain they were specially protected against assault or imprisonment while hunting: anyone who killed, injured or seized a huntsman, even if he was in a situation of formal dispute or challenge with him, could be imprisoned or exiled. Huntsmen were protected against hunger and thirst: they could demand food for their hounds, and bread and wine for themselves (one loaf, and enough wine to fill a hunting-horn) from any householder during the course of a hunt, or when benighted, either with payment or simply on the promise of it (see Appendix IV, p. 267).

The huntsman's perquisites could be unconnected with the course and success of a hunt, or directly linked to them and to his individual role. The hunting establishment of Alfonso V of Portugal in Santarem benefited from the fines imposed for poaching in the forest, and was probably thereby encouraged to be more vigilant in suppressing it. There appears to have been some dispute in the matter; Alfonso's decree of 1435 mentions that in the reign of his father the fine for killing a boar or piglet, burning undergrowth or setting traps in the Santarem reserve had been twenty-five *libras*, which had gone to the local huntsmen, but that more recently the fine had increased to five hundred *libras* and had been paid to Lopo Vaasques, his own Master of Game. He readjusts matters, altering the amount of the fine to two thousand *reis* (the new currency), and allotting a thousand to Lopo Vaasques, five hundred to Vicente Esteves, Master Huntsman of the Santarem reserve, and the rest to the huntsmen; the one who caught the poacher or fire-raiser was to have a double share. There were to be similar share-outs of the fines imposed for deer-poaching (half the penalty for killing a boar) and for stealing wood (two hundred *reis* for firewood; five hundred for large timbers).[22]

Whenever the King visited Lisbon (but not more than once a year) the Moorish population of the city paid a special tax to furnish various household necessities – pots, candlesticks, etc. – to the huntsmen (mounted and on foot) and the pages of the King's Chamber who looked after dogs. Vicente Esteves, again, received a double share (see Appendix v, p. 270).

In France, Spain, England and Germany certain persons associated with the hunt had the right to certain perquisites after the kill. In the case of a *par force* hunt, this was relatively straightforward, and the number of items to be disposed of was limited by the fact of there being only one beast. Different authorities vary considerably in their instructions, and it is difficult to know whether this is due to lapse of time or to national and regional custom. Twiti simply states that the huntsman in charge of the hounds has the hide as his right or *droit*, and whoever flays the hart takes a shoulder. Certain titbits were reserved for the lord's table (see p. 42), according to Phoebus. The presentation of the head or foot of the hart to a lady is a literary commonplace,[23] though in the practicalities of the everyday hunt the first right to the head went to the lymer, which was allowed to worry it while the running-hounds were receiving their *curée* (see Fig. 7). In the practice of some hunts, however, the head was the right of the lord, and if especially fine it might be carried into the hall at supper.

Phoebus mentions in passing that the neck of the hart (with perhaps the shoulders; the wording is ambiguous) should go to the *veneurs* and *varlets*, but here as elsewhere the hounds had the greater right: if there were many hounds, or if they had worked exceptionally well, or were thin, the neck and shoulders were chopped up and mixed with the offal for the *curée*.[24] According to a manuscript in the Bodleian Library, Oxford,[25] the left shoulder goes to the huntsman who unmakes the hart, the right shoulder to the forester, the liver to the 'Foster knave' (probably the forester's assistant), and the rest of the carcass, the head, numbles and *fourchée* are taken to the lord's gate, where the prise is blown before they are taken inside. The 'bone' in the middle of the heart is given to the lord or to a child, since it is 'medecynable for many emaladis [maladies]'. After the *par force* hunt described by Gace de la Vigne the king, delighted by the magnificent head of the hart, which is brought in during supper, rewards the huntsman who unharboured it with a large supply of firewood.[26]

After *par force* hunting in Spain the rewards were rather more generous and more widely distributed: a substantial proportion of the carcass, after a boar-hunt, was dispersed to huntsmen who had fulfilled particular roles such as unharbouring the boar, releasing the first relay, finding the boar again when hounds had lost him, striking the first blow with a spear, etc. If the quarry was a stag, the reward might be a joint of venison or the hide; if it was a bear, the head and paws, or the hide, which could then be sold to the king or to the lord (see Appendix IV).

After a bow and stable hunt, with rows of dead deer to consider, matters became more complex and, at times, litigious. Archers, huntsmen and fewterers had to be rewarded, 'eche freke [man] for his fee, as fallez to have'.[27] The *Master of Game*, consequently, goes to some lengths in describing a system of 'fees' which preserves certain aspects of the procedures recommended by Phoebus, but which is complicated by the participation of archers and fewterers and by the need to reward the handlers of two distinct packs of hounds. It is clear that disputes were commonplace: 'Every man, bowe and feutrere, that hath out [i.e. anything] slayn shuld mark it [it is not clear whether he means "mark it down" or "put a mark on it"] that he myghte chalaunge his fee, and have it at quirre, but that he be ware that he mark no lordes marke ne feutreres ne hunters for lesyng of his fee'; 'And as of fees it is to wete that what man be sette or smytt a deere at his tree with a deethes stroke, and he be rekeveryd bi the sonne goyng doun, he shal have the skynn, and if he be not sette or goo from his tree or do other wise than it is sayde he shalle non have. And as of feutrers if thei be sette, the first teisoure and the reseeyvour that draweth hym doun shal part the skyn'; 'And the deeres nekkis ben the hunters, and that oon shulder and the chyne is his that undoth the deere and that other chuldere is the forsters or the parkers fee that kepeth the baly that is hunted, and alle the skynnes of hertis slayn with strength of the hert hounds ben the maister of the hert houndes fee.'

Practices varied. In the matter of the reward for the participation of the greyhounds, 'nathelees, in other lordis huntyng who pincheth [i.e. bites the deer] first and gooth therwith to the deethe he shalle have the skyn'. The question of whether a slain beast was a hart or a younger animal was a matter with substantial financial implications for the Master of the

Harriers, since the latter had as his right (possibly for dispersal among his subordinates) the skins of the rascal: 'The fees of alle the folies ben the maisters of the eirers, if so be that he be or his depute at the huntyng and blow .iii. mote, and ellis not. . . . And al shalle be juged foly of rede deer bineth hert and of falowe deer bynethe the buk.' The disputes went to arbitration: 'Nathelees if the eirere wil chalaunge a deer for foly that were noon, if he be a strif with hym that asketh the fee therof, the maister of the game shal deme [judge] it, and right so shal he do of alle the strives for fees bitwene bowe and bowe, and feutrere and fewtrere, and of alle other strives and discordes that longen to huntyng.'[28]

The *Craft of Venery* disperses rewards with a slightly different system (here again the instructions relate to the large numbers of deer killed in bow and stable hunting). The rewards differ according to whether the quarry is red or fallow deer: '. . . the greyhound that pynchithe hym furst and cometh to the dethe of the beste [beast] schall have the hide by ryght, be it buk or do, but nought of herte ne hynde, for he that restreynethe it schall have the hide evermore.' The rules for rewarding the bowmen, too, are more complex:

he that draweth furst blode of hym, yf it be withyn the IIII quarters, schall have the hide, and yf he smyte without the IIII quarters and another smyte withynne the IIII quarters, he that smytithe last schall have the hide, be it hert or bucke. And if the lordes hunt[er] be present and have blowe his mots with his horne, he schall have the necke and the hedde of every beste that is taken in his presens thoughe none of his houndez be uncoupled. And yf the hunter be not present, he that settithe the wanles schall have the same fee of the bests that been take at the wanles of grey houndez.

Here again there are hints of conflicting claims:

. . . yf it be hurt with archers and the lord have a barcelet and sue the beste, he schall have the fee, and ellys the master forster schall have the fee or els he that makithe the sute best. . . . Moreover, yf the quarter be sett as y seid be fore and the beste come into the launde and the greyhoundez pynche it and the beste ascapithe and wodithe and comethe to the archers and be y hurte with eny ercher, and the greyhound sue and take the best, the greyhound schall have the fee and the archer a peny for his schote. In parke may no man ask no fee but with the will of the lord. . . . The hunter schall have his fee, and every man aftur his right. Yf eny of this bests ben takyn in forest or parke out of sesonne, the hed is forfet to hym that ownithe the chace and the fee is the master forsters or parkers.[29]

Medieval accounts of hunting, be they literary or practical, convey an impression of a special occasion, enjoyed by all. They were written, mostly, by men who could choose to hunt or not, as they pleased. The attitudes of the employed huntsmen must have been much more workaday; historical records reveal that they spent much of their time not as partners in royal sport, but as providers of the royal venison. In England, particularly, huntsmen and hounds were sent all over the country, accompanied by a lardener who took charge of and normally salted the slaughtered deer. The sheriff of the shire had to provide not only salt and barrels, but the wages of the huntsmen while they were in his area. On 1 July 1311, for example, King Edward ordered the Sheriff of Southampton

> to pay to the King's yeoman John Lovel, whom the King is sending with twenty-four running-hounds, six greyhounds, two berners and a fewterer to take the King's fat venison in the said county, his wages from midsummer last at the rate of 12d. daily whilst in his bailiwick, and 3d. daily for the two berners, 2d. daily for the fewterer and 1/2d. daily for each of the above hounds and greyhounds. He is also to deliver to him salt for the said venison and carriage for the same to London.

On the same day an order went to the Sheriff of Northampton regarding 'William de Balliolo and Robert Squyer, huntsmen whom the King is sending with twenty-four harriers, eighteen greyhounds, two berners, two fewterers, a berceletter, a bercelet and a lardener to take harts in Whitlewode forest'.[30]

The three men alluded to in these documents were the most important figures in the royal hunting establishment. John Lovel was Master of the Buck-hounds, with kennels at Hunter's Manor, Little Weldon, Northamptonshire. Robert Squyer or Le Squier was Master of the Harriers, and William de Balliolo probably Master of the Hart-hounds; all had the same wages of 12d. per day. They were much travelled men, if one can accept the year 1313 as typical. On 26 January Lovel was sent to Wiltshire with two berners, a fewterer, twenty-four buck-hounds and six greyhounds. On 12 February Balliolo went to hunt in Norfolk and Suffolk with two berners, two fewterers, twenty-four running-hounds, twelve greyhounds and a bercelet. On 16 May Squyer was sent to take deer in Huntingdon with two berners, two fewterers, twenty-four running-hounds, twelve greyhounds and a bercelet. On 27 July all three were despatched, with precise orders. Lovel set off for Wiltshire, Southampton and Berkshire with twenty-four buck-hounds, sixteen greyhounds and a bercelet; he was to take the following deer: twelve harts and six bucks in Windsor Forest, six bucks at Asshele, six bucks in Bristol Chase, twelve bucks and four harts in

Wolvemere Forest, six bucks in Freemantel Park, six bucks and eight harts in Pambere Forest and twelve bucks in Claryndon Forest. Balliolo and Squyer set off for Nottinghamshire, Derbyshire, Huntingdon, Northampton and Essex, with orders for a total of sixty bucks, thirty-four harts and forty hinds. On 13 October Lovel was sent to Wiltshire, and on 10 November he went to Wolmere to take eight hinds and ten bucks. On the same day Squyer left for Windsor and Essex with orders for another twenty-six bucks and fourteen hinds.[31]

It is hard to see how these numbers could be achieved by such small groups of huntsmen without local help. Such hunting cannot have been done in the classic *par force* manner. The large numbers of greyhounds accompanying the running-hounds, the presence of bercelets rather than lymers, and the fact that Balliolo and Squyer often travelled together all suggest that the hunting would be done with bow and stable, and that local help must have been provided. It would be impossible, for example, for a couple of fewterers to handle all the greyhounds in the hunting field. For the huntsmen, waking in the morning far from home, with their quota of deer unachieved, these hunts for the larder must have been a wearisome business, and they probably awaited with a grim fatalism days such as 14 and 15 July 1313, when they received orders for the taking of 646 deer in thirty-three different forests and parks.[32]

A Master Huntsman's power over those under him was not limited to settling disputes; in Portugal, at least, Vicente Esteves could deprive a huntsman of his office and replace him, punish him, and even send him to prison for dereliction of duty (see Appendix v, p. 270). Cowardice might endanger one's fellows; Alfonso XI of Castile's *Fuero de los monteros* lays down that 'if two huntsmen go to strike a beast, and one of them runs away instead of helping his companion, and it is proved by the testimony of another, he shall have no fee. Moreover, he shall not eat with his fellow huntsmen for a month.'[33]

Alfonso's punishments are directed, too, at huntsmen who lose either their hounds or themselves: 'Any man releasing a hound, whether his own or someone else's, should not come home without it, or without at least bringing information as to its whereabouts; otherwise his master should punish him and cast him out'; 'Any huntsman returning home without the lord with whom he went to the forest, unless he is bringing a dead beast or a wounded hound, or is wounded or lame himself, should lose his ration for a month and be upbraided or beaten.' The theft of another huntsman's hound was a shameful thing, and earned a suitably humiliating punishment: the thief was made to *sorrabar* the hound, i.e. to kiss it under its tail, and the hound was returned to the owner. If the culprit was of noble birth, his humiliation was limited to the publication of his infamous conduct.[34]

Alfonso had a very short way with huntsmen who failed to make the grade, rather like tearing off an officer's buttons on the parade-ground:

> Take him to the forest, and put him on the day-old trail of a bear or boar, with his spear in his hand, and his leash, and his horn around his neck, and order two huntsmen to go with him some little way, and then to snatch his spear and his leash from him, and to break his horn over his head. And thenceforth he shall have nothing to do with hunting, and his companions shall look on him as ill-omened, and if he tries to join in any hunting he shall be turned away.[35]

In contrast, the bond of respect between a keen hunting monarch and his older huntsmen could be considerable. John I of Portugal stresses the importance of the king knowing every one of his huntsmen by name, and of their loving him as well as fearing and respecting him.[36] Alfonso XI looks back with affection on the huntsmen, now dead, who sought the bear and boar with him through the snowy sierras. It is when he is listing the most difficult things for a trainee hunter to do well: 'A huntsman who can find and move a quarry under such circumstances . . . will be fit to be ranked with Martín Gil and Diego Bravo when they were alive.' Diego Bravo died fighting the Moors at the siege of Algeciras.[37]

The fellowship of everyone connected with the hunt is exemplified in the custom of celebrating the first and last hart of the season with a special supper for the huntsmen:

> The shergeant or the yemen shul goo on theire offices bihalfe and axe theire fees, the which I reporte me to the old statutis and custumes of the kyngges hous, and . . . the Maister of the Game ougt to spekis to the officers that alle the hunters soper be well ordeyned, and that thei drynk non ale, for nothing but alle wyne that nyght, for the good and grete labour that thei have had for the lordes game and disport, and for the exploit and makyng of the houndes, and also that thei the more merily and gladly telle what ech of hem hath don of alle the day, and which houndes have best ronne and boldliest.[38]

Loyalty and efficiency also had their long-term rewards. On reaching the age of seventy, retired Portuguese royal huntsmen continued to receive the same protection and privileges as the working huntsman (see Appendix V, p. 270). In England, William Twiti was accommodated in retirement in Reading Abbey, with a royal pension. His presence there seems to have been short-lived: he was still receiving the wages of a working huntsman in 1326, but already in 1328 he was probably dead. The Abbot of Reading was asked to provide for Alan de Leek, another royal huntsman, the same hospitality which Twiti had had.[39] Monastic surroundings and idleness may have been too much for William; he lived too soon to learn from Gaston Phoebus that huntsmen do not need to hear the prayers of monks and the cloister bell to find Paradise.

14

Hawk Species and Social Imagery

Mirry Margaret,
As mydsomer flowre,
Jentill as fawcoun
Or hawke of the towre;

With solace and gladnes,
Moche mirthe and no madnes,
All good and no badnes,
So joyously,
So maydenly,
So womanly
Her demeyning
In every thynge,
Far, far passynge
That I can endyght,
Or suffice to wryght
Of mirry Margarete
As mydsomer flowre,
Jentyll as fawcoun
Or hawke of the towre.[1]

'Jentill as fawcoun'. Nothing to do with gentleness, clearly. Gentility, rather; nobility. John Skelton's allusion is to the term 'falcon gentle', usually a synonym for the peregrine, which is one kind of 'hawk of the tower'. The first term is generic; the second alludes to the mode of flight. The distinction between the *hawk of the tower* and the *hawk of the fist* is, broadly, the same as that between the falcons (*falconidae*) and the hawks (*accipitridae*). It is partly clarified in the well-known list of the *Boke of St Albans*:

Theys be the names of all maner of hawkes. First an Egle, a Bawtere, a Melowne. The symplest of theis .iii. will flee an Hynde calfe, a Fawn, a Roo, a Kydde, an Elke, a Crane, a Bustarde, a Storke, a Swan, a Fox in the playn grownde. And theis be not enlured ne reclaymed, because that thay be so ponderowse to the perch portatiff. And theis .iii. by ther nature belong to an Emprowre.

Ther is a Gerfawken. A Tercell of a gerfauken. And theys belong to a Kyng.

Ther is a Fawken gentill, and a Tercell gentill, and theys be for a prynce.

Ther is a Fawken of the rock. And that is for a duke.

Ther is a Fawken peregryne. And that is for an Erle.

Also ther is a Bastarde and that hauke is for a Baron.

Ther is a Sacre and a Sacret. And theis be for a Knyght.

Ther is a Lanare and a Lanrett. And theys belong to a Squyer.

Ther is a Merlyon. And that hawke is for a lady.

Ther is an Hoby. And that hauke is for a yong man. And theys be *hawkes of the towre*: and ben both Ilurid to be calde and reclaymed.

And yit ther be moo kyndis of hawkes. Ther is a Goshawke, and that hawke is for a yeman. Ther is a Tercell. And that is for a powere man. Ther is a Spare Hawke, and he is an hawke for a prest. There is a Muskyte. And he is for an holiwater clerke. *And theis be of an oder maner kynde*, for thay flie to Querre and to fer Jutty and to Jutty fferry.[2]

To a working falconer, much of this list would appear as pretty fair nonsense. Eagles have been trained to take prey, but are to all intents and purposes useless, and are generally ignored by the medieval practical treatises; so are the 'bawtere' (vulture) and the 'melowne' (kite?). A prince or a nobleman of any social level would be unlikely to use the highly temperamental and physically fragile musket (the male sparrowhawk), or perhaps the hobby, but with these exceptions he might use any or all of the birds in the list, including the tercels (males), depending on his means, the terrain surrounding his home, the availability of quarry and the season of the year. The Spanish epic hero, El Cid, a member of the lower nobility, unjustly disgraced, exiled by his king and leaving his desolate home near Burgos, turns his head and sees:

> . . . open doors and gates without locks,
> empty perches, stripped of cloaks and mantles,
> stripped of their falcons and their mewed goshawks.[3]

The author of the *Boke of St Albans* would have been surprised by the credulity with which its now hackneyed allocation of species continues to be accepted. It is partly a piece of fun: the musket would suit the holy-water clerk because it hardly eats anything and because its neurotic behaviour would drive a profane layman to perdition. King Modus divides the birds rather differently between the two basic categories: for him the hawks of the tower are the falcon, lanner, saker and hobby, and he includes among the hawks of the fist not only the goshawk and sparrowhawk but, surprisingly, the gyrfalcon and merlin.[4]

Nevertheless, the social vision exemplified in the list of the *Boke of St Albans* is important in the interpretation of medieval imaginative literature in which falconry motifs occur. In its simplest form, the division of the eagle from the rest, it is the basis of the various medieval versions of the tale of the punished falcon. In Bandello's *Novellino* the Emperor Frederick's falcon, 'worth more to him than a city,' is cast off after a crane, but kills an eagle instead. Frederick hastens to the kill, expecting a dead crane; when he finds the eagle he has the falcon ceremonially beheaded, 'because it had killed its lord'.[5] In Bandello's other, more sympathetic version of the same tale, the hunter is the King of Persia. He has a special dais, richly decorated, erected after the death of the eagle; a small golden crown is placed on the falcon's head, in recognition of its valour, and it is then decapitated.[6] In a version involving an unspecified king of England, an eagle pursues a hunting falcon which takes refuge in a flock of sheep; the eagle pokes its head through the hurdle of the sheepfold and the falcon kills it. The courtiers, *tam milites quam adolescentes nobiles* ('both knights and young noblemen') praise the deed; the king, seeing it as an example of *lèse-majesté*, orders the falcon to be hanged.[7]

The Spanish fifteenth-century court poet Villasandino concocted, with an obscure collaborator, a political debate in verse in which the eagle represents John II of Castile; the two gyrfalcons his princely cousins of Aragón; the tercel saker Alvaro de Luna, the court favourite; the owl a plotting prelate.[8] The Scottish *Book of the Howlett*, of the same period, personifies the eagle as an emperor, the erne or sea-eagle as king, gyrfalcons as dukes, the falcon as Earl Marischal, goshawks as military leaders and sparrowhawks as knights.[9]

Less self-consciously hierarchical are the views of the birds of prey expressed by the aristocratic but practical Chancellor of Castile, Pero López de Ayala. He sees falconry as an intrinsically superior activity, an appropriate pastime for the aristocracy.[10] To be a falconer, like adhering to the code of courtly love, or jousting, implies nobility.[11] Furthermore, one sees in his view of the natural world and of the use made of it by the falconer a confirmation of the structure of human society, with certain natural and ineradicable divisions; he accepts that there are beings inherently superior to others, over which they have the power of life and death; beings stronger, abler, cleaner and more refined; in a word, more 'gentle': 'Men saw every day that certain birds, by their nature, take and live on others; and these are the birds of prey, and include the eagle, the goshawk, the falcon, the sparrowhawk . . . they eat no flesh other than the birds which they kill for themselves . . . and of all birds the cleanest are those which live only on live birds.'[12] Within the order of raptors, moreover, Pero López expresses the differences of physical characteristics in social terms:

> The *borní* and *alfaneque* are called lanners; all these are not called falcons, but rather villeins, or, as it were, bastard falcons; only the *neblí* is called falcon gentle, having longer and more slender fingers and a nobler shape, with a smaller head, more pointed wings and a shorter tail, and being less bulky in the back, and more dashing and strong; in its feeding it is more delicate than the other birds, and wishes always to be fed on finer food, and to be borne on the wrist, through its great pride . . . and its heart is likewise great.[13]

> Some think it wrong to speak of the *baharí* before the gyrfalcon . . . but they should not be surprised, for . . . in every land but Spain the *baharí* is called a falcon gentle, because of its conformation and hands and fingers and bravery, in which it resembles the peregrine; this is not true of the gyrfalcon, which, if one studies it, is just like a large lanner, and . . . is a villein in having coarse hands and short fingers.[14]

How much more penetrating an observation than that of the *Boke of St Albans*. For Pero López the greatest glory of falconry is not the imperial eagle, not the gyrfalcon with its kingly robe of ermine, but the peregrine, *neblí*; smaller, less magnificent, but faster, bolder; lofty in two senses; full of pride: 'I have worked more with the *neblí* . . . for in truth this is the noblest and best of the birds of prey, the lord and prince of hunting-birds, and whoever may govern and control the *neblí* may more easily govern the rest.' 'Do not hasten to put up the quarry before your falcon attains her height, for all the nobility and goodness of the falcon lies in her being as lofty as you can make her.'[15]

The peregrine, *cabalgando el viento* (riding the wind), looking down on the world from above, or gentled and caressed on the falconer's wrist with its finely worked hood, its crest of feathers, its distinctive plumage, with those curved, cruel weapons which destroy inferiors at a blow, is almost a physiological extension of its master; an image, conscious or unconscious, of the knight, helmeted and armed in the panoply of the late-medieval passage of arms: 'And the *neblís* are called, in every country, gentle falcons, which means *hidalgos*, and in Spain and Portugal they are called *neblís*; but originally they were called *nobles* and the word became corrupted by time.'[16]

For practical purposes, then, the falconer relied principally on the following birds (the female being, in all cases, larger, more useful and more valuable than the male):

The peregrine

It had many different names, based less on scientific criteria than on plumage, which in turn depended largely on country of origin. In Spain, for example, the northern race (*neblí*), the Mediterranean race (*baharí*) and the African race (*tagarote*) were seen as different species, and used to some degree in different ways. The peregrine was trained to two contrasting modes of flight. It could be made to 'wait on', i.e. to attain altitude over a place where game had been seen or might be expected, so that when the game (such as partridge or wildfowl) was flushed by beaters or dogs the falcon could descend in its brilliant stoop and either kill the prey with a blow of its talons or bind to it and bring it to earth; in a region where the main quarry was what is now classed as wildfowl such a hawk might be called simply 'a hawk for the river'. The other admired sport was heron hawking, in which the quarry tried to escape in a climbing, spiralling (or 'ringing') flight, the falcon pursuing a sometimes apparently unrelated series of upward gyrations until it gained an advantage in height which enabled it to stoop down on the heron, which in the wild it would not have contemplated as prey. This improvement on nature was part of the falconer's pride; the quarry in some areas included other large birds such as the stork, crane, bustard and wild goose.

The gyrfalcon

Despite the reservations of King Modus[17] its quarries and mode of flight were generally similar to those of the peregrine. Heavier and less dashing, and somewhat harder to train, it could exceed the peregrine in a ringing flight, needing fewer gyrations to attain height. The gyrfalcon breeds in Greenland, Iceland and Scandinavia; Scandinavian birds and the occasional birds caught on passage furnished the main supply of what for the average falconer was never more than an expensive rarity. The more beautiful gyrfalcons, sometimes pure white, or with flecks of black which reminded Pero López of the letters of a manuscript and provided such birds with their familiar name of *letrados*, were sometimes kept simply as decorative royal accoutrements.[18]

The saker

The saker was and is the main hunting-bird of Arab falconers. Its breeding grounds are in Eastern Europe and the Middle East, but there were clearly lines of supply from these areas to Western Europe; Pero López de Ayala was fully conversant with the bird's habits and use. Although it was hardier and easier to keep than the peregrine, he thought it not a good hawk for the river. Even modern ornithologists find it difficult to distinguish a light-coloured saker from a dark gyrfalcon, which may account for Pero López's statement that sakers came from Norway, and his description of a favourite bird (notice again the hunter's preoccupation with whiteness as something wondrous): 'I had a Romanian saker which I gave to Don Alvar Pérez de Guzmán, and with its fourth moult two of the main primaries of each wing, and all the feathers around the neck and one tail feather turned as white as a white dove. It was lost, but I believe that had it been moulted again it would have had more white feathers, and eventually turned completely white, for it already had many feathers flecked with white.'[19]

The lanner

This bird, whose range in Europe is now restricted to south-eastern areas, was clearly more widely distributed in the Middle Ages. Pero López mentions many areas of France and Spain as sources of lanners, and says that the finest were taken on passage in the Crau of Arles, in Provence, where their capture seems to have been a minor industry.[20] Humbler in appearance than the peregrine, they were hardier, less choosy in their feeding, and they were useful for the partridge, the heron and, at least in Spain, the hare. They were sometimes flown at the river in company with the peregrine, being less prone to fly off after birds other than those selected as quarry by the falconer, and so acting as a restraining influence on the more wayward and more precious peregrine. Conversely, by flying it regularly with the peregrine, one could teach a lanner to wait on at height, against its normal nature. Once trained to this lanners were commonly flown in couples, working in harmony and acquiring consider-able joint value: one hundred francs of gold for a good couple, according to Pero López.[21]

The alphanet

They bred in North Africa, and were probably infrequently used in Europe, with the exception of Spain; Alicante was one fourteenth-century point of entry. They were flown at the river, and also took partridge and, used in couples, the Spanish hare. Pero López tells us, ruefully, that as soon as they felt the sun on their backs they tended to disappear and fly back to Africa.[22]

The merlin

This pretty little falcon is like a miniature peregrine; easily manned, it would take small birds, and a good hen bird would take partridges. Against a rising lark its flight resembled that of the peregrine against the heron, and lark and falcon might climb up and up until almost lost sight. A good princeling's hawk: 'Prince Philip, son of the King of France, Duke of Burgundy and Count of Flanders, told me that his merlin, a gift from the Duchess of Brittany, had taken two hundred or more partridges that winter' (Pero López again, after one of his French journeys).[23]

The hobby

Another pretty toy, not of great use. It could take small birds, hoopoes in Spain, perhaps partridges in exceptional cases. Flying a hobby must have been very much a fringe activity, or a way of teaching a boy the basics. Pero López includes a very brief chapter on the bird, which is omitted as useless by nearly all the manuscripts of his book.[24]

The goshawk

This bird and the sparrowhawk are the short-winged or true hawks. Their trainer was properly called an austringer, or in the case of the sparrow-hawk, if one was being very pernickety, a sparviter. The goshawk was cast from the fist, usually after the quarry rose, and was not hooded as often as the long-winged hawks. It was generally ill-natured and difficult to man, but was a great slayer of ground game and low-flying birds, its most sporting flight being against walked-up partridge and, in grander country, bustard and pheasant; a great asset to the kitchen, but rather on the level of modern rough-shooting as compared to driven game. A good female could take hares, perhaps not always killing them, though her grip was prodigious, but binding to them until a dog arrived to help. The best birds came from Scandinavia, and consequently the further south one lived the more highly a good goshawk was prized; Pero López expresses astonishment at the hurly-burly performance expected of a goshawk in more northerly countries in contrast to its use in Spain, where it was used to take herons, and where in value and literary symbolism the bird rivals the peregrine.[25]

The sparrowhawk

Only the female was of much use. A good one could take partridges, woodcock and young pheasants; blackbirds and thrushes were a more regular quarry; sometimes larks. Sparrowhawks were often carried by ladies in aristocratic, country-picnic hunts, but were a great nuisance to their trainer, with the same unpredictable personality as the goshawk. It was difficult to assess and regulate their feeding, 'for the leest mysdyetyng and mysentendyng sleth her'.[26] Even when apparently well they were prone to go rigid, fall off the perch and even die out of what seemed to their master to be simply the ultimate manifestation of their innate perversity.

This small but savage little hawk was of great benefit in providing sport when the lordlier goshawks were in their 'soore age', i.e. moulting or mewing, 'for all the whyle thay bene on a butt, the spare hawke occupithe the sseson and fleth the partrich weel, that is to say froom Saynt Margaritys day [10 June] until it be lammas, and so forth in the yere'.[27] She was a provider of welcome titbits; small birds enlivened the medieval diet of the comfortably-off, such as the well-fed fifteenth-century schoolboy who wrote in one of his schoolbooks: 'I have no deleyte in beffe and motyn and such daily metes. I wolde onys have a partrige set before us, or sum other such, and in especiall litell small birdes that I love passyngly well.'[28]

15

The Acquisition and Trading of Hawks

How did one come by one's hawk? If it bred locally, one could catch it oneself; regular nest-sites were carefully guarded. Punishment for disturbing hawks could be savage: in Wartenstein in Austria, in the fifteenth century, a peasant who disturbed hawks was to be blinded if he had no property to confiscate.[1] The local legislation of towns in central and southern Spain, in areas reconquered from the Moors, was concerned to preserve hawks in their nesting season: the *ordenanzas* of Baeza forbid all taking of birds suitable for falconry between 1 March and the end of July; around Granada the ban began in mid-February. In Seville it was forbidden to shoot a bird of a species used in falconry with a bow or crossbow within a league of the city.[2] When Robert of Avenel gave Eskdale to the Church of St Mary of Melrose, he reserved the game rights and *accipitrum et sperveriorum nidos*, the nests of hawks. In a dispute in 1235 about the monks' rights, the document was interpreted as prohibiting them from frightening hawks away or felling trees in which they were known to have previously nested.[3] Abbot's Craig at Stirling was a regular nesting site for falcons, and was raided at royal instigation; James IV's accounts for 1496 include the sum of two shillings, 'giffin to the boy that brocht the towis [ropes] to clym the halk nest in the Abbotiscrag' (see Fig. 35).[4] In July 1508 James paid fourteen shillings 'to Alexander Law, falconar, to tak the hawks of Cragorth', and the same sum 'to Pate Fat Bak, falconar, to bide with him'.[5]

Hawks taken from the nest ('eyasses'), though more easily tamed, caused problems; they had to be taught everything, and were prone to tiresome screaming. The longer one could leave their capture, the better. Young sparrowhawks were available in the wild in all countries of Europe, and were netted or snared shortly after leaving the nest: 'Anoon . . . they will draw somwatt out of the nest, and draw to bowis and come agayn to ther nest, and then thay be clepit Bowessis. And after saynt Margaretis day

thay will flie fro tre to tre, and then thay bene calde Brawncheris. And then
it is time for to tak hem. And .vii. nighttis before Saynt Margaritis day and
.vii. nightis after is beste takyng of sparehawkes.'[6]

Sparrowhawks were occasionally the subject of early breeding experi-
ments. In 1240 the Emperor Frederick ordered all the sparrowhawks in the
county of Molise to be brought together under a special keeper, Walter of
Cicala.[7] The finest sparrowhawks in Spain were those of El Pedroche, near
Córdoba. Pero López tells us that Ruy Páez de Biedma, returning
northward from the Moorish wars, gathered a score of hawks in El
Pedroche, took them home to Galicia and released them in his own woods,
causing a permanent improvement in the quality of the local birds.[8]

Falcons following the migrating flocks of smaller species were commonly taken in the nets of bird-catchers in France and Spain, and might then be
offered to the local nobleman; there is a graphic description of the delight
and clumsy lust for money of a netsman finding a falcon in his net in Gace
de la Vigne's poem.[9] There are copious examples of countrymen turning
up with hawks or falcons at the royal courts in the expectation of reward.
James IV gives three shillings 'to a man of David Ogilviys in Inchmartyne
that brocht a spar halk to the King'.[10] In 1334 Philip VI of France orders the
Baillie of Rouen to 'pay to Guillaume Tanegot and Pierre de la Pommeraie,
for a sore falcon which they caught and brought to us, whatever sum of
money is customary in such a case'.[11] Certain areas, such as the Crau of
Arles and the plains of Brabant, provided a good living for men netting
falcons; the family of Mollen, in Valkenswaard (Holland), still carried on
the profession, using ancient methods of netting with decoy pigeons, in the
twentieth century.[12] The medieval treatises depict various ingenious nets
and engines for the purpose.

With a royal treasury at one's disposal, one could despatch one's own
falconers to the wilder parts of one's kingdom, or even abroad, to catch
birds of prey. James IV sends men away repeatedly: '. . . Downy, falconar,
to pass in the Northland for halkis'; 'Alexander Law . . . to pas in Caithnes
for hawkes'; 'Robert . . . to pas to the Ilis'; '. . . a man that brocht halkis to
the King out of Noroway . . .'. Other sources of his hawks include
Whithorn, Arran, Blebo, Ross, Berwick, Shetland, Atholl, Galloway,
Carrick, Orkney and 'our the Mounth' (the eastern Grampians).[13] The
Emperor Frederick used to send falconers away en masse; in May 1240 he
sent nineteen of them to Malta for hawks.[14] Fernando of Portugal was
another who did things on the grand scale: 'When he sent abroad for birds,
they never brought him fewer than fifty; goshawks, peregrines and
gyrfalcons, all females.'[15]

Hunting-birds were a favourite kingly or aristocratic gift in both literature
and practice.[16] Pero López mentions several such cases: a gyrfalcon sent by

the Grand Master of Prussia to a French aristocrat; a lanner given by the Bishop of León to Pedro the Cruel.[17] The *Tresslerbuch* of Marienburg mentions white goshawks sent as gifts between noblemen, and the despatch of falcons from Königsberg in 1406 as a gift from the Hofmeister of the Deutscher Orden to Henry IV of England.[18] James IV of Scotland pays eight angels 'to Downy, falconar . . . quhen he past to the King of Inglande with halkis', and six angels 'to the Erle of Oxfurdis man that cam for halkis'; he himself receives repeated gifts of hawks from his Scottish nobles, and on one occasion dispenses ten French crowns 'to ane man of Odoneillis of Irland brocht halkis to the King'. [19] King John received a cast of gyrfalcons from the King of Norway.[20] The town of King's Lynn sent a gift of two falcons, with falconer's gloves, to King Edward III in 1344, by the hand of William of Lakenham, when His Majesty was at Castle Rising.[21]

Birds died; birds were lost; the demand for replacements was constant. Enterprising men carried on an exacting but lucrative trade, moving about Scandinavia, the Baltic, Western Europe, the Balkans, the Middle East and North Africa with falcons and hawks. Pero López tells us of his conversations in the ports of the Mediterranean with seafaring men bringing alphanets from Barbary; in Paris with a Genoese merchant resident in Damascus, who was employing German falconers to convey eighty gyrfalcons caught near the Arctic Circle to the Sultan of Babylon for his crane-hawking (after a previous similar enterprise, to maintain his supplier's resolution, the Sultan had paid as much for birds which died during the journey as for those which arrived in good health).[22] The Catalan Ramón Llull describes 'men travelling from the extreme bounds of the Earth [he probably means Scandinavia] with falcons and gyrfalcons to sell them to the Tartars to grow rich'.[23]

There was a general recognition that the finest birds of prey came from Norway and the other Scandinavian countries. This awareness underlies part of the narrative machinery in Gottfried's *Tristan*: the hero's abduction is achieved through the lure of a merchant ship newly arrived from Norway, whose principal cargo is 'fine hunting birds . . . peregrines, merlins, sparrowhawks, both mewed and eyass birds'. Tristan goes on board to buy falcons, becomes absorbed in a chess game, and finds himself kidnapped.[24]

In the fourteenth century the principal staging-post for this trade was Flanders, and particularly Bruges; the new season's birds were brought from Scandinavia and Germany and bought by merchants who dispersed them throughout Europe. In some cases the birds were trained before their further dispersal, especially by the professional falconers of Brabant, the finest in the world according to Pero López: 'They go to Bruges and buy many falcons to train in their own country, and when Lent arrives the birds are manned and flying, and they take them off to Paris, to England, to Cologne and to the Empire to sell them to the nobility . . . I have bought falcons in Paris from Brabantine falconers who came back to Castile with me.'[25] An important centre for the gathering and despatch of birds caught in the Baltic area (Gotland, Livland, Samland and Brandenburg) was Königsberg; records show the departure of consignments of birds for Saxony, Württemberg, the Rhineland, Bavaria, Austria, Bohemia, Hungary, Holland, Burgundy, France and England.[26]

In England, the port of King's Lynn was a point of entry for falcons from Scandinavia; they were sometimes shipped from Norway in direct exchange for East Anglian corn. The royal falcons were often bought there in the thirteenth century, as was the royal wine, and the keeper of the king's gyrfalcons enjoyed rights to the proceeds from a specific shipping tax.[27]

The birds were transported on cadges, rectangular frames carried by a man walking inside with straps over his shoulders. The falcons sat on padded bars. The Königsberg records suggest that a cadge held about a dozen birds, but Pero López's Genoese merchant needed only four cadges for his eighty gyrfalcons.[28] Frederick II gives detailed instructions for the transporting of falcons over long distances: they should have their eyelids seeled (closed by stitching with a thread), and in summer and autumn should preferably be carried at night to avoid the heat of the day and the distractions of birdsong; because of the disruption of their normal digestion they should be fed several times a day on cool, moist meat. In the event of rain the falconer should take the brunt of it himself to protect the birds; one should keep to the woods if possible, shun rustling undergrowth and roaring water, and generally avoid villages and towns.[29]

The commonness of the sparrowhawk meant that nowhere was its value very high. Why, then, did its presence in a cargo of falcons absolve a merchant from paying import dues on them? Pero López is unequivocal on the practice:

> . . . I saw it myself in Cañete, in Aragón; a boat arrived from Provence with seventeen merchants, bringing sakers from Romania and Germany, and Provençal lanners, eighty birds in all, and they had one sparrowhawk with them. As they came into port the sparrowhawk died, and they would not leave the place with their falcons until someone went to Perpignan, gave a Provençal falcon to a knight and took a sparrowhawk in exchange, and brought it back; then off they went with their falcons, being now secure from paying duty on them.[30]

An attempt by the importing country to ensure good treatment of the more precious falcons by the merchants, since only by careful treatment and feeding could a sparrowhawk be kept alive? The sparrowhawk also has a role as a tournament prize, and is used in medieval literature for narrative and symbolic purposes with a frequency disproportionate to its practical usefulness.[31]

Values of trained birds could be surprisingly high, varying with the degree of exoticism and rarity of the bird in question, its plumage, the number of moults it had undergone and its state of training. A mewed or moulted bird was worth more because the moult was a toilsome business and birds often died in the course of it. Hen birds were invariably worth more than the tercel or male. James IV pays three pounds ten shillings 'for ane goshalk at the Rede Castell', but only twenty-eight shillings 'for ane tersell of ane goshalk bocht in Ros'.[32]

The *Tresslerbuch* records of around 1400, as interpreted by Dalby,[33] give the values of a gyrfalcon as four Prussian marks, a male gyr as two marks, a peregrine as one or occasionally two marks, a merlin as half a mark, and a lanner as between one-thirtieth and three-twentieths of a mark. This last figure is difficult to square with Pero López, who tells us that in Paris he saw a pair of trained tercel lanners valued at one hundred gold francs, whereas a first-year trained peregrine was worth only forty, and one trained for heron-hunting seventy, though if mewed they were worth more.[34]

Medieval codes of law give an idea of comparative, though not necessarily market, values. The thirteenth-century German *Schwaben-spiegel* gives the value of a sparrowhawk as one-sixth of that of a goshawk, and a goshawk as equal in value to a peregrine.[35] The Spanish *Fuero de los fijosdalgo* (laws relating to the nobility) lists the fines payable for killing or injuring various birds of prey: for a goshawk trained to take herons, a hundred *sueldos*; a hen goshawk not so trained, sixty; a tercel goshawk thirty; a falcon for heron-hunting three hundred; a good lanner sixty; a sparrowhawk two or three *maravedíes*; an owl (possibly used as a lure for taking other birds of prey, or small birds for the table, as seen in Figure 51) one *maravedí*.[36] Falconers were given special consideration by rural bye-laws; the *Fuero* of Teruel in Aragón specifies a fine of ten *sueldos* for treading down crops, but only five if the accused was carrying a hawk at the time.[37]

There are examples of hawks forming part of rents and ransoms.[38] In an extreme, fictionalized case in a thirteenth-century Spanish epic, the *Poema de Fernán González*, the subject county of Castile gains its independence through the King of León's desire for a horse and a hawk belonging to Count Fernán González; it is agreed that if the price is not paid on time, it will double each day; as a result the King cannot pay and Castile is freed instead, soon to become an independent kingdom and subsequently to dominate León.[39]

16

The Training and Manning of Hawks

Eyasses might be put initially in a hack house, an outbuilding in a quiet area. Once used to it, they were allowed to fly free from it in the daytime, returning to take food and to roost; flying at hack strengthened their feathers and muscles, while maintaining some contact with the world of man. When ready, they were taken from the house at night and seeled or hooded to make them more amenable. Seeling consisted of putting one neat stitch through the lower eyelids with a linen thread and tying the ends over the head (or, as recommended by the *Boke of St Albans*, stitching through the upper lids and tying under the beak[1]). This was commonly done before transportation by the merchants, so as to keep the birds calmer.[2] The eyass or newly-purchased passage bird was then fitted with the following accoutrements:

The jesses: a pair of leather strips tied around the hawk's legs with a special knot, and bearing at their end a metal ring or 'tyret', 'like the mesh of chainmail'.[3] They were about six inches long for a sparrowhawk, ten for a goshawk. The leather had to be soft but durable. In 1508 John Forman supplied James IV with 'twa dog skinnis to be chessis for halkiz', and the Earl of Northumberland's hunting accounts, similarly, include a payment of two shillings for '.ii. doggeskynnes',[4] but jesses were commonly made of calf.

The leash: a long leather strap with a rolled knot at the end; it was passed through the rings on the jesses, and served to tie the bird to its perch. A swivel was sometimes interposed between the leash and the jesses.

The bells. They were tied to the bird's legs with special leather straps called bewits. They were made in different sizes and served to reveal the bird's position to the falconer when hunting, especially after killing in cover, and to warn him if she had bated off her perch in the mews. Making them was a specialized craft. In the fourteenth and fifteenth centuries Milan was celebrated all over Europe for exporting hawk bells,[5] but the

Boke of St Albans recommends those from Dordrecht: 'Off spare hawke bellis ther is choice and lytill charge of thaym, for there beeth plenty. Bot for Goshawkes sometyme Bellis of Melen were calde the best, and thay be full goode for thay comunely be sownden with silver and solde ther after. Bot ther be now used of Duchelande bellys, of a towne calde Durdright, and thay be passing goode, for thay be wele sortid, well sownded, sonowre of ryngyng in shilnes and passing well lastyng.'[6] Pairing bells for pitch was important. Pero López tells us that one should be alto and the other bass, 'to make sweet melody'; the *Boke of St Albans* has a slightly different idea: 'Looke also that thay be . . . not both of oone sowne, bot that oon be a semytoyn under anoder.'[7]

Bells were possibly used less in Germany than elsewhere; they are not mentioned in German practical treatises, though they do appear in literary sources. It may be that the bells were largely for decoration and ostentation, being sometimes of gold, and that the German treatises were aimed principally at the lower gentry, who would be less concerned with this aspect than the aristocracy who were the public for more imaginative literature.[8] German falcons sometimes had a small silver escutcheon, a *schildechin*, attached to their leg, bearing the owner's coat of arms.[9]

James IV of Scotland usually paid six to eight shillings for 'ane dozan halk bellis'.[10] Some bells, however, seem to have been very cheap; a 1431 scrutineer's list of a ship's cargo at Wolfreton, England, includes: '13 duodenarum [dozen] de haukes bellys . . . 13d.'; the same list includes seven dozen thimbles at sevenpence and eleven dozen curtain rings at fivepence halfpenny, so that a bell (presumably imported) was the same price as a thimble and only twice the price of a curtain ring. Obviously inferior goods to those recommended by the *Boke of St Albans*.[11]

The hood was made of leather, sometimes plain and workaday, sometimes of contrasting colours and decorated with a plume of feathers. In France the recommended material was a soft calfskin called *cuir d'abaie*, in Spain *cuero de abadía*, 'abbey leather', so called, according to Pero López, because it was made by the comfortable monks for their own shoes.[12] In Scotland hoods were made of different kinds of leather, and were a sideline of the shoemaker: James IV pays nine shillings 'for ane Portugall skin to be halk hudis', three shillings 'for ane done basand [sheep; cf. French *basane*] skyn, to be halk hudis', and two shillings 'til a sowtar [shoemaker] that sewyt halk hudis to the King'. The large payment of fifty-six shillings to 'Richard Justice, Inglisman, for the making of halk hudis', however, suggests that he may have made a living solely from falconry furnishings.[13]

The lure was a device of weighted leather on a long cord; it was garnished with feathers, often a pair of wings of the intended quarry (Figs. 38,. 39, 47). Its purpose was to recall the hawk after an unsuccessful flight, for which purpose meat was attached to it, and also the bird could be exercised by whirling the lure and snatching it away as the bird passed. A lure received some rough treatment. James IV's were made by John Lethane, 'sadillar'; in 1505 a lure cost five shillings.[14] In the royal or imperial courts, however, lures were sometimes finely embroidered and extremely decorative The falconer himself needed a strong leather glove to protect his left fist from the falcon's talons (James IV paid only sixteen pence for one; eighteen shillings 'to the skynnar of Lythgow' for an unspecified number[15]), and carried a bag of standardized form containing tools, medicines, spare hoods and bells, etc., and perhaps a live hen or two for reward or emergency; courtly falconers had lavishly embroidered bags.[16]

The perch varied according to circumstances and the species of the bird. Indoors the safest perch was a bar supported firmly on uprights at both ends, often with a sheet suspended from it to assist the bird to regain the perch (to which it was tied with the leash) if it bated. Pero López recommends wrapping the bar with a scarlet cloth.[17] During the day falcons might be set on a wooden block like an inverted cone with a spike in the bottom, out of doors (Figs. 37, 39). Short-winged hawks were usually given a bow-perch instead, a stick curved into a semicircle, its ends pushed into the ground, with linen padding to save the bird's feet from corns.

The mews. The medieval writers are vague about dimensions. No doubt if one had only one or two hawks, one kept them in any suitable outhouse or spare room, but the royal falcons were housed in purpose-built mews. James IV pays his Master Falconer, Sir James McCullough, only thirty-six shillings 'to big [i.e. build] ane gallery for halkis'.[18] This was possibly not a very sophisticated structure; James had permanent and temporary establishments of hawks in various places. Some manuscript illuminations, particularly the illustrations to the Emperor Frederick's *De Arte Venandi*, suggest something quite elaborate, at times almost on the lines of a Victorian Gothic folly (Fig. 37). The practical essentials, according to Pero López, were that the mews should be free of draughts, dust and smoke; that the walls should not be lime-washed inside; that there should be at least one window, and that the floor should be clear except for clean sand, so that one could easily find the pellet of fur, feather or bones regurgitated after a meal, on the presence and consistency of which the falconer relied as an indication of the bird's condition. If one really loved one's falcon, however, 'it should sleep in your bedchamber, or that of its keeper, and there should be a lamp burning all night. In Spain falconers leave their birds untied, because if they flew off the perch at night, dreaming that they were hunting, it would be dangerous.' Endearing man; no doubt he dreamed of hunting himself, and took it for granted that his falcons did the same. 'I always left [past tense; he is writing in a Portuguese prison] my falcons loose and near my bed, if they were my favourites.'[19]

Before any training could be done, a hawk had to be made vermin-free. Both Pero López and the *Boke of St Albans* recommend bathing a newly acquired hawk with yellow arsenic ('orpement') to get rid of lice picked up during the congested transportation by the merchants.[20] It then had to be induced to accept the proximity of man. As long as it was seeled or hooded, it would sit reasonably calmly on the fist or perch. One method of manning involved gradually unseeling the eyelids by slackening the thread, so that the bird's vision was progressively restored; Frederick II recommends accustoming the bird to being carried about over several days, introducing it increasingly to noises, conversations, horseback, etc., until it could be completely unseeled.[21] The *Boke of St Albans* combines a complete unseeling with a period of preventing the bird from sleeping:

> . . . cast her on a perch and let hir stande ther a night and a day and on that other day towarde eeven then take and cut eseli the thredes and take hem a way softeli for brekynge of the lyddis of the ighen. Then softe and faire begynne to fede her, and fair fare with her till she will sitte weell uppon the fist, for it is drede for hurtyng of hir wengys. And then the same night after fedyng wake her all nyght and the morow all day. Then she will be previ inowgh to be reclamed.[22]

'Softe and faire': the essence of the whole trepidatious business. Pero López recommends carrying the unseeled hawk on the fist continually for twenty days and nights, hooding and unhooding her frequently, and waking her for the first ten. 'It takes an *hombre sofrido*, a long-suffering man,' he says several times. A subordinate, of course, did most of the suffering, but at least his master had some thought for his comfort: 'Let the man who wakes her through the night have a lamp in his hand, or beside him, and forget not some wine for the falconer and his assistants.'[23]

The bird was fed on the fist, and given its 'tirings' (chicken's wings, or something similar, which involved the hawk in a good deal of tugging and exercise without it consuming much except feathers or fur to provide essential roughage); after a while it was encouraged to jump from the perch to the fist for food, and then to fly from a distance with a long line, the *creance*, attached to its jesses. A long-winged hawk had to be made to fly to the lure; one secured its interest in the lure by allowing it to feed on meat attached to it, then it might be put on a perch outside with some slack in the leash, and made to jump to the lure, and subsequently to fly to it on a creance (Fig. 38), and eventually to fly to the lure unsecured in some quiet, treeless spot and devour some special titbit. 'And all this effort to prepare and tame a peregrine will take thirty days, so that it may be flown at the river,' says Pero López, 'but all depends on the skill of the hunter, and the species and heart of the falcon.'[24] The bird had to be made confident and to come to the lure in the presence of men, horses and dogs, to take the lure thrown in the air, and to fly in company with other falcons, after which it might be entered at live quarry, possibly magpie or partridge, with an experienced, good-tempered and reliable falcon to show it what to do, and then to feed on the prey.[25]

Special techniques were used to persuade a falcon to take the heron or the crane. If one had a good heron-hawk, one allowed the trainee bird to join it in the flight at a point at which the heron was obviously about to be beaten, and then let it eat the heart and wing-bone marrow of the heron on the carcass, supplemented by a chicken leg.[26] King Modus commends the heartless method of taking a live heron and breaking its beak and legs for the initiation of the falcon, and he too mentions the delight taken by the falcon in the bone marrow.[27] Captive birds were evidently commonly used in the training of hawks; we find James IV giving nine shillings 'to ane man brocht herons to the King'; fourteen shillings 'to ane man that brocht quik [live] herons fra the Lard of Dawick'; fourteen pence 'for ane gus to make ane trane to ane halk'; nine shillings to 'falowis to seik bwtoris [probably bitterns] in Baythcartbog'.[28]

Bitterns were also used for human food, however, as were herons; indeed both birds were thought to have restorative properties: 'Wodcok, Betowre, Egret, Snyte and Curlew, heyrounshaw, restoratiff they ar and so is the brewe.'[29] Cranes, too, provided meat for the table: the *Tacuinum Sanitatis* states that they should only be eaten by 'people who do physical work', and that those caught by falcons were preferable, and should be hung to make them palatable (though the illustration of crane-hunting in the *Tacuinum* shows the birds being stalked and shot by a cross-bowman).[30]

When Frederick II needs live cranes, he orders the justiciars of Terra di Lavoro, Bari and the Capitanata to supply as many as possible to be kept at the royal residence.[31] We see his reasons for this in the *De Arte Venandi*, in which Frederick gives instructions for burning off the tip of a crane's claws, binding its beak, seeling its eyes, and weakening its knees by bending the legs into a sling, before mooring it to a stake with meat tied to its back, all for the initiation of a gyrfalcon. Having killed an immobilized crane, the gyrfalcon was allowed to kill a walking crane, similarly weakened, and then a crane flying with a creance.[32]

Frederick also describes an Armenian method for training the less courageous sakers and lanners to take hares: a live piglet was disguised in a hare skin and let loose in the fields; the falcon was slipped, seized the fleeing pig, and received a titbit. It must have provided all-round hilarity, except to the confused and innocuous target. The pig might be spared for future initiations, but the falcon was sometimes allowed to kill it; after a few such flights the bird was ready for the sterner test against a real hare.[33]

17

Food and Medicine

Much of the falconer's craft lay in assessing the amount and type of food which his hawk's species, size, condition, state of health and flying programme demanded. One essential was that it should consume each day some fur or feather, which was later regurgitated. A hawk which had become too bumptious, or prone to wander, or reluctant to come to the lure, might be reduced a little in condition by being given less nutritious meat, a smaller quantity, or meat which had been washed, i.e. soaked in water and wrung out. A convalescent bird might be given something rich and easily digested, such as the breasts of young pigeons.

Not all falconers were rural landowners; in the towns of Spain, for instance, the availability of food for falcons depended partly on the butchers. In the late fifteenth century the town of Avila had a racially mixed population of some three thousand Christians, two thousand Jews and two thousand Muslims. The town ordinances state, specifically for the benefit of falconers, that 'meat for hunting-birds' shall be sold by the Christian butchers every day of the year except on Fridays and Saturdays and during Lent; by the Jewish butchers only during Lent and on other Fridays; and by the Muslims only on Saturdays. The hawks and falcons of the town, therefore, need never go unfed, even on those days when their masters were fasting.[1] The essential standby was the chicken: 'Never forget that the day the falcon was born, that same day was born the chicken,' says Pero López; James IV's treasurer records repeated payments for 'ane hen to the Kingis halkis'.[2]

The trickiest time for feeding was the moult; a closed and fretful season for the hawks, and a worrying one for the falconer. He had two main aims during the moult: to keep his bird in good health and spirits, and to restore it to flying condition as soon as possible. Frederick II's barons probably worried more than most; the Emperor used to disperse his falcons among them to be cared for during the moult.[3] It was not impossible to fly one's birds when they were moulting, but regular flying prolonged the period of the moult, and it was easy to damage the young and tender feathers and thus to affect the bird's appearance and flying ability for the ensuing season.

Some species started and ended their moult earlier than others, and the latitude of the bird's origins and the climate of the area probably affected the dates; Pero López mentions the Mediterranean peregrines and the tartarets as early moulters. Frederick II says that the moult began in the spring. The principal moult, however, according to Pero López, began in the first week of June. He recommends feeding the bird liberally, giving it the rich meat of turtle-doves and pigeon squabs, especially when its main replacement feathers are emerging. The hawk should be housed in a dry, secluded mews, away from noise and smoke, except for the lanners, 'which moult best where they see men'. 'Put in a rock, and sand, and let the bird have a lamp burning through the night; and sometimes give her some green turves, as if it were a meadow, for her pleasure. Feed her on your fist, as much as she will take . . . and observe always whether she is content, and how she bears herself, so that you may aid her with medicines if she needs them.'[4] The *Boke of St Albans*, too, stresses calm seclusion: 'Sett and dispose yowre mew in this maner so that no wesell ner pulcatt ner non other vermyn entre therto, Ner none wynde, ner no grete colde . . . Also that she be not evexed ner greved withe mych noyse, ner with song of men, and that no manner folkes come to hir, but oonly he that fedyth hir.'[5]

Peace, quiet, good feeding, with interesting titbits to keep the bird happy (Pero López suggests the glands from a goat's neck; Modus, green wagtails; the *Boke of St Albans*, cygnets, goslings, mice and eels[6]); thus one achieved one's aim of restoring her to good flying condition early, as the unwitting partridges grew fat on the stubble fields, and the wildfowl further north grew restive for their migration in the shortening days. There were recipes for decoctions to speed the process; several involve adders:

> Take .ii. or .iii. of theym and smyte of ther hedes and thendys of theyr taylis. Then take a new erthen pot that was never used, and cut them into small gobbettys, and put those same therin, and let hem sethe stronglich a grete while at good layser, and let the pot be covered, that no ayre com owte of it ner no breth, and let it sethe so long that the saame colpons seth to grece, then cast it out and doo away the bonis, and geder the grece, and put it in a clene vessill. And as oft as ye fede yowre hawke, anoynt her meete therin, and let hir ete as moch as she will, and that meete shal mewe her at yowre awne will.[7]

Even more deviously, one could stew adders, soak wheat in the gravy, feed chickens on the wheat, and feed the hawk on the chickens. Paradoxically, the *Boke of St Albans* recommends feeding the bird on chopped adder's skin to *postpone* the onset of the moult.[8]

Having one's bird re-feathered and flying early was the mark of a good falconer, and the occasion for comment. Pero López recalls, from decades earlier, 'a falcon of King Pedro's called Doncella [meaning Maiden], a Romanian peregrine . . . mewed and enseamed [rid of the fat which built up during the moult], and killing a heron, in the first week of August'.[9] An Aragonese owner of one manuscript of Pero López's book had something even more noteworthy to boast of, and wrote proudly in the margin: 'I, Pedro Pérez, hunter in Aragón, on the third of July of the year 1561 had a Catalan peregrine from Peña Groguera mewed and clean after her first moult. And so wondrous a thing was set down in this book in commemoration.'[10]

The craft and mystery of medieval falconry was pervaded by a vicarious hypochondria. 'Your eyes should be constantly on your hawk, as a woman's on her mirror,' says Pero López.[11] Descriptions of ailments and medications form substantial sections of the medieval treatises; some works, such as the *Livro de Falcoaria* of the Portuguese royal falconer Pero Menino, consist of nothing else. Cures for mites: 'Take the Juce of wormewode and put it thir thay be and thei shall dye'; for 'an hawke that has the goute: Fede yowre hawke with an Irchyn [hedgehog] onys or twyes, and it shall helpe hir';

> for an hawke that has the stoon: Anoynt her fundement with Oyll, and put the powder of alym with an hole straw. Also take an herbe callid Cristis lardder, and anoynt hir mowthe within and she shall be hooll. Also take smale flambe [iris] rotis and polipodi and the cornes of sporge and grinde it weell and seeth it in butter, and drawe it through a clooth, and make thereof .iii. pellettis of the grettenes of a Not, and put it in hir mowth in the morowtide, and looke that she be voide, and then let hir fast till evensong, and fede hir littill and littill, and she shall be hooll'.[12]

A hawk was prey to endless ailments, many of them no doubt imagined or caused by an unwillingness to let well alone: aggrestyne (itch), agrum (rheum), anguellis (worms), artetik (arthritis?), booches (mouth ulcers), fallera (liver disease), filanders (worms), frounce (mouth sores), gleth (phlegm), podagre (gout?), poose (cough), teyne (asthma?) and general debility or 'unlustynesse'. Most of the cures are based on herbs or spices and a few minerals: saffron, shepherd's purse, canell (cinnamon), gelofre (gillyflower), kersis (watercress), maryall (black nightshade), neppe (catmint), puliall (pennyroyal), venecreke (fenugreek), quicksilver, coral, ashes, urine, heron fat, pigeon or even human dung. The *Boke of St Albans* suggests a searching remedy for 'an hawke that castys wormes at the foundement . . . Take lymayll [filings] of iren and medyll [mix] it with flesh of poorke and yeve it to the hauke ii days for to heete, and she shall be hooll.'[13] And perhaps a little startled.

A treasured ingredient in ointments and pills was mummy, bought from the apothecaries, 'the most precious medicine for falcons' wounds; it is prepared from the flesh of dead men, and the finest is made from the head.' Pero López lists almost sixty ingredients with which the falconer should always be equipped.[14]

Great attention was paid to maintaining the condition of the plumage. A period of poor feeding could result in a visible hunger trace, a weak spot where feathers might break; the *Boke of St Albans* calls this a *taynt*, 'a thyng that gooth overwarte the federis of the wynges and of the tayll, lyke as and it were eetyn with wormys; and it begynyth first to brede at the body in the penne, and that same penne shall frete asonder and falle away thurrow the ssame taynte, and then is the hawke disparagid for all that yere'.[15] Feathers suffered, too, in the struggles of the kill, the bating of the hawk from the perch and the overcrowded conditions of transport by the merchants. A broken feather had to be 'imped': a feather from another bird was cut to size and fixed to the part of the broken feather remaining in the bird with a serrated iron needle glued inside the slanting joint with pine resin. Pride was taken in an invisible mend; Pero López devotes a whole chapter to the technique: 'Take an identical feather, a primary for a primary, a secondary for a secondary, and the colouring must be the same; you must not imp a peregrine with a gyrfalcon's feather, nor vice versa. If the bird is an eyass, find an eyass feather; if mewed, a feather from a mewed bird. It must come from the same wing, and the same position: first primary, second primary, and so forth.'[16] When the quills of the two feathers were fixed together, one then 'married' the strands by stroking them between thumb and finger, much as a man tying salmon flies makes the composite wing of, say, a Green Highlander. In a large mews one needed a ready store of feathers; James IV despatches 'Fatbak, falconar' on a special excursion 'to pas agane fro Dunottir to seik halk federis'.[17] The cliffs near Dunottar Castle, Stonehaven, were still a haunt of peregrines in the nineteenth century.

18

Flying the Hawk

When one reached the stage of flying one's hawk loose in the hunting field, or of flying her again after the moult, one had probably invested in her large expense and long hours of sometimes frustrating devotion. Sometimes one saw all this vanish literally into the blue, and supernatural protection might be sought in advance. *Prince Edward's Book* recommends verbal safeguards: 'In the morowe tyde when ye goo owt and hawkyng sey *In nomine Domini volatilia celi erunt sub pedibus tuis*' (In the name of the Lord the birds of the heavens shall be beneath thy feet);[1] 'Also yf your hawke be rebukyd of any man, sey *quem iniquus homo ligavit dominus per adventum suum soluit*' (Whom the unjust man bound the Lord by his coming set free);[2] 'Also lest she be hurt of the heyron say

> *Vicit leo de tribu iuda*
> *radix david aleluia*

> [The lion conquered, of the tribe of Judah;
> the root of David; Alleluia]'[3]

Falconers were superstitious in other ways. The Spanish version of *Moamin* includes a chapter on avine augury, with much more detail than the well-known evil omen of the crow on the left of the road. An eagle or other bird of prey seen perched on the left indicated plentiful game and a successful hunt. A crow perched on the left indicated a little game, one on the right a larger amount, and one calling on the left meant even more game. If, on leaving home to hunt, one saw snow in front, behind or on the left, it meant that there would be game, but only a little.[4]

If one omitted verbal precautions and disaster ensued, divine help could still put things right. There are several cases in the *Cantigas de Santa María* of Alfonso the Wise of Castile of a falconer's prayer to the Virgin resulting in a minor miracle. If one lost one's hawk, one way of regaining it was to make a short pilgrimage and to offer a wax model of the bird to the Virgin, as did the knight of Vila Sirga, who then had his hawk miraculously restored to him.[5] The Virgin was also disposed to help falconers who were themselves in danger (Fig. 40).

There were more mundane ways of recovering a hawk. Any country-man coming across a hawk with jesses and bells would know that the local aristocrat, or the king if he was in the area, would be pleased to have it. Rewards for such services are a minor but recurring drain on James IV's purse: five shillings 'to ane man that fand ane goshalk of the kingis'; eighteen to 'a man that brocht the kingis halk furth of Tuedale [Tweeddale] that flew away'; three shillings and twopence (probably the available loose change) 'to ane man that fand the kingis sparhalk'.[6] The frequent wayward behaviour of hawks was the main reason for the scorn of falconry expressed by the *Treatyse of Fysshynge wyth an Angle*: 'For often the fawkener leseth his hawkes as the hunter his houndes. Thenne is his game and his dysporte goon. Full often cryeth he and whystlelyth tyll that he be right evyll athurste. His hawke taketh a bowe and lyste not ones on hym rewarde.'[7]

If one could locate the tree in which one's errant hawk had perched, one left the bird alone until night, and captured it with 'a praty craft': 'Looke where an hawke perchith . . . and softe and layserly clymbe to her with a sconce or a lanterne that hath bot oon light in yowre hande, and let the light be towarde the hawke so that she se not yowre face, and ye may take hir by the leggys.'[8] A Persian treatise recommends a breathless variation on this, using a noose:

> Now, my son . . . let hand and foot be steady; think not you are after a goshawk; say to yourself, 'It is the leaf of a tree, or a barn-door fowl.' Do not let your hand shake. This is the advice I can give you; I cannot myself act up to it, nor do I believe that any falconer can. Well, hold the light close to the goshawk's breast. If she is asleep, head under wing, gently, ever so gently, stroke her breast with the horsehair noose to awaken her . . . till she withdraws her head from under her wing. Then pass the noose onto her neck, and pull her down to you.[9]

Dogs were used in falconry, sometimes to find and flush game, sometimes to assist the struggling hawk by seizing large prey which it had brought to the ground. A fresco in the Palazzo Publico in Siena shows two mounted falconers in the middle distance; two black and white dogs resembling pointers are quartering a stubble field, noses to the ground, presumably in search of partridge or quail. The two dogs accompanying the fashionably dressed Italian lady hunting partridges in the *Tacuinum Sanitatis* also look very like modern pointers (Fig 41). The Devonshire tapestries' falconry scene shows a motley variety of dogs: small hounds, greyhounds, spaniels and indeterminate terrier-like beasts with hairy faces.[10]

'Of gentle dogs serving the hawke,' the *Treatise of Englishe Dogges* tell us, '. . . such as play their parts eyther by swiftness of foote, or by often questing, to search out and to spying the byrde for further hope of advauntage, or else by some secrete signe and privy token bewray the place where they fall . . . some be called dogges for the Falcon, the Pheasant, the Partridge and such like; the Common sort of people call them by one generall word, namely *Spaniells*.' Evidently different colours of spaniel were national characteristics:

> The most part of their skynnes are white, and if they be marcked with any spottes, they are commonly red, and somewhat great there- withall . . . othersome of them be reddishe and blackishe, but of that sorte there be but a very few. There is also at this day among us a newe kind of dogge broughte out of France . . . and thay been speckled all over with white and black, which mingled colours incline to a marble blewe, which bewtifyeth their skinnes and affordeth a seemly show of comlynesse. These are called French dogges.[11]

The *Treatise* also gives a graphic picture of setters:

> making no noise either with foote or with tounge, whiles they followe the game. These attend diligently on their Master and frame their conditions to such beckes, motions, and gestures as it shall please him to exhibite and make, either going forward, drawing backeward, inclining to the right hand, or yealding toward the left; . . . when he hath found the byrde, he keepeth sure and fast silence, he stayeth his steppes and wil proceede no further, and with a close, covert, watching eye layeth his belly to the grounde and so creepeth forward like a worm. . . .[12]

For Gaston Phoebus, bird-dogs and spaniels (*espaignoulx*, from *Espaigne*, Spain) are synonymous: 'They love their master . . . and willingly go before him all day, questing and wagging their tails, and put up all manner of birds and animals, but their true calling is the partridge and the quail; a fine thing for a man with a good goshawk or falcon, lanner or saker, or for flushing small birds for the sparrowhawk.' Phoebus, however, used to the single-minded running-hound, has had grievous experiences with spaniels, 'as one would only expect from dogs of their country of origin'. They chase sheep, hens and cattle, bark, riot . . . 'They have so many evil traits that if I had not a goshawk on my fist, or a falcon or sparrowhawk . . . I should have nothing to do with them.'[13]

To assist hawks trained to take the larger birds such as heron, crane or bustard, Frederick II recommends a medium-sized greyhound, mainly because of its speed in reaching a struggling quarry in time to prevent it from injuring the falcon. The dog should be male, brave in nature, totally obedient, and must never be used in hunting quadrupeds. It should be in the company of the falcon from puppyhood, fed at the same time and from the same hand; it should be aware of the master's love for the bird, and should recognize her scent. Then it should be trained to follow the falcon, first to the lure (garnished with a piece of cheese), then to a captive wild or domestic goose, and eventually to wild quarry.[14]

The more aristocratic hunts also needed beaters. Fernando of Portugal used Moorish slaves;[15] James IV of Scotland used the local children, but did at least pay them: two shillings 'giffin to the laddis that ran with the King at the halking', the same 'to .ii. childer that chasit dukis in the dubbis [bogs] and set thaim up to the halkis'.[16] One of the beaters' or under-falconers' jobs was to swim to retrieve game, or a hawk which had killed across water; one such unfortunate, the subject of one of Alfonso the Wise's *Cantigas*, needed the assistance of the Virgin to survive (Fig. 40).

Gace de la Vigne, with whose misanthropic summary of hunting this book began, is in cheerier vein in his description of three typical fourteenth-century hunts, of differing degrees of quality and formality, which encapsulate and probably somewhat idealize his own experiences as a hunter and a member of the French court. We sense that, appealingly, his enjoyment increases in inverse proportion to the magnificence and predictable success of the proceedings.

The first (ll. 9407–10086) is a hunt involving King John of France himself, in which the stress is on grandeur and variety, the provision of a range of quarry to enable what were, no doubt, the finest falcons in France to demonstrate the most brilliant contemporary achievements of the falconer's craft. The King rises early, hears Mass, mounts his horse, takes on his wrist a falcon of exemplary beauty, a recent gift, and, in company with his Master Falconer (a nobleman), examines his falconers and their birds (over thirty, including white gyrfalcons), and decides which of them shall fly together and at which quarry. The company of over a hundred, some of them with dogs, proceeds to the river marshes, where the King proposes to the Master Falconer that the two of them should fly their falcons together; the birds are cast into the wind and fly up almost into the clouds, the duck are flushed from the river, and each falcon kills a mallard a bow-shot from its master. The King allows his falcon only the heart of the duck, as he wishes to fly it again later, at heron.

Three falcons are then cast off together over a lake where there are more duck; the duck are flushed by beating a little drum (see Fig. 44), and three of them are killed. Again the falcons are allowed only a titbit, to keep them hungry for flying again in the afternoon. Next, three tercel peregrines mount almost higher than the eye can see (*'bien près de Paradis'*), more duck are flushed, and two or three are killed. Two *moretons* (tufted ducks?) fall in the water, and Gace describes the jocular competition among the courtiers to fish them out with swords, as if they were slaying a boar or wolf and not *'deux petis oyseaulx'*. Eventually someone has to swim to retrieve the ducks, and their blood is given to the falcons as a prophylactic against the filanders (see above, p. 208).

The party moves to where a falconer has marked down two herons in a field; again the King puts his own falcon into competition with the Master Falconer's finest heron-hawk. He allows the herons so much time that everyone thinks a kill impossible; by the time the falcons are unhooded and cast off, the herons are in the clouds, but each falcon binds to a heron and brings it down almost at the King's feet, much to his joy. The *curée* of the heron is done there and then (see p. 204), and the falcons, having recovered their breath, are allowed to feed.[17]

The next flight, at cranes, involves some previous organization: men with greyhounds are stationed in the direction in which the cranes are expected to fly. Four falconers with birds specially trained for crane-hawking approach the feeding birds as closely as possible, each with one or two greyhounds, and cast off their falcons. The cranes rise, two falcons take one crane, two another, and the greyhounds race in to subdue the struggling prey. The cranes' hearts are cut up and put on a white gauntlet, then the marrow of the wing-bones, and the falcons feed. Gace suggests that they might also have been given some of the flesh of the thigh, or of a freshly killed hen.

After two more passing cranes have been taken by a pair of gyrfalcons, one of the austringers suggests that there may be bustard in the nearby fields, and the King agrees to his trying his fine white goshawk against them. The austringer approaches the birds carefully, with the King some way behind him, and throws the bird carefully to increase its initial impetus; the hawk seizes a bustard and the austringer runs in to help. The King marvels at the weight of the quarry, and the hawk is given the heart.

It is now midday. The company retires to a nearby village to dine lightly; the main meal is to be supper. In the afternoon the King is keen to try a recent, exotic gift from Bertrand de Claquin, Constable of France: a pair of tartarets, from 'Barbary, beyond the seas'. Small and reddish, no bigger than tercel peregrines, they are cast off against a flock of cranes, and are so well trained that one seizes a crane by the head and the other by the belly, and the three birds come battling down to earth, where a well-trained greyhound takes over. The Count of Tancarville, a celebrated authority on falconry, declares the flight perfect, worth a thousand florins.[18]

And so it continues until evening and the laying out of the bag at the hunting lodge: cranes, bustards, herons, mallard, pheasant, partridges . . . We should perhaps take the unfailing consistency of the falcons' success with a grain of salt, but in its pattern and its range of quarry this hunt is probably authentic enough. It is the kind of hunt which Pero López, as Castilian Ambassador, probably experienced in France, and which caused him to include the Duke of Burgundy and the Count of Tancarville in his list of famous experts. Many of his detailed reminiscences are of exploits witnessed in France.[19]

So much for splendour; what about fun? Gace finds much more of this in his second hunt (ll. 10087–199), an informal affair with his friends, 'for folk of modest estate often have as much pleasure from their falcons as the great, or more. . . . No prince or lord was with us; none was rich, but all loved birds: gentlemen, canons, burghers, squires – about a dozen. We spent a week together, a week as pleasurable as men ever had.' He tells us that there were good birds and good falconers, but not all were experts; some were new to the sport, but all was amity and 'no man was too frightened of his fellows.' They had a score of birds between them; they ate in a cheerful inn, and argued good-humouredly, and laughed, as hunters still do, at one who had fallen in the river; above all they were free from that lurking unease which a medieval subordinate always felt in the company of the powerful, for 'if one is with one's lords, one feels obliged to pay them such respect that one dare not speak until they do, and if one does speak, one goes pale with worry that one will make a slip, and this is why our company was so happy. We were in revelry; men exchanged birds . . . a falcon for a lanner; a lanner for a tercel . . . and so we spent the week and thought of nothing but the honest and profitable delight which we took in our hunting-birds.'

Gace's third account (ll. 10257–344) is of hunting with sparrowhawks, and this is where the ladies come to share the foreground. After a description of the ideal sparrowhawk, we learn that to make the most of the bird a man should be between twenty and forty years of age, mature but agile; one should also, because of the social nature of the sport, be courteous and debonair, since it is a great revealer of personality. One needs a stout, steady-going horse, another in reserve, and four spaniels to quest and retrieve, two in the morning and two in the afternoon. The other requirements are good country and good company; lone hawking is poor sport. The company should be blithe and beautiful: knights and squires not overburdened with wealth, ladies and maidens, each bearing a sparrowhawk. They pass through the champaign landscape in the high summer, hunting at random: partridges, quails, larks, young pheasants, in a friendly and flirtatious competitive spirit, until the game-bags are filled. 'As long as game lasts, there is no sport to compare with that with the sparrowhawk.' King Modus gives a very similar description of communal sparrow-hawking. He too stresses the participation of ladies, explaining the term *espreviers a dames* ('ladies' hawks') as 'hawks which carry their dead prey back to the hand of their bearer'.[20] Indeed, for some medieval artists such hunting serves as a symbol of all the pleasures of worldly life, its participants unconscious of the looming death whose quarry they are (Fig. 34).

As a culminating joy, the right true end of hunting, Gace passes on for the special benefit of the young his own recipe for:

Sparviter's Pie

Make the centre of your pie three plump partridges, with six fat quails to give them support; around the quails set a dozen larks; then take wheatears and small birds, as many as you have, and scatter them around. Then take fresh-smelling fat bacon, cut it into dice, and strew it over the birds. As an extra improvement, add verjuice grapes, and sprinkle with salt for savour. The case should be a rough pastry of pure wheaten flour, with eggs. Add no spices; add no cheese; put it in a good hot oven, well-cleared of ashes, and you will find no food to rival it. [ll. 10353–82]

19

The Falconer's Life

The post of Lord Falconer, like that of Master of the King's Hunting, was in several countries a high office of the royal household. In cases where the holder was a really notable member of the aristocracy, the post was clearly a grand honour, involving a flattering role in ceremonial and precedence but no actual bloodying of the hands. It is unlikely that Pedro the Cruel's Lord Falconer, Ruy González de Illescas, for example, had any active role in training the king's hawks; this would have ill befitted his even more dignified position as *Comendador de Santiago*, the leader of the most distinguished order of Spanish chivalry.[1] In the Welsh *Laws of Howel Dha* of around 900, the king was obliged to stand to receive the *Penhebogyd* (Lord Falconer) when he entered the hall after a good day; in the seating at meals the holder of the office was only fourth from the king himself, though he was restricted to three drinks per meal to ensure that his dedication to the hawks did not waver.[2] The man who directly supervised the day-to-day running of the mews, a highly demanding job in a royal household, suitably remunerated, might also be a minor aristocrat. James IV's larger payments to do with falconry, including a bi-annual stipend of fifty pounds, are made to a knight, 'Schir Alexander Makcullo' (Sir Alexander MacKulloch of Myreton or Merton), alluded to by the Lord High Treasurer more simply and dismissively as 'Makcullo'.[3]

Even the royal falconers of lower status, without a title, were sometimes drawn from the landed gentry, and in some cases held lands in consequence of their office. Robert Hannay of Sorby, whose Whitsunday (half-yearly) stipend was only ten pounds – when a mason received twenty, the Master of the Wardrobe thirty-five, and the Queen's lute-player eleven pounds thirteen shillings and fourpence[4] – was a member of a landed family, the occupants of Sorbie Place in Wigtownshire. Some of James IV's other highly-ranked falconers, Dande (i.e. Andrew) Dowle, John Man, John Baty and Donald Falconer, held lands near the royal hunting lodge of

Falkland in Fife, and received remission of rent in consequence of their employment.[5]

In England a royal falconer could have unexpected ties with commerce: in 1291 three men were called to account for refusing to pay to Thomas de Hauvyle the *lastage* dues which he had the right to collect from all ships leaving King's Lynn for foreign ports, by virtue of his sergeanty of keeping the king's gyrfalcons. The case involved 140 laden ships.[6] Thomas must have enjoyed a substantially grander life-style than the average single-handed falconer employed by a member of the aristocracy; the powerful Earl of Northumberland laid out only five shillings and elevenpence on the clothing of Hew the falconer in a period of sixteen months when even Robert the lackey was clothed to the tune of twenty-eight shillings, and ten shillings was spent merely on 'thred for nettes'.[7]

Like the royal huntsmen of France, the falconers of the Scottish court were clothed by the king. The Exchequer Rolls record the provision of a robe to Matthew, a falconer, in 1329,[8] and the treasurer's accounts for 1491 record the provision of cloth for several falconers' clothing: gowns, doublets and hose. Notice the evidence of a hierarchy marked by quality and colour: Dande Dowle receives more cloth than the others, of several different kinds, some of it imported, some of it red; Downy, Reid and John Man, presumably his subordinates, receive only grey cloth, less of it and a lower quality; Downy himself has a subordinate, Lang Thom:

Leverais to Falconaris

In primis, to Dande Dowle, xx° Septembris, .iii. elne of Rowane tanny to a gowne; price of the elne .xxii. s.; summa .iii. li. .vi. s.

Item, .ii. elne fustiane, to be him a dowblat, price .vi. s.

Item, til him, .v. quartaris of Inglis caresay to hoyss [hose]: price .vii. s. .vi. d.

Item, the xxi° Decembris, to Dande Dowle, .ii. elne .iii. quartaris of braid Inglis reid to a gowne and hoyss, price the elne .xx. s., summa .ii. l. .xv. s.

Item, to Downy falconar, Thome Reid, Johne the Man, and Lang Thom, Downeis man, .xi. elne and dimid. of gray, to be thaim gownis and hoyss; price the elne .x. s.; summa .v. li. .xv. s.

Item, to Downy and his man, and Thome Reid, .vi. elne of fustiane to thare dowblatis; price .xviii. s.

Item, to Johne of Callindar, falconar, to be him a gowne, .ii. elne and dimid. of gray; price .xxv. s.

Item, to Pryngill and Caryk, to be thaim gownis, .iiii. elne of braid Inglis reid; price .iiii. li.

Item, to Domynico, .ii. elne and dimid. of gray; price of the elne .ix. s.; summa .xxii. s. .vi. d.

Item, .ii. elne quyt fustiane; price .vi. s.

Item, .v. quartaris and dimid. of Inglis cayrsay; price .viii. s. .iii. d.

Item, a bonat; .xxxii. d.

Item, for a sark; .iii. s. .vi. d.[9]

What of this Domenico? How did this exile come to share the grey livery of these men of the north, remaining so conspicuously foreign as to have no further need of his surname? Did he arrive as the bearer of some ducal gift to the king, and remain to impart fresh techniques at a time when Italian falconry was beginning to acquire new celebrity?[10] Certainly a falconer's skills were internationally marketable; there were many falconers in the royal mews of Europe who, however halting their mastery of the language of their employer, were welcome immigrants because of their way with a hawk. We have heard from Pero López of the Brabantines whom he persuaded to enter his service in Paris and to return to Spain with him. Domenico's move to Scotland may have mirrored the earlier emigration to Italy of Frederick II's Alexander Henrici (possibly Alexander Henry, and, like his namesake the famous nineteenth-century Edinburgh rifle-maker, a Scot).[11]

Frederick certainly had two English falconers, Master Walter, specified as 'Gualterius Anglicus', and his son.[12] Possibly Walter was the informant in the conversation reported by Frederick in his *De Arte Venandi* about English methods of luring: 'Those who live in Britain and are called Anglians do not use the lure in the manner just described, because they never lure on horseback, nor do they call out when luring. We inquired why they do not call out, but they could only reply that it is their customary practice.' Unconvinced, Frederick discusses this at length, and finally dismisses the English way imperiously. If Walter and his son knew which side their bread was buttered, they probably started using horse and voice rather more.[13]

Frederick's mews was probably the most cosmopolitan in history, as a result of the Emperor's obsessive appetite for information: '. . . we, at great expense, summoned from the four quarters of the Earth masters in the practice of the art of falconry. We entertained these experts in our domains, meantime seeking their opinions, weighing the importance of their knowledge, and endeavouring to retain in memory the more valuable of their words and deeds.'[14] Englishmen, certainly, possibly a Scot, possibly Spaniards (Frederick mentions the use of live hens as lures in Spain[15]), Germans, and the native Italians; but his greatest debt, especially in hooding techniques, was probably to Muslim falconers: 'The Arabian chiefs not only presented us with many kinds of falcons, but sent with them falconers expert in the use of the hood. In addition . . . we have imported, partly from Arabia, partly from other countries, both birds and men skilled in the art, from whom we have acquired a knowledge of all their accomplishments.'[16]

Royal falconers must have dreaded the king's foreign wars, to which they were dragged willy-nilly. Edward III took thirty falconers with him when he invaded France.[17] The Bayeux Tapestry shows a hawk and two hounds being carefully conveyed into the ship in which King Harold is embarking.[18]

Frederick's court was a most important centre for the transmission of oriental methods into Europe, rivalled probably only by Spain. His interpreter, Theodore of Antioch, translated into Latin works by the Arab falconer Moamin and the Persian Ghatrif; the former was corrected personally by the Emperor during the siege of Faenza, and was subsequently translated into French and Spanish.[19] Other European treatises sometimes cite obscure foreign and especially oriental falconers as sources; exoticism adds authority. The introduction to the work of Jean de Francières alludes to 'Moloxin, falconer to the Prince of Antioch, Michelin, falconer to the King of Cyprus, and Ayme Cassan, falconer to the King of Rhodes and the Grand Turk'.[20]

Frederick gives detailed specifications,[21] mostly predictable, about the physical and personal traits necessary in a falconer: medium height; nimble but not nervous; shrewd and inventive; above all, good-tempered and patient. Essentials were keen eyesight and hearing, a strong carrying voice and an ability to swim. He had to be a light sleeper, so as to hear the falcons if they were restless in the night, and an early riser. Drunkenness was anathema: 'Inebriety is one of those minor forms of insanity that soon ends in destroying the usefulness of a bird.' It seems to have been generally held that falconers were more sober men than huntsmen. In the argument on the subject in *Modus* one accusation from the falconers before the descent to blows is that huntsmen return home so thirsty after their hunting cries and hornblowing that they habitually drink themselves into oblivion.[22]

The social distinction between hawks of the tower and hawks of the fist was reflected in the relations between the men who trained and worked them: falconers appear to have been rather scornful of austringers. In a large mews there were usually only a few goshawks, and in Gace de la Vigne's *Roman des Déduis* the lone austringer appears as a coarse, farouche figure, hunched and secretive, as unapproachable as the bird he handles, indiscriminate in his choice of quarry, spoiling the sport of his betters, and only slightly redeemed by his efficiency in filling the larder. 'You do need goshawks,' says Gace:

> but please do not house your graceless austringers in the falconers' room. They are cursed in Scripture, for they hate company and go alone about their sport. They wear a cloak to cover up their bird, the better to deceive the bird they seek to take. When they go to hunt, you think they are behind the falconers, but instead they are ahead, beating their drum. When you hear that noise and see the birds flying in all directions, you know that there will be nothing left in the area for the falconers. So I beg all landed gentlemen to put two restrictions on their austringer: firstly, that he shall come always after the falconers when hunting, and secondly, that the grey herons shall be left for the falcons. Let the austringer, by all means, take bitterns, spoonbills, egrets, white herons, seagulls, cormorants, crows, rooks, swans, bustards, cranes, geese large and small, partridge, pheasant, curlew . . . and if they want rabbit to eat, let them seek them, well away from their holes.

Above all, the austringers should leave the herons alone, 'so that we may often see them rising in the meadows, and see no more the austringers taking their sport and beating their drum in the heron's broad valleys with their beautiful river-banks; let them rather take their ease and their sport in the town and the castle, pursuing their own wives; that is where they should do their drum-beating.'

For Gace, 'austringer' is a term of abuse akin to 'scarecrow'; austringers do not look like falconers or even normal human beings:

> When one sees an ill-formed man, with great big feet and long shapeless shanks, built like a trestle, . . . hump-shouldered and skew-backed, and one wants to mock him, one says, 'Look, what an austringer!' I know the austringers would like to beat me for this, but there are two dozen of us falconers to one of them, so I have no fear. Nonetheless, it is a wise man who keeps a goshawk in his house, good kitchen-bird that it is! [ll. 841–930]

Like the huntsman, a falconer commonly followed in his father's footsteps, after an apprenticeship of menial duties. We have seen an English boy installed in Italy with his father. In James IV's accounts we find not only 'Johne the Man, falconer in Abirdene' being clothed and horsed as a qualified falconer, but also payments of a few pence to 'Johne the Mannis boy, to pas to the Laird of Stanywood [about five miles away] for ane halk', and 'the samyn boy, to pas agane for ane dog'; 'Young Hannay' is mentioned between 1501 and 1512 as well as, presumably, his father, Robert Hannay of Sorby, between 1495 and 1508.[23] Frederick II concedes that boys may be good carriers of falcons, but recommends against their being allowed to participate in taming and training.[24] Women, too, might be employed in a mews: James IV's treasurer pays five shillings and fourpence in 1496 to 'the wif that kepis the Kingis halkis'.[25] Frederick provides clothing not only for his falconers, but also for their wives and families.[26]

One of the most humane and evocative sections of the Devonshire tapestries is the picture of the old falconer (Fig. 47). Simply clad among a throng of spendthrift coxcombs, bowed and a little wearied, he goes unsmiling about his practical task, more in tune with the hawk and hound which are his charges than with the pretty folk he serves. No doubt many such men, well-travelled and surrounded by finery in their working lives, often separated from or lacking friends and family, came to a poor end. James IV's treasurer dispensed thirteen shillings to Dande Dowle, 'to ger erd [to bury] ane pur falconer'.[27]

20

The Symbolism of Falconry

Literary comparison of the medieval knightly hero to a bird of prey is commonplace, so much so that it can be treated humorously by Wolfram von Eschenbach in his description of Segramors:

> His horse jumped over the high bushes,
> Many a golden bell rang out on it
> Both on the caparison and on the man himself.
> You could well have cast him
> After a pheasant into a thorn-bush;
> Whoever wanted to run to seek him
> Would have found him by the bright ringing
> Of the bells.[1]

The hawk- or falcon-like warrior is a durable motif, exemplified by Homer's description of Achilles in his pursuit of Hector:

> And Peleus' son went after him in the confidence of his quick feet.
> As when a hawk in the mountains who moves lightest of things flying
> Makes his effortless swoop for a trembling dove, but she slips away
> From beneath and flies and he shrill screaming close after her
> Plunges again and again, heart furious to take her;
> So Achilles went straight for him in fury, but Hector
> Fled away under the Trojan wall.[2]

Consider, too, Fig. 42, in which we see the knight transformed, the exaggerated device on the helmet and trappings turning him into a huge mounted bird of prey, and conveying on him the transfixing power of that bird. The association of knight with hawk frequently occurs in medieval poetry. In the fourteenth-century version of the Spanish epic of the *Seven Infantes of Lara* one can perceive the use of the goshawk motif as a narrative device with more than one function. In the earlier version of this epic, which describes the treacherous betrayal of the seven Infantes by their wicked uncle Ruy Velázquez, who deceives them into a fatal foray against the Moors, the bulk of the heroic activity is centred on the youngest brother, Gonzalo González. The later version extends the story with an account of the birth of a half-Moorish step-brother, Mudarra, who eventually returns from Córdoba to take revenge for the crime. There is an obvious problem for the author in the potential lack of heroic unity; to overcome this Mudarra is presented as a reincarnation of Gonzalo González. Their physical similarity is commented on by several characters. Furthermore, the link is stressed by the use of the goshawk motif. In both early and late versions, there is a strong link between the hawk and Gonzalo González: in a dispute at the wedding of Ruy Velázquez and Doña Llambra the young hero uses his goshawk as a weapon with which to strike his uncle; he is carrying it to bathe it when Doña Llambra makes a sarcastic comment prolonging the ill-feeling; and when she orders a servant to insult him ritually she identifies him as 'the one you see with a goshawk on his fist'. In the later version, this element is continued into the Mudarra section, in an identification of the avenging hero with the goshawk. His arrival is presaged by the dream of Doña Sancha, mother of the Infantes; she tells her husband: 'I dreamed that . . . high in the mountains . . . I saw a goshawk flying towards me from the direction of Córdoba, and it settled on my hand, and spread its wings, and it seemed to me that it was so large that its shadow covered me and you; and it rose, and perched on the shoulder of Ruy Velázquez, the traitor, and gripped him so tightly with its talons as to tear off his arms from his body, and rivers of blood gushed out, and I knelt to drink it.' The final encounter comes when the fleeing traitor thinks himself safe enough to go hunting; he loses his goshawk (generally an omen of trouble to come, in traditional Spanish literature), and as he looks for it finds Mudarra instead, who wounds him in single combat and takes him to the court of the Count of Castile for a bloody, ceremonial vengeance.[3]

Similarly, in a Spanish ballad version about the death of Roland, his wife Doña Alda has a prophetic dream in which one bird is savaged by another; initially comforted by her maid, who interprets the dream through the symbolism of the *caza de amor*, the hunt of love (see pp. 229–30), she receives a letter on the following day with the news of the hero's death in the bloody *caza* of Roncevaux.[4] The falcon dream has precedents in medieval Germany.[5]

Hawk and hound are sometimes almost physiological extensions of the knight. In one Spanish ballad, a knight is punished by the gouging out of his eyes and the severing of the foot he uses to mount his horse and the hand on which he bears his hawk.[6] Extreme deprivation is exemplified in

British balladry by separation from one's hawks, hounds and land, as in Young Beichan's plaint:

> My hounds they all run masterless,
> My hawks they flie from tree to tree,
> My youngest brother will heir my lands;
> Fair England again I'll never see![7]

In Serbo-Croatian epic poetry the falcon sometimes protects its owner, in one case bringing him water in its beak and shading him from the sun when he is ill,[8] and in the English ballad *The Three Ravens* the hawks play their part in the protection of their master against dark forces, sharing the burden with his hounds and the doe who is his grieving and pregnant lover:

> There were three ravens sat on a tree,
> They were as black as they might be.
>
> The one of them said to his make,
> 'Where shall we our breakfast take?'
>
> 'Down in yonder greene field
> There lies a knight slain under his shield;
>
> 'His hounds they lie down at his feet,
> So well do they their master keep;
>
> 'His hawks they flie so eagerly,
> There's no fowl dare come him nigh.
>
> 'Down there comes a fallow doe
> As great with young as she might goe.
>
> 'She lifted up his bloudy head
> And kist his wounds that were so red.
>
> 'She gat him up upon her back
> And carried him to earthen lake.
>
> 'She buried him before the prime;
> She was dead herself ere evensong time.
>
> 'God send every gentleman
> Such hounds, such hawks, and such a leman!'[9]

Compare this with the knight's utter loneliness and vulnerability in death in the Scottish version, *The Twa Corbies*; his hawk, his hound and his lady have all abandoned him, and the dark forces triumph:

> As I was walking all alane,
> I heard twa corbies making a mane:
> The tane unto the tither did say,
> 'Whar sall we gang and dine the day?'
>
> '– In behint yon auld fail dyke
> I wot there lies a new-slain knight;
> And naebody kens that he lies there
> But his hawk, his hound, and his lady fair.
>
> 'His hound is to the hunting gane,
> His hawk to fetch the wild-fowl hame,
> His lady's ta'en anither mate,
> So we may mak' our dinner sweet.
>
> 'Ye'll sit on his white hause-bane,
> And I'll pick out his bonny blue e'en:
> Wi' ae lock o' his gowden hair
> We'll theek our nest when it grows bare.
>
> 'Mony a one for him maks mane,
> But nane sall ken whar he is gane;
> O'er his white banes, when they are bare,
> The wind sall blaw for evermair.'[10]

Such linkages are not purely literary. In the medieval laws of Teruel, in Aragón, the confiscation of the goods of a noble widower guilty of a particular offence stops short of the things socially and emotionally dearest to him: he is allowed to retain his warhorse, his weapons, the bed in which he first slept with his wife, and his hunting-birds.[11]

This association of knight with hawk is sometimes used in a contrastive way. A fifteenth-century statue of St Gorgonius shows him hesitating between the worlds of the spirit and the flesh, between the missal in his right hand and the falcon on his left fist, as if literally weighing one against the other.[12] More explicit still is the representation of the contemplative life and the active life in a manuscript in the Heiligenkreuz monastery, near Vienna (Fig. 43). At the foot of the page we see on the left a priest reading, representing *contemplativa vita*; on the right a mounted nobleman with a goshawk on his fist, symbolising *vita activa*. The purpose is not to praise one and decry the other; above them we see a perch with, left and right, a dove and a goshawk, and the rubric *Ecce in eadem pertica sedent accipiter et columba* ('See how hawk and dove sit on the same perch'); the perch is the properly balanced life.[13]

The hawk plays a similar role in medieval iconography of death. In frescos, paintings and sculpture, hunting and especially falconry exemplify those earthly joys which blind man to his future fate: the sweetness of carefree, limber youth; the worldly status of the powerful, defenceless against death. In the famous fresco in the Campo Santo in Pisa, *The Triumph of Death*, we see the members of a merry hunting party silenced by an encounter with their own coffins; the horses' eyes roll as they sniff the rotting corpses.[14] In paintings of the Dance of Death, the knight or nobleman called to join the Dance often carries a hawk.[15] Mary of Burgundy lost her life in a hunting accident; a miniature in her Book of Hours, completed after her death, shows her riding in a hunting party, dainty and pretty, with a hawk on her fist; behind her loom three dark figures of Death, their skeletal arms raised to throw hunting-spears into their victim (Fig. 34).

The hawk has a less solemn role as messenger, usually between two lovers. The sparrowhawk often plays this part, sometimes simply as a confidant requested by its despairing master to convey his love, sometimes as the bearer of a written message, like a modern carrier pigeon.[16] The bird of prey's characteristics of physical beauty and independence of mind enable falconry practices to serve, as symbol or in simile, to express the emotional and physical attractiveness of woman to man: the man's obsessive wish to bend a free-ranging spirit to his own desires. Shakespeare's images of luring the hawk/lady, finding her haggard,[17] casting her off, etc., are well known. He has English predecessors, such as the anonymous author of a poem pervaded by the anguish and joy of a simple man at losing and regaining his hawk:

> The Lover compareth himself to the painful Falconer
>
> The soaring hawk from fist that flies,
>   Her Falconer doth constraine
> Sometime to range the ground unknown,
>   To find her out againe:
> And if by sight or sound of bell
>   His falcon he may see:
> 'Wo, ho!' he cries, with cheerful voice,
>   The gladdest man is he.

By Lure then, in finest sort,
   He seekes to bring her in:
But if that she ful gorged be,
   He cannot so her win:
Although her becks and bending eies,
   She manie proffers makes:
'Wo ho ho!' he cries, awaie she flies,
   And so her leave she takes.

This wofull man with wearie limmes,
   Runnes wandring round about:
At length by noise of chattering Pies
   His hawke againe found out,
His heart was glad his eies had seen
   His falcon swift of flight:
'Wo ho ho!' he cries, she emptie gorgde
   Upon his Lure doth light.

How glad was then the falconer there,
   No pen nor tongue can tel:
He swam in blisse that lately felt
   Like paines of cruel hel.
His hand somtime upon her train,
   Somtime upon her brest:
'Wo ho ho!' he cries with cheerfull voice,
   His heart was now at rest.

My dear, likewise, beholde thy love,
   What paines he doth indure:
And now at length let pitie move,
   To stoup unto his Lure.
A hood of silk, and silver belles,
   New gifts I promise thee:
'Wo ho ho!' I crie; 'I come,' then saie,
   Make me as glad as hee![18]

Some of the medieval predecessors of this are even simpler, such as Kürenberc's lapidary summary:

Women and falcons are easily tamed:
If you lure them the right way, they come to meet their man.[19]

Others, as is the wont of allegory based on the minutiae of specific activities, are too clever for their own good. In the fourteenth-century

German *Der Minne Falkner* the poet depicts himself as a falconer who has lost his falcon/lady; he is advised by a more experienced falconer to find a less valuable and more suitable hawk, and by a bad falconer to trap the bird in a net (i.e. to use unworthy methods of seduction), which he declines to do on the grounds that it might damage her wings. He is still unsuccessful at the end of the poem, after luring the falcon by tying his own heart to the lure, which the bird seizes and carries away.[20] A more resourceful and striking range of comparisons is used by Wolfram von Eschenbach, particularly in *Parzival*. His imagery, based on a deep practical knowledge of the workaday process of keeping a hawk in trim, and therefore fully meaningful only for someone with the same experiences, is varied and imaginative. Feeding the hawk, for instance: to describe starving men, he says with understatement that if they had been hawks their crops would not have been over-full. The falcon's moult is used variously to describe the earth at the onset of spring, girls at puberty and a man's loss of *werdekeit* (the quality of being worthily esteemed).[21]

In the Iberian peninsula the commonest falconry imagery in poetry is that of the *caza de amor*, the hunt of love, in the traditional and oral lyric. Instead of the toilsome quest which is the substance of *Der Minne Falkner*, we have a briefer and more intense imagery of the triumphant falcon, not now the sought but the seeker, mantling and panting over its prey: love-making as a killing and love as a chase, a flight of heart- stretching endeavour which ends with the two participants enmeshed on the earth; a soaring and a stooping. Some of the brief lyrics are ambiguous, depending on an awareness in the reader of a wider tradition in which the heron is used as a comparison for the beauty of woman:

> The heron was wild
> and lofty of flight;
> there is none who can take her.   [Juan del Encina]

> If so many falcons
> pursue the heron,
> let them take her, by God!

> The heron complains
> as she sees her fortune,
> which denies her the joy
> of a loftier flight.
> With pleasure and sadness

they pursue the heron.
Let them take her, by God!   [Luis de Narvaez]

The heron was wounded,
alone and crying.

On the banks of the river,
where the heron nests,
she goes alone and crying.   [Diego Pisador]

Other poems make the link with the erotic clearer:

Two goshawks pursue me;
one of them will die of love.

Two goshawks of mine
move round me in this dance;
one of them will die of love. [From the Portuguese of Gil Vicente]

Noble-gazing heron,
how I should like to take you
for your pleasure and for mine!   [Juan de Timoneda][22]

In one French romance this symbolism becomes a narrative transformation. The future mother of Yonec, the hero of one of the lays of Marie de France, is immured by her jealous husband in a tower, watched over by his old sister. The knight who fathers Yonec gains access to the lady by flying in through her narrow window in the form of a mature goshawk ('of five or six moults'), wearing jesses, then to take on human form and make love to her. The affair goes on until the old woman sees the arrival of the bird and the love-making. The husband has razor-sharp spikes fitted to the outside of the window and pretends to go hunting; the eager hawk flies unsuspecting to the window and receives a fatal wound.[23]

Linkages between falconry and love-making are common in medieval miniatures and carvings. Frequently one of a pair of lovers, usually but not invariably the man, will be holding a falcon (Fig. 45).[24] In sources in which calendars appear, even in Books of Hours, falconry motifs are commonly used as illustrations of activities befitting the month of May (Fig. 46). In Spain there is a further dimension of this imagery: the love of God for man.

In one anonymous lyric the falcon is both God and Christ; the thicket and the crown of thorns are one:

> To the flight of a heron
> the peregrine stooped from the sky,
> and, taking her on the wing,
> was caught in a bramble-bush.
>
> High in the mountains
> God, the peregrine, came down
> to be closed in the womb
> of Holy Mary.
> The heron screamed so loudly
> that *Ecce ancilla* rose to the sky,
> and the peregrine stooped to the lure
> and was caught in a bramble-bush.
>
> The jesses were long
> by which he was caught;
> cut from those webs
> which Adam and Eve wove.
> But the wild heron
> took so lowly a flight
> that when God stooped from the sky
> He was caught in a bramble-bush.[25]

St John of the Cross, seeking a means to convey the indescribable, the mystic union of his soul with God, uses the image of the falcon grasping its prey among the clouds, blinded by glory, after a stoop in two senses: the peregrine's hurtling descent which gives it the momentum to soar up almost vertically, and the individual's self-abasement and relinquishing of individuality which enable the soul to rejoin the divine:

> The nearer I came
> to this lofty quarry,
> the lower and more wretched
> and despairing I seemed.
> I said: 'No-one can reach it';
> and I stooped so low, so low,
> that I soared so high, so high,
> that I grasped my prey.[26]

Just occasionally the idea of the falcon as an emotional treasure, an object of tenderness and wistful nostalgia, is expressed from the woman's viewpoint. In the mid-twelfth century the German Kürenberc produced this compressed lyric drama, which has the merit of leaving much of the creative process to the reader:

I nurtured a falcon   for more than a year.
When I had him tamed   exactly as I wished
And had gracefully decked   his feathers with gold,
he raised himself so high   and flew to other lands.

Since then I've seen that falcon   flying superbly;
he was wearing silken   fetters on his feet
and the whole of his plumage   was all red gold.
May God bring those together   who want each other's love.

Is this a dialogue, between the bird's first mistress and a confidant, or an internal monologue? Is a second, more blatant mistress implied in the second stanza, or only the loss of the lover, all previous tenderness wasted? Is the second stanza admiring, bitter or both? Whatever our interpretation, its foundation is the combination of tenderness and fear felt by the falconer for his hawk as he strives to balance the paradox of taming a bird whose wildness is its most admired feature.[27]

A similarly enigmatic mingling of the tender and the wild is seen in a Serbian folk-song quoted by Peter Dronke:

A falcon is perched on the fortress of Salonika,
his talons yellow right up to the spur,
his wings golden right up to the shoulder,
his beak bloody right up to the eyes.
The girls of Salonika question him:
'In God's name, you grey-green falcon,
who is it who has yellowed your talons,
who is it who has gilded your wings,
who is it who has bloodied your beak?'
'Leave me alone, you girls of Salonika!
It was a good master whom I served,
and he had daughters three:
the first was she who yellowed my talons,
the second, she who gilded my wings,
and the third was she who bloodied my beak.'[28]

Beauty and bloodiness once again; the pride of ownership and tender care are there in the actions of the first two daughters, but the relationship with the third is enigmatic. Is the falcon proud of a conquest, or is he suffering? Is his beak bloody from generous feeding, or is the blood that of the girl herself? Why 'Leave me alone'?: has he a lover already, the youngest daughter, or does his use of the past tenses imply desertion, and, if so, who deserted whom?

So our Serbian falcon gentle leaves us puzzling over the complexities of love, the way of a man with a maid; we are almost back to Merry Margaret, with whose gentler virtues our examination of medieval falconry began.

21

The Lower Courts of Paradise

One could compile a useful handbook for the twentieth-century poacher on the basis of the information contained in the medieval manuals. Those written in English would contribute relatively little; the works of William Twiti, Edward, Duke of York, Dame Juliana Berners and the anonymous author of the *Craft of Venery* are all pervaded by the procedural and linguistic snobbery which excludes from consideration the lower social orders and their inglorious methods. The French works, in contrast, and most notably the *Livre du Roy Modus* and Gaston Phoebus's *Livre de chasse*, are significantly more catholic in their attitude; they address the needs, not only of the courtier and the aristocratic landowner, but of the general rural population; they accept that, while *par force* hunting is a glory without parallel, less fortunate men find a valid fulfilment in creeping along hedges with a bundle of rabbit-nets, sitting inside a bush to lure small birds to their innocent doom, or devising subtle contrivances of hazel-twigs or bent saplings which work for a man's dietary or agricultural benefit during the hours of night. Some German works, too, provide considerable information about methods which would have appealed little to the mounted aristocrat. The royal authors of Spain and Portugal ignore the methods of the common man, but the local codes of law of Iberia reveal that not only the villager, but the townsman, too, had his sport.

In its essential form, *par force* hunting involved pitting a pack of hounds against a quarry which was unhampered in the direction or length of its flight. Bow and stable hunting, in its purity, used men and hounds to drive the quarry towards and through a line of archers; if the beast came unscathed through the winnowing arrows it went free. Nevertheless, the French huntsman's training covered the making of nets. The royal hunting accounts' references to the purchase of cord usually specify that it is for couples and leashes,[1] but one miniature in the *Livre de chasse* shows men working on nets of a varied range of patterns for different quarries and methods; one man is spinning the rope from which the nets are made. Phoebus includes a long chapter on making hayes and nets, though not without reservations based partly on conservationist considerations: 'I speak of this against my will, for I should not teach you how to take game except in noble and gentle fashion, and to have good sport, so that there may always be plenty to hunt and that beasts may not be killed ignobly.[2]

It is quite clear, despite this protestation, that some French aristocratic hunting involved the use of nets. The use of the long-net or haye, supported by stakes, dates back to classical times: there are Roman mosaics showing hunters carrying rolled long-nets, and the netsman plays an important role in Xenophon's description of hare-hunting.[3] The long-net might be used as an adjunct to the other forms of hunting to prevent the quarry escaping in an undesired direction, so avoiding the relays in a *par force* hunt or the archers in bow and stable hunting. At the lower social levels it was used, as it is today, as a principally nocturnal method of taking rabbits, hares and even partridges, a light net being hung in a strategic position (in rabbiting, between the feeding-ground and the burrows), and the quarry driven towards it by men with or without dogs. Deer, too, were driven into fixed nets and killed while they were entangled – an unworthy method, according to Phoebus, 'and properly the sport for fat men, old men, idle men and churchmen, not of men who wish to hunt with skill and true venery'.[4]

At the aristocratic level, sturdier and smaller nets were used in a particular form of deer- and boar-hunting involving the process called in France *tailler le buisson*, 'shaping the covert'.[5] This involved cutting apparent escape routes for the game and placing in them sturdy nets of large mesh, strung on forked posts with a crossbar, which extended the nets into a rectangle. The cord of the nets was dyed green, and its thickness varied, as did the height of the nets, for different quarries. Some nets had a drawstring round the edge so that the animal was enveloped as if by a bag. A combination of the haye and the small net was also used, with two of the small nets at each end of the haye and two in the middle. For boar, bear and wolf two feet of the bottom of the net lay flat on the ground to prevent the quarry going under it, but for deer a gap of a foot was left. Large snares sometimes replaced the nets in the apertures in the haye.

Driving deer into nets was also practised in Germany (the stag Fidelity is about to run into one in Fig. 32). The method is accepted as sporting by some German authors, but is condemned by Hadamar. It appears that the acceptability of netting in Germany varied with the abundance of game and the nature of the terrain.[6] It is likely that the method was used in England, too, though the *Master of Game* is haughtily dismissive of it as means of taking deer: 'Men take hem . . . with nettis, and with cordes [probably meaning snares, running nooses, also shown in Phoebus[7]], and with other harnays . . . and with other gynnes [devices], but in Engelonde thei ben not slayn but with houndes, or with shotte [i.e. bow and arrow] or with strength of rennyng houndes.'[8]

The use of nets to take deer is criticized by certain Scottish authors. Both Boece's *Histories* and Bellenden's *Chronicles* describe the contrasting hunting methods of the Picts, who set nets and drove the deer into them, and the Scots, who despised this method and used hounds alone. Bellenden also says that hares should not be taken with nets or traps, but hunted only with hounds. Long before, Arrian had likened the use of greyhounds to a properly fought battle, and the use of nets to mere pillaging.[9] The Duke of York is similarly critical of various pragmatic methods used by the depraved foreigner against the hare: 'Men sle hares with greyhoundes and with rennyng houndes by strengthe *as in Engelonde, but ellis where thei slee hem Also* with pursnetes and with smale nettis, *with hare pipes* and with long nettis and with smale cordis that men casten where thei make her brekyng of the smale twygges when thei goon to hure pasture.'[10]

The italicized words in this extract are Edward's additions to Phoebus, his source, and though he does not allude directly to Phoebus here, this passage is a criticism of those chapters of the *Livre de chasse* which describe several crafty but inglorious methods of taking a hare. They include lurking with a leash of greyhounds on the fringe of a wood around the hour of vespers; flushing the hares from standing corn with greyhounds and shooting them with round-headed arrows; snaring them at dawn and dusk on their regular routes to and from their feeding-grounds; setting small nets across the four arms of a crossroads, waiting for a hare to pass and then banging the ground with a stick to bolt it into one of the nets; waiting until hares have entered an enclosed vineyard or orchard at night to feed, setting nets across the gates, and sending in a couple of dogs; and hanging a long-net between a wood and a cornfield and driving the hares out of the corn with bells hung on a long rope held at either end by a man walking towards the wood.[11] All disgraceful, in the eyes of the Duke of York: 'Trewly I trowe that a good hunter wold sle hem so for no good.'[12]

Nor has Edward much affection for rabbit-hunters, nor indeed for the rabbit, called in the Middle Ages the coney or conyng: 'Of conynges speke I not, for no man hunteth for hem but yit it be *bisshhunters* [fur-hunters], and thei hunte hem with ferettis and with long smale haies.'[13] For true hunting men the rabbit was a pest, a distraction to the undisciplined hound; the word 'rioting' is derived from the misbehaviour of hounds led astray from their path of vocational rectitude by the zigzagging scut of a bolting rabbit: 'What racches that rennen to a cony in ony tyme, hym ought to be astried, sayeng to him loude *Ware, Riot, Ware*; for non other wilde best in Engelonde is called *ryot* sauf the conynge alonly.'[14]

Edward's reference to 'ferettis and long smale haies' does not mean that the two were used together; ferreting is a daytime sport, and was carried out in the Middle Ages just as it is today: purse-nets were pegged over the mouths of the holes of a burrow, possibly identified as being occupied with the help of a spaniel (Phoebus recommends working a spaniel through the hedges and thickets to drive the rabbits *into* the holes first[15]), a ferret was put down one hole, and the rabbits bolted in terror into the nets. The tapestry of ferreting reproduced in Fig. 48 represents the participants, male and female, very clearly as peasants. The method of taking rabbits with hayes is nowadays called long-netting; it works best at night, when the rabbits are out feeding, and involves no ferrets, only men and perhaps a dog or two.

If one had no ferret, one could still set purse-nets over the holes and burn a mixture of sulphur and yellow arsenic in the hole furthest upwind to drive out the rabbits.[16] King Modus, in one of his least regal chapters, recommends mixing the chemicals with scraps of charred linen or old parchment, putting them in a special earthenware vessel with an aperture at each end, placing the mouth of the pot in the hole in the warren and introducing a burning coal through the other aperture.[17]

In some areas not even the destructive rabbit was conceded to the poor man as a legitimate quarry, and ferreting was banned. The poacher's eternal defence – poverty and an empty belly – is the basis of the objections raised by Juan Rodríguez and some of his neighbours against the prohibition of ferreting by the town of Jerez de la Frontera, to the detriment of 'many poor persons who earn a living through such hunting, because in the months when they were formerly allowed to hunt they had no crops or other means of earning a living, and it would mean that the wretched poor folk who hunt rabbits to sell them would die of hunger; and hunting with the ferret causes no threat to the breeding of the rabbit'.[18] This suggests, however, that the use of the ferret was normally permitted. Rural Spaniards also employed the *losa*, the stone fall-trap, though attempts were made to restrict its use or phase it out; existing *losas* were an ancient heritable right in some areas, but the ordinances of Carmona prohibit the construction of new ones, or the setting of old ones in the close season (roughly corresponding to Lent) on pain of destruction.[19]

The enclosed rabbit-warren was of great importance in the Middle Ages and later, both the flesh and the skin of the rabbit having a significant value, but the warren falls more into the field of livestock husbandry than hunting.

Southern Spain in the late Middle Ages presents a picture of considerably more democratic hunting practices than the more northerly countries of Europe. As the Moors, who had occupied the area from the early eighth century, were gradually pushed southward (they were not finally driven out of the Kingdom of Granada until 1492), their towns were taken over by the victorious Christians from the north, and new towns were founded. These settlements retained a sense of their own considerable importance, which was reinforced by the codes of law and privileges granted to them by successive monarchs in the far-distant centres of government in León, Castile and Aragón as an incentive to northerners to move southward and consolidate the Christian reoccupation. A farmer, merchant or artisan moving into such an area enjoyed considerably greater freedom to hunt than his counterpart in northern Europe.

This does not mean that the monarchy ignored the potential of the reconquered areas for their own hunting; Alfonso xi's *Libro de la montería*'s description of boar- and bear-hunting areas includes the southern mountain ranges. Subject to this overriding royal prerogative, however, the population of the towns and villages appears to have enjoyed considerable freedom to hunt small game, to engage in falconry, and even, in some areas and periods, to take *caza mayor*, i.e. deer, boar and bear. The towns themselves issued ordinances to restrict particular hunting practices, but the forbidding or suspension of an activity is useful information that that activity was taking place. Much of it would not have found favour with the French or English aristocrat.

The right to hunt in the *coto* of a Spanish town was normally restricted to the residents; the *coto* was the area of countryside over which the town's laws and privileges were applicable (the word survives today almost exclusively in the phrases *coto de caza* and *coto de pesca*, 'shooting- and fishing-reserves'). Some towns, such as Carmona, allowed an outsider to hunt if he obtained written permission from the town council. Others had reciprocal agreements, *hermandades*, which included hunting among those rights (grazing, woodcutting, charcoal-burning) extended to another town; such pairings included Carmona and Seville, Madrid and Manzanares el Real, and Gibraleón and Huelva. Otherwise, strangers found hunting in the *coto* had their game and equipment taken from them, and were fined and sometimes flogged or imprisoned.

Freedom to hunt small ground game and all feathered game in the vicinity of many Spanish towns, though normally unrestricted in areas of common ground and most privately owned land, varied not only with the season of the year, but with the growing of certain crops, the state of the weather and even one's occupation. A general close season operated from the beginning of Lent, but it ended on widely differing dates, in some places as early as 31 May, elsewhere as late as 29 September. Even in the thirteenth century a pragmatic conservationism underlay some of the additional prohibitions: most towns forbade the taking of quail and partridge eggs, and several places in the mountainous areas of Avila and Segovia made it a crime to hunt hares, rabbit and partridge in time of snow. There were ordinances to protect arable land; in Peñafiel hunting in vineyards was banned from 1 May until the grape harvest, and Toledo prohibited hunting in both vineyards and olive groves. Carmona, where a similar ban operated in the vineyards, allowed the owners to protect their vines from the depredations of animals by setting up to two dozen snares. The town of Baeza allowed beekeepers to hunt all the year round and to sell what they killed. This privilege was evidently a compensation for their lonely life in the hills; they were allowed to bring back two brace of rabbits and partridges whenever they returned to their homes.

The devices permitted, or more often temporarily or partially banned, around these Spanish municipalities include the *cebadero* (probably an area of straw fed with grain to lure partridges); nets of various kinds for taking small birds; the *cepo* or large trap for bear, deer and boar; the *callejo*, a type of wolf-trap (probably a pit with fences to guide the wolf into it); stone deadfall traps; the *buey* or ox, of which more later; and the *lazo* or *cuerda*, the snare. Snares appear to have been set for everything from bear and deer down to small birds; it was forbidden to set snares within a league of a dovecote in Cuéllar, and several towns give the domestic pigeon special protection against other forms of hunting. The crossbow, sometimes used with *yerva*, a herbal poison, on the arrowhead, and hunting-birds (the sparrowhawk and, less often, the goshawk are mentioned) were also common in the hunting excursions of the men of these developing towns, as was the use of scenting-hounds and, probably more commonly, greyhounds.

In the lands of the major aristocrats, who acquired vast areas of central and southern Spain in the process of the Reconquest, the men of the towns and villages might find that they were allowed to hunt any game, small game only, or no game at all. Penalties, severe enough in the case of a person of noble birth or a *ciudadano honrado* (a citizen of good repute) who was simply fined, could involve flogging in the case of a lower-class person, and were commonly doubled if the offence took place at night or if the transgressor was an incomer.

Royal edicts, too, nationally applicable, were severe on certain offences. In contrast to the apparent freedom enjoyed by the townspeople to employ snares and traps unless there was some local ban for specific reasons, the *Cortes* of 1348 decreed a punishment of six months in prison, in chains, for anyone setting traps for bear, boar or deer. For a second offence this was augmented by sixty lashes, and for a third by the loss of a hand.[20]

In Germany one finds a similar contrast: severe penalties for certain offences, but an overall acceptance of the validity of the hunting aspirations of the lower classes of society, sufficient to cause the existence of the word *weide-man*, sometimes meaning an employed huntsman but often simply a hunter from the lower reaches of society (especially the free peasantry), in contrast to the more generally applicable term *jeger*.[21]

For both Germany and France there is abundant documentary and pictorial information on methods of killing game and vermin by methods other than hunting with hounds or bow and stable. Stalking deer with the bow or crossbow was marginally acceptable, but was a lonely method, often used by the silent poacher. Even the local clergy might engage in a purposeful, crepuscular foray around the pale of a deer-park (see p. 262). The boar was commonly shot at its wallow at dawn or by moonlight, sometimes from a specially constructed hide with a raised floor which reduced the chances of the hunter's scent betraying him (Fig. 21). King Modus recommends that the hide should be two feet above the ground, and suggests mid-October to the end of November as the suitable season.[22]

As a refinement to stalking, Phoebus[23] suggests making a framework in the shape of a bullock and covering it with a cloth, suitably dyed. It is not clear from the accompanying illustration (Fig. 53), in which the device looks more like an apprehensive anteater in its first ball-gown, whether the hunter moved it towards the quarry himself or had the help of an assistant walking inside it. The hunter, hidden by the cloth bullock, was enabled to approach the deer close enough to shoot even in an area devoid of cover. In the miniature in question he is shooting with a crossbow, but the text also mentions the use of the same contraption against partridges, without stating how the birds were caught or killed. King Modus alludes to the wearing of a 'partridge horse',[24] and an Italian source shows a man wearing an ox's head and a cape, and carrying a cowbell, shepherding partridges into a tunnel-net.[25] The Spanish town legislation sometimes mentions a method called the *buey*, 'the ox', which may have been similar. It, too, was probably used against partridges, since one document banning its use mentions the legitimate alternative of falconry.[26]

Deer are again the target of a pair of hunters in a miniature in the *Livre de chasse* which shows an open-sided cart drawn by a horse. One man is astride the horse; the other crouches on the cart, armed with a crossbow. Both are dressed in green and festooned with leafy branches around waist and head, and more branches are stuck in the cart-shafts and the horse's harness. The instructions are that the cart-wheels should be a little tight on the axles, so as to squeak; the deer, fascinated by the noise, will stand listening until the camouflaged chariot of death is close enough to simplify the hunter's shot.[27]

Marauding boar, raiding an orchard, could be taken in a fall-trap. A low wall of turves or stones was made around a heap of apples, so that the invader had to jump it to reach them. He was allowed to do this unmolested for two or three nights, then a pit was dug at his landing-point and covered with brushwood.[28] It is not easy to convey surprise simply with a rump and a curly tail, but the miniaturist of the *Livre de chasse* somehow achieves it in his picture of the boar vanishing into the hole. When one thinks that many a peasant spent much of the year fattening a domestic pig in preparation for winter, an autumn windfall such as this in one's orchard was probably as welcome as the apples themselves.

Phoebus describes pitfall-traps three *toises* deep (a toise is six feet), shaped like a bottle-dungeon, into which boar were guided by wattle fences ('a form of hunting fit for villeins, common people and peasants').[29] Presumably the height was sufficient to kill or at least to immobilize them; the thought of being lowered into such a pit to dispose of an enraged boar is unappetizing, though they may have been killed with the crossbow or spear. In Germany pitfall-traps were made to take bears and wolves as well as boar.[30] Wolves, despite their value as an exciting *par force* quarry, were destroyed everywhere, without mercy, as vermin. The methods included traps, some consisting of a flat block or board with hinged wooden or metal sections which gave way under the animal's foot and pierced its leg with their toothed edges when it tried to withdraw it,[31] others of a hole containing a snare into which the wolf's foot slipped when it approached a bait.[32] Wolves were also caught in wattle enclosures, lured through one-way gates by the scent of a dead or tethered animal.[33] and others died after eating poisoned cakes[34] or lumps of meat containing large S-shaped needles, or leaping up to seize a bait hanging from a tree only to find that it had a barbed hook inside it.[35]

The *Livre de chasse* shows a horrific device for killing a bear which is making regular nightly raids on a vineyard or orchard: one restricted the point of entry and set in the opening a spring-trap made of a bent bough with the end of a hunting-spear fixed to it at right-angles, and a trip device like that which releases the spring of a mouse-trap. Having shown us this, Gaston Phoebus recoils: 'I do not wish to say any more about this; a most villainous form of hunting.'[36] This device was just one of many which employed the natural materials available in the woods as inconspicuous engines of death. Snares tightened by bent branches or by pivoted beams with a counterweight were used against wolves, foxes, badgers and small game.[37] Birds such as thrushes were also taken with a more delicate version involving a horsehair noose, baited with berries, and a bent sapling, bow or pivot.[38]

A special ingenuity was brought to bear on the capture of small birds.

Those trays of miniature carcasses which horrify the squeamish tourist in Continental market-halls are evidence of the continued existence of an activity which provided variety in the medieval diet and a living for men for whom the seasonal migrations of bird flocks were an unquestioned and recurring harvest. A monarch or aristocrat commonly had his own bird-catcher or 'fowler'; James IV of Scotland, as well as frequently paying men who brought him live herons, etc. for use in training hawks (see p. 204), made payments 'to the fowler in Dernway: .xiii. s.'; 'to the fowler to pass in through Fiff with his nettis and to remane thare on fowlis taking, be the Kingis command: .xxviii. s.'.[39] Here the fowler is clearly distinguished from James's falconers, but elsewhere such a distinction is not always clear. In Germany the word *vogeler* might be applied to a falconer of low rank, sometimes mounted; in some cities the *vogeler* had a paid post, and might be employed in menial work such as letter-carrying as well as in his principal role in stocking the larders with feathered game.[40] In Spain, town legislation laid down prices which fowlers might charge for different birds, and specified places of sale.[41]

As well as providing food, the hunting of small birds was seen as an agricultural necessity. We find Córdoba permitting the killing of thrushes, sparrows, finches and other small birds all the year round, without regard to the normal close season for hunting, because of the damage they did to the fields and their usefulness as a food for the citizens; Lorca allowed the netting of all small birds except domestic pigeons right up to the town walls, to protect the orchards.[42] A fowler had to take large numbers of birds to make a living. In Granada in 1520 a thrush or small bird was worth a *maravedí* and a half (the price of a hen's egg) if fat; one *maravedí* if thin. Domestic pigeon squabs were worth twelve *maravedíes* a brace, wood-pigeons eight. Partridges, much better eating, cost seventeen *maravedíes* apiece, still less than a domestic hen.[43] Partridges were very common as a food in Spain, at least in middle-class society; they figure largely in the evidence presented to the Inquisition concerning the dietary habits of converted Jews in the late fifteenth century.[44]

Pero López de Ayala mentions that the Spanish *rederos* (netsmen) sometimes took the falcons which had flown from northern Europe pursuing the migrating flocks, but wild pigeons and small birds were their bread and butter.[45] To take a falcon must have been a financial bonanza; compare the prices of small birds quoted above with the values of birds of prey (p. 199). The fowlers used numerous varieties of net; some worked unattended, others needed the constant vigilance and shrewd timing of a concealed operator. The spider-net had a fine mesh and was hung in the flight path of the flocks. Birds were caught on the ground with a clap-net, which used either a trip-and-spring device or the action of a man or boy hauling on a rope to throw a net spread by a framework over small birds feeding on grain, or a bird of prey lured to attack a tethered pigeon or a decoy owl. The cage-net allowed crows, etc. to enter through a one-way tunnel to reach a bait, or employed a falling door. Another type of net was suspended over a baited area and dropped when enough birds had accumulated beneath it. Tunnel-nets with a wide mouth and diminishing diameter were used to take waterfowl and partridges.[46]

As well as the random netting carried out to protect individual crops, certain sites were productive enough year after year to become established as 'fowling-floors'. In Germany permanent wooden platforms were built in forest clearings, with very large clap-nets operated by two tension-poles of beech or pine. These poles were bent when the net was set, and released by a tug on the rope when enough birds were on the fowling-floor. Fieldfares were a frequent quarry, and a particular delicacy at the time of the juniper berries. William Turner's *A New Herbal* says that the juniper 'groweth in Germany in many places in greate plentye, but in no place in greater than a lytle from Bon, where as at the time of year the feldfares fede only of junipers berries, the people eate the feldefares undrawen with guttes and all because they are full of the berries of juniper'.[47]

Along the Rhine, areas on or near the riverbank were allocated annually by the civic authorities to fowlers who paid a rental for the exclusive right to net birds. The hamlet of Vogelgrün on a backwater of the river takes its name from the word for such a site, *vogel-grien*. An alternative term, *löz-grien* suggests that the sites may have been distributed by drawing lots.[48]

A widespread and long-lived method of taking small birds was the clap-stick (German *klobe*; French *breulet*; see Fig. 51). It consisted of a cloven stick or of two rods fixed together at one end, pierced with staggered holes through which a zigzag cord was threaded. The fowler hid in a bush from which the stick protruded; he held the end of the stick in one hand and the cord in the other. Small birds were lured to perch on the open stick by a birdcall whistle or a live or stuffed owl decoy, and were trapped by feet or wings with a tug on the cord. King Modus describes the stick in detail: it should be of heart of oak, four feet long, and the inner face of one side should be grooved to take the other so as to grip the birds better. He says that the best time and place were in a vineyard when the grapes were ripe, and suggests other possibilities such as making portable hides to be set in the open where the birds were feeding or, in periods of drought, beside a watering-place.[49]

The birdcall was also used in conjunction with birdlime, which was already in use in the classical period and which is described by King Modus as 'the best, most delightful and most pleasant of all ways of taking birds'.[50] To the twentieth-century reader it appears one of the least delightful, and certainly the messiest. It was best done in the late summer and early autumn, since it was essential to restrict the available perching places for the birds, and the bare boughs of winter gave them too wide a choice, as well as revealing the fowler. The *pipée* or piping-spot was prepared a day or two in advance by stripping suitable boughs, while leaving sufficient leaves elsewhere on the branches to preserve an attractive appearance and to conceal the fowler. On the day itself one had to arrive at dawn and place one's lime-sticks along the stripped boughs. The lime was made from mistletoe berries or the juice of holly bark, and was smeared on short sticks of birch which were arranged in a criss-cross pattern to ensure that no bird could perch on the bough without touching the lime. The birds were attracted by a decoy owl and by the noise made by the fowler blowing either on a piece of grass or leaf between his thumbs, or on a wooden whistle.[51]

A procedure frowned upon, at least intermittently, in Spanish municipal legislation is hunting at night with the *calderuela*,[52] a lantern with which game, for example partridge, was dazzled to allow it to be easily netted. The lantern was commonly used in several countries in conjunction with a bell, for taking larks, partridges, etc. One went 'low-belling', as it was called in England,

> with a great light of cressets or ragges of linnen dipt in Tallow that will make a goode light, and you must have a panne of plate, made like a Lanterne, to carrye your light in . . . and carrie it before you on your brest, with a Bell in your other hand of a great Bignesse, made in manner like to a Cowbell . . . and you must ring it allwayes after one order, with two to goe with Nets one of each side of him that carries the Bell, and what with the light that so doth amaze them, and the Bell that so doth astonish them, they will, when you come neere them, turn up their white bellies, which you shall quickly perceive, then lay your nets on them and take them; but the Bell must not stint going: for if it cease, then the birds will flye up if there be any more nigh. This is a good way to catch Larkes, Woodcockes, and Partriches, and all other land-Birdes.[53]

Some of King Modus's most delightful contrivances are explained in the chapters in which he replies to a poor man's questions about methods of taking birds. Some of his devices have survived the centuries unmodified. His way of capturing partridges by luring them with a trail of grain which leads them via a tunnel of netting into a cage is used today by gamekeepers to catch up pheasants in January for the laying season. So is the wicker basket supported by a figure-of-four support which collapses on the pheasant when it steps on a bar, lured again by a trail of grain.[54] Modus's version has a refinement which has later been abandoned: a mirror under the basket which induces the cock pheasant, taking its own reflection for a rival, to rush in to attack it (Fig. 50). This would probably work, at least in the mating season; less convincing is an alternative scheme to paint a pheasant on a sheet, hang it between the bushes and wait until a real cock pheasant came along and became intent on browbeating its own effigy; one then jumped out of hiding to knock the bird on the head.

The King's most appealing suggestion, so bizarre as to lead one to question whether it was ever successfully applied (even Modus himself says that it is 'astonishing and little used'), is the taking of woodcock *a la folletoere* (Fig. 49). The aim appears to have been either to disguise oneself as a woodcock (a difficult role, since the bird is only some nine inches tall) or to provide the bird with a spectacle so inexplicable that its instinct for survival was suspended by curiosity. The instructions are that the hunter should wear a short cloak, coloured like the autumn leaves, and a hood of the same cloth completely covering his head and shoulders, but with two eyeholes. Some manuscripts show the hood with a long nosepiece, like a Spanish penitent's headdress upside down, reinforcing the birdlike appearance. The hunter is to carry two short sticks, bound with russet, with red cloth at the ends, and a rod with a horsehair noose. He approaches the woodcock slowly on his knees, presumably making the sticks work like a pair of bird's legs; the woodcock becomes intrigued by this gigantic version of itself 'and grows so stupid that the hunter can come close enough to take his rod and gently put the noose over the bird's neck, and so it is taken'.[55]

This would be fun to try if one could only locate a woodcock, a shy and secretive bird, in an open space and persuade it sufficiently to suspend its disbelief to join in the game. One's first inkling of the presence of a woodcock is usually a whirr of wings and a brief glimpse of it jinking away through the trees. Doubt has been cast as to whether Modus is alluding to the woodcock in his use of the word *videcoc*, [56] and some of the manuscript illustrations of his method certainly show a larger long-beaked bird, which tempts one to think that he means the curlew, but his description of the *videcoc*'s habitat and habits in his previous chapter certainly fits the woodcock.

A more reliable way of taking woodcock, and common enough for its name to have been used in a synonym for the twilight, was the cock-shut. In *Richard III* Lord Northumberland and the Earl of Surrey,

> Much about cock-shut time, from troop to troop,
> Went through the army, cheering up the soldiers.
>
> [Act V, Scene 3]

The cock-shut or 'cock-road' was a ride through a wood, sometimes specially cut. The woodcock, whose twilight flight or 'roding' along such places is characteristic of the species, were taken in high nets raised on cords and pulleys. George Owen of Henllys enthuses about the method as used in Wales:

> Yf anie Easterly winde be alofte, wee shal be sure to have him a fortnight and sometimes three weeke before Michaelmas, and for plentie yt is allmost incredible, for when the chiefe time of haunte ys, wee have more plentie of that kinde of foule onely, than of all other sortes layed together, the chiefest plentye ys betweene Michaelmas and Christmas; . . . their chiefe takinge is in cockeroades in woodds, with nettes erected up betweene two trees, where in cocke shoote tyme (as yt is tearmed) which is the twylight (a litle after the breakinge of the daye, and before the closinge of the night) they are taken, sometymes ii. iii. or iiii. at a fall. I have my selfe oftentimes taken vi. at one fall, and in one roade, at an eveninge taken xviii, and yt ys no strange thinge to take a hundred or sixe score in one woodd in xxiiii. houres.[57]

The gullibility of the woodcock, and especially its reputed susceptibility to Modus's cloak-and-noose technique, prompts the King himself to preempt Queen Ratio's normal didactic role with harsh words on human frailty:

> The woodcock is the stupidest bird in the world, which many people on this earth resemble in being so foolish as to take pleasure in earthly delights [probably an allusion to the woodcock's eating habits: it plunges its beak into the soft ground in search of worms]; they think not of God, nor of heavenly rewards, and the Devil, who hunts them, puts his noose around their neck and draws them to him; thus one can say that they are caught *a la folletoere*, like the woodcock.[58]

This stricture is just one of many cases of the medieval use of the imagery of fowling to express the spiritual vulnerability of man. Queen Ratio delivers a graduation address on this theme to the apprentice hunters who have listened to Modus's practical expositions.[59] Fleshly delights, fine wines, rich food, estates and wealth are the baits which lure us into the nets of the devil. Human greed and lust for power turn men into *gens de proie*, 'people of prey', from whom others flee in fear; when they perch in their lonely isolation, like the falcon, they are taken in Satan's snare.

Birdlime, too, is easily made symbolic of man's flesh, by which he is so easily and irrevocably captured, and for Ratio the owl decoys used in liming are comparable to the great lords who encourage the poor into difficulties from which there is no escape. In Germany, where the nets and snares of the fowler are commonly used as images to enliven descriptions both of the devil seizing souls and of Love or the beloved seizing the lover's heart,[60] birdlime imagery symbolizes the trapping of the lover. In some German examples this image is more overtly physical: the lime-stick, smeared with lime, acquires a phallic implication, especially when used in conjunction with the clap-stick or *klobe*, which has the obscene sense of 'vagina'.[61]

Queen Ratio, ever resourceful, has a solution to free man from his adherence to the flesh:

> Birdlime is such that when it is softened it cannot stick to or capture anything. So it is with the flesh: when the flesh of Man is diluted with the tears of contrition and repentance it can capture nothing except that which is its own by right and reason, and so the evil lust of the flesh, the great enemy of Man, is destroyed. And so, if you would defend yourself against these three enemies, the world, the flesh and the Devil, clothe yourself in three things: Faith, Hope and Charity; and be armed likewise with three weapons: Confession, Repentance and Contentment. And thus your enemies will be powerless to do you harm or hurt.[62]

The latter part of the Middle Ages saw a curtailment of the hunting rights of the common man. In France there was a rapid shrinkage: an act of Charles v (1322–28) allowed everyone to hunt, at least for rabbits and hares, in areas other than warrens, but in 1396 Charles vi prohibited the non- nobleman from hunting any game unless he had specific permission, and an attempt to reverse this in 1414 was defeated by the nobles. In England, Richard ii decreed in 1390 that hunting with hounds, ferrets and even snares was to be restricted to those with an estate worth forty shillings a year and to clerks with an income of ten pounds.[63] The attitude underlying such prohibitions is summed up by John of Portugal: 'Kings should prize hunting highly, and ensure that it be not brought down so low as it is nowadays; for every cowherd, priest, or vile fellow seeks to be a hunter, and it is a sorry thing that it should be permitted that such lowborn folk should take part in a thing which was elevated by many good men to preserve the status of kings.'[64]

Gaston Phoebus, a rarity in combining the tastes of an aristocrat with a perception of the feelings of his social inferiors, would have viewed this curtailment of the pleasures of the common man with regret. His own delight in hunting, as we have seen, impelled him to try to increase that of all his fellow men. He is, one feels, not speaking entirely tongue-in-cheek in his expression of concern for the posthumous welfare of those less fortunate than himself on earth, though he is much less solemn about it than Ratio, and clearly his goodwill stops short of egalitarianism:

It would be a great sin on my part if I let people go to Hell when I could save them and let them gain Paradise; and if I let them die when I could prolong their life; and if I made them sad and wretched if I could make them joyful instead. I said at the start of my book [see p. 11] that good hunters live long and merrily and go to Paradise when they die, and therefore I wish to teach *every* man to be a hunter, in one fashion or another [This is at the start of his description of nets, snares, traps and other ignoble devices]. . . . But in whatever fashion they hunt, it is my firm belief that they will enter into Paradise; not the centre of Paradise, but some corner; or at the very least they will be lodged in the outskirts or the lower courts of Paradise, merely by having been saved from idleness, which is the root of every evil.[65]

Explicit

Nowe prey I unto every creature that hathe herde or redde this lytell tretys, what ever he bee of estate or condicyoun, that ther as to lytel is of good langage, that of theyre benignytee and grace they wol more adde, and ther as to is to muche superfluytee, that they wol also abregge hit as hem seme the best, by hure goode and wyse discrecion; nought presumyng upon me that I hade other ful knowelegge or konnynge for to put in wryting this ryale, desportful and noble game of huntyng so effectuelly, but alwey to be submitted under the correccoun of alle gentyle hunters; and in my symple manere as I best koude and might bee lerned of olde and many dyvers gentyl hunters, did my bysynesse in this rude maner to put the crafft, the termes ond thexercyse of this sayde game more in remembraunce, oponly to the knowlegge of alle lordes, ladyes, gentylmen and wymmen.

[From the Shirley manuscript of the *Master of Game*]

The French Royal Hunting Accounts[1]

THE ACCOUNT [of] Philippe de Courguilleroy, Knight, Master Huntsman to Our Lord the King and Master of His Waters and Forests, made in respect of the wages and maintenance which are his right as Master of the said Waters and Forests, and for the wages, clothing, maintenance, boots and axes of six huntsmen, two aides and the Clerk of Venery, and of the varlets and pages of the King's running-hounds and greyhounds, for the third part of a year, namely the term beginning on the Day of the Ascension of Our Lord, 1398, and ending on All Saints' Day in the same year; and also for the expenses of the running-hounds, lymers and greyhounds, both for the hart and for the boar, at home and away from home, from the day after Ascension Day to the day after All Saints'.

RECEIPT given by me, Philippe de Courguilleroy, Knight, Master Huntsman to the King, for the pay of myself and my fellow-huntsmen of the said Office of the Venery and the expenses of the King's hart-hounds and boar-hounds, at home and away from home, from the day after Ascension Day to the day after All Saints':

Received by me, Philippe de Courguilleroy, from Jean Auber, Viscount of Rouen, by order of the King's Treasurers, for the Venery in the term ending on All Saints' Day, 1398, against my receipt given at Rouen on the last but one day of October: 800 l.p.[2]

Received by me, Philippe de Courguilleroy, from Pierre Courtin, Receiver of Senlis, by order of the King and His Treasurers, for the term ending at All Saints', against my receipt given at Senlis on the first of December of the said year: 320 l.p.

Total received: 1120 l.p.

EXPENSES of this present account

WAGES of Officers
Philippe de Courguilleroy, Knight, Master Huntsman to Our Lord the King, for his wages earned in the said office of Master Huntsman and Master of Waters and Forests for the third part of a year, being the term beginning on the Day of the Ascension of Our Lord, 1398, and ending on All Saints' Day:

.x. s.p. per day, making 182 l. 10 s.p. per year, and for the one third of the year at the said term: 60 l. 16 s. 8 d.p.

Maintenance of the said Philippe de Courguilleroy: 100 l. per year, and for the term   33 l. 6 s. 8 d.p.

[HUNTSMEN]
Robert de Franconville, Squire, Huntsman to the King, for his wages in the said office for the third of a year ending at the term of All Saints': 3 s. per day, making 54 l. 15 s.p. per year, and for the third of a year of this term 18 l. 5 s.p.[3]

Clothing 100 s.p. per year, and so for this term 33 s. 4 d.p.

Maintenance at 80 l.p. per year, and so for this term 26 l. 13 s. 4 d.p.

Boots and axes at 17 s.p. per year, and so for this term 5 s. 8 d.p.

Total, paid to him against his receipt, 12 November 1398:   46 l. 17 s. 4 d.p.

[Identical payments follow to:]
Mahieu de Franconville, Squire, Huntsman to the King
Jehan de Courguilleroy, Squire, Huntsman to the King
Loys Cochet, Squire, Huntsman to the King
Gillet Brossart, Huntsman to the King
Richart Potier, Huntsman to the King

AIDES AND THE CLERK OF VENERY
Jehan Villart, Aide of Venery to Our Lord the King, for his wages in the said office for the third of a year ending on All Saints' Day: 2 s.p. per day, making 36 l. 10 s.p. per year, and so for the present term 12 l. 3 s. 4 d.p.

Clothing at 100 s. per year, and for the present term 33 s. 4 d.p.

Maintenance at 40 l.p. per year, so for the present term 13 l. 6 s. 8 d.p.

Total paid to him against his receipt, 12 November 1398:   27 l. 3 s. 4 d.p.

[Identical payments to:]
Philippot le Prouvencel, Aide of Venery
Gervaisot de la Chambre, Clerk of Venery

VARLETS OF HOUNDS AND GREYHOUNDS
Robin Rasson, Varlet of Hounds to Our Lord the King for his wages in the said office for the third of a year ending at the term of All Saints: 8 d.p. per day, making 12 l. 3 s. 4 d.p. per year, and so for one third of a year 4 l. 13 d.p.

Clothing at 40 s.p. per year, and so for the one-third term 13 s. 4 d.

Maintenance at 16 l. per year, and so for this term 106 s. 8 d.p.

Total paid against his receipt: 10 l. 13 d.p.

[Identical payment to:]
Jehan Corneprise

Gillet Parquier,[4] appointed Varlet of Hounds to Our Lord the King, replacing Guillaume Gloret deceased. For the wages of the said Gillet in the said office from 19 August 1398 inclusive, who was employed, as is more fully explained in a transcript of the ledgers of Our Lord the King collated by the Chamber of Accounts, to the 1st November, the Feast of All Saints, i.e. 74 days at 8 d.p. per day, making 49 s. 4 d.p.

Clothing at 40 s.p. per year, making for the said period 7 s. 8 d.p.

Maintenance at 16 l.p. per year, making for the said period 113 s. 8 d.p.

Total paid to him against his receipt, as is confirmed in the said transcript of the Royal Accounts: 6 l. 8 d.p.

[The following receive the same payments as Robin Rasson:]
Perrin Parquier, Varlet of Hounds
Jehan de Bouchevillier, Varlet of Hounds
Guillaume le Prouvencel, Varlet of Hounds
Jehan Huelievre, Varlet of Hounds
Adam Rasson, Varlet of Greyhounds
Edouart Stratton, Varlet of Greyhounds
Guillot Sonot, Varlet of Greyhounds

PAGES OF HOUNDS AND GREYHOUNDS
Jehan Alanaine, Page of Hounds to Our Lord the King, for his wages in the said office for one third of a year ending at the All Saints' term: 8 d.p. per day, making 12 l. 3 s. 4 d.p. per year, and so for the term 4 l. 13 d.p.

Maintenance at 8 l.p. per year, making for the term 53 s. 4 d.p.

Total paid to him against his receipt on 12 November 1398: 6 l. 14 s. 5 d.p.

[The following receive the same payments:]
Regnault Bouchart, Page of Hounds
Perrin de la Rue, Page of Hounds
Jehan le Comte, Page of Hounds
Perrin le Cornal, Page of Hounds

Robin Hennoquel, appointed Page of Hounds to Our Lord the King in place of Gillet Parquier, now Varlet of Hounds. For the wages of the said Robin

Hennoquel in the said office of Page of Hounds from 19 August 1398
inclusive, who was appointed, as is confirmed in a transcript of the royal
ledgers issued by the Chamber of Accounts, until the 1st of November, the
Feast of All Saints, i.e. 74 days, at 8 d.p. per day, making 49 s. 4 d.p.

Maintenance at 8 l. per year, making for the said period 31 s. 10 d.p.

Total paid to him against his receipt on 19 August, as is confirmed in the
transcript of the Royal Accounts: 4 l. 1 s. 2 d.p.

[The following receive the same payments as Jehan Alanaine:]
Massiot Brisset, Page of Hounds
Jehan Regnault, Page of Greyhounds
Guillaume de la Bourne, Page of Greyhounds
Gieuffroy le Masson, Page of Greyhounds

EXPENSES incurred in respect of Our Lord the King's 108 running-hounds,
8 lymers and 24 greyhounds for the hart-hunting, with 20 greyhounds of
the King's Chamber hunting the hart in the forests of France, plus the
expenses of a number of running-hounds, greyhounds and mastiffs hunting
the boar for the King in his boar-hunts, and of a number of hounds, mastiffs
and varlets borrowed for the said boar-hunts. These present expenses were
incurred for the royal hounds while deer-hunting and at home, and for the
hounds, greyhounds and mastiffs in boar-hunting, and in buying bread for
the hounds, rope, salt for salting venison, expenses of varlets and sundry
other necessities of the hounds, both at home and away from home, in the
hart-hunting and the boar-hunting, as set down in the accounts of M.
Philippe de Courguilleroy, Knight, Master Huntsman to the King, for the
term running from Ascension Day to All Saints', 1398.

Michel de Soissons, baker in Senlis, for bread supplied for 108 running-
hounds, 8 lymers and 24 greyhounds, and for 20 greyhounds of the King's
Chamber, all being together in the town of St Christophe to hunt the hart in
the Forest of Halatte and the country around, for 50 days from 27 May to 16
July 1398: 72 l.p.

Jehan de Bosne of St Christophe, for the cost of 3 varlets who kept the 20
greyhounds of the King's Chamber at the hunting with the hart-hounds for
6 days, from 27 May to 2 June: 18 s.p.

Perrin le Cordier of Senlis, for 60 *toises* of rope to make couples for the
hounds, lymers and greyhounds when they were at St Christophe. Paid on
4 June, at 2 d.p. per *toise*: 10 s.p.

For 4 lb. of candles bought at Pont Sainte Maxence so as to enable the
hounds to be prepared at night when they were in the said town; at 12 d.p.
per pound: 4 s.p.

Perrin le Cordier of Senlis, for three cowhide traces for three of the King's lymers when they were in that town; at 16 d.p. per length: 4 s.p.

For 16 ox and sheep plucks bought in the butcher's in Senlis to make soup to give to certain lean hounds which refused bread. Paid on 10 June at 4 d.p. apiece: 5 s. 4 d.p.

To Guillaume le Mercier in Senlis, for four pots of oil of hemp, camphor [?], quicksilver and sulphur, all mixed together, to anoint the wounds of the hounds when they were in that town. Paid on 12 June, total: 16 s.p.

To the same, for 12 wooden combs to groom and clean the hounds; paid on 16 June at 4 d.p. apiece: 4 s.p.

Michel de Lie, innkeeper in St Christophe, for the expenses of the said three varlets lodged there to serve the King in his hunting in the forest by keeping the greyhounds of the Chamber; 6 days: 14 s.p.

Jehan Bonnevoie, for the supply of a cart to convey the bread for the hounds from Senlis to St Christophe for 6 days; paid on 18 June: 12 s.p.

To the same, for a two-horse cart to carry bread from Senlis to St Christophe for 4 days; paid on 20 June: 8 s.p.

Robin le Cordier of Senlis, for 50 *toises* of rope to make couples for the hounds, lymers and greyhounds when they were in that town; paid on 22 June, at 2 d.p. per *toise*: 8 s. 4 d.p.

Pierre Hardy of Fleurines, for the expenses of the three varlets keeping the greyhounds of the King's Chamber at Fleurines for the King's hunting in the said forest in the months of June and July; paid against his receipt on 13 June 1398: 68 s.p.

Jehan Joli and Thevenon le Songeur, bakers in Fontainebleau, for bread for the King's running-hounds, lymers and greyhounds, with 20 greyhounds of the Chamber, being all at Fontainebleau to hunt the hart in the Forest of Bière and the country around; 63 days from 16 July to 17 September 1398, while these dogs were kennelled in the town; paid as appears in their receipt: 102 l.p.

Adam Rasson of Fontainebleau, for the cost of bread, wine and meat for the said three varlets keeping the greyhounds of the King's Chamber, at Fontainebleau with the King's Venery for the hart-hunting; 63 days from 16 July to 17 September; paid against his receipt: 6 l. 18 s.p.

Guillaume Cordelette, ropemaker in Moret, for 80 *toises* of rope to make couples for the hounds; paid on 20 July at 2 d.p. per *toise*: 13 s. 4 d.p.

For 2 pairs of breeches and 2 pairs of new shoes bought from Jehan Ouvry, shoemaker in Moret, for two of the varlets keeping the greyhounds of the

King's Chamber for his hunting in the said forest . . .; paid in total on 24 July: 20 s.p.

For 6 lb. of candles bought from Thevenon de Loperon of Moret, to light the kennels to attend to the hounds at night . . .; paid on 24 July at 12 d.p. per pound: 6 s.p.

For a pair of breeches bought in Moret for a poor varlet who lies with the hounds at night and has no wages; paid on 25 July: 8 s.p.

For a pair of new shoes bought in Moret for the same poor varlet; paid on 26 July: 3 s. 4 d.p.

For 2 bushels of salt bought in Moret to salt for the King in Fountainebleau a hart taken in the said forest; paid on 27 July at 4 s.p. per bushel: 8 s.p.

For 24 sheep plucks bought at the butcher's in Moret and Fontainebleau to make soup for certain lean hounds which refused bread; 31 July, at 3 d.p. apiece: 6 s.p.

For 2 bushels of salt to salt for the King a hart taken in the said forest on the last day of July: 8 s.p.

Raoulet Tabone, in silver given to him for seeking three hounds of the King's Venery which had run away in pursuit of a hart in the Forest of Stenart [?], for which purpose he was away 4 days; paid to him on 6 August: 7 s.p.

Davisot Durant of Fontainebleau, for the use of his horse to carry the hounds' bread to Ury for the *curée* of a hart killed there on 8 August: 2 s.p.

Jehan le Roy of Fontainebleau, for the use of his horse to carry the bread for the hounds to the *curée* of a hart taken at Soisy sur Ecole; paid to him on 24 August: 2 s. 8 d.p.

For two lengths of cowhide bought at Moret for two of the King's lymers in Fontainebleau; 30 August 1398; at 16 d.p. per length: 2 s. 8 d.p.

For 4 lb. of candles bought from Thevenon de Loperon of Moret to light the kennels to attend to the hounds at night; 1 September; at 12 d. the pound: 4 s.p.

Gontier Gontier, store-keeper of the salt store established for the King at Montereau-faut-Yonne, for 9 *minots*[5] of salt, local measure, taken by me, Philippe de Courgulleroy, from the said store, after salting venison for the supply of the King's household at Fontainebleau; namely several carcasses of deer taken by the King's hounds; paid to the said store-keeper . . . on 8 September 1398, at 19 s.p. per *minot*: 8 l. 11 s.p.

[EXPENSES] for 98 running-hounds, 8 lymers and 30 greyhounds, all kennelled at Fontainebleau, being expenditure on wheat for bread for the said hounds, lymers and greyhounds, rope, salt, candles and sundry other necessities for the said hounds; set down in the accounts of Philippe de Courguilleroy for the term beginning on Ascension Day and ending on All Saints' Day, 1398.

Gillet Parquier and Edouart Stratton, varlets of hounds and greyhounds to the King, in money supplied to them by me, Philippe de Courguilleroy, Master Huntsman to the King, to buy in Nemours market 16 *minots* of wheat, Gâtinais measure, to make bread for the King's 98 running-hounds, 8 lymers and 30 greyhounds for the hart-hunting, all kennelled at Fontainebleau for the period of 38 days from 17 September to 25 October 1398; . . . at 58 s.p. per *minot*:   46 l. 8 s.p.

Hennequin Videl of Fontainebleau, for 3 *minots* of wheat, by the measure of that town, received from him to make bread for the King's hounds kennelled in Fontainebleau for 7 days from 25 October to 1 November, the Feast of All Saints, 1398; at 64 s.p. per *minot*:   9 l. 12 s.p.

Guillaume Cordelette, ropemaker in Moret, for 80 *toises* of rope to make couples for the running-hounds, lymers and greyhounds kennelled at Fontainebleau; paid to him on 20 September, at 2 d.p. per *toise*:   13 s. 4 d.p.

To the same, for 12 *toises* of thick rope to raise water from the well to water the hounds . . .; paid on 21 September at 4 d.p. per *toise*:   4 s.p.

Thevenon de Loperon of Moret, for 8 lb. of candles . . .; paid on 24 September at 12 d.p. the pound: 8 s.p.

Jehan Bon, varlet of Fontainebleau, for his work in making 2 dozen hazel hurdles for the kennels of the said hounds and greyhounds . . . to raise the beds so that the hounds should not sleep on the ground, and so as to use less straw; paid on 26 September: 20 s.p.

Perrin Bon, varlet of the said town, for his labour in seeking and cutting down several hazel trees in the King's woods for making the hurdles for bedding the hounds; paid on 26 September: 16 s.p.

Adam Margolet of Ury, for a *minot* of beans for making bean broth for the hounds and greyhounds; paid on 28 September: 12 s.p.

To Le Magneur, butcher, for 8 pints of pig's blood for strengthening the bean broth for the hounds . . .; paid on 29 September, at 16 d.p. per pint:
10 s. 8 d.p.

Thevenon de Loperon of Moret, for 2 bushels of salt to flavour the bean broth for the hounds; paid on 29 September, at 6 s. per bushel: 12 s.p.

For 4 earthenware pots bought in Moret to prepare the bean broth and other things for the hounds; paid on 29 September, at 8 d.p. per pot:
2 s. 8 d.p.

For 4 round wooden tubs, bought in Moret for use in the kennels for watering the hounds; paid on 4 October at 2 s. 8 d.p. apiece: 10 s. 8 d.p.

For 4 new pails bought in Moret for carrying water from the well to the kennels; paid on 8 October at 2 s.p. apiece: 8 s.p.

For 24 sheep and ox plucks bought in the butchers' in Moret and Fontainebleau to give to certain lean hounds which refused bread . . .; paid on 10 October, at 4 d.p. apiece: 8 s.p.

For two pairs of new breeches bought in Moret . . . for the two poor varlets who lie at night with the hounds and have no wages; paid on 16 October at 8 s.p. per pair: 16 s.p.

For two pairs of new shoes bought in Moret for the same two varlets . . .; paid on 16 October at 4 s.p. per pair: 8 s.p.

For 4 lengths of cowhide bought in Moret for 4 of the King's lymers in Fontainebleau, paid on 15 October at 16 d.p. per length: 5 s. 4 d.p.

For 8 lb. of candles bought in Moret so as to be able to see to attend to the hounds at night; paid on 16 October at 12 d.p. per pound: 8 s.p.

For 16 wooden combs bought from Thevenon de Loperon in Moret for grooming and cleaning the hounds; at 4 d.p. apiece: 5 s. 4 d.

For 2 bushels of salt bought in Moret for salting the soup for the hounds . . .; paid on 21 October, at 6 s.p. per bushel: 12 s.p.

For 48 *toises* of rope bought from Guillaume Cordelette of Moret to make couples for the hounds and greyhounds . . .; paid on 21 October at 2 d.p. per *toise*:   8 s.p.

For 4 carcasses of old, worn-out horses bought in Nemours market to feed several thin and ailing hounds kennelled at Fontainebleau; paid on 23 October at 3 s.p. per carcass: 12 s.p.

[EXPENSES] for 48 boar-hounds, 8 lymers and 48 mastiffs borrowed from various persons, namely from the Abbot of Châalis, from Le Galois d'Aulnay, and others of the town of St Leu and elsewhere, hunting the boar for the King's pleasure; this outlay being for bread for the hounds, rope, salt for preserving venison, candles, expenses of varlets keeping the hounds and mastiffs, as described in these accounts of myself, Philippe de Courguilleroy, Knight, for the term beginning on Ascension Day, 1398, and ending at All Saints' in the same year.

Michel de Soissons, baker in Senlis, for bread supplied for the 48 running-hounds, 8 lymers and 48 mastiffs borrowed from various persons, namely the Abbot of Châalis, Le Galois d'Aulnay and other persons of the town of

St Leu and elsewhere, when the hounds were at St Christophe to hunt the black beasts in the Forest of Halatte and the lands around for 20 days from 22 October 1398, when boar-hunting began, until 1 November, the Feast of All Saints; paid against his receipt on 25 November: 38 l. 18 s.p.

Guillot le Mastinier, called Sonot, for his expenses in the Forest of Dyrmon [?] in seeking 24 mastiffs borrowed for the King's sport in his boar-hunting in the Forest of Halatte, and for his lodging for this purpose and for bringing these mastiffs to the Forest of Halatte with the boar-hounds for ten days; also for the bread supplied by him for the mastiffs and the expense of 4 varlets of the Forest of Dyrmon who came to serve the King with the mastiffs; paid to him for all his time, including his journeys from and back to St Christophe: 116 s.p.

For 60 *toises* of rope bought in Senlis to make couples, lyams and hardes for the hounds, greyhounds and mastiffs when they were at St Christophe for the King's hunting; paid on 16 October at 2 d.p. per *toise*:   10 s.p.

For 6 lengths of cowhide bought from Robin le Cordier for 6 of the King's lymers . . .; paid on 18 October at 16 d.p. per length: 8 s.p.

For 8 billhooks bought in Senlis from Jehan Sale of that town to make the hayes for the King's boar-hunting in the Forest of Halatte; paid on 20 October at 2 s.p. apiece: 16 s.p.

For 6 deerskin mittens bought from Jehan Sale in Senlis for making the hayes for the King's boar-hunting in the Forest of Halatte; paid on 20 October at 16 d.p. apiece: 8 s.p.

Jehan de Bosne of St Christophe, for the expenses of the varlets borrowed to serve the King in his sport in the said forest; paid on 20 October: 20 s.p.

Michel de Lie, innkeeper, for the expenses of the varlets borrowed to serve the King . . .; paid on 20 October: 20 s.p.

For 2 pairs of breeches and 2 pairs of new shoes, bought in Senlis for 2 of the borrowed varlets . . .; total: 20 s.p.

[2 further pairs of breeches and shoes were bought on 24 October, and two more pairs of each on 26 October.]

Girardin le Mercier of Senlis, for 3 bushels of salt to salt down for the King's larder 3 boars taken in the Forest of Halatte; paid on 22 October at 6 s.p. per` bushel: 18 s.p.
[More salt was bought in Senlis on 23 October (2 boars); 24 October (3); 25 October (1); 26 October (2); 27 October (2).]

Jehan Bonnevoie of Senlis, for the use of his two-horse wagon for bringing the hounds' bread from Senlis to St Christophe . . .; paid on 23 October:
6 s.p.

Pierre Mollevite of St Christophe, for the expenses of the varlets borrowed to guard hounds and mastiffs of the persons named above in St Christophe; paid on 24 October: 20 s.p.

Perrin de la Mare of Senlis, for the use of his two-horse wagon for bringing the hounds' bread from Senlis to St Christophe on two days; paid on 25 October: 4 s.p.

For a prime pig bought in Senlis market and given to the hounds in the place of a boar salted for the King on 25 October: 18 s.p.

Perrin Hardy of Fleurines, for the expenses of the varlets borrowed to serve the King in his sport in the Forest of Halatte for three days . . .; paid on 26 October: 20 s.p.

Guillaume Terot, for his expenses in bringing the boar-hunting equipment from Fontainebleau to St Christophe for 3 days . . .; paid on 26 October:
                                                                                                                        20 s.p.

Jehan de Bosne, for the costs of the carters and horses bringing the equipment for the King's boar-hunting in the said forest . . .; paid on 26 October: 18 s.p.

For 10 lb. of candles bought in Senlis from Pierre le Mercier . . .; paid on 26 October at 12 d.p. per lb.:   10 s.p.

For 40 *toises* of rope bought from Colin Dotens of Senlis to make couples for the hounds . . .; paid on 27 October at 2 d.p. per *toise*:   6 s. 8 d.p.

To Jehan de Fleurines, for the expenses of the varlets borrowed to serve the King in his hunting in the Forest of Halatte for 3 days, 27, 28 and 29 October: 20 s.p.

To Gervaisot de la Chambre, for the expenses of himself and one other in going to Rouen and Senlis to the Viscount and the Receiver there to request and obtain the moneys for the present account, his accommodation there and his journeys to and from these places; 16 days, namely to Rouen 10 days, from 22 October to 1 November 1398, and to Senlis 6 days, from 28 November to 3 December, at 12 s.p. per day   9 l. 12 s.p.

To the same for parchment, paper and ink for making 3 copies of these accounts, one on paper and two on parchment, and for the labour of a clerk to do this . . .

The Framlingham Park Game Roll[1]

[1515]

In the .vii. yere of our soferen lord Kyng Herry the .viii. and in the .xxiii. yer of Rychard Chambyr, parker of Framlingham

Item My Lord of Norwyche	i buk
Item My Lord Wylleby	ii bukkis
Item be the commaundment of My Lord Wylleby Sir Lyenell Demok	i buk
Item My Lady Vere	i buk
Item the Abbot of Sypton	i buk
Item Sir Wylliam Rows	i buk
Item the Abbas of Brusyzard	i buk
Item the master of Metyngham	i buk
Item Iohan Henyngham	i buk
Item Sir Arthur Hopton	i buk
Item Sir Edmond Jeney	i buk
Item Sir John Wyllebye	i buk
Item Anthony Hansart	i buk
Item Sir Robert Cotton	i buk
Item Sir Tomas Lovell	i buk
Item the Prior of Hey and the scoellmastyr	i buk
Item for Iohan Teye	i buk
Item the Balys of Ypswyche	i buk
Item Robert Cheke	i buk
Item the gyld of Framlingham	i buk
Item the Abbot of Bery	ii bukkis
Item the Prior of Buttley	i buk
Item the Prior of Seynt Peters	i buk
Item the Prior of Woodbrege	i buk
Item the Prior of Elye	i buk
Item Edmond Wyngfeld	i buk
Item Wylliam Jeney	i buk
Item Crystoper Harman	i buk
Item Edmond Gelgatt	i buk
Item Robert Forthe the helder	i buk

Item Doctor Call	i buk
Item the Parson of Framlingham, for his tythe	i buk
Item My Lord Curson was her and kylled a buk and a sowrell, and I gave the sowrell to Lord Cursons servauntis and Sir Rychyard Wentforthys servauntys	i buk
Item Sir Rychard Wentforthe	i buk
Item Sir Anthony Wyngfeld	i buk
Item Sir Rychard Cawndysche	i buk
Item Sir Iohan Awdeley	i buk
Item Sir Iohan Glemham	i buk
Item Sir Iamys Framyngham	i buk
Item the townschepe of Ypswyche	i buk
Item Master Lane	i buk
Item the towne of Wodbrege	i buk
Item the Priories of Campsey	i buk
Item Master Commysary	i buk
Item be a warrant of My Lordis, Iohan Draper gentylman	i buk
Item be a warrant of My Lordis, Iohan Mascall of the Chancery	i buk
Item be a warrant of My Lordis, Rychard Warton	i buk
Item the Person of Orforthe and Johan Garlond	i buk
Item be a warrant of My Lordis	i buk
Item Sir Edward Ichyngham	i buk
Item Regnold Lytylprow	i buk
Item Iohan Rychere of Bongay	i buk
Item Sir Crystofer Wyllebye	i buk
Item Herry Kooke	i buk
Item My Lady Bowser	i buk
Item be warrant of My Lordis, Mastyr Chauncy	i buk
Item Master Lucas	i buk
Item Thomas Benet and Robert Mellis	i buk
Item Mr Thomas Fyncham	i buk
Item Wylliam Mekylfeld	i buk
Item Mr Prior of Thelforthe	i buk
Item Robert Browne	i buk
Item Thomas Sporne	i buk
Item the towne of Harleston	i buk
Item Sir Thomas Tyrrell	i buk
Item Thomas Cok, for hys dowtyris marryage	i buk
Item for Mastrys Marget Hasset	i buk
Item Edmond Rookwood	i buk
Item Nycholas Call	i buk

Item be a warrant of My Lordis, Wylliam Crane
    gentylman   i buk
Item Humfrey Everton   i buk
Item Thomas Russche   i buk
Item Sir Thomas Wysche   i buk

Lossys thys somer ded of the wyppys
Item of buks   iii
Item of sowers   v
Item of preketys   i
Item of dooys   viii
Item a dog came in and kyllyd a do
Item Dallyng of Laxfeld Merser, .ii. doggis of hys came
    in and kyllyd a doo and a fawne
Item on Holy Rood evyn I found in the parke Sir Iohan
    Bowse, parysch pryst of Tanygton, with hys bow bent
    and an arrow in yt, betyng at the herd.¯

These be the doys that I have kyllyd thes seson
Item My Lord Wylleby   ii doys
Item for the Awdyt   ii doys
Item to My Lordis Grace to Lambethe   viii doys
Item aftyr that the second tyme   vi doys
Item at the .iii. tyme   vi doys
Item my Lord Wyllebye   i do
Item . . .
[presents to various individuals; 64 does in all]
My Lord Wylleby cam from London and he schewyd me
    that My Lordys Grace was content thatt he sholde kyll
    doys her, and for as many doys as he kyllyd heere he
    shulde put quyke [i.e. live] doys in Hersham Park for
    them as wyche he had   x doys
Also he seyd My Lordys Grace was content thatt My
    Lord Byrsschope schuld have   ii doys
He seyd that My Lordys Grace schulde have to putt in
    Hersham Park   vi doys
Also he schewyd me that My Lordys Grace was content
    that Iohan Henyngham schuld have .iii. doys and he
    schulde put in Hersham Parke for them   viii doys

Thees be the lossys thatt I have had thys wynter
Item of bukkys   vii
Item of sowrellys   iiii
Item of preketys   x
Item of dooys   xvii

Item of fawnys	iii score xi
These be dede be Candylmes	
Thes be the lossys sythe Candylmes	
Item of bukkys	iii
Item a buk dyed drownyd in the moote	i
Item sowrells	ii
Item sowers	i
Item prekettys	iiii
Item doys	v
Item of ye last yer fawnys morkyns	xlix
Thes be ded syn Wytson Day	

[1516]
In the .viii. yer

Lossys this fawning tym

Item of fawnys	xlx^te [sic]

Thes be the bukkys y^t I have kyllyd thys yer

Item the Frensche Quene	i buk
Item .ii. fawnys.	
Item she sent to me for a fawne.	
Item the Duke sent to me for a	i buk
Item the Quene cam agayn and kyllyd	iiii bukys
Item . . . [various other persons, making a total of 99 bucks, 2 sores, 3 sorrells, a pricket, 2 does and a fawn]	

Thes be ye lossys thys somer of the garget

[A list totalling 9 bucks, 3 sores, 4 sorrells and a pricket]	
Item doys dyed of fawning and the garget	xi

Thes be the dere that I have begon to kyll this seson

[9 does for various persons]	
Item for the audyte	ii dois
Item to My Lordys Grace to London before the awdyte and aftyr	xxxvi doys
[25 more does to various persons]	

Thes be the dere that be ded in the same place

[7 bucks, 3 sores, 5 sorrells, 8 prickets, 23 does, 59 fawns]
Item Johan Pulsham thelder cam rydyng be the wey and fownd a do without and hys doge kyllyd hym

[*sic*] and he hyng hys dog.

Also Watyr Warnere, the sone of Ane Warnere of
    Denyngton, forstallyd My Lordys dere wan I was
    settyng them home and put hys byche to hyr and
    browt hyre in to the parke and kyllyd here.

Also on Seynt Markys Day Johan Foxe and yonge
    Thomas Hyllys, laddys, and William Tendyclone, they
    went forthe to the releffyng [?] of the hare and had a
    sowre, and browt hyr in to the parke and kyllyd a do
    with fawne and another fawne.

[1517]
Thes be the deere that I have kyllyd thys somere
[Entries totalling 93 bucks, 1 doe, 1 sorrell, including
    the following]

Item My Lord Edmond Howard	vi bukkys
Item for the comyng of My Lord Cardenall	i buk
Item he cam trow the parke and kyllyd	i buk and a do
Item on the next day I was sygned to kyll for hym	xii bukkys

Dead of the garget
[11 bucks, 6 sores, 7 sorrells, 43 prickets, 67 does, 50
    fawns]

On the Thourisday after Mycholmes Daye at night I toke
    the persone [parson] of Ketylweris Brege in the
    parke.
[Killed for various persons 22 does]

*These be the lossys of quyke deere to Wyndferdyng for My
    Lorde of Surrey*
[121 deer taken at various times, including bucks, sores,
    sorrells, does, prickets, 'malefawnys' and 'rascall
    fawnys']

Deer had to Hersham for My Lord of Norfolk at four times
[120 and one 'quyk dere']

Dead this winter in Framlingham Park
[44 bucks, 19 sores, 28 sorrells, 54 prickets, 89 does, 165
    fawns]

[1518]
[68 bucks killed]

Died of the garget and the rotte thys somore
[15 bucks, 6 sores, 9 sorrells, 4 prickets, 11 'of dooges']

[31 fawns lost at fawning and in the summer]

[93 does killed for various persons, including the
    following]
Item for My Lorde of Norffolks Grace to Lambeth afore
    the audite and senys   xxx doys
Item the Abbot of Bery sent to me for a doo, upon Sent
    Johanis Day in Cristismes, and I kyllyd hyr and
    delyveryd hyr to Johan Crispe and to Johan Chyrie,
    and in the whey homeward they took a corse in
    Holfereth and broute a souerell in to the parke and
    kyllyd hyme ther. At wich I toke up the one doge in
    the parke and keppyd hym, they made labor to Sir
    Wylliam Rowces for the dog and I delyveryde the dog
    to hym.   i doo

[Lost in the winter in Framlingham Park: 23 bucks, 16
    sores, 19 sorrells, 16 prickets, 38 does and 'of faunys
    .lx xxxv.' (*sic*). A doe and 9 fawns were killed by
    dogs.]

[1519]
Losses this fawning time
[53 fawns died, and one was killed by 'a mastife beche
    and a spanyell'.]

[96 bucks were killed for various persons, including the
    following]
Item Sir Johan Rowe for syngynge of hys fyrst messe   i bucke
Item George Baker for his mariage   i bucke

Item the Mundaye afore Mychaelmes Daye cam in a
    dogge of Iohnsons of Denyngtone, the shoemaker,
    and kyllyd .ii. dooes, and there the dogge was take
    up, and I sende to hym to wete wether he wold have
    the dogge agayne and he sende me word naye, and
    then I hynge hym upon a tre.

An English Royal Hunt Wages Account[1]

This indenture made at Dorchester the third October the year of our Lord the King Henry Fourth since the Conquest Ninth. Witness by Waut Rodeney sheriff of the counties of Somerset and Dorset by virtue of a writ under privy seal of our said lord the king has paid for the wages of the huntsmen and the puture of the dogs of our said lord the king, one hundred and thirty one pounds eleven pence and one maille [halfpenny] in the manner be shewn below thus:

To Edward Duke of York,[2] Count of Canterbury, Rutland and Cork and lord of Tyndale, Master of harthounds of our said lord the king, twelve pence daily.

To Robert Hurlebat and Edward Banet, Yeoman berners at horse for the said office, to each of them four pence daily.

To Roger Cheneston, John Hayne, William Milbourne and Henry Digge, yeoman berners on foot, of the same office, to each of them two pence daily.

To Edmond Rokesbury and John Bowier, yeoman veautrers [fewterers] of the said office, to each of them two pence daily.

To Thomas Benchesham, Robert Bailly, William Cawet and John Cawet, grooms of the same office, to each of them one penny halfpenny daily for their wages.

And to the aforesaid Robert Hurlebat and Edward Benet for the expenses of two horses in their charge, for each horse 3 pence one farthing daily; and for the puture of forty dogs of our lord the king and twelve greyhounds, for each of them three farthings daily; and for three limers, for each of them one penny daily; commencing the above said wages, expenses and puture of the aforesaid dogs from the thirtieth day of September, the year of our lord the king the eighth, and ending on the twenty ninth day of the same month in the following year for a whole year counting both days.

In witness of which to this indenture the said sheriff and the aforesaid Duke has put the seal of his office, etc.

Alfonso XI's *Code of the Freedom and Rights of Huntsmen*[1]

Firstly, in order that those who go to hunt shall do so in safety, any man who seeks a huntsman to injure him, take him prisoner or kill him, even if he is his enemy or formally in dispute with him, or has been challenged by him, and injures, seizes or kills him while he is occupied in hunting, shall be punished for injuring him by three months in the royal prison; for taking him prisoner, by six months in the royal prison; and for killing him, by exile from our realms for one year, unless the man hunting be a known malefactor and the man who pursues him be one of our officers of justice.

Item: any huntsman in pursuit of a game animal shall be entitled to demand a loaf of bread and enough wine to fill his horn [from a house] on the road at a fair price; and if he has no money, he may take them without penalty. And if a huntsman or huntsmen are overtaken by night and come on a house in the forest and have no money, and the people of the house refuse them bread for the hounds or food for themselves, they may take them, undertaking to pay later.

Item: hunting may be of two kinds: firstly when a lord, knight or squire hunts with his company; secondly, when two or three squires, or more, hunt together. In a hunt in which the lord, knight or squire hunts with his company, the huntsmen's rights shall be as follows: the huntsman who blows the horn to start the hunt in the morning, who should be one of those who take part in the quest, . . . shall have a joint of the beast killed that day, if it is a hart or a boar; if it is a bear, he shall have a meal at the table of the lord or knight who has been hunting. The man who moves the beast, if it is a boar or a hart, shall have its head and feet; if it is a bear, he shall have the skin, and the lord will buy it from him.

Item: the huntsman who releases the first relay shall have a joint, if it is a hart or a boar; if it is a bear, he shall have a meal at the lord's table. A huntsman on foot who wounds the beast first, if it is a hart or a boar, shall have a joint of it; if it is a bear, he shall receive one-third of the value of the skin from the man who first moved it.

Item: if the hunting is done by a group of squires in company, the huntsman who blows for the start in the morning shall have a joint from the haunch. The man who moves the beast shall have the head and a joint from the shoulder, if it is a boar; the hide, if it is a hart; and the head and feet, if it is a bear. And those who release the first relay shall likewise have a joint. And if it should happen that all the hounds give up, those uncoupled at first and the relays alike, and some huntsman finds and takes the beast with his own hound, he shall have a joint from the shoulder and a joint from the haunch. And he who strikes the first blow shall have a shoulder, if it is a hart or a boar; if it is a bear, he shall have the skin.

Item: he who strikes the second blow, if it is a hart or a boar, shall have a joint from the shoulder; if it is a bear, the huntsman who delivered the first blow shall give the second one one third of the value of the skin.

Item: if two huntsmen go to strike a beast, and one of them runs away instead of helping his companion, and this is proved by the testimony of another, he shall have no rights. Moreover, he shall not sit to eat with his fellow-huntsmen for a month.

Item: if a beast goes from one man's land to another's, taking the hounds with it, the people on the land to which it has gone, if it is not killed, shall feed the hounds and return them to their owner. If the owner is unknown, they shall make a proclamation so that he may claim them. If the beast is killed, they shall carry out the *curée* and feed the hounds well, and keep the carcass four days for the huntsmen who hunted it, and proclaim in the neighbourhood that they may claim it and the hounds. And if they fail to perform the *curée*, they shall pay the owners of the hounds fifty *maravedíes*, for the dishonour done to the hounds. And if they are not claimed after four days, they may use the flesh of the carcass, and keep the skin nine days, and proclaim that the hounds may be claimed by their owners. And if they refuse to return the hounds, they shall pay a hundred *maravedíes* per hound. If they refuse to return the carcass, they shall pay twice what it is worth in the reasonable estimation of the man who hunted it.

Extracts from the Hunting Ordinances of Alfonso V of Portugal[1]

Book I, Chapter 67: *The Master Huntsman, and certain things pertaining to his office*

My father the King, of blessed memory, made in his time certain Ordinances concerning the Master Huntsman and his office, as appears in certain documents signed by his hand, and in a deposition made by Vicente Esteves, at that time Master Huntsman of the Forest of Santarem, who was asked especially about the rights of the Master Huntsman, the mounted huntsmen, the foot huntsmen, and the squires of our hounds . . .; and these documents and deposition are as follows:

1. We the King make it known . . . that we find discrepancies in the charters given to our huntsmen in the days of our most virtuous father the King, of blessed memory, since in the earlier ones it was stated that anyone who killed boar or piglets in the reserves, or set fire to the undergrowth, or set traps in the reserves, should pay twenty-five pounds, old money, to the huntsmen; whereas in the more recent it states that they should pay five hundred pounds of the new money to us, which moneys go to Lopo Vaasques, our Master Huntsman.

2. Wishing to moderate these penalties, but to cause the woods to be properly guarded, . . . we order that anyone offending in the ways described shall pay two thousand *reis* of the present money for each offence, of which a thousand shall go to Lopo Vaasques, five hundred to the Master Huntsman of the forest, and the other five hundred to the huntsmen of the forest, with the man who discovered the offence receiving a double share.

3. And the said Huntsman of the forest shall demand such penalties before the *Almoxarife* of that area, to whom we order that he shall have this properly applied; and in cases of appeal the Master Huntsman of that forest shall bring it to our Court, before our own Inspectors of the Treasury, and our own Master Huntsman shall pursue the case until it is decided.

4. If the deer in any forest are reserved, the penalties for killing a deer or a fawn shall be half those above, and shall be divided in the same proportions.

5. As it is forbidden to cut timber or firewood in the forests . . . we order that for each trunk or other large timber hauled out by oxen the culprit shall pay four hundred *reis*, and for a load of firewood two hundred, to be divided in the same way.

. . .

8. The Master Huntsman, the foot-huntsmen, the mounted huntsmen, the King's squires and the grooms of the King's Chamber who keep the hounds of the King shall have in perpetuity the right to receive the following items from the Moors of Lisbon: a small pot with its lid; a stewpot; an earthenware water-jug; a cauldron with its lid; a wine-jar with its lid; . . . a metal oil-jug; and a candlestick; and the Master Huntsman shall have all this twice over. These things shall be given every time the King visits the city, and Vicente Esteves shall be responsible for seeing that this is done, as it has always been done since the days of King John, God rest his soul.

9. King Duarte, whom God preserve in Holy Paradise, ordered that since he visited the city four or five times a year, or more, this gift should only be given once annually, and not at all if the King did not visit.

. . .

11. And if any huntsman reached the age of seventy, he was to be lodged by the Master Huntsman, and given a document preserving his privileges.

. . .

16. Item: The said Vicente Esteves further states that the Master Huntsman had jurisdiction, as he has now, over the huntsmen of the Chamber, the mounted huntsmen and the foot-huntsmen who failed to carry out their office . . . and the right to deprive them of their post, to replace them, to send them to prison, and to punish them in any way he thought they merited, as appears in a letter from him to the said Lopo Vaasques.

17. Item. Anyone killing a bear anywhere in the kingdom without permission of the King shall pay a thousand pounds of good money.

Notes

The following abbreviations have been used:

BSA: The Boke of St Albans

La Chasse: Jacques de Brézé, *La Chasse.*

CV: The Craft of Venery

DAB: Guicennas, *De Arte Bersandi*

DAV: The Art of Falconry, being the De Arte Venandi cum Avibus of Frederick II of Hohenstaufen

Débat: Le Débat des herauts d'armes de France et d'Angleterre

Debate: John Coke, *The Debate between the Heralds of England and France*

ER: The Exchequer Rolls of Scotland

Gace: Gace de la Vigne, *Le Roman des déduis*

Gawain: Sir Gawain and the Green Knight

LHT: Accounts of the Lord High Treasurer of Scotland

Livro: John I of Portugal, *Livro da montaria*

MG: Edward, Duke of York, *The Master of Game*

Moamin: Moamin et Ghatrif: Traités de fauconnerie et des chiens de chasse

Modus: Les Livres du Roy Modus et de la Royne Ratio

Montería: Alfonso XI of Castile, *Libro de la montería*

Noble Arte: George Turbervile, *The Noble Arte of Venerie or Hunting*

PEB: Prince Edward's Book

Phoebus: Gaston Phoebus, *Livre de chasse*

PLA: Pero López de Ayala, *Libro de la caça de las aves*

TED: Iohannes Caius, *Treatise of Englishe Dogges*

Thiébaux, *Stag:* Marcelle Thiébaux, *The Stag of Love*

Tristan: Gottfried von Strassburg, *Tristan*

Twiti: William Twiti, *La Vénerie de Twiti*

Introduction

1 Gace, ll. 8365–66.
2 Phoebus, p. 51.
3 See *LHT*, especially the indexes to Vols. II, III, and IV; Gilbert, *Hunting and Hunting Reserves*, pp. 66–71, 77–79.
4 *Livro*, pp. 458–59.
5 *Regesta*, nos. 2857, 3082.
6 Baillie-Grohman, *Sport in the Alps*, pp. 9–10.
7 *PLA*, pp. 51–52.
8 Phoebus, pp. 52–53.
9 See *Gawain*, especially ll. 1179ff., 1469ff., 1731ff.; *Canterbury Tales*, Vol. III, p. 583. For other instances of this conventional criticism of idleness see Thiébaux, *Stag*, pp. 76–80.
10 *Modus*, pp. 59–60.
11 Surtees, *Handley Cross*, Chap. 6.
12 Llull, *Libre del ordre de cavayleria*; for the hunting reference, see Caxton's translation (under Llull in Bibliography), p. 31.
13 *Montería*, p. 3.
14 See Chapter 6, pp. 101–02.
15 *Livro* pp. 21–32. Compare Xenophon, pp. 443–44: 'For it makes the body healthy, improves the sight and hearing, and keeps men from growing old; and it affords the best training for war. In the first place, when marching over rough roads under arms, they will not tire: accustomed to bearing arms for capturing wild beasts, they will bear up under their tasks. Again, they will be capable of sleeping on a hard bed and of guarding well the place assigned to them. In an attack on the enemy they will be able to go for him and at the same time to carry out the orders that are passed along, because they are used to do the same things on their own account when capturing game . . .'
16 *DAB*, pp. 24–25.
17 Haskins, 'The *De Arte*', p. 349.
18 *PLA*, p. 53; Bertelli, *Italian Renaissance Courts*, pp. 172–73.
19 *Livro*, pp. 459–60.
20 Keen, *Chivalry*, pp. 172–73.
21 *Livro*, p. 18.
22 *MG*, p. 93.
23 Gace, ll. 8347–62.
24 Phoebus, p. 272.
25 Delbouille, *Le Roman du Châtelain de Coucy*, ll. 460ff.
26 Translated by D. G. Rossetti, *The Early Italian Poets*, p. 88. Another sonnet in similar vein appears on p. 79 of the same work.
27 For an extreme example of the ritualized homecoming, see *Tristan*, pp. 83–84, where it is depicted as specifically French, a refinement strange to Tristan's Cornish hosts and, possibly, Gottfried's German readers.
28 E.g. *LHT*, II, p. 396; IV, p. 85.
29 Gace, ll. 8309–13.
30 Baillie-Grohman, *Sport in the Alps*, p. 11.
31 *La Chasse*, pp. 24–26.
32 *Debate*, p. 59; *Débat*, pp. 5–6.
33 *LHT*, IV, p. 134.
34 Quoted in Thiébaux, 'The Mediaeval Chase', p. 263.
35 See Lindner, *Die Jagd im frühen Mittelalter*, pp. 412–14; Thiébaux, 'The Mediaeval Chase', pp. 263–65.
36 Bertelli, *Italian Renaissance Courts*, p. 175.
37 *MG*, pp. 203–04. For other poaching clerics, see Appendix II, pp. 262 and 264.
38 Anderson, *History of Scottish Forestry*, pp. 112–13.
39 Anderson, p. 110.
40 Anderson, p. 130.
41 Anderson, p. 100.
42 *LHT*, III, p. 156.
43 *MG*, p. 111; see also my Appendix II, pp. 260ff.
44 Shirley, *Some Account of English Game Parks*, p. 7.
45 *MG*, pp. 6–9 (a translation of Phoebus).

Chapter 1

1 *MG*, p. 44.
2 For the list, see *BSA*, p. 80; on the nature and origins of the *veltre* and the greyhound, and on the *zwickdarm*, see Dalby, pp. 311–12, and *BSA*, p. 149.
3 Gace, ll. 8832–42; cf. Phoebus, pp. 128–29.
4 British Library, MS. Egerton 1995, fol. 55v. Other versions in *BSA*, p. 80; Cambridge University Library, MS. Ll. I. 18, fol. 55.
5 Phoebus, p. 129.
6 *MG*, p. 66.
7 For references on the Scottish greyhound, and on Scottish hounds generally, see Gilbert, pp. 64–65.
8 *Montería*, Plate 6.
9 *Livro*, pp. 54–76.
10 *Montería*, p. 22.
11 *MG*, p. 64.
12 *Devonshire Tapestries*, Plate 22 and Fig. 30.

13 See Migeon, *Les Tapisseries*, Plate x.
14 See the Casariego edition of the *Libro de la montería* (under Alfonso in Bibliography), p. 16.
15 On alaunts, see Phoebus, pp. 125–27; *Montería*, pp. 48–50; *MG*, pp. 64–65; *Livro*, pp. 58–59, 67–76.
16 There are some fine examples of such collars in the Jagd- und Fischereimuseum in Munich (Inventory nos. 3002–05).
17 Phoebus, p. 134.
18 Phoebus, p. 129; *Montería*, p. 22; *Livro*, p. 56; *Moamin*, p. 245; *MG*, p. 58.
19 Xenophon, pp. 377–87, 421; Grattius, pp. 165–73; Nemesianus, p. 505; Oppian, pp. 39–53.
20 Charles ix, *La Chasse royale*, pp. 31–38.
21 For speculations on the relationship of English hounds to the French strains, see Paget, *Beagles and Beagling*, pp. 3–10.
22 See *MG*, p. 61; also my Chapter 3.
23 Oppian, p. 49.
24 Oppian, p. 51.
25 Phoebus, pp. 129–35.
26 *TED*, p. 4.
27 *Modus*, pp. 70, 98–99; *Montería*, pp. 19–20.
28 Phoebus, pp. 132–33.
29 *Les Dits du bon chien Souillard* is included in *La Chasse*, pp. 56–58.
30 See especially *La Chasse*, stanzas 13, 20, 24, 25, 30, 34, 40, 51, 52.
31 *La Chasse*, p. 96.
32 *Twiti*, pp. 38, 48; *MG*, p. 95.
33 Oppian, p. 47.
34 Xenophon, p. 415.
35 *Modus*, p. 14.
36 The French royal hunting accounts, mainly concerned with areas immediately to the north and south of Paris (especially Senlis and Fontainebleau), survive in the Bibliothèque Nationale, MSS. Fr. 7839–46 and Fr. 11202–04. See Appendix I. ·
37 On training the lymer, see *DAB*, pp. 21–25; *Montería*, pp. 32–33.
38 See *TED*, p. 5; Dalby, pp. 135–36.
39 Dalby, p. 135.
40 See *Montería*, p. 16; *Livro*, pp. 81–84; Dalby, p. 135.
41 *MG*, p. 70.
42 Bibliothèque Nationale, MS. Fr. 7845.
43 *MG*, p. 70.
44 Quoted by Baillie-Grohman, *MG*, p. 172, from the household expenses of Princess Mary (probably Mary,

daughter of Henry vii, though this is not clear).
45 Queen's Wardrobe Accounts for 1400, quoted in Wyllie, *History of England*, Vol. iv, p. 196.
46 *Modus*, p. 108.
47 *Montería*, pp. 74, 78, 117; see also my Chapter 8, p. 126. For another example of a hound being carried on horseback, see Fig. 7.
48 *Montería*, p. 92.
49 See e.g. *Livro*, p. 459.
50 *La Chasse*, p. 58, ll. 43–44.
51 *Montería*, p. 21.
52 *The Knight's Tale*, in Chaucer, Vol. iii, p. 55.
53 *Cronica del rei D. Fernando*, Chap. 100, quoted in *Livro*, pp. 463–64.
54 Wardrobe Accounts 14, 15, Edward i, quoted in *MG*, p. 173; *LHT*, iii, pp. 167, 168.
55 See Appendix i, p. 259.
56 *LHT*, i, p. 390; iii, p. 167.
57 Bibliothèque Nationale, MS. Fr. 7845 (many similar entries elsewhere in the accounts); see also Appendix i and Phoebus, p. 183.
58 *Manners and Meals*, p. 320.
59 See *MG*, p. 187.
60 *MG*, p. 187.
61 *MG*, p. 188; *LHT*, iii, p. 176 (and see also i, p. 390); Gilbert, p. 66.
62 Xenophon, pp. 413–15.
63 Grattius, pp. 169–71; see also Nemesianus, pp. 495–97.
64 Phoebus, pp. 111–12.
65 Phoebus, pp. 111–12; cf. *Montería*, pp. 21, 41.
66 *Montería*, p. 23; *Moamin* in Fradejas Rueda, *Tratados de cetrería*, p. 172; Nemesianus, pp. 497–99.
67 *Montería*, p. 21; Phoebus, p. 112.
68 'That a bitch ever bore'.
69 *BSA*, pp. 80–81.
70 *Moamin*, in Fradejas Rueda, *Tratados de cetrería*, p. 173.
71 Bibliothèque Nationale, MS. Fr. 11203, fol. 8v.
72 Grattius, pp. 185–87.
73 Grattius, pp. 189–91; Nemesianus, pp. 503–05.
74 *MG*, p. 47.
75 *MG*, p. 48.
76 *MG*, p. 49.
77 Quoted in *MG*, p. 174.
78 Phoebus, p. 116.
79 *MG*, p. 49. For other references to rabies, see *Moamin*, ed. Tjerneld, p. 243; *Modus*, pp. 102–03; *Montería*, pp. 43–44.

80 Grattius, p. 191.
81 Bibliothèque Nationale, MS. Fr. 7845; MS. Fr. 11204 contains a similar example.
82 Musée Condé, Chantilly, MS. XVI B³; Bertelli, *Italian Renaissance Courts*, p. 173; Klingender, *Animals*, p. 484; Klingender, *Animals*, p. 480.
83 *Regesta*, nos. 2661, 2783, 3029; Klingender, *Animals*, p. 480. On the cheetah as a hunting animal, see Friedmann, *A Bestiary for St Jerome*, p. 202.

Chapter 2
1 *BSA*, pp. 78, 144; *La Chace dou cerf* (see Tilander in Bibliography), ll. 393ff.; *Modus*, pp. 69, 117.
2 MS. Bodley 546, fol. 2v.
3 *MG*, pp. 17–18.
4 *CV*, in *Twiti*, p. 54.
5 British Library, MS. Landsdowne 85, quoted in *MG*, p. 117. On the hart's antlers, see *MG*, pp. 116–17; Phoebus, p. 51; *Twiti*, pp. 45–46; *CV* in *Twiti*, pp. 53–54; *BSA*, pp. 119–20.
6 *BSA*, p. 65.
7 *Modus*, p. 12; Phoebus, p. 60.
8 Phoebus, pp. 149–70.
9 For examples of German tracking techniques, see Lindner, *Die Lehre von den Zeichen des Hirsches*, numerous entries in Dalby (especially his pp. lvi–lvii), and my Fig. 10.
10 *MG*, p. 84.
11 *La Chasse*, stanza 10.
12 *MG*, p. 73.
13 *MG*, pp. 83–84.
14 *MG*, p. 94.
15 *MG*, p. 95.
16 *MG*, p. 97.
17 *MG*, p. 96.
18 *MG*, p. 98.
19 *MG*, pp. 98–99.
20 *La Chasse*, stanza 47.
21 *MG*, p. 99.
22 Phoebus, pp. 177–81; see also *Modus*, pp. 50–55.
23 *Noble Arte*, p. 135.
24 *BSA*, p. 77.
25 *La Chasse*, stanzas 42–46.
26 Phoebus, p. 183.
27 *MG*, p. 100.
28 *Tristan*, pp. 78–82. See Thiébaux, *Stag*, pp. 130–33.
29 *BSA*, ll. 1214–16.
30 British Library, MS. Yates Thomson 13; see Klingender, *Animals*, pp. 415–16.
31 British Library, MS. Royal 10E. IV. see

32 See Phoebus, pp. 181–83; *Modus*, pp. 56–58; *La Chasse*, stanzas 48–53; *MG*, pp. 100–01; *BSA*, p. 79.
33 Phoebus, p. 183; *Modus*, p. 56.
34 *MG*, pp. 100–01; for a vivid depiction of a *curée* in one of the hunts of Maximilian I, see Migeon, *Les Tapisseries*, Plate IV.
35 *La Chasse*, stanza 48.
36 *Modus*, pp. 57–58.
37 See Chapter 4, pp. 71–73; *Neptalym cervus emissus*, p. 72.
38 *Tristan*, pp. 83–85.
39 *MG*, pp. 101–02; *BSA*, p. 79.
40 See Phoebus, pp. 194–96.

Chapter 3
1 See Bibliography, Guicennas.
2 *DAB*, pp. 19–21.
3 See Dalby, pp. 36–37.
4 Phoebus, pp. 273, 430; *Modus*, pp. 412–13.
5 *Modus*, pp. 128–30.
6 Phoebus, pp. 273–74.
7 Gilbert, p. 60.
8 Cranach, Plates 281, 411, 412.
9 See Dalby, pp. 26–27.
10 Quoted by Dalby, p. 24.
11 See e.g. Dalby, p. 24.
12 *Twiti*, pp. 57, 98.
13 Gilbert, p. 52.
14 *LHT*, IV, p. 137.
15 Gilbert, p. 7.
16 Gilbert, p. 52.
17 Dalby, p. 186.
18 Gilbert, p. 53.
19 Cranach, Plate 411.
20 The hart attacked the King's horse, and as the King fell he seized, by chance, a cross between the hart's antlers which came away in his hand. The cross was then worshipped in thanks for his deliverance, and the Monastery of Holyrood founded on the spot. For the original Latin version, see *The Holyrood Ordinale*, pp. 64–66; see also Gilbert, p. 53. Another example of the role of a deer-hunt in a monastery foundation legend is the incident depicted on an altarpiece in the Alte Pinakothek, Munich (see Fig. 19). For similar examples involving a boar, see p. 106.
21 Phoebus, pp. 269–73.
22 I.e. in the close season.
23 *Gawain*, ll. 1133–77.
24 On teasers and receivers, see *MG*, p. 112.
25 Shirley, *Some Account of English Game Parks*, p. 19, n. 1.

26 *Modus*, pp. 62–64.
27 Phoebus, p. 64.
28 Anderson, *History of Scottish Forestry*, I, p. 83.
29 Phoebus, p. 263.
30 Shirley, p. 12.
31 Shirley, pp. 11–12.
32 Holinshed, *Chronicles*, p. 89.
33 Shirley, p. 33.
34 For a list of Scottish royal and baronial game-parks, see Gilbert, pp. 356–59.
35 Gilbert, p. 216.
36 Gilbert, p. 218.
37 Gilbert, p. 218.
38 Shirley, pp. 20–21.
39 See Gilbert, pp. 82–87 and Figures 16 and 17.
40 *ER*, I, p. 38; XII, pp. 277, 441, 521.
41 *ER*, IX, p. 54.
42 *LHT*, III, p. 152.
43 *LHT*, IV, p. 76.
44 To 'ratch about' is still used in north-eastern Scotland in the sense of hunting around, especially of a wandering dog.
45 *LHT*, III, pp. 172, 181, 171.
46 *LHT*, III, p. 181.
47 *LHT*, III, pp. 180, 171.
48 *LHT*, II, pp. 407, 475, 424.
49 *ER*, XII, p. 205.
50 Forsyth, *The History of Bradgate*, pp. 3–6.
51 Forsyth, p. 7.
52 *LHT*, III, p. 171.
53 *ER*, I, p. 38.
54 Phoebus, p. 241.
55 *Débat*, p. 3. On deer-parks in Germany, see Dalby, pp. 56, *ge-hege*; 76, *hac*; 85–86, *hege, hege-wilt*; 96, *hüeten*; 240, *tiergarte*.
56 *MG*, pp. 15–16.
57 Chapter XXXVI, *MG*, pp. 107–12.
58 From Andrew Borde's *Regyment or Dietary of Helth*, quoted in *Manners and Meals*, pp. 210–11.

Chapter 4
1 *Modus*, pp. 116–19.
2 On the legend of the serpent and the stag, see Thiébaux, *Stag*, pp. 41–42, especially 42 n.
3 Aelfric, *Lives of Saints*, Vol. II, p. 192.
4 See Thiébaux, *Stag*, pp. 60–66, for an illuminating semantic analysis of Aelfric's version.
5 *Oxford Dictionary of Saints*, p. 198. See also Randall, *Images*, Fig. 614.
6 E.g. Randall, *Images*, Fig. 649.
7 Phoebus, p. 64.

8 *MG*, p. 20.
9 Le Clerc, *Le Bestiaire divin*, ll. 2761–62.
10 *MG*, p. 153; Klingender, p. 453.
11 Oppian, p. 81. Oppian says that the stag lives four lifetimes of the crow; he appears to be relying on Hesiod, who says the same and gives the crow's lifetime as nine generations of man (a generation then being reckoned as forty years).
12 Chaucer, III, p. 534.
13 Quoted in Thiébaux, *Stag*, pp. 45–46.
14 See Picot, 'Le Cerf allégorique'.
15 For the details of Kurt Lindner's edition, with introduction, see Bibliography under *Neptalym cervus emissus*.
16 Malory, *Works*, pp. 717–18.
17 Migne, *Patrologia Graeca*, Vol. 105, pp. 375–412; Aelfric's version is in his *Lives of Saints*, Vol. II, p. 192.
18 *Ormulum*, II, p. 113.
19 Rogers, *The Perilous Hunt*, pp. 6–40, especially p. 25; Smith, *Spanish Ballads*, nos. 63, 67, 70.
20 Smith, *Spanish Ballads*, no. 58.
21 See Diego Catalán, *Por campos del romancero*, Madrid, 1970, pp. 94–96.
22 See Entwistle, 'The Adventure of *Le Cerf au pied blanc*'.
23 Malory, pp. 76–91.
24 Malory, pp. 33–34.
25 *Oxford Book of Ballads*, pp. 664–75.
26 Housman, *Of Aucassin and Nicolette*, p. 39.
27 Boccaccio, *The Decameron*, pp. 457–62.
28 Klingender, pp. 416, 471–72.
29 *Neptalym cervus emissus*, p. 66.
30 For the text, see Thiébaux, 'An Unpublished Allegory'.
31 Reproduced in Thiébaux, *Stag*, p. 150.
32 For a full and sensitive analysis, see Thiébaux, *Stag*, pp. 145–53.
33 See Bibliography under Acart, Jean.
34 See Bibliography under Hadamar.
35 For a full analysis, see Thiébaux, *Stag*, pp. 185–228.
36 Quoted in Klingender, p. 471.
37 *MG*, p. 20.
38 I cannot locate this work exactly; I saw it in the course of a visit to either the Alte Pinakothek, Munich, or the Kunsthistorisches Museum, Vienna.
39 Jacobs, *Mythological Painting*, p. 48.
40 Jensen, *The Earliest Portuguese Lyric*, p. 70.
41 Cummins, *The Spanish Traditional Lyric*, pp. 54–55.
42 Shipman, *The Abbots Bromley Horn Dance*, pp. 6–7.

43 Cranach, Plates 281, 411, 412.
44 Reproduced in *Treasures from the Burrell Collection*, Item 9.
45 See Cranach, especially Plates 191–93, 196–99, 201–02, 261, 270–71.

Chapter 5
1 Phoebus, p. 67.
2 *MG*, pp. 22–23; cf. Phoebus, p. 69.
3 *BSA*, p. 63.
4 Bodleian Library, MS. Rawlinson Poet. 143, printed in *BSA*, p. 180, ll. 367–68.
5 *Modus*, p. 66.
6 *BSA*, p. 63.
7 *BSA*, pp. 65, 86.
8 *Modus*, p. 65.
9 *BSA*, p. 57.
10 *Twiti*, p. 28 (and cf. p. 44, 'enchased', 'aquilled'; *CV*, in *Twiti*, p. 51, 'enchased', 'encoylid').
11 See Tilander, *Julians Barnes*, p. 77.
12 *BSA*, p. 63.
13 The Rawlinson manuscript has 'buk'; see *BSA*, p. 173, l. 160.
14 Phoebus, p. 68.
15 *Modus*, pp. 65–66.
16 Phoebus, pp. 213–14.
17 *Modus*, p. 66.
18 *Modus*, p. 66.
19 Phoebus, p. 68.
20 *Modus*, p. 66.
21 Phoebus, p. 69.
22 It was certainly not so in Scotland; see pp. 59–61 for the keeping of red deer in parks.
23 *MG*, p. 25. This traditional belief goes back via Phoebus to *Modus*, where it is attributed to Avicenna (*Modus*, p. 68).
24 *BSA*, pp. 59–60, 63–65.
25 Rawlinson Poet. 143, in *BSA*, p. 180, ll. 373–74.
26 *MG*, p. 24.
27 *MG*, p. 24; cf. Phoebus, p. 75.
28 *BSA*, p. 65.
29 *Noble Arte*, p. 143, and see *BSA*, pp. xlii–xliv.
30 *BSA*, p. 64.
31 *BSA*, p. 64.
32 Phoebus, p. 73.
33 *BSA*, p. 64.
34 Phoebus, p. 74.
35 Cranach, Plates 184, 186.
36 Pope-Hennessy, *The Complete Works of Paolo Uccello*, p. 26 and Plates 97–102.
37 Pope-Hennessy, p. 26.
38 *Tacuinum sanitatis*, I, fol. 71v. This is entitled *Carnes gazelarum*, but the animals look very like roe-deer; they are being pursued and savaged by a combination of running-hounds and greyhounds, and speared by hunters on foot.
39 *Modus*, p. 68; Phoebus, pp. 75, 219–20; *MG*, p. 24.
40 *Modus*, p. 68; Phoebus, p. 216.
41 Phoebus, p. 216.
42 *MG*, p. 25.
43 Phoebus, p. 218.
44 *BSA*, p. 60; 'croyses' and 'tresouns' in Rawlinson Poet. 143 (see *BSA*, p. 171).
45 *Modus*, p. 69.
46 Phoebus, p. 220.
47 *Twiti*, p. 42.
48 *MG*, p. 26.
49 *BSA*, p. 60. For another version, probably more accurate, see Rawlinson Poet. 143 in *BSA*, p. 171.
50 Phoebus, pp. 66–67, 212.
51 Phoebus, p. 66.
52 Phoebus, p. 212.
53 Phoebus, p. 73.
54 He may be referring to chamois in this passage (p. 73), or to ibex and chamois together.
55 Phoebus, p. 214. In the bestiaries the two horns of the ibex are likened to the two Testaments of the Bible, which save men when they fall (see e.g. British Library, MS. Harleian 4751, fol. 10).
56 Phoebus, p. 71.
57 Phoebus, p. 215.
58 See Bibliography under Maximilian I, and Spaur and Hohenleiter.
59 Cranach, Plate 281.
60 The sword is illustrated in Thomas, Gamber and Schedelmann, *Die schönsten Waffen*.
61 Baillie-Grohman, *Sport in the Alps*, p. 12.
62 Cranach, Plates 281, 411, 412.
63 Baillie-Grohman, *Sport in the Alps*, p. 9.
64 Baillie-Grohman, *Sport in the Alps*, p. 10.

Chapter 6
1 *Modus*, p. 60.
2 *MG*, p. 28.
3 Phoebus, p. 88.
4 Phoebus, p. 91.
5 *Montería*, pp. 19–20.
6 Quoted in *Livro*, p. 445; similar examples on pp. 446–47.
7 *Débat*, p. 6.
8 *Debate*, p. 59.
9 Phoebus, p. 90; *Modus*, p. 73; *BSA*, ll. 1434–35.
10 *Twiti*, p. 51. The boar is *singularis ferus*

in Psalm LXXX. It seems likely that in France his horrific reputation may have been increased by an association in popular etymology between *sanglier* and *sang*, 'blood'.

11 *BSA*, ll. 1436–44; see also *Modus*, pp. 74–77.

12 *MG*, p. 29.

13 *MG*, p. 28. On the tracks of the boar, see a very full description in *Livro*, pp. 96ff.

14 *Gawain*, ll. 1437–53, 1464–67.

15 Phoebus, p. 231. The French royal hunting accounts include items such as the purchase of 'eight dozen needles for stitching up the hounds wounded by wild boar' (Bibliothèque Nationale, MS. Fr. 11203, fol. 8v).

16 *Livro*, pp. 300–01. Xenophon, p. 435, also mentions the eyes.

17 *Livro*, pp. 301–02.

18 *Livro*, pp. 320–22.

19 Phoebus, p. 234. Xenophon, p. 437, describes the blade of the spear as being toothed to prevent it penetrating too far.

20 *Livro*, p. 302.

21 Menen, *Cities in the Sand*, p. 106, reproduces a Roman mosaic of a lion-hunting scene from Djemila, Algeria, showing the technique. A mosaic from Oudna, Tunisia, reproduced on p. 180 of the same work, shows a man killing a boar in the style recommended by John I, accompanied by another hunter and two hounds, and a very similar scene appears on a Roman glass dish (see Donald B. Harden, *Glass of the Caesars*, Milan, 1987, pp. 226–27).

22 *Gawain*, ll. 1583–1600.

23 *Livro*, pp. 316–17.

24 Phoebus, p. 234.

25 *Livro*, pp. 27–28.

26 Phoebus, p. 187.

27 Phoebus, pp. 231–32. The Oudna mosaic (see above, n. 21) shows mounted hunters throwing spears at (possibly) a lion.

28 *Livro*, pp. 334–35.

29 Phoebus, p. 232.

30 *Montería*, p. 62.

31 *Livro*, p. 297.

32 *Modus*, pp. 104–11. Driving boar into nets is an ancient practice, described by Xenophon, p. 439.

33 *Modus*, pp. 86–87; Phoebus, p. 92.

34 *Modus*, pp. 82–86; Phoebus, pp. 185–88.

35 *Twiti*, p. 40. One of the tapestries of the

Hunts of Maximilian in the Louvre is a vivid depiction of the burning off of the boar's bristles over a huge bonfire (see Migeon, Plate XI).

36 *Twiti*, pp. 55, 75–76; see a fuller analysis by Rachel Hands in *BSA*, pp. 139–40.

37 Phoebus, p. 188.

38 Henish, *Fast and Feast*, p. 229.

39 *MG*, p. 28. For the pagan cults, see Beck, *Das Ebersignum*, pp. 74, 177, 193.

40 See Hatto, 'Snake-swords and Boar-helms'.

41 Dalby, p. xvii; Beck, pp. 131ff.; Thiébaux, 'The Mouth of the Boar', pp. 285–86. The Thiébaux article is a cogently organized survey, to which this chapter owes a substantial debt.

42 Thiébaux, 'The Mouth of the Boar', p. 287, especially n. 25.

43 *Nibelungenlied*, pp. 124–32.

44 Thiébaux, 'The Mouth of the Boar', p. 289.

45 *Livro*, p. 36. For the Scriptural commentaries, see Thiébaux, 'The Mouth of the Boar', pp. 291–92.

46 *Modus*, pp. 104ff. In this chapter of *Modus* the phrase alludes specifically to the boar, rather than to the five black beasts described by the King in pp. 73ff. For an allusion to the boars as 'the black beasts' in the hunting accounts see Appendix I, p. 258.

47 Oppian, p. 145. Xenophon, p. 437, says the same. For the dragon associations, see Thiébaux, 'The Mouth of the Boar', pp. 290–91. Alexander the Great was said to have fought great herds of gryphons, dragons and boars during his advance into India (a miniature in the Petit Palais, showing his battle against large numbers of the three beasts, is reproduced in Anon., *Dragons*, p. 122). A case of the boar as a beneficent guide is found in the Spanish epic *Poema de Fernán González*, stanzas 225–49, in which the hero receives divine aid in battle after chasing a boar which takes refuge behind the altar of the hermitage of the monk Pelayo; later he founds the Monastery of San Pedro de Arlanza as a thank-offering. This more sympathetic role may be due to the preference for the boar over the deer in Spain, which in turn could be a relic of pre-Christian Germanic cults imported by the Visigoths.

48 See Remon Vidal, *La Chace aux mesdisans*, pp. 465–94; summarized in

Thiébaux, 'The Mouth of the Boar', pp. 293–94.

49 Oppian, p. 145.
50 Phoebus, p. 186.
51 *Troilus and Criseyde*, Book v, stanzas 177–79, in Chaucer, Vol. II, p. 223; Boccaccio, *Il Filostrato*, p. 179. See also Hatto, ' "Venus and Adonis" – and the Boar', in his *Essays*, pp. 221–32.
52 *Tristan*, pp. 219–20.
53 Klingender, *Animals*, Figure 262, p. 429.
54 *Modus*, pp. 144–50.

Chapter 7

1 These lines are from the *Craft of Venery* (*CV*); for the full text, see *Twiti*, pp. 51–58.
2 *BSA*, p. 61. See also *MG*, p. 103.
3 Flaying involved slitting the skin up the belly and the inside of each leg, and peeling it back from the sides towards the spine; stripping was cutting the skin around the neck or snout and just above the feet, and pulling it off inside-out like a sock, with the tail attached. Deer and foxes are still skinned in these two contrasting ways.
4 The hare is not strictly a ruminant, since it does not chew the cud, but it does consume its food twice to extract full benefit, by eating its own droppings. The reference to 'four teeth above' is to the fact that the hare has four upper incisors instead of two.
5 *BSA*, p. 62.
6 Edward Topsell, *The Historie of Four-footed Beasts*; quoted by G. Ewart Evans in *The Leaping Hare*, pp. 24–25, q.v.
7 Phoebus, pp. 77–82.
8 *BSA*, p. 62.
9 Xenophon, pp. 391–93; Oppian, p. 159.
10 *MG*, p. 103.
11 Phoebus, pp. 78–79.
12 *Modus*, p. 69.
13 *MG*, p. 13.
14 Phoebus, pp. 77, 221; *Twiti*, p. 50. See also *CV*, p. 57; *MG*, p. 13.
15 *BSA*, p. 65.
16 Phoebus, p. 221.
17 Xenophon, pp. 407–09. See also Phoebus, pp. 77–79, 221–26; *Modus*, pp. 69–70; *MG*, pp. 103–06.
18 Phoebus, p. 79.
19 *CV*, pp. 52–53. See also a versified version in *BSA*, pp. 66–68.
20 *LHT*, III, p. 156. Another monarch who

shows similar concern is John I of Portugal, who mentions the need to recompense the countryfolk (*Livro*, p. 328).
21 *Modus*, pp. 70–71.
22 *MG*, p. 104.
23 *Treatyse of Fysshynge with an Angle*, fol. 5.
24 *MG*, p. 106.
25 See Courtney-Williams, *Beagles*, pp. 3–12.
26 *MG*, pp. 105–06.
27 Phoebus, p. 226.
28 *Noble Arte*, p. 175.
29 *BSA*, p. 62.
30 Quoted in George Ewart Evans' splendid study, *The Leaping Hare*, p. 146.
31 Evans, *The Leaping Hare*, pp. 147–77.
32 Anson, *Fisher Folklore*, pp. 101, 104.
33 On the marginal illustrations, see Randall, *Images in the Margins of Gothic Manuscripts*, pp. 105–10, for references, and her Figs. 32, 33, 158, 217, 218, 224–29, 302, 354, 357, 365, 569. See also Varty, *Reynard the Fox*, pp. 83–84 and Fig. 140.
34 'Scot' is a synonym for hare (perhaps associable with 'scut'?); '-art' is a pejorative suffix. See Ross, 'The Middle English Poem', pp. 353, 355.
35 A proper name (see Ross).
36 Compare the cry about the hound Beamont in the *Craft of Venery* (see above, p. 114).
37 A proper name (see Ross).
38 But see Ross for a different translation.
39 A reference to the hare's habit of turning uphill when hard pressed, to make use of the advantage given it by its longer hind legs.
40 There is a Welsh poem of a similar nature, published by Ross in his 'The Middle English Poem', pp. 374–77.
41 *Tacuinum sanitatis*, II, p. 101.
42 A cook writing, not a properly educated hunter; see note 3 above.
43 British Library MS. Harleian 279, fol. 15a, printed in *Manners and Meals*, p. 60.

Chapter 8

1 See *Devonshire Tapestries*, Plates 20, 22, 23, 25; folding plates I and III.
2 The bear, however, is included among the 'bestis of the chace of the swete fewte' in *BSA*, p. 80; the boar and wolf are omitted.
3 See Dalby, pp. xvii–xviii for the literary

references; Lindner, 'Die Hohenlohesche Handschrift', pp. 94–95.

4 Phoebus, pp. 83–88.
5 *Devonshire Tapestries*, Plates 26 and III.
6 Oppian, pp. 125–27.
7 Phoebus, p. 85.
8 *Montería*, p. 14.
9 Phoebus, p. 86. See also *Montería*, p. 14.
10 Reproduced in H. Blackmore, *The World's Finest Sporting Guns*, Geneva, 1983, p. 8.
11 *Livro*, pp. 462–63, 451.
12 Thiébaux, *Stag*, pp. 66–68, 47.
13 Phoebus, pp. 86–87.
14 Oppian, pp. 189–93.
15 Phoebus, p. 230; *Montería*, p. 14.
16 *Montería*, p. 19; Phoebus, p. 84.
17 *Montería*, p. 13.
18 *Montería*, p. 18.
19 Phoebus, p. 230.
20 *Montería*, pp. 78–79.
21 *Montería*, pp. 74–75.
22 This account is taken from Tilander's edition of the *Livre de chasse*, p. 24.
23 *Montería*, pp. 74, 79.
24 Malory, pp. 33–34.
25 Malory, p. 90.
26 The original has 'Adelantado de los Galeses'. The writer may have in mind a punning association between Galicia in north-western Spain and *Gales*, the Spanish word for Wales. Wales, like Cornwall, was a common setting for Arthurian legend in the Middle Ages.
27 A free rendering. The original has *Ladrón*, 'thief', a common term of abuse in Spain.
28 The original text is in *Montería*, p. 135.

Chapter 9
1 Phoebus, p. 92.
2 *MG*, p. 35.
3 *MG*, pp. 33, 34.
4 Phoebus, p. 97.
5 Phoebus, pp. 92–93.
6 Phoebus, p. 94.
7 Phoebus, pp. 94–95.
8 *MG*, p. 35.
9 Phoebus, p. 97.
10 *Modus*, pp. 150–51.
11 *BSA*, p. 57.
12 *Modus*, p. 9.
13 *BSA*, p. 68.
14 Quoted in *MG*, p. 189.
15 Phoebus, p. 238.
16 Phoebus, pp. 60, 67.
17 Phoebus, p. 75.

18 E.g. Lindner, 'Die Hohenlohesche Handschrift', pp. 99–100.
19 *Tresslerbuch*, pp. 503, 531.
20 See Dalby, p. xviii.
21 Paget, *Beagles*, pp. 17–18.
22 *MG*, p. 31.
23 Vol. I, p. 19.
24 *ER*, I, p. 38.
25 Gilbert, p. 232.
26 *Acts of the Parliament of Scotland*, II, pp. 51–52.
27 *ER*, VI, p. 540; Gilbert, p. 232; *LHT*, I, p. 182.
28 Gilbert, pp. 255–56.
29 *Modus*, pp. 88–89. For a German description of wolf-tracks, see Lindner, 'Die Hohenlohesche Handschrift', p. 99.
30 *Modus*, pp. 87–88.
31 Phoebus, pp. 236–42.
32 Phoebus, p. 239.
33 Phoebus, p. 240.
34 Phoebus, p. 241.
35 *Modus*, pp. 111–14.
36 Phoebus, p. 241.
37 See *MG*, pp. 250–52 for a list.
38 *MG*, p. 37.
39 See Varty, *Reynard the Fox*, pp. 27–30 and Figs. 5, 8, 12, 13–17, 38–42, 45–46, 48–52, 61–62 and frontispiece; also Klingender, *Animals*, pp. 367–68, 395.
40 Varty, pp. 91–94 and Figs. 151–53, 156–57.
41 Quoted in Varty, p. 91.
42 See Varty, Fig. 11.
43 See Varty, pp. 51–59 and Figs. 35, 61, 65–83, 86–88, 128.
44 *Modus*, pp. 151–52.
45 See Bibliography under Lancaster.
46 Lancaster, p. 111.
47 Lancaster, p. 115.
48 *MG*, p. 36.
49 Phoebus, p. 101.
50 *BSA*, p. 65; *Twiti*, p. 50; *CV*, p. 57.
51 *CV*, p. 57.
52 Dalby, p. xviii.
53 *Modus*, p. 90; cf. Phoebus, pp. 243–44.
54 *BSA*, p. 63.
55 *Modus*, pp. 90–91; cf. Phoebus, pp. 244–45.
56 Phoebus, pp. 100, 244.
57 Phoebus, p. 245.
58 *Gawain*, ll. 1694–1916.
59 *MG*, p. 37.

Chapter 10
1 *MG*, p. 40.
2 *Modus*, pp. 153–56.
3 Friedmann, *A Bestiary for St Jerome*, pp. 273–74.

4 *Modus*, p. 93.
5 See Phoebus, pp. 247–49.
6 *Modus*, p. 92.
7 The weapons may be bill-hooks, and the hunters peasants.
8 *Devonshire Tapestries*, Plate III.
9 Gace, ll. 9059–142.
10 *MG*, pp. 178–79.
11 *MG*, p. 179.
12 *MG*, p. 180.
13 Phoebus, pp. 103–04, 246–47.
14 Phoebus, p. 104.
15 *MG*, p. 39.
16 *MG*, p. 38.
17 *BSA*, p. 74.
18 Phoebus, p. 102.
19 See *BSA*, pp. 130 (n. 1426) and 186, ll. 611–12.

Chapter 11
1 Yule, *The Book of Ser Marco Polo*, II, p. 285.
2 Bibliothèque Nationale, MS. Fr. 2810, fols. 59, 85; reproduced in Freeman, *The Unicorn Tapestries*, p. 36.
3 Reproduced (from B. von Breyderbach, *Peregrinationes in Montem Syon*, Mainz, 1486) in Freeman, p. 37.
4 Numbers XXIII. 22; Deuteronomy XXXIII. 17; Job XXXIX. 9–11; Psalm XCII. 10; Daniel VIII, 5–7.
5 See Freeman, p. 39.
6 Freeman, p. 40; Klingender, *Animals*, p. 170; Cranach, Figs 191, 202.
7 E.g. Cranach, Fig. 191.
8 Migne, *Patrologia Latina*, XIV, col. 1099.
9 Way, *Exegetic Homilies*, pp. 204–05; quoted in Freeman, p. 17.
10 See McCulloch, *Medieval Latin and French Bestiaries*.
11 See Shepard, *The Lore of the Unicorn*, pp. 41–69.
12 See Schultz, *Die Legende vom Leben der Jungfrau Maria*, pp. 55–56.
13 See Freeman, p. 49.
14 See Freeman, p. 50; Klingender, pp. 465–66. Similar depictions include an embroidered reading-desk and the carved centre panel of an altarpiece in Lübeck Cathedral, in which Gabriel, unusually, is on the right. See Appuhn, *Die Jagd als Sinnbild*, Figs. 9 and 10, and pp. 35–36.
15 Freeman, pp. 50–51.
16 Freeman, pp. 57–59. See also Raphael's *Lady with a Unicorn* (R. Cocke and P. de Vecchi, *The Complete Paintings of Raphael*, London, 1987, Plate VII).
17 Klingender, p. 399; Freeman, p. 45.

18 Klingender, p. 94.
19 Freeman, pp. 46–48.
20 Translated from Cesare Segre's edition (see under Fournival in Bibliography), pp. 42–44. For similar imagery of the lover as unicorn and Love as the hunter, see *Les Chansons de Thibaut de Champagne, Roi de Navarre*, ed. A. Wallensköld, Paris (SATF), 1925, pp. 112–13.
21 Freeman, p. 27.
22 See especially Freeman, pp. 29, 31.
23 Reproduced in splendid colour and detail in Freeman. See also Rorimer, *The Unicorn Tapestries*; Klingender, pp. 464–65.
24 See Freeman, pp. 155–74.
25 E.g. Cranach, Figs. 191, 202; Klingender, Fig. 152.
26 Cranach, Fig. 201.
27 Freeman, p. 83.
28 Friedmann, pp. 285–86.

Chapter 12
1 *Livro*, pp. 18–19.
2 *MG*, p. 154.
3 *Modus*, p. 231.
4 *MG*, p. 155.
5 Phoebus, pp. 144–45.
6 *MG*, p. 72.
7 *MG*, p. 154.
8 Dalby, p. 103.
9 *MG*, p. 154.
10 *MG*, p. 155; see also Appuhn, *Die Jagd als Sinnbild*, Plate 14, for a particularly fine example from Lüneburg.
11 Phoebus, pp. 144–45.
12 Gace, ll. 8298–304.
13 The 'hocket' will be explained shortly.
14 *Modus*, pp. 48–49.
15 *Montería*, p. 5.
16 *Twiti*, p. 34.
17 *Twiti*, pp. 46–47.
18 *Twiti*, pp. 54–55.
19 *MG*, p. 96.
20 *MG*, p. 95.
21 *MG*, p. 96.
22 *MG*, p. 97.
23 *MG*, p. 97.
24 *MG*, p. 98.
25 *MG*, pp. 96, 98, 99.
26 *MG*, pp. 101–02.
27 *MG*, p. 160.
28 The miniature on folio 9 shows these six elements in sequence. The *Trésor* is MS. Fr. 855 in the Bibliothèque Nationale, Paris.
29 For the descriptions and miniatures, see *Trésor*, fols. 9v (*chemin*); 10v–11r

(*asemblee*); 11v–12r (*queste*); 12r–13r (*chasse*); 13v–14r (*vehue*); 14v–15r (*mescroy*); 15v–16v (*requeste*); 17r–17v (*leaue*); 18r–18v (*relaies*); 19r–19v (*ayde*); 20r–21r (*prise*); 21v–22r (*retraite*); 22v–23r (*appel de chiens*); 23v–24v (*appel de gens*). There is an occasional discrepancy between the textual instructions and the miniatures. In such cases I have preferred the description in the text.

30 *Modus*, pp. 49–50.
31 *Montería*, pp. 12–13.
32 See Phoebus, pp. 132–35.
33 Gace, ll. 8073–92.

Chapter 13

1 Bibliothèque Nationale, MSS. Fr. 7839–46, 11202–04. The details given so far are from MS. Fr. 7843. For a translation of one complete set of accounts, see Appendix I.
2 Keen, *Chivalry*, pp. 16, 23–26, 104, 213, 226.
3 *Livro*, pp. 442, 444.
4 *Livro*, p. 47.
5 Bibliothèque Nationale, MS. Fr. 7843.
6 See Appendix I, p. 252.
7 Appendix I, p. 257.
8 *Montería*, pp. 114, 78.
9 *Regesta*, nos. 2661, 2783, 3029 (the last item concerns the making of coats for the leopards).
10 The instructions begin in Phoebus on p. 138.
11 Phoebus, pp. 140–42; *Modus*, p. 99.
12 *MG*, p. 69.
13 Phoebus, p. 189.
14 Phoebus, pp. 194, 344 n.
15 *Montería*, pp. 5–7.
16 *Montería*, p. 5.
17 *Livro*, pp. 442, 444.
18 Phoebus, p. 194.
19 *Livro*, pp. 331–34.
20 Gace, ll. 8007–12.
21 Bibliothèque de l'Arsénal, MS. 3252, especially fol. xxxv.
22 See Appendix V, p. 269.
23 For references see Dalby, p. 169.
24 Phoebus, p. 181.
25 Printed in *BSA*, pp. 168–86, especially lines 331–34, 351–56.
26 Gace, ll. 8327–44.
27 *Gawain*, l. 1358.
28 *MG*, pp. 111–12.
29 *CV*, pp. 57–58.
30 *MG*, p. 203.
31 *MG*, p. 202.
32 *MG*, p. 203.

33 *Montería*, p. 24.
34 *Montería*, pp. 20–21.
35 *Montería*, p. 21.
36 *Livro*, pp. 326–30.
37 *Montería*, pp. 6–7, 136.
38 *MG*, p. 102.
39 *Twiti*, pp. 10–11.

Chapter 14

1 John Skelton, *The Complete English Poems*, pp. 340–41.
2 *BSA*, pp. 54–55.
3 *Poema de Mío Cid*, ll. 3–5.
4 *Modus*, pp. 173–74.
5 See Devoto, 'El halcón castigado', for this and other examples of the rebellious falcon punished.
6 Devoto, p. 141.
7 Neckam, *De Naturis rerum*, pp. 75–76.
8 Academia de la Historia, Madrid, MS. 2–7–2, fols. 455v–465v.
9 Gilbert, p. 74.
10 *PLA*, p. 52.
11 See also Dalby, pp. xx, xxvi–xxviii.
12 *PLA*, p. 57.
13 *PLA*, pp. 61–62.
14 *PLA*, p. 68.
15 *PLA*, pp. 82, 91.
16 *PLA*, p. 62.
17 See above, n. 4.
18 *PLA*, pp. 71–72.
19 *PLA*, pp. 74–75.
20 *PLA*, pp. 76–77.
21 *PLA*, p. 78.
22 *PLA*, pp. 79–80.
23 *PLA*, p. 190.
24 *PLA*, p. 191.
25 *PLA*, pp. 183–84.
26 *BSA*, p. 48.
27 The Feast of St Margaret of Antioch is 20 July; from then to Lammas is a very short time, which leads me to suppose that the reference is to the Feast of St Margaret of Scotland, 10 June, by which date the moult was probably under way.
28 Nelson, *A Fifteenth-Century Schoolbook*, pp. 7–8.

Chapter 15

1 Dalby, p. 279.
2 Ladero Quesada, 'La caza', p. 209.
3 *LHT*, I, p. ccxlix.
4 *LHT*, I, p. 227.
5 *LHT*, IV, p. 134.
6 *BSA*, pp. 3–4. See also *DAV*, p. 128.
7 *Regesta*, no. 3056.
8 *PLA*, pp. 187–88.
9 *PLA*, p. 194; Gace, ll. 61ff.

10 *LHT*, I, p. 45; cf. III, p. 167.
11 Bibliothèque de l'Arsénal, MS. 6589, Item 12.
12 See Michell, *The Art and Practice of Hawking*, pp. 5, 16, 42, 48, 79, 144, 276.
13 *LHT*, I, pp. 95, 332; III, p. 387; see also I, index, pp. 483–84.
14 *Regesta*, no. 3082.
15 *Livro*, p. 459.
16 See Dalby, p: xxviii, n. 112.
17 *PLA*, pp. 72, 76.
18 *Tresslerbuch*, pp. 384, 469, 586.
19 *LHT*, I, p. 26; IV, p. 135.
20 Glasier, *Falconry and Hawking*, p. 13.
21 Owen, *The Making of King's Lynn*, p. 386.
22 *PLA*, pp. 79, 195.
23 Ramón Llull, *Felix*, p. 893.
24 *Tristan*, pp. 70–71.
25 *PLA*, p. 89.
26 Dalby, pp. 116–17.
27 Owen, *The Making of King's Lynn*, pp. 42, 386, 433.
28 Dalby, p. 116; *PLA*, p. 195.
29 *DAV*, pp. 195ff.
30 *PLA*, pp. 188–89.
31 See Dalby, pp. 212–13.
32 *LHT*, III, p. 167.
33 Dalby, pp. 253–55.
34 *PLA*, pp. 78, 89.
35 See Dalby, pp. xxvii–xxviii.
36 Bibliothèque Nationale, Paris, MS. Esp. 335, fols. 47r–48r.
37 *Fuero de Teruel*, paragraph 405.
38 Gilbert, p. 70.
39 *Poema de Fernán González*, stanzas 569–74, 730–33.

Chapter 16

1 *BSA*, p. 4.
2 *DAV*, p. 137–38.
3 *DAV*, p. 139.
4 *LHT*, IV, p. 136; Hodgson, *Percy Bailiff's Rolls*, p. 99.
5 *PLA*, pp. 97, 202.
6 *BSA*, ll. 1154–61.
7 *PLA*, p. 98; *BSA*, ll. 1149–50.
8 Dalby, p. 190.
9 Dalby, pp. 190, 193.
10 See e.g. *LHT*, III, pp. 161, 172, 331.
11 Owen, *The Making of King's Lynn*, p. 364.
12 *Modus*, pp. 178, 349; *PLA*, p. 202.
13 *LHT*, I, pp. 182, 365; III, pp. 169, 402.
14 *LHT*, III, pp. 164, 352.
15 *LHT*, I, p. 92; III, p. 172; see also IV, p. 136.
16 There are splendid examples in the Waffensammlung in Vienna; see also *Devonshire Tapestries*, Plates 8, 11, II.
17 *PLA*, p. 90.
18 *LHT*, III, p. 384.
19 *PLA*, pp. 99–100.
20 *PLA*, p. 83; *BSA*, p. 25.
21 *DAV*, pp. 170ff.; *Modus*, pp. 179–82, also recommends progressive unseeling.
22 *BSA*, pp. 4–5.
23 *PLA*, p. 85.
24 *PLA*, p. 87.
25 *PLA*, p. 90; *Modus*, pp. 184–93.
26 *PLA*, pp. 101–02.
27 *Modus*, pp. 194–95.
28 *LHT*, I, pp. 94, 363; III, pp. 158, 385.
29 John Russell's *Boke of Nurture*, ll. 421–22, in *Manners and Meals*, p. 143; see also pp. 211, 276.
30 *Tacuinum sanitatis*, I, fol. 70v; II, p. 99.
31 *Regesta*, no. 2801.
32 *DAV*, pp. 257–67.
33 *DAV*, p. 255.

Chapter 17

1 Ladero Quesada, 'La caza', p. 209.
2 *PLA*, pp. 94, 203; *LHT*, III, pp. 128, 138, 169, 182, etc.
3 *Regesta*, no. 2903.
4 *PLA*, pp. 176–77.
5 *BSA*, p. 32.
6 *PLA*, p. 179; *Modus*, p. 204; *BSA*, p. 34.
7 *BSA*, pp.35–36.
8 *BSA*, p. 36.
9 *PLA*, p. 176.
10 Academia de la Historia, Madrid, MS. C–74 9/5495, fol. 79r.
11 *PLA*, p. 112.
12 *BSA*, pp. 40–41.
13 *BSA*, pp. 30–31.
14 *PLA*, pp. 202–05.
15 *BSA*, p. 20.
16 *PLA*, pp. 196–201.
17 *LHT*, III, p. 168.

Chapter 18

1 *PEB*, fol. 319v. Gerardus recommends a similar, briefer wording to protect a hawk when its feathers are growing (see Hands, ' "Dancus Rex" in English'), and there is a garbled version in the Spanish *Moamin* (Fradejas Rueda, *Tratados de cetrería*, p. 165).
2 Gerardus recommends saying this as one takes one's hawk from the perch, as does the Spanish *Moamin*.
3 Gerardus and the Spanish *Moamin* say that this will ward off eagles.
4 Fradejas Rueda, *Tratados de cetrería*, p. 130.

5 Alfonso x, *Cantigas*, no. 232. Other examples of Marian assistance to falconers are nos. 44, 142, 243, 352 and 366. See Seniff, 'Falconry, Venery and Fishing'.

6 *LHT*, I, p. 98; III, pp. 155, 185; see also I, p. 359; II, p. 454; III, p. 176.

7 *Treatyse of Fysshynge with an Angle*, fols. 5–6.

8 *BSA*, p. 52.

9 From the *Baz-Nama-Yi Nisiri*, transl. D. C. Phillott, London, 1908, quoted in *DAV*, p. 449.

10 *Devonshire Tapestries*, Plates 6–14, II.

11 *TED*, p. 14–15.

12 *TED*, pp. 15–16.

13 Phoebus, pp. 135–37. See also Dalby, p. 16, *beiz-hunt*; p. 274, *vogel-hunt*. James IV of Scotland pays a reward of five shillings 'to ane man that socht ane spanyell dog, be the kingis command' (*LHT*, III, p. 156).

14 *DAV*, pp. 267–70. See also Dalby, pp. 75–76, *habech-wint*.

15 *Livre*, p. 459.

16 *LHT*, I, pp. 288, 305.

17 Compare *Modus*, p. 195, and *PLA*, p. 102, on the dangers of heron-flesh. It was not usual for the same bird to take both heron and mallard, since the two flights were so different and falcons were usually trained for one of them and kept to it. Pero López does mention an exceptional falcon of Pedro the Cruel's which was both *garcero* and *altanero* (*PLA*, p. 176).

18 The Count of Tancarville appears in Pero López's list of famous falconers (*PLA*, p. 60), and is the arbiter in the debates between falconers and huntsmen in *Modus*, pp. 233–65, and Gace, ll. 12175–94.

19 *PLA*, pp. 60, 66, 67, 70, 71, 72, 75, 77, 78, etc.

20 *Modus*, p. 227.

Chapter 19

1 *PLA*, p. 69.

2 Glasier, p. 13.

3 *LHT*, III, pp. 331, 332, 384; IV, pp. 267, 443.

4 *LHT*, III, pp. 118, 121, 125.

5 *ER*, x, pp. 203, 257, 316, 449; see also XI, pp. 78, 155, for other falconers renting lands in Fife.

6 Owen, *The Making of King's Lynn*, p. 331.

7 Hodgson, *Percy Bailiff's Rolls*, pp. 96–101.

8 *ER*, I, p. 216.

9 *LHT*, I, p. 194. See also I, p. 234, for further payments for clothing for Andrew Dowle.

10 George Turbervile, writing only a few decades later, leans heavily on Italian sources.

11 *Regesta*, nos. 2539, 2706, 2749, 2807, 2811, 2814, 2817, 2856, etc.

12 *Regesta*, no. 2857.

13 *DAV*, pp. 243–44.

14 *DAV*, p. 3.

15 *DAV*, p. 227.

16 *DAV*, pp. 205–06.

17 Glasier, p. 12.

18 *Bayeux Tapestry*, Plate 5; see also Plates II, 15, 17.

19 See the Introduction to Tjerneld's edition of *Moamin et Ghatrif*; Fradejas Rueda, *Tratados de cetrería*, pp. 107–73; Haskins, 'The *De Arte Venandi*', p. 348.

20 Bibliothèque Nationale, Paris, MS. Fr. 618, fol. 113r.

21 *DAV*, pp. 150–51.

22 *Modus*, p. 230. For other debates on the relative merits of falconry and the chase, see Gace; Robert de Herlin, *Le Débat du faucon et du lévrier*.

23 *LHT*, I, pp. 194, 363.

24 *DAV*, p. 151.

25 *LHT*, I, p. 275.

26 *Regesta*, no. 2814.

27 *LHT*, IV, p. 73.

Chapter 20

1 See Dalby, p. xxix.

2 Homer, *Iliad*, transl. Lattimore, Book 22, ll. 138–44.

3 See Menéndez Pidal, *Reliquias*, pp. 181–239, especially pp. 183, 184, 218–19, 226; Cummins, 'The Chronicle Texts'.

4 Smith, *Spanish Ballads*, no. 44.

5 See Dalby, p. xxix, for references.

6 Quoted in E. Randam Rogers' stimulating study of ballad symbolism, *The Perilous Hunt*, p. 7.

7 *Young Beichan*, in *Oxford Book of Ballads*, pp. 199–205.

8 See Rogers, *The Perilous Hunt*, p. 9.

9 *Oxford Book of Ballads*, p. 294.

10 *Oxford Book of Ballads*, p. 293.

11 *Fuero de Teruel*, paragraph 458.

12 See *DAV*, pp. 154–55.

13 See Maiwald, 'Das Stift Heiligenkreuz und die Handschrift Codex 226'.

14 See Boase, *Death in the Middle Ages*, p. 105.

15 See various illustrations in Dreyer, 'Der

mittelalterliche Totentanz und die
Falknerei'.

16 See Dalby, p. xxxi, n. 131, and p. 213;
Bec, *La Lyrique*, no. 141 and note.

17 A haggard falcon is one not taken as an
eyass.

18 Tydeman, *English Poetry 1400–1550*, pp.
149–50.

19 Dronke, *The Mediaeval Lyric*, p. 115.

20 Dalby, p. xxxi and n. 127.

21 For references and further details, see
again the splendid Dalby, pp. xxxii-
xxxiii; Hatto, 'Wolfram von
Eschenbach and the Chase', in his
Essays, pp. 200–17.

22 For the originals, see Cummins, *The
Spanish Traditional Lyric*, pp. 81–82.

23 Marie de France, *Lais*, pp. 82–96.

24 For other examples, see *Manesse Codex*,
fols. 69r, 164v, etc.

25 Alonso and Blecua, *Antología*, no. 144.

26 For a fuller analysis of the poem and its
relationship with its secular sources,
see Cummins, '*Aqueste lance divino*'.

27 For detailed analyses, see Dronke, *The
Mediaeval Lyric*, pp. 113–14, 258;
Dalby, pp. xxxii-xxxiii, notes 132–35;
Sayce, *The Mediaeval German Lyric*, pp.
86, 88.

28 Dronke, *The Mediaeval Lyric*, p. 114.

Chapter 21

1 See Appendix i, pp. 254, 256.

2 Phoebus, p. 250.

3 Menen, *Cities in the Sand*, p. 86;
Xenophon, pp. 403–13.

4 Phoebus, p. 251.

5 *Modus*, pp. 105–15.

6 See Dalby, pp. 84–85, *hecke*; 264–65,
ver-binden.

7 Phoebus, pp. 143, 252.

8 *MG*, p. 18.

9 See Gilbert, p. 57.

10 *MG*, p. 14.

11 Phoebus, pp. 283–89.

12 *MG*, p. 14.

13 *MG*, p. 41.

14 *MG*, p. 41.

15 Phoebus, p. 227.

16 Phoebus, p. 228.

17 *Modus*, pp. 164–65.

18 Ladero Quesada, 'La caza', p. 207.

19 Ladero Quesada, 'La caza', pp. 206–07.

20 On all these aspects of Spanish
municipal hunting laws, see Ladero
Quesada, 'La caza'.

21 See Dalby, pp. 291–93.

22 *Modus*, pp. 135–36; cf. Phoebus, pp.
280–82.

23 Phoebus, p. 278.

24 *Modus*, p. 293.

25 Macpherson, p. 350.

26 Ladero Quesada, 'La caza', p. 213.

27 Phoebus, p. 275.

28 Phoebus, pp. 265–66; *Modus*, pp. 157–
58.

29 Phoebus, pp. 257–58.

30 Dalby, pp. 71–72, *gruobe*; Lindner, *Die
Jagd im frühen Mittelalter*, p. 315;
Lindner, *Deutsche Jagdtraktate*, i, pp.
131ff.

31 Phoebus, p. 262; Dalby, p. 314, *wolf-
segense*.

32 Dalby, pp. 45–46, *druch*; for full
descriptions and illustrations, see
Lindner, *Deutsche Jagdtraktate*, i, pp.
135–48.

33 Phoebus, p. 263.

34 Lindner, *Die Hohenlohesche Handschrift*,
pp. 99–100; similar cakes, containing
yew leaves, broken glass, mercury
compounds, etc., sweetened with
honey, were used against foxes (see pp.
102–03, 108, in the same work).

35 Phoebus, pp. 267–69; *Modus*, pp. 159–
60; Dalby, p. 316, *wolves-angel*.

36 Phoebus, pp. 259–60.

37 Dalby, pp. 196, *shupf-reitel*; 206, *snel-
reitel*; 246–47, *üf-slac*; Phoebus, p. 261.

38 Dalby, pp. 33, *bogel*; 43, *done*; 206,
sneller. For thrush-snaring, see
Macpherson, pp. 91–97.

39 *LHT*, iii, pp. 167, 168.

40 Dalby, pp. 272–73.

41 Ladero Quesada, 'La caza', pp. 218–19.

42 Ladero Quesada, 'La caza', p. 203.

43 Ladero Quesada, 'La caza', p. 219.

44 There are numerous examples in
Beinart, *Records of the Trials of the
Spanish Inquisition*, e.g. iii, pp. 454–57.

45 *PLA*, p. 194.

46 On different types of net, see Dalby,
pp. 55, *garn*; 68, *ge-ziuc*; 79–80, *ham*;
118, *kevje*; 160, *netze*; 166–67, *poms*;
201, *slac*; 214, *spinne-webbe*; 226,
stözgarn; 285–86, *want*; Macpherson,
pp. 19–23, 26–34, 36–39, 62–71, etc.
On the tunnel-net, see Lindner, *Das
Jagdbuch des Petrus de Crescentiis*, pp.
171, 185–86.

47 Quoted in Macpherson, p. 98. See
Dalby, pp. 88–89.

48 Dalby, p. 274.

49 *Modus*, pp. 295–96. See also Dalby, pp.
119–20, *klobe*; 161, *nicklïn*; and
especially Lindner, *Deutsche
Jagdtraktate*, i, pp. 27–43. For a
mechanically superior version, see
Macpherson, p. 72.

50 *Modus*, pp. 298–300.
51 See also Dalby, pp. 137–38, *lïm, lïm-ruote*; Lindner, *Die Jagd im frühen Mittelalter*, pp. 339ff.; Macpherson, pp. 23–25.
52 Ladero Quesada, 'La caza', p. 208.
53 Macpherson, p. 61.
54 See Macpherson, pp. 41–42.
55 *Modus*, pp. 293–94.
56 See *Modus*, notes to Chap. 130, Vol. I, pp. 374–75.
57 From *The Description of Pembrokeshire*, London, 1892, quoted in Macpherson, pp. 448–49.
58 *Modus*, p. 294.
59 *Modus*, pp. 307–11.
60 See Dalby, *garn, ham, klobe, masche, netze* II, *phifen, reizel, reizen, stric*, etc.
61 Dalby, p. 137, *lïm*.
62 *Modus*, pp. 310–11.
63 Gilbert, p. 38.
64 *Livro*, p. 31.
65 Phoebus, pp. 250–51.

Appendix I

1 With the exception of a few recurring items, this is a complete translation of Bibliothèque Nationale MS. Fr. 7846.
2 The sums of money are given in livres, sous and deniers. The letter 'p' means 'Paris money'.
3 If the figure of three sous per day is correct, de Franconville and the other *veneurs* appear to have been underpaid. The figures should have been 57 l. 15 s.p. per year, and 19 l. 5 s.p. per term.
4 As a varlet he received the same wages as a page, but a larger maintenance allowance, and a clothing allowance which the pages did not receive.
5 A *minot* was about 39 litres.

Appendix II

1 Quoted from a private source by Shirley, *Some Account of English Game Parks*, pp. 29–33. Framlingham belonged to the Duke of Norfolk. The Park Keeper was Richard Chambyr.

Appendix III

1 This modernized version of an account of Henry IV is as printed in *MG*, pp. 169–70.
2 The author of the *Master of Game*.

Appendix IV

1 *Montería*, pp. 23–24.

Appendix V

1 *Livro*, pp. 439–44.

Bibliography of Works Consulted

Manuscripts

British Library: mss.: 16.392; Cotton Vespasian B xii; Royal 2B vii; Royal 10E iv; Yates Thomson 13; Landsdowne 85; Egerton 1995; Add. 16.165.

Bodleian Library, Oxford: mss.: Bodley 264; Bodley 546; Douce 219 and 220; Douce 335 and 336; Rawlinson C.506; Rawlinson Poet. 143.

Cambridge University Library: mss.: FF.6.13; Ll.I.18.

Bibliothèque Nationale, Paris: mss.: Lat. 1156B; Fr. 614–20; Fr. 622; Fr. 855; Fr. 1289–95; Fr.. 1297–303; Fr. 1593; Fr. 1614–20; Fr. 1995; Fr. 7839–46; Fr. 11202–04; Fr.19113; Fr. 12397–12400; Fr. 24271–72; Esp. 286; Esp. 292; Esp. 335.

Bibliothèque de l'Arsénal, Paris: mss.: 3252; 6589.

Musée Condé, Chantilly: mss.: Lat. 368; XVI B³.

Biblioteca Nacional, Madrid: mss.: 3350; 7195.

Biblioteca del Palacio, Madrid: mss.: ii–1366; ii–1370; ii.g.3/2105.

Biblioteca del Monasterio de San Lorenzo del Escorial: mss.: K.iii.31; T.i.1; V.ii.19; Y.ii.19.

Academia de la Historia, Madrid: mss.: 2–7–2; C.74 9/5495.

Österreichische Nationalbibliothek, Vienna: mss.: 2573; 2611; Ser. N. 2644.

Kunsthistorisches Museum, Vienna: Abteilung f. Plastik, No. 4984.

Printed sources

Acart, Jean, *L'Amoureuse prise*, ed. E. Hoepffner, *Gesellschaft für romanische Literatur*, Vol. 22, Dresden, 1910.

Accounts of the Lord High Treasurer of Scotland, ed. T. Dickson and Sir J. Balfour Paul, Edinburgh, 1877–1916.

Acts of the Parliament of Scotland, ed. T. Thomson and C. Innes, Edinburgh, 1814–75.

Aelfric, *Lives of Saints*, ed. W. W. Skeat, 2 vols., Early English Texts Society, London, 1881–1900.

Alexander, The Romance of (ms. Bodley 264); facsimile edition by M. R. James, Oxford, 1933.

Alfonso x of Castile, *Cantigas de Santa María*, ed. W. Mettman, 4 vols., Coimbra, 1959–72.

Alfonso xi of Castile, *Libro de la montería*, ed. Dennis P. Seniff, Madison, 1983. The edition by J. E. Casariego, Madrid, 1976, is inferior but reproduces the miniatures in colour.

Alonso, Dámaso, and Blecua, J. M., *Antología de poesía española: Poesía de tipo tradicional*, Madrid, 1956.

Anderson, J. K., *Hunting in the Ancient World*, Berkeley and Los Angeles, 1985.

Anderson, M. L., *History of Scottish Forestry*, 2 vols., London, 1967.

Anon., *Dragons*, Time–Life Books, Amsterdam, n.d.

Anson, Peter F., *Fisher Folklore*, London, 1965.

Appuhn, Horst, *Die Jagd als Sinnbild in der norddeutschen Kunst des Mittelalters*, Hamburg and Berlin, 1964.

The Art of Falconry, being the De Arte Venandi cum Avibus of Frederick ii of Hohenstaufen, transl. and ed. C. A. Wood and F. M. Fyfe, Stanford, 1943; reissued 1961; reprinted 1981.

Baillie-Grohman, W. A., 'Ancient Weapons of the Chace', *The Burlington Magazine*, iv, 1904, pp. 157–67.

Baillie-Grohman, W. A., Sport in Art, London, 1913.

Baillie-Grohman, W. A., *Sport in the Alps in the Past and Present*, London, 1896.

Bayeux Tapestry: Sir Frank Stenton *et al.*, *The Bayeux Tapestry: A Comprehensive Survey*, London, 1957; 2nd edn 1965.

Bec, P., *La Lyrique française au moyen âge*, Paris, 1977.

Beck, H., *Das Ebersignum in Germanischen: Ein Beitrag zur germanischen Tiersymbolik*, Berlin, 1965.

Beinart, Haim, *Records of the Trials of the Spanish Inquisition in Ciudad Real*, 4 vols., Jerusalem, 1974–85.

Bernheimer, Richard, *Wildmen in the Middle Ages*, Cambridge, Mass., 1952.

Bertelli, S., *Italian Renaissance Courts*, London, 1986.

Blackmore, Howard, *Hunting Weapons*, London, 1971.

Boase, T. S. R., *Death in the Middle Ages*, London, 1972.

Boccaccio, *The Decameron*, transl. G. H. McWilliam, Harmondsworth, 1972.

Boccaccio, *Il Filostrato e Il Ninfole Piesolano*, ed. V. Pernicone, Bari, 1937.

The Boke of St Albans, facsimile edition in Rachel Hands, *English Hawking and Hunting in 'The Boke of St Albans'*, Oxford, 1975.

Book of the Howlett, The, in *The Bannatyne MS.*, Scottish Texts Society, 4 vols., 1928–30: iv, 138.

Brézé, Jacques de, *La Chasse*, ed. Gunnar Tilander, Cynegetica, vi, Lund, 1959.

Caius, Iohannes, *Treatise of Englishe Dogges*, London, 1576; new edn, London, 1880.

Charles ix of France, *La Chasse Royale: Livre du Roy Charles de la chasse du cerf*, ed. H. Chevreul, Paris, 1859.

La Chasse Royale: see Charles ix of France.

Chaucer, Geoffrey, *Works*, The World's Classics, 3 vols., London, 1903.

Coke, John, *The Debate between the Heralds of England and France*, ed. L. Pannier in *Le Débat des hérauts*.

Courtney-Williams, A., *Beagles: Their History and Breeding*, 2nd edn, Ilkley, 1974.

The Craft of Venery, published in *La Vénerie de Twiti*: see Twiti, William, *La Vénerie de Twiti*.

Cranach: Max J. Friedländer and Jakob Rosenberg, *The Paintings of Lucas Cranach*, London, 1978.

Cummins, J. G., '*Aqueste lance divino*: San Juan's falconry images', *What's Past is Prologue: a Collection of Essays in Honour of L. J. Woodward*, ed. S. Bacarisse *et al.*, Edinburgh, 1984.

Cummins, J. G., 'The Chronicle Texts of the Legend of the *Infantes de Lara*', *Bulletin of Hispanic Studies*, LIII, 1976, pp. 101–16.

Cummins, J. G., *The Spanish Traditional Lyric*, Oxford, 1977.

Dalby, David, *Lexicon of the Mediaeval German Hunt*, Berlin, 1965.

Daltrop, George, *Die kalydonische Jagd in der Antike*, Hamburg, 1966.

Le Débat des hérauts d'armes de France et d'Angleterre, ed. L. Pannier, Société des Anciens Textes Français, Paris, 1877.

Delbouille, M. (ed.), *Le Roman du Châtelain de Coucy et de la dame de Fayal*, Société des Anciens Textes Français, Paris, 1936.

Devonshire Tapestries: George Wingfield Digby, *The Devonshire Hunting Tapestries*, London, 1971.

Devoto, Daniel, 'El halcón castigado', in his *Textos y contextos*, Madrid, 1974.

Dreyer, Hans-Jürgen, 'Der mittelalterliche Totentanz und die Falknerei', *Der Falkner: Zeitschrift des Österreichischen Falknerbundes*, 23–24, 1973–74, pp. 14–19.

Dronke, Peter, *The Mediaeval Lyric*, London, 1968.

du Fouilloux, Jacques, *La Vénerie et l'adolescence*, ed. Gunnar Tilander, Cynegetica XVI, Karlshamn, 1967.

Edward, Duke of York, *The Master of Game*, ed. W. A. and F. Baillie-Grohman, London, 1904. There is a second edition in modern English, Edinburgh, 1909. My references are to the first edition.

Entwhistle, W. W., 'The Adventure of *Le Cerf au pied blanc* in Spanish and elsewhere', *Modern Language Review*, XVIII, 1925, pp. 435–48.

Evans, George Ewart and Thomson, David, RA, *The Leaping Hare*, London, 1972.

The Exchequer Rolls of Scotland, ed. J. Stuart *et al.*, Edinburgh, 1878–1908.

Fontaines-Guérin, Hardouin de, *Trésor de Vénerie*, ed. H. V. Michelaut, Paris, 1865.

Forsyth, Marie A., *The History of Bradgate*, the Bradgate Park Trust, 1974.

Fournival, Richard de: *Li Bestaires d'Amours di Maistre Richart de Fornival*, ed. Cesare Segre, Milan, 1957.

Fradejas Rueda, José M., *Ensayo de una bibliografía de los libros españoles de cetrería y montería*, Madrid, 1985.

Fradejas Rueds, José M., 'Precisiones a una nueva edición del *Libro de la monteria*', *Epos*, I, 1984, pp. 283–92.

Fradejas Rueda, José M. (ed.). *Tratados de cetrería*, Madrid, 1985.

Frederick II of Hohenstaufen: see *The Art of Falconry*. . .

Freeman, Margaret B., *The Unicorn Tapestries*, New York, 1976.

Friedmann, Herbert, *A Bestiary for St Jerome*, Washington D.C., 1980.

Fuero de Teruel, ed. Max Gorosch, Stockholm, 1950.

Gace de la Vigne (or de la Buigne), *Le Roman des déduis*, ed. A. Blomqvist, Studia Romanica Holmiensia, III, Karlshamn, 1951.

Gaston Phoebus (Gaston III, Count of Foix), *Livre de chasse*, ed. Gunnar Tilander, Karlshamn, 1971.

Gilbert, John M., *Hunting and Hunting Reserves in Medieval Scotland*, Edinburgh, 1979.

Glasier, Phillip, *Falconry and Hawking*, London, 1978.

Gottfried von Strassburg, *Tristan*, transl. and ed. A. T. Hatto, London, 1960.

Grattius, *Cynegetica*, in *Minor Latin Poets*, transl. J. Wight Duff and A. M. Duff, Loeb Classical Library, London, 1934, pp. 143–205.

Grimani Breviary, The, facsimile edition by M. Salmi, London, 1972.

Guicennas, *De Arte Bersandi*, ed. Gunnar Tilander, Cynegetica III, Uppsala, 1956.

Hadamar von Laber, *Die Jagd*, ed. J. A. Schmeller, Stuttgart, 1850; reprinted Amsterdam, 1968.

Hands, Rachel, ' "Dancus Rex" in English', *Mediaeval Studies*, XXXV, 1973, pp. 354–69.

Haskins, Charles H., 'The *De Arte Venandi cum Avibus* of the Emperor Frederick II', *English Historical Review*, 36, 1921, pp. 334–55.

Hatto, A. T., *Essays on Mediaeval German and Other Poetry*, Cambridge, 1980.

Hatto, A. T., 'Snake-swords and Boar-helms in *Beowulf*', *English Studies*, XXXVIII, 1957, pp. 145–60; reprinted in his *Essays . . .* , pp. 239–54.

Henisch, Bridget A., *Fast and Feast: Food in Medieval Society*, Pennsylvania State University, University Park and London, 1976.

Herlin, Robert de, *Débat du Faucon et du lévrier*, Bibliothèque Nationale, Paris, MS. Fr. 1995.

Hodgson, J. C. (ed.), *Percy Bailiff's Rolls of the Fifteenth Century*, Surtees Society, Durham, 1921.

Holinshed, Raphael, *Chronicles of England, Scotlande and Irelande*, 3 vols., London, 1577.

Holyrood Ordinale, The, ed. F. C. Eeles, *The Book of the Old Edinburgh Club*, VII, 1914.

Homer, *Iliad*, transl. Richmond Lattimore, Chicago, 1962.

Housman, Laurence (transl.), *Of Aucassin and Nicolette*, London, n.d.

Hull, Denison Bingham, *Hounds and Hunting in Ancient Greece*, Chicago, 1964.

Jacobs, Michael, *Mythological Painting*, Oxford, 1979.

Jagd einst und jetzt (catalogue of Niederösterreichische Landesmuseum exhibition, Schloss Marchegg, 29 April–15 November 1978), Vienna, 1978.

Jensen, Frede, *The Earliest Portuguese Lyric*, Odense, 1978.

John I of Portugal, *Livro da montaria*, ed. Francisco M. Esteves Pereira, Coimbra, 1918.

Keen, Maurice, *Chivalry*, Yale University Press, New Haven, 1984.

Klingender, Francis, *Animals in Art and Thought to the End of the Middle Ages*, London, 1971.

La Chasse: see Brézé, Jacques de.

Ladero Quesada, M. A., 'La caza en la legislación municipal castellana', *En la España medieval, I. Estudios dedicados al profesor D. Julio González González*, Madrid, 1981, pp. 193–221.

Lancaster, Henry of, *Livre des seyntz medecines*, ed. E. J. Arnold, Oxford, 1940.

le Clerc, Guillaume, *Le Bestiaire divin*, ed. Robert Reinsch, Leipzig, 1892; reprinted Wiesbaden, 1967.

Libro de la montéria: see Alfonso XI of Castile.

Lindner, Kurt, *Beiträge zu Vogelfang und Falknerei in Altertum*, Quellen und Studien zur Geschichte der Jagd, XII, Berlin, 1973.

Lindner, Kurt, *Bibliographie der deutschen und der niederländischen Jagdliteratur von 1480 bis 1850*, Berlin, 1976.

Lindner, Kurt (ed.), *Das Jagdbuch des Petrus de Crescentiis*, Quellen und Studien zur Geschichte der Jagd, IV, Berlin, 1957.

Lindner, Kurt, *Deutsche Jagdschriftseller*, Quellen und Studien zur Geschichte der Jagd, IX, Berlin, 1964.

Lindner, Kurt (ed.), *Deutsche Jagdtraktate des 15. und 16. Jahrhunderts*, 2 vols., Quellen und Studien zur Geschichte der Jagd, V and VI, Berlin, 1959.

Lindner, Kurt (ed.), *Die deutsche Habichtslehre*, Quellen und Studien zur Geschichte der Jagd, II, Berlin, 1964.

Lindner, Kurt, 'Die Hohenlohesche Handschrift. Ein deutsches Jagdbuch des 16. Jahrhunderts', in *Deutsche Jagdtraktate*, Vol. I, Berlin, 1959, pp. 49–152.

Lindner, Kurt, *Die Jagd im frühen Mittelalter* (Vol. 2 of *Geschichte des deutschen Weidwerks*), Berlin, 1940.

Lindner, Kurt (ed.), *Die Lehre von den Zeichen des Hirsches*, Quellen und Studien zur Geschichte der Jagd, III, Berlin, 1956.

Lindner, Kurt, *Geschichte des deutschen Weidwerks*, 2 vols., Berlin and Leipzig, 1937–40.

Lindner, Kurt, *Von Falken, Hunden und Pferden*, 2 vols., Quellen und Studien zur Geschichte der Jagd, VII and VIII, Berlin, 1962.

Les Livres du Roy Modus et de la Royne Ratio, ed. Gunnar Tilander, 2 vols., Société des Anciens Textes Français, Paris, 1932. Page references are to Vol. I. See also Nordenfalk.

Livro da montaria: see John I of Portugal.

Llull, Ramón, *Felix*, transl. A. Bonner in *Selected Works of Ramón Llull (1232–1316)*, Vol. 2: *Felix, or the Book of Wonders.* . . . Princeton, 1985.

Llull, Ramón, *Libre del ordre de cavayleria*, ed. J. Ramón de Luanco, Barcelona, 1901. Translated by Caxton as *The book of the Ordre of Chyvalry*, ed. A. T. P. Byles, Early English Texts Society, London, 1926.

López de Ayala, Pero, *Libro de la caça de las aves*, ed. J. G. Cummins, London, 1986.

McCulloch, Florence, *Medieval Latin and French Bestiaries*, Chapel Hill, 1962.

Macpherson, H. A., *A History of Fowling*, Edinburgh, 1897.

Maiwald, Theo, 'Das Stift Heiligenkreuz und die Handschrift Codex 226, um 1220'. *Der Falkner: Zeitschrift des Österreichischen Falknerbundes*, 33–34, 1983–84.

Malory, Sir Thomas, *Works*, ed. E. Vinaver, Oxford, 1954.

Manesse Codex (Heidelberg University Library, Cod. Pal. Germ. 848): *Codex Manesse: die grosse Heidelberger Liederhandschrift*, ed. W. Koschorrek and W. Werner, Kassel, 1981.

Manners and Meals in Olden Times, ed. Frederick J. Furnivall, Early English Texts Society, London, 1868.

Marie de France, *Lais*, ed. A. Ewert, Oxford, 1952.

Master of Game: see Edward, Duke of York.

Maximilian I, Emperor of Germany: *Das Fischereibuch Kaiser Maximilians*, Innsbruck, 1901.

Maximilian I, Emperor of Germany, *Der Weisskunig*, ed. A. Schultz, Vienna, 1888.

Maximilian I, Emperor of Germany, *Teuerdank*, facsimile edition, Vienna, 1971.

Menen, Aubrey, *Cities in the Sand*, London, 1972.

Menéndez Pidal, Ramón, *Reliquias de la poesía épica española*, Madrid, 1951.

Menino, Pero, *Livro de falcoaria*, ed. M. Rodrigues Lapa, Coimbra, 1931.

Michell, E. B., *The Art and Practice of Hawking*, London, 1900; reprinted 1964.

Migeon, Gaston, *Les Tapisseries des chasses de Maximilien*, Paris, 1920.

Migne, J. P., *Patrologia Graeca*, 162 vols., Paris, 1857–1912.

Migne, J. P., *Patrologia Latina*, 221 vols., Paris, 1844–64.

Moamin et Ghatrif: Traités de fauconnerie et des chiens de chasse, ed. H. Tjerneld, Studia Romanica Holmiensia, 1–2, Stockholm, 1945–49.

Modus: see *Les livres du Roy Modus et de la Royne Ratio*.

Möller, Detlef, *Studien zur mittelalterlichen arabischen Falknerei-Literatur*, Quellen und Studien zur Geschichte der Jagd, x, Berlin, 1965.

Neckam, Alexander, *De Naturis rerum libri duo*, ed. Thomas Wright, London, 1858.

Nelson, W. (ed.), *A Fifteenth Century Schoolbook*, Oxford, 1956.

Nemesianus, *Cynegetica*, in *Minor Latin Poets* (see Grattius), pp. 484–512 (and see pp. 512–15 for two fragments on bird-snaring).

Neptalym cervus emissus, ed. Kurt Lindner, Quellen und Studien zur Geschichte der Jagd, i, Berlin, 1966, pp. 41–99.

Nibelungenlied: The Nibelungenlied, transl. and ed. A. T. Hatto, London, 1965.

The Noble Arte of Venerie or Hunting: see Turbervile, George.

Nordenfalk, Carl (ed.), *Kung fraktiks och drottning teoris jaktbok: Le Livre des deduis du Roi Modus et de la Reine Ratio*, Stockholm, 1955.

Oppian, *Cynegetica*, transl. and ed. A. W. Moir, Loeb Classical Library, London, 1928; reprinted 1963.

Ormulum, ed. Robert Holt, 2 vols., Oxford, 1898.

Owen, Dorothy M., *The Making of King's Lynn: A Documentary Survey*, Records of Social and Economic History, New Series, 9, London, 1984.

Oxford Book of Ballads, ed. A. Quiller-Couch, Oxford, 1955.

Oxford Dictionary of Saints: David Hugh Farmer, *The Oxford Dictionary of Saints*, Oxford, 1978.

Paget, John O., *Beagles and Beagling*, London, 1931.

Phoebus: see Gaston Phoebus.

Picot, Emil, 'Le Cerf allégorique dans les tapisseries et les miniatures', *Bulletin de la Société française de réproductions de manuscrits à peintures*, 3e. année, Paris, 1913, pp. 57–67.

Poema de Fernán González, ed. A. Zamora Vicente, Madrid, 1946.

Poema de Mío Cid, ed. Colin C. Smith, Oxford, 1972.

Pope-Hennessy, J., *The Complete Works of Paolo Uccello*, London, 1950.

Prince Edward's Book (Bodleian Library MS. Rawlinson C.506).

Pschmadt, C., *Die Sage von der verfolgte Hinde*, Greifswald, 1911.

Randall, Lillian M. C., *Images in the Margins of Gothic Manuscripts*, Berkeley and Los Angeles, 1966.

Regesta: J. F. Böhmer (ed.), *Regesta Imperii (Die Regesten des Kaiserreichs unter Philipp, Otto IV, Friedrich II, . . . 1198–1272)*, 2 vols., Innsbruck, 1881–1901.

Remnant, G. L., *A Catalogue of Misericords in Great Britain, with an Essay on their Iconography by M. D. Anderson*, Oxford, 1969.

Rogers, E. Randam, *The Perilous Hunt: Symbols in Hispanic and European Balladry*, Kentucky U. P., 1980.

Rorimer, James, *The Unicorn Tapestries at the Cloisters*, 4th edn, New York, 1962.

Ross, A. S. C., 'The Middle English Poem on the Names of a Hare', *Proceedings of the Leeds Philosophical and Literary Society, Literary and Historical Section*, III–IV, 1932–38; III, pp. 347–77.

Rossetti, Dante Gabriel, *The Early Italian Poets*, London, 1861.

Sayce, Olive, *The Mediaeval German Lyric, 1150–1300*, Oxford, 1982.

Schultz, Alwin, *Die Legende vom Leben der Jungfrau Maria*, Leipzig, 1878.

Seniff, D. P., 'Falconry, Venery and Fishing in the *Cantigas de Santa María*', *Studies on the Cantigas de Santa María: Art, Music and Poetry*, ed. I. J. Katz and J. E. Keller, Madison, 1987, pp. 459–74.

Shepard, Odell, *The Lore of the Unicorn*, London, 1930.

Shipman, E.R., *The Abbots Bromley Horn Dance*, Rugeley, 1982.

Shirley, E. P., *Some Account of English Game Parks*, London, 1867.

Sir Gawain and the Green Knight, ed. J.R.R. Tolkien and E.V. Gordon; 2nd edn ed. Norman Davis, Oxford, 1967; reprinted in paperback, 1972.

Skelton, John, *The Complete English Poems*, ed. J. Scattergood, London, 1983.

Smith, Colin C., *Spanish Ballads*, Oxford, 1964.

Spaur, C. von, and Hohenleiter, W., *Das Jagdbuch Kaiser Maximilians I*, Innsbruck, 1901.

Surtees, R. S., *Handley Cross*, London, 1843.

Tacuinum sanitatis: Tacuinum sanitatis in medicina: MS. Series Nova 2644 of the Austrian National Library, Vienna; facsimile edition by Franz Unterkircher, 2 vols., Graz, 1967.

Thiébaux, Marcelle, 'The Mediaeval Chase', *Speculum*, 42, 1967, pp. 260–74.

Thiébaux, Marcelle, 'The Mouth of the Boar as a Symbol in Medieval Literature', *Romance Philology*, XXII, 1969, pp. 281–99.

Thiébaux, Marcelle, *The Stag of Love: The Chase in Medieval Literature*, Cornell University Press, 1974.

Thiébaux, Marcelle, 'An Unpublished Allegory of the Hunt of Love: *Li dis dou cerf amoreus*', *Studies in Philology*, 62, 1965, pp. 531–45.

Thomas, Bruno, Gamber, O., and Schedelmann, H., *Die schönsten Waffen und Rüstungen aus europäischen und amerikanischen Sammlungen*, Heidelberg and Munich, 1963.

Tilander, Gunner (ed.), *La Chace dou cerf*, Cynegetica, VII, Stockholm, 1960.

Tilander, Gunnar (ed.), *Dancus Rex, Guillelmus Falconarius, Gerardus Falconarius*, Cynegetica, IX, Lund, 1963.

Tilander, Gunnar, *Essais d'étymologie cynégétique*, Cynegetica, I, Lund, 1953.

Tilander, Gunnar, 'Etude sur les traductions en vieux français du traité de fauconnerie de l'empéreur Frédéric II, *Zeitschrift für Romanische Philologie*, XLVI, 1926, pp. 211–90.

Tilander, Gunnar (ed.), *Julians Barnes, Boke of Huntyng*, Cynegetica, XI, Karlshamn, 1964.

Tilander, Gunnar, *Mélanges d'étymologie cynégétique*, Cynegetica, V, Lund, 1958.

Tilander, Gunnar, *Nouveaux essais d'étymologie cynégétique*, Cynegetica, IV, Lund, 1957.

Tilander, Gunnar, *Nouveaux mélanges d'étymologie cynégéique*, Cynegetica, VIII, Lund, 1961.

Topsell, Edward, *The Historie of Four-footed Beasts*, London, 1607.

Treasures from the Burrell Collection (Catalogue of Arts Council Exhibition at the Hayward Gallery), London, 1975.

Treatyse of Fysshynge with an Angle, edited in facsimile by M. G. Watkins, London, 1880.

Tresslerbuch: Das Marienburger Tresslerbuch der Jahre 1399–1409, ed. Joachim, Königsberg, 1896.

Tristan: see Gottfried von Strassburg.

Turbervile, George, *The Booke of Faulconrie or Hauking* (1575); facsimile edn, New York, 1969.

Turbervile, George, *The Noble Arte of Venerie or Hunting* (1576); Tudor and Stuart Library reprint, Oxford, 1908.

Twiti, William, *La Vénerie de Twiti*, ed. Gunnar Tilander, Cynegetica, II, Uppsala, 1956.

Twiti, William, *The Art of Hunting: 1527*, ed. Bror Danielsson, Stockholm Studies in English, XXXVII, Cynegetica Anglica, I, Stockholm, 1977.

Tydeman, W. (ed.), *English Poetry 1400–1550*, London, 1970.

Varty, Kenneth, *Reynard the Fox: A Study of the Fox in Medieval English Art*, Leicester, 1967.

Vidal, Remon, *La Chace aux mesdisans*, ed. A. Mercier, *Annales du Midi*, VI, 1894, pp. 465–94.

Way, A. C. (transl.), *Exegetic Homilies*, Washington D.C., 1963.

Werth, H., 'Altfranzösische Jagdlehrbücher nebst Handschriften-bibliographie der abendländischen Jagdliteratur überhaupt', *Zeitschrift für Romanische Philologie*, XII, 1888, pp. 146–91, 381–415; XIII, 1889, pp. 1–34.

White, T. H., *The Book of Beasts*, London, 1954.

Wyllie, J. H., *History of England under Henry IV*, 4 vols., London 1884–98.

Xenophon, *Scripta minora*, transl. and ed. E. C. Marchant, Loeb Classical Library, London,, 1925.

Yule, Sir Henry (transl. and ed.), *The Book of Ser Marco Polo, the Venetian*, 3rd edn, London, 1903.

Sources of illustrations

Index

(numbers in **bold** indicate illustrations)